C++ Windows Prograr

Develop real-world applications in Windows

Stefan Björnander

BIRMINGHAM - MUMBAI

C++ Windows Programming

First published: September 2016

Production reference: 1020916

Published by Packt Publishing Ltd.
Livery Place
35 Livery Street
Birmingham
B3 2PB, UK.
ISBN 978-1-78646-422-4

www.packtpub.com

Credits

Author

Stefan Björnander

Reviewer

Lou Mauget

Commissioning Editor

Kunal Parikh

Acquisition Editor

Chaitanya Nair

Content Development Editor

Zeeyan Pinheiro

Technical Editor

Pratish Shetty

Copy Editor

Pranjali Chury

Project Coordinator

Suzanne Coutinho

Proofreader

Safis Editing

Indexer

Rekha Nair

Graphics

Jason Monteiro
Disha Haria

Production Coordinator

Melwyn Dsa

About the Author

Stefan Björnander holds a master's degree in computer science, and has worked with software development for many years. He has lectured on programming for the industry and universities. He has also authored Microsoft Visual C++ Windows Applications by Example for Packt Publishing, which gained great acclaim.

About the Reviewer

Lou Mauget learned to program long ago at Michigan State University as a physics major, learning to use software to design a cyclotron. He worked at IBM for 34 years, and after that, he went on to work for several consulting firms, including a long-term engagement with the railroad industry. He is currently consulting for Keyhole Software of Leawood, Kansas. Recently, he designed and coded MockOla, a drag-drop wire-frame prototyping tool for Keyhole Software. Lou has coded in C++, Java, JavaScript, Python, and newer languages, as each was conceived. His current interests include reactive functional programming, containers, Node JS, NoSQL, geospatial systems, mobile, and any new language or framework. Occasionally, Lou blogs about software technology for Keyhole Software. He has coauthored three computer books and authored two IBM DeveloperWorks XML tutorials and a WebSphere Journal LDAP tutorial. Lou coauthored several J2EE certification tests for IBM. He has reviewed books for Packt Publishing, as well as other publications.

www.PacktPub.com

eBooks, discount offers, and more

Did you know that Packt offers eBook versions of every book published, with PDF and ePub files available? You can upgrade to the eBook version at www.PacktPub.com and as a print book customer, you are entitled to a discount on the eBook copy. Get in touch with us at customercare@packtpub.com for more details.

At www.PacktPub.com, you can also read a collection of free technical articles, sign up for a range of free newsletters and receive exclusive discounts and offers on Packt books and eBooks.

https://www2.packtpub.com/books/subscription/packtlib

Do you need instant solutions to your IT questions? PacktLib is Packt's online digital book library. Here, you can search, access, and read Packt's entire library of books.

Why subscribe?

- Fully searchable across every book published by Packt
- Copy and paste, print, and bookmark content
- On demand and accessible via a web browser

Free access for Packt account holders

Get notified! Find out when new books are published by following @PacktEnterprise on Twitter or the Packt Enterprise Facebook page.

I dedicate this book to my parents Ralf and Gunilla, my sister Catharina, her husband Magnus, and their sons Emil and Rasmus.

Table of Contents

Preface

Application development has gained massive popularity because of the immense impact it has on various sectors. In this booming market, it has become critical to have the right set of tools to enable developers to build practical, user-friendly, and efficient applications. This book is focused on the use and implementation of Small Windows, which is a C++ object-oriented class library that eases the development of interactive Windows applications.

What this book covers

Chapter 1, *Introduction*, gives an introduction to Small Windows, which is a class library that encapsulates a part of the Win32 API.

Chapter 2, *Hello, Small World!*, starts by building a (very) small application—the Small Windows version of the famous Hello World program. Then, we will continue with a (still rather small) application that handles circles in a window. The user can add and move circles, change their colors, and save and load circles.

Chapter 3, *Building a Tetris Application*, explores a version of the classic Tetris game. Seven different kinds of figure are falling down the screen and the user's task is to move or rotate them so that as many rows as possible can be completely filled and removed.

Chapter 4, *Working with Shapes and Figures*, teaches you how to build a drawing program, which can be regarded as a more advanced version of the circle application. It is possible to create and remove figures as well as mark and drag figures.

Chapter 5, *The Figure Hierarchy*, continues to build the drawing program. We can define a class hierarchy with lines, arrows, rectangles, and ellipses.

Chapter 6, *Building a Word Processor*, describes a word processor capable of formatting individual characters.

Chapter 7, *Keyboard Input and Character Calculation*, discusses how the word processor handles many keyboard input combinations and calculates the size and position of each individual character.

Chapter 8, *Building a Spreadsheet Application*, talks about the final application, which is a spreadsheet program capable of calculating formulas with the four rules of arithmetic. It is also possible to cut and paste blocks of cells.

Chapter 9, *Formula Interpretation*, explains that when the user inputs a formula, we need to interpret it. The process is divided into scanning and parsing, which we will look into in this chapter.

Chapter 10, *The Framework*, describes the most central part of Small Windows. This chapter begins the description of Small Windows. The Application class handles the message loop of the application and the registration of Windows classes. The Window class handles basic window functionality.

Chapter 11, *The Document*, talks about the document-based Window subclasses, that is, the Document class that provides basic document functionality, such as menus and accelerators, and the Standard Document framework, which provides a document-based framework.

Chapter 12, *The Auxiliary Classes*, explores a set of small auxiliary classes handling points and sizes, rectangles, colors and fonts, dynamic lists, and tree structures.

Chapter 13, *The Registry, Clipboard, Standard Dialogs, and Print Preview*, explains the implementation of the registry and clipboard, the standard dialogs to save and load files, choosing color or font, or printing a document. The chapter also explains the implementation a class for print previewing.

Chapter 14, *Dialogs, Controls, and Print Setup*, describes the possibility to design custom dialogs with controls such as push buttons, check boxes, radio buttons, list boxes, combo boxes, and text field. The input of a text field can be converted to any type. Finally, the Print Setup dialog is a custom dialog annotated with suitable controls.

What you need for this book

First of all, you need to download Visual Studio on your computer. I suggest you download and install Express for Desktop, which is free, and is available at `https://www.visualstud io.com/en-us/products/visual-studio-express-vs.aspx`.

Then, there are two ways to install Small Windows:

1. If you want to follow the chapter structure of this book you can download it from `https://github.com/PacktPublishing/Cpp-Windows-Programming`. It is made up by a set of Visual Studio projects holding the applications of this book.
2. If you want all the code in one Visual Studio solution you can download the C++ Windows Programming solution in the Cpp Windows Programming file.

3. If you want to write code with Small Windows on your own, you can download the Empty project in the Empty Project file. It is an application holding only the Small Windows source code with a very simple application. You can change the name of the project and add your own application-specific code.

Who this book is for

This book is for application developers who want a head-first approach into Windows programming. It will teach you how to develop an object-oriented class library in C++ and enhanced applications in Windows. Basic knowledge of C++ and the object-oriented framework is assumed to get the most out of this book.

Conventions

In this book, you will find a number of text styles that distinguish between different kinds of information. Here are some examples of these styles and an explanation of their meaning.

Code words in text, database table names, folder names, filenames, file extensions, pathnames, dummy URLs, user input, and Twitter handles are shown as follows: "The first part of a Small Windows application is the `MainWindow` function."

A block of code is set as follows:

```
void MainWindow (vector<String>argumentList,
                SmallWindows::WindowShow windowShow);
```

New terms and **important words** are shown in bold. Words that you see on the screen, for example, in menus or dialog boxes, appear in the text like this: "For instance, often, the **Open** item in the **File** menu is annotated with the text **Ctrl+O**."

Warnings or important notes appear in a box like this.

Tips and tricks appear like this.

Reader feedback

Feedback from our readers is always welcome. Let us know what you think about this book-what you liked or disliked. Reader feedback is important for us as it helps us develop titles that you will really get the most out of. To send us general feedback, simply e-mail feedback@packtpub.com, and mention the book's title in the subject of your message. If there is a topic that you have expertise in and you are interested in either writing or contributing to a book, see our author guide at www.packtpub.com/authors.

Customer support

Now that you are the proud owner of a Packt book, we have a number of things to help you to get the most from your purchase.

Downloading the example code

You can download the example code files for this book from your account at http://www.packtpub.com. If you purchased this book elsewhere, you can visit http://www.packtpub.com/support and register to have the files e-mailed directly to you.

You can download the code files by following these steps:

1. Log in or register to our website using your e-mail address and password.
2. Hover the mouse pointer on the **SUPPORT** tab at the top.
3. Click on **Code Downloads & Errata**.
4. Enter the name of the book in the **Search** box.
5. Select the book for which you're looking to download the code files.
6. Choose from the drop-down menu where you purchased this book from.
7. Click on **Code Download**.

Once the file is downloaded, please make sure that you unzip or extract the folder using the latest version of:

- WinRAR / 7-Zip for Windows
- Zipeg / iZip / UnRarX for Mac
- 7-Zip / PeaZip for Linux

The code bundle for the book is also hosted on GitHub at `https://github.com/PacktPubl ishing/Cpp-Windows-Programming`. We also have other code bundles from our rich catalog of books and videos available at `https://github.com/PacktPublishing/`. Check them out!

Downloading the color images of this book

We also provide you with a PDF file that has color images of the screenshots/diagrams used in this book. The color images will help you better understand the changes in the output. You can download this file from `https://www.packtpub.com/sites/default/files/down loads/CppWindowsProgramming_ColorImages.pdf`.

Errata

Although we have taken every care to ensure the accuracy of our content, mistakes do happen. If you find a mistake in one of our books-maybe a mistake in the text or the code-we would be grateful if you could report this to us. By doing so, you can save other readers from frustration and help us improve subsequent versions of this book. If you find any errata, please report them by visiting `http://www.packtpub.com/submit-errata`, selecting your book, clicking on the **Errata Submission Form** link, and entering the details of your errata. Once your errata are verified, your submission will be accepted and the errata will be uploaded to our website or added to any list of existing errata under the Errata section of that title.

To view the previously submitted errata, go to `https://www.packtpub.com/books/conten t/support` and enter the name of the book in the search field. The required information will appear under the **Errata** section.

Piracy

Piracy of copyrighted material on the Internet is an ongoing problem across all media. At Packt, we take the protection of our copyright and licenses very seriously. If you come across any illegal copies of our works in any form on the Internet, please provide us with the location address or website name immediately so that we can pursue a remedy.

Please contact us at `copyright@packtpub.com` with a link to the suspected pirated material.

We appreciate your help in protecting our authors and our ability to bring you valuable content.

Questions

If you have a problem with any aspect of this book, you can contact us at questions@packtpub.com, and we will do our best to address the problem.

1
Introduction

The purpose of this book is to learn how to develop applications in Windows. In order to do so, I have developed Small Windows, which is a C++ object-oriented class library for graphical applications in Windows.

The idea is to guide you into Windows programming by introducing increasingly more advanced applications written in C++ with Small Windows, thereby hiding the technical details of the **Windows 32-bit Applications Programming Interface (Win32 API)**, which is the underlying library for Windows development. With this approach, we can focus on the business logic without struggling with the underlying technical details. If you are interested in knowing how the Win32 API works, the second part of this book gives a detailed description of how Small Windows is implemented.

This book is made up of two parts, where the first part describes the applications developed in C++ with Small Windows. While some books have many examples, this book only includes six examples, among which the last four are rather advanced: the Tetris game, a drawing program, a word processor, and a spreadsheet program. Note that this book is not only a tutorial about Windows programming, but also a tutorial about how to develop object-oriented graphical applications.

The second part holds a detailed description of the implementation of Small Windows in the Win32 API. Note that the Win32 API is not introduced until the second part. Some of you may be satisfied with the high level aspects of Small Windows and only want to study application-specific problems, while others may want to read the second part in order to understand how the classes, methods, and macros of Small Windows are implemented in the Win32 API.

Naturally, I am aware of the existence of modern object-oriented class libraries for Windows. However, the purpose of those libraries is to make it easier for the developer by hiding the details of the architecture, which also prevents the developer from using the Windows architecture to its full extent. Even though the Win32 API has been around for a while, I regard it as the best way to develop professional Windows applications and to understand the Windows architecture.

All source code is given in this book; it is also available as a Visual Studio solution.

The library

This section gives an introduction to Small Windows. The first part of a Small Windows application is the `MainWindow` function. It corresponds to `main` in regular C++. Its task is to set the name of the application and create the main window of the application.

In this book we talk about **definitions** and **declarations**. A declaration is just a notification for the compiler, while a definition is what defines the feature. Below is the declaration of the `MainWindow` function. Its definition is left to the user of Small Windows.

```
void MainWindow(vector<String>argumentList,
                SmallWindows::WindowShow windowShow);
```

Simply put, in Windows the application does not take any initiative; rather, it waits for messages and reacts when it receives them. Informally speaking, *you do not call Windows, Windows calls you.*

The most central part of Small Windows is the `Application` class. In Windows, each event generates a message that is sent to the window that has input focus at the moment. The `Application` class implements the `RunMessageLoop` method, which makes sure that each message is sent to the correct window. It also closes the application when a special quit message is sent.

The creation of a window takes place in two steps. In the first step, the `RegisterWindowClasses` method sets features such as style, color, and appearance. Note that Windows classes are not C++ classes:

```
class Application {
  public:
    static int RunMessageLoop();
    static void RegisterWindowClasses(HINSTANCE instanceHandle);
};
```

The next step is to create an individual window, which is done by the `Window` class. All `virtual` methods are empty and are intended to be overridden by sub classes shown as follows:

```
class Window {
  public:
```

A window can be visible or invisible, enabled or disabled. When a window is enabled, it accepts mouse, touch, and keyboard input:

```
void ShowWindow(bool visible);
void EnableWindow(bool enable);
```

The `OnMove` and the `OnSize` methods are called when the window is moved or resized. The `OnHelp` method is called when the user presses the *F1* key or the **Help** button in a message box:

```
virtual void OnMove(Point topLeft);
virtual void OnSize(Size windowSize);
virtual void OnHelp();
```

The **client area** is the part of the window that it is possible to paint in. Informally, the client area is the window minus its frame. The contents of the client area can be zoomed. The default zoom factor is 1.0:

```
double GetZoom() const;
void SetZoom(double zoom);
```

The **timer** can be set to an interval in milliseconds. The `OnTimer` method is called on every interval. It is possible to set up several timers, as long as they have different identity numbers:

```
void SetTimer(int timerId, unsigned int interval);
void DropTimer(int timerId);
virtual void OnTimer(int timerId);
```

The `OnMouseDown`, `OnMouseUp`, and `OnDoubleClick` methods are called when the user presses, releases, or double-clicks on a mouse button. The `OnMouseMove` method is called when the user moves the mouse with at least one button pressed. The `OnMouseWheel` method is called when the user moves the mouse wheel with one click:

```
virtual void OnMouseDown(MouseButton mouseButtons,
                Point mousePoint, bool shiftPressed,
                bool controlPressed);
```

```
virtual void OnMouseUp(MouseButton mouseButtons,
                Point mousePoint, bool shiftPressed,
                bool controlPressed);
virtual void OnDoubleClick(MouseButton mouseButtons,
                Point mousePoint, bool shiftPressed,
                bool controlPressed);
virtual void OnMouseMove(MouseButton mouseButtons,
                Point mousePoint, bool shiftPressed,
                bool controlPressed);
virtual void OnMouseWheel(WheelDirection direction,
                bool shiftPressed, bool controlPressed);
```

The OnTouchDown, OnTouchMove, and OnTouchDown methods work in the same way as the mouse methods. However, as the user can touch several points at the same time, the methods takes lists of points rather than an individual point:

```
virtual void OnTouchDown(vector<Point> pointList);
virtual void OnTouchMove(vector<Point> pointList);
virtual void OnTouchUp(vector<Point> pointList);
```

The OnKeyDown and OnKeyUp methods are called when the user presses or releases a key. If the user presses a graphical key (a key with an ASCII value between 32 and 127, inclusive), the OnChar method is called in between:

```
virtual bool OnKeyDown(WORD key, bool shiftPressed,
                    bool controlPressed);
virtual void OnChar(TCHAR tChar);
virtual bool OnKeyUp(WORD key, bool shiftPressed,
                    bool controlPressed);
```

The Invalidate method marks a part of the client area (or the whole client area) to be repainted; the area becomes **invalidated**. The area is cleared before the painting if clear is true. The UpdateWindow method forces a repainting of the invalidated area. It causes the OnPaint method to be called eventually:

```
void Invalidate(Rect areaRect, bool clear = true) const;
void Invalidate(bool clear = true) const;
void UpdateWindow();
```

The OnPaint method is called when some part of the client area needs to be repainted and the OnPrint method is called when it is sent to a printer. Their default behavior is to call the OnDraw method with Paint or Print as the value of the drawMode parameter:

```
virtual void OnPaint(Graphics& graphics) const;
virtual void OnPrint(Graphics& graphics, int page,
                     int copy, int totalPages) const;
virtual void OnDraw(Graphics& graphics, DrawMode drawMode)
                 const;
```

The OnClose method closes the window if TryClose returns true. The OnDestroy method is called when the window is being closed:

```
virtual void OnClose();
virtual bool TryClose();
virtual void OnDestroy();
```

The following methods inspect and modify the size and position of the window. Note that we cannot set the size of the client area; it can only be set indirectly by resizing the window:

```
Size GetWindowSize() const;
void SetWindowSize(Size windowSize);
Point GetWindowPosition() const;
void SetWindowPosition(Point topLeft);
Size GetClientSize() const;
```

In the word processor and spreadsheet programs in this book, we handle text and need to calculate the size of individual characters. The following methods calculate the width of a character with a given font. They also calculate the height, ascent, and average character width of a font:

```
int GetCharacterWidth(Font font, TCHAR tChar) const;
int GetCharacterHeight(Font font) const;
int GetCharacterAscent(Font font) const;
int GetCharacterAverageWidth(Font font) const;
```

The ascent line separates the upper and lower part of a letter, shown as follows:

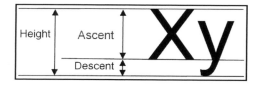

Finally, the MessageBox method displays a simple message box in the window:

```
Answer MessageBox(String message,
            String caption = TEXT("Error"),
            ButtonGroup buttonGroup = Ok,
            Icon icon = NoIcon, bool help = false) const;
};
```

The `Window` class also uses the `Graphics` class responsible for drawing text and geometrical objects in the window. A reference to a `Graphics` object is sent to the `OnPaint`, `OnPrint`, and `OnDraw` methods in the `Window` class. It can be used to draw lines, rectangles, and ellipses and to write text:

```
class Graphics {
  public:
    void DrawLine(Point startPoint, Point endPoint,
                  Color penColor, PenStyle penStyle = Solid);
    void DrawRectangle(Rect rect, Color penColor,
                       PenStyle = Solid);
    void FillRectangle(Rect rect, Color penColor,
                       Color brushColor, PenStyle penStyle=Solid);
    void DrawEllipse(Rect rect, Color penColor,
                     PenStyle = Solid);
    void FillEllipse(Rect rect, Color penColor,
                     Color brushColor, PenStyle penStyle=Solid);
    void DrawText(Rect areaRect, String text, Font font,
                  Color textColor, Color backColor,
                  bool pointsToMeters = true);
};
```

The `Document` class extends the `Window` class with some functionality common to document-based applications. The scroll thumbs are automatically set to reflect the visible part of the document. The mouse wheel moves the vertical scroll bar one line-height for each click. The height of a line is set by the constructor. The code snippet for it is shown as follows:

```
class Document : public Window {
  public:
```

The **dirty flag** is `true` when the user has made a change in the document and it needs to be saved. In `Document`, the dirty flag is set manually, but in the following `StandardDocument` subclass it is handled by the framework:

```
bool IsDirty() const;
void SetDirty(bool dirty);
```

The **caret** is the blinking marker that indicates to the user where they should input the next character. The keyboard can be set (with the Insert key) to insert or overwrite mode. The caret is often a thin vertical bar in insert mode and a block with the width of an average character in overwrite mode.

The caret can be set or cleared. For instance, in the word processor, the caret is visible when the user writes text and invisible when the user marks text. When the window gains focus, the caret becomes visible if it has earlier been set. When the window loses focus, the caret becomes invisible, regardless of whether it has earlier been set:

```
void SetCaret(Rect caretRect);
void ClearCaret();
void OnGainFocus();
void OnLoseFocus();
```

A document may hold a menu bar, which is set by the SetMenuBar method:

```
void SetMenuBar(Menu& menuBar);
```

The OnDropFiles method is called when the user drops one or several files in the window. Their paths are stored in the path list:

```
virtual void OnDropFile(vector<String> pathList);
```

The keyboard mode of a document can be set to **insert** or **overwrite** as follows:

```
KeyboardMode GetKeyboardMode() const;
void SetKeyboardMode(KeyboardMode mode);
```

The OnHorizontalScroll and OnVerticalScroll methods are called when the user scrolls the bar by clicking on the scroll bar arrows or the scroll bar fields, or dragging the scroll thumbs. The code snippet for it is shown as follows:

```
virtual void OnHorizontalScroll(WORD flags,WORD thumbPos=0);
virtual void OnVerticalScroll(WORD flags, WORD thumbPos =0);
```

There is a large set of methods for inspecting or changing scroll bar settings. The size of a line or page is set by the constructor:

```
void SetHorizontalScrollPosition(int scrollPos);
int GetHorizontalScrollPosition() const;
void SetVerticalScrollPosition(int scrollPos);
int GetVerticalScrollPosition() const;

void SetHorizontalScrollLineWidth(int lineWidth);
int GetHorizontalScrollLineHeight() const;
void SetVerticalScrollLineHeight(int lineHeight);
int GetVerticalScrollLineHeight() const;

void SetHorizontalScrollPageWidth(int pageWidth);
int GetHorizontalScrollPageWidth() const;
void SetVerticalScrollPageHeight(int pageHeight);
int GetVerticalScrollPageHeight() const;
```

```
      void SetHorizontalScrollTotalWidth(int scrollWidth);
      int GetHorizontalScrollTotalWidth() const;
      void SetVerticalScrollTotalHeight(int scrollHeight);
      int GetVerticalScrollTotalHeight() const;
};
```

The Menu class handles the menu bar, a menu, a menu item, or a menu item separator (a horizontal bar) in the document. The selection listener is called when the user selects the menu item. The enable, check, and radio listeners are called (unless they are null) when the item is about to become visible. If they return true, the item is enabled or annotated with a check box or radio button:

```
class Menu {
  public:
    void AddMenu(Menu& menu);
    void AddSeparator();
    void AddItem(String text, VoidListener selection,
                 BoolListener enable = nullptr,
                 BoolListener check = nullptr,
                 BoolListener radio = nullptr);
};
```

An **accelerator** is a shortcut command. For instance, often, the **Open** item in the **File** menu is annotated with the text **Ctrl+O**. This means that you can obtain the same result by pressing the *Ctrl* key and the *O* key at the same time, just as if you selected the **Open** menu item. In both cases, the Open dialog is displayed.

The Accelerator class holds only the TextToAccelerator method. It interprets the menu item text and adds the accelerator, if present, to the accelerator set:

```
class Accelerator {
    public:
      static void TextToAccelerator(String& text, int idemId,
                                    list<ACCEL>& acceleratorSet);
};
```

The StandardDocument class extends the Document class and sets up a framework that takes care of all traditional tasks, such as load and save, and cut, copy, and paste, in a document-based application:

```
class StandardDocument : public Document {
  public:
```

The StandardDocument class comes equipped with the common **File**, **Edit**, and **Help** menus. The **File** menu can optionally (if the print parameter is true) be equipped with menu items for printing and print previewing:

```
Menu StandardFileMenu(bool print);
Menu StandardEditMenu();
Menu StandardHelpMenu();
```

The `ClearDocument` method is called when the user selects the **New** menu item; its task is to clear the document. The `WriteDocumentToStream` method is called when the user selects the **Save** or **Save As** menu item and the `ReadDocumentFromStream` method is called when the user selects the **Open** menu item:

```
virtual void ClearDocument();
virtual bool WriteDocumentToStream(String name,
                                   ostream& outStream)const;
virtual bool ReadDocumentFromStream(String name,
                                    istream& inStream);
```

The `CopyAscii`, `CopyUnicode`, and `CopyGeneric` methods are called when the user selects the **Cut** or **Copy** menu item and the corresponding `ready` method returns `true`. The code snippet for it is shown as follows:

```
virtual void CopyAscii(vector<String>& textList) const;
virtual bool IsCopyAsciiReady() const;
virtual void CopyUnicode(vector<String>& textList) const;
virtual bool IsCopyUnicodeReady() const;
virtual void CopyGeneric(int format, InfoList& infoList)
                        const;
virtual bool IsCopyGenericReady(int format) const;
```

In the same way, the `PasteAscii`, `PasteUnicode`, and `PasteGeneric` methods are called when the user selects the **Paste** menu item and the corresponding `ready` method returns `true`:

```
virtual void PasteAscii(const vector<String>& textList);
virtual bool IsPasteAsciiReady
            (const vector<String>& textList) const;
virtual void PasteUnicode(const vector<String>& textList);
virtual bool IsPasteUnicodeReady
            (const vector<String>& textList) const;
virtual void PasteGeneric(int format, InfoList& infoList);
virtual bool IsPasteGenericReady(int format,
                                 InfoList& infoList) const;
```

The `OnDropFile` method checks the path list and accepts the drop if exactly one file has the suffix of the document type of the application (set by the constructor):

```
void OnDropFile(vector<String> pathList);
};
```

In Small Windows, we do not care about the pixel size. Instead, we use **logical units** that stay the same, regardless of the physical resolution of the screen. We can choose from the following three coordinate systems:

- `LogicalWithScroll`: A logical unit is one hundredth of a millimeter, with the current scroll bar settings taken into account. The drawing program and word processor use this system.
- `LogicalWithoutScroll`: A logical unit is one hundredth of a millimeter also in this case, but the current scroll bar settings are ignored. The spreadsheet program uses this system.
- `PreviewCoordinate`: The client area of the window is set to a fixed logical size when the window is created. This means that the size of the logical units changes when the user changes the window size. The Tetris game and the `PreviewDocument` class uses this system.

Besides the `StandardDocument` class, there is also the `PrintPreviewDocument`, which class that also extends the `Document` class. It displays one of the pages of a standard document. It is possible for the user to change the page by using the arrow keys and the *Page Up* and *Page Down* keys or by using the vertical scroll bar:

```
class PrintPreviewDocument : Document {
  public:
    PrintPreviewDocument(StandardDocument* parentDocument,
                int page = 1, Size pageSize = USLetterPortrait);
    bool OnKeyDown(WORD key, bool shiftPressed,
                bool controlPressed);
    void OnVerticalScroll(WORD flags, WORD thumbPos = 0);
    void OnPaint(Graphics& graphics) const;
};
```

There are also the simple auxiliary classes:

- `Point`: It holds a two-dimensional point (x and y)
- `Size`: It holds two-dimensional width and height
- `Rect`: It holds the four corners of a rectangle
- `DynamicList`: It holds a dynamic list
- `Tree`: It holds a tree structure
- `InfoList`: It holds a list of generic information that can be transformed into a memory block

The `Registry` class holds an interface to the **Windows Registry**, the database in the Windows system that we can use to store values in between the execution of our applications. The Clipboard class holds an interface to the **Windows Clipboard**, an area in Windows intended for short-term data storage that we can use to store information cut, copied, and pasted between applications.

The Dialog class is designed for customized dialogs. The Control class is the root class for the controls of the dialog. The CheckBox, RadioButton, PushButton, ListBox, and ComboBox classes are classes for the specific controls. The TextField class holds a text field that can be translated to different types by the Converter class. Finally, the PageSetupDialog class extends the Dialog class and implements a dialog with controls and converters.

Summary

This chapter has given an introduction to Small Windows. In Chapter 2, *Hello, Small World*, we will start to develop applications with Small Windows.

2
Hello, Small World!

This chapter introduces Small Windows by presenting the following two small applications:

- The first application writes "Hello, Small Windows!" in a window
- The second application handles circles of different colors in a document window

Hello, Small Windows!

In *The C Programming Language* by Brian Kernighan and Dennis Richie, the hello-world example was introduced. It was a small program that wrote "hello, world" on the screen. In this section, we shall write a similar program for Small Windows.

In regular C++, the execution of the application starts with the `main` function. In Small Windows, however, `main` is hidden in the framework and has been replaced by `MainWindow`, whose task is to define the application name and create the main window object. The following `argumentList` parameter corresponds to `argc` and `argv` in main. The `commandShow` parameter forwards the system's request regarding the window's appearance:

MainWindow.cpp

```
#include "..\\SmallWindows\\SmallWindows.h"
#include "HelloWindow.h"

void MainWindow(vector<String> /* argumentList */, WindowShow windowShow) {
  Application::ApplicationName() = TEXT("Hello");
  Application::MainWindowPtr() =
    new HelloWindow(windowShow);
}
```

In C++, there are to two character types, char and wchar_t, where char holds a regular character of 1 byte and wchar_t holds a wide character of larger size, usually 2 bytes. There is also the string class, which holds a string of char values, and the wstring class, which holds a string of wchar_t values.

However, in Windows, there is also the generic character type TCHAR, which is char or wchar_t, depending on system settings. There is also the String class, which holds a string of TCHAR values. Moreover, TEXT is a macro that translates a character value to TCHAR and a text value to an array of TCHAR values.

To sum it up, the following table shows character types and string classes:

Regular character	Wide character	Generic character
char	wchar_t	TCHAR
string	wstring	String

In the applications of this book, we always use the TCHAR type, the String class, and the TEXT macro. The only exception to that rule is clipboard handling in Chapter 13, *The Registry, Clipboard, Standard Dialogs, and Print Preview*.

Our version of the hello-world program writes "Hello, Small Windows!" in the center of the client area. The client area of the window is that part of the window where it is possible to draw graphical objects. In the following window, the client area is the white area:

The `HelloWindow` class extends the Small Windows `Window` class. It holds a constructor and the `Draw` method. The constructor calls the `Window` constructor with suitable information regarding the appearance of the window. The `Draw` method is called every time the client area of the window needs to be redrawn:

HelloWindow.h

```
class HelloWindow : public Window {
  public:
    HelloWindow(WindowShow windowShow);
    void OnDraw(Graphics& graphics, DrawMode drawMode) const;
};
```

The constructor of `HelloWindow` calls the constructor of `Window` with the following parameters:

- The first parameter of the `HelloWindow` constructor is the coordinate system. `LogicalWithScroll` indicates that each logical unit is one hundredth of a millimeter, regardless of the physical resolution of the screen. The current scroll bar settings are taken into consideration.
- The second parameter of the `Window` constructor is the preferred size of the window. It indicates that a default size should be used.
- The third parameter is a pointer to the parent window. It is null since the window has no parent window.
- The fourth and fifth parameters set the window's style, in this case overlapped windows.
- The last parameter is `windowShow`, given by the surrounding system to `MainWindow`, which decides the window's initial appearance (minimized, normal, or maximized).
- Finally, the constructor sets the header of the window by calling the `Window` class's `SetHeader` method.

HelloWindow.cpp

```
#include "..\\SmallWindows\\SmallWindows.h"
#include "HelloWindow.h"

HelloWindow::HelloWindow(WindowShow windowShow)
 :Window(LogicalWithScroll, ZeroSize, nullptr,
         OverlappedWindow, NoStyle, windowShow) {
  SetHeader(TEXT("Hello Window"));
}
```

The `OnDraw` method is called every time the client area of the window needs to be redrawn. It obtains the size of the client area and draws the text in its center with black text on a white background. The `SystemFont` parameter will make the text appear in the default system font.

The Small Windows `Color` class holds the constants `Black` and `White`. The `Point` class holds a two-dimensional point. The `Size` class holds `width` and `height`. The `Rect` class holds a rectangle; more specifically, it holds the four corners of a rectangle:

```
void HelloWindow::OnDraw(Graphics& graphics,
                          DrawMode /* drawMode */) const {
  Size clientSize = GetClientSize();
  Rect clientRect(Point(0, 0), clientSize);
  graphics.DrawText(clientRect, TEXT("Hello, Small Windows!"),
                    SystemFont, Black, White);
}
```

The circle application

In this section, we look into a simple circle application. As the name implies, it enables the user to handle circles in a graphical application. The user can add a new circle by pressing the left mouse button. The user can also move an existing circle by dragging it. Moreover, the user can change the color of a circle as well as save and open the document:

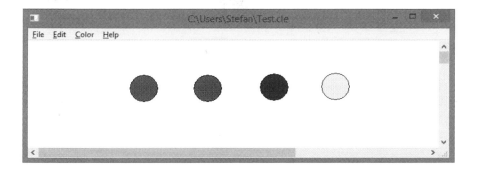

The main window

As we will see throughout this book, the MainWindow function always does the same thing: it sets the application name and creates the main window of the application. The name is used by the **Save** and **Open** standard dialogs, the **About** menu item, and the registry.

The difference between the main window and other windows of the application is that, when the user closes the main window, the application exits. Moreover, when the user selects the **Exit** menu item, the main window is closed, and its destructor is called:

MainWindow.cpp

```cpp
#include "..\\SmallWindows\\SmallWindows.h"
#include "Circle.h"
#include "CircleDocument.h"

void MainWindow(vector<String> /* argumentList */,
                WindowShow windowShow) {
  Application::ApplicationName() = TEXT("Circle");
  Application::MainWindowPtr() =
    new CircleDocument(windowShow);
}
```

The CircleDocument class

The CircleDocument class extends the Small Windows StandardDocument class, which, in turn, extends the Document and Window classes. In fact, the StandardDocument class constitutes a framework, that is, a base class with a set of virtual methods with functionality that we can override and further specify.

The OnMouseDown and OnMouseUp methods are overridden from the Window class and are called when the user presses or releases one of the mouse buttons. The OnMouseMove method is called when the user moves the mouse. The OnDraw method is also overridden from the Window class and is called every time the window needs to be redrawn.

The ClearDocument, ReadDocumentFromStream, and WriteDocumentToStream methods are overridden from the StandardDocument class and are called when the user creates a new file, opens a file, or saves a file:

CircleDocument.h

```
class CircleDocument : public StandardDocument {
  public:
    CircleDocument(WindowShow windowShow);
    ~CircleDocument();

    void OnMouseDown(MouseButton mouseButtons,
                     Point mousePoint,
                     bool shiftPressed,
                     bool controlPressed);
    void OnMouseUp(MouseButton mouseButtons,
                   Point mousePoint,
                   bool shiftPressed,
                   bool controlPressed);
    void OnMouseMove(MouseButton mouseButtons,
                     Point mousePoint,
                     bool shiftPressed,
                     bool controlPressed);

    void OnDraw(Graphics& graphics, DrawMode drawMode) const;

    bool ReadDocumentFromStream(String name,
                                istream& inStream);
    bool WriteDocumentToStream(String name,
                               ostream& outStream) const;
    void ClearDocument();
```

The DEFINE_BOOL_LISTENER and DEFINE_VOID_LISTENER macros define **listeners** which are methods without parameters that are called when the user selects a menu item. The only difference between the macros is the return type of the defined methods: bool or void.

In the applications of this book, we use the common standard whereby listeners called in response to user actions are prefixed with On, for instance, OnRed, as shown in the following code snippet. The methods that decide whether the menu item should be enabled are suffixed with Enable, and the methods that decide whether the menu item should be marked with a check mark or a radio button are suffixed with Check or Radio.

In the following application, we define menu items for the red, green, and blue colors. We also define a menu item for the color standard dialog:

```
DEFINE_VOID_LISTENER(CircleDocument,OnRed);
DEFINE_VOID_LISTENER(CircleDocument,OnGreen);
DEFINE_VOID_LISTENER(CircleDocument,OnBlue);
DEFINE_VOID_LISTENER(CircleDocument,OnColorDialog);
```

When the user has chosen one of the colors, red, green, or blue, its corresponding menu item is checked with a radio button. The RedRadio, GreenRadio, and BlueRadio parameters are called before the menu items become visible and return a Boolean value indicating whether the menu item should be marked with a radio button:

```
DEFINE_BOOL_LISTENER(CircleDocument, RedRadio);
DEFINE_BOOL_LISTENER(CircleDocument, GreenRadio);
DEFINE_BOOL_LISTENER(CircleDocument, BlueRadio);
```

The circle radius is always 500 units, which corresponds to 5 mm:

```
static const int CircleRadius = 500;
```

The circleList field holds the circles, where the topmost circle is located at the beginning of the list. The nextColor field holds the color of the next circle to be added by the user. It is initialized to minus 0ne to indicate that no circle is being moved at the beginning. The moveIndex and movePoint fields are used by the OnMouseDown and OnMouseMove methods to keep track of the circle being moved by the user:

```
private:
  vector<Circle> circleList;
  Color nextColor;
  int moveIndex = -1;
  Point movePoint;
};
```

In the `StandardDocument` constructor call, the first two parameters are `LogicalWithScroll` and `USLetterPortrait`. They indicate that the logical size is hundredths of millimeters and that the client area holds the logical size of a US letter: *215.9*279.4 millimeters (8.5*11 inches)*. If the window is resized so that the client area becomes smaller than a US letter, scroll bars are added to the window.

The third parameter sets the file information used by the standard save and open dialogs; the text description is set to `Circle Files` and the file suffix is set to `cle`. The `nullptr` parameter indicates that the window does not have a parent window. The `OverlappedWindow` constant parameter indicates that the window should overlap other windows, and the `windowShow` parameter is the window's initial appearance passed on from the surrounding system by the `MainWindow` class:

CircleDocument.cpp

```
#include "..\\SmallWindows\\SmallWindows.h"
#include "Circle.h"
#include "CircleDocument.h"

CircleDocument::CircleDocument(WindowShow windowShow)
 :StandardDocument(LogicalWithScroll, USLetterPortrait,
                   TEXT("Circle Files, cle"), nullptr,
                   OverlappedWindow, windowShow) {
```

The `StandardDocument` class adds the standard **File**, **Edit**, and **Help** menus to the window menu bar. The **File** menu holds the **New, Open, Save, Save As, Page Setup, Print Preview**, and **Exit** items. **Page Setup** and **Print Preview** are optional. The seventh parameter of the `StandardDocument` constructor (the default value is `false`) indicates their presence. The **Edit** menu holds the **Cut, Copy, Paste**, and **Delete** items. They are disabled by default; we will not use them in this application. The **Help** menu holds the **About** item, and the application name set in `MainWindow` is used to display a message box with a standard message **Circle, version 1.0**.

We add the standard **File** and **Edit** menus to the menu bar. Then we add the **Color** menu, which is the application-specific menu of this application. Finally, we add the standard **Help** menu and set the menu bar of the document.

The **Color** menu holds the menu items used to set the circle colors. The OnRed, OnGreen, and OnBlue methods are called when the user selects the menu item, and the RedRadio, GreenRadio, and BlueRadio methods are called before the user selects the **Color** menu in order to decide if the items should be marked with a radio button. The OnColorDialog method opens a standard color dialog.

In the &Red\tCtrl+R text in the following code snippet, the **ampersand (&)** indicates that the menu item has a **mnemonic**; that is, the letter R will be underlined and it is possible to select the menu item by pressing **R** after the menu has been opened. The **tabulator character** (**\t**) indicates that the second part of the text defines an **accelerator**; that is, the text Ctrl+R will occur right-justified in the menu item and the item can be selected by pressing Ctrl+R:

```
Menu menuBar(this);
```

The false parameter to StandardFileMenu indicates that we do not want to include the file menu items.

```
menuBar.AddMenu(StandardFileMenu(false));
```

The AddItem method in the Menu class also takes two more parameters for enabling the menu item and setting a checkbox. However, we do not use them in this application. Therefore, we send null pointers:

```
Menu colorMenu(this, TEXT("&Color"));
colorMenu.AddItem(TEXT("&Red\tCtrl+R"), OnRed,
                  nullptr, nullptr, RedRadio);
colorMenu.AddItem(TEXT("&Green\tCtrl+G"), OnGreen,
                  nullptr, nullptr, GreenRadio);
colorMenu.AddItem(TEXT("&Blue\tCtrl+B"), OnBlue,
                  nullptr, nullptr, BlueRadio);
colorMenu.AddSeparator();
colorMenu.AddItem(TEXT("&Dialog ..."), OnColorDialog);
menuBar.AddMenu(colorMenu);

menuBar.AddMenu(StandardHelpMenu());
SetMenuBar(menuBar);
```

Finally, we read the current color (the color of the next circle to be added) from the registry; red is the default color in case there is no color stored in the registry:

```
nextColor.ReadColorFromRegistry(TEXT("NextColor"), Red);
}
```

The destructor saves the current color in the registry. In this application, we do not need to perform the destructor's normal tasks such as deallocating memory or closing files:

```
CircleDocument::~CircleDocument() {
  nextColor.WriteColorToRegistry(TEXT("NextColor"));
}
```

The `ClearDocument` method is called when the user selects the **New** menu item. In this case, we just clear the circle list. Every other action, such as redrawing the window or changing its title, is taken care of by the `StandardDocument` class:

```
void CircleDocument::ClearDocument() {
  circleList.clear();
}
```

The `WriteDocumentToStream` method is called by the `StandardDocument` class when the user saves a file (by selecting **Save** or **Save As**). It writes the number of circles (the size of the circle list) to the output stream and calls the `WriteCircle` method for each circle in order to write their states to the stream:

```
bool CircleDocument::WriteDocumentToStream(String name,
                           ostream& outStream) const {
  int size = circleList.size();
  outStream.write((char*) &size, sizeof size);

  for (Circle circle : circleList) {
    circle.WriteCircle(outStream);
  }

  return ((bool) outStream);
}
```

The `ReadDocumentFromStream` method is called by the `StandardDocument` method when the user opens a file by selecting the **Open** menu item. It reads the number of circles (the size of the circle list) and for each circle it creates a new object of the `Circle` class, calls the `ReadCircle` method in order to read the state of the circle, and adds the circle object to the `circleList` method:

```
bool CircleDocument::ReadDocumentFromStream(String name,
                              istream& inStream) {
  int size;
  inStream.read((char*) &size, sizeof size);
```

```
    for (int count = 0; count < size; ++count) {
      Circle circle;
      circle.ReadCircle(inStream);
      circleList.push_back(circle);
    }

    return ((bool) inStream);
}
```

The OnMouseDown method is called when the user presses one of the mouse buttons. First we need to check that they have pressed the left mouse button. If they have, we loop through the circle list and call the IsClick method for each circle in order to decide whether they have clicked on a circle. Note that the topmost circle is located at the beginning of the list; therefore, we loop from the beginning of the list. If we find a clicked circle, we break the loop.

If the user has clicked on a circle, we store its index moveIndex and the current mouse position in movePoint. Both values are needed by that OnMouseMove method that will be called when the user moves the mouse:

```
void CircleDocument::OnMouseDown
          (MouseButton mouseButtons, Point mousePoint,
           bool shiftPressed /* = false */,
           bool controlPressed /* = false */) {
  if (mouseButtons == LeftButton) {
    moveIndex = -1;
    int size = circleList.size();

    for (int index = 0; index < size; ++index) {
      if (circleList[index].IsClick(mousePoint)) {
        moveIndex = index;
        movePoint = mousePoint;
        break;
      }
    }
  }
```

However, if the user has not clicked on a circle, we add a new circle. A circle is defined by its center position (mousePoint), radius (CircleRadius), and color (nextColor).

An invalidated area is a part of the client area that needs to be redrawn. Remember that in Windows, we normally do not draw figures directly. Instead, we call the Invalidate method to tell the system that an area needs to be redrawn and force the actual redrawing by calling the UpdateWindow method, which eventually results in a call to the OnDraw method. The invalidated area is always a rectangle. The Invalidate method has a second parameter (the default value is true) indicating that the invalidated area should be cleared.

Technically, it is painted in the window's client color, which in this case is white. In this way, the previous location of the circle is cleared and the circle is drawn at its new location.

The SetDirty method tells the framework that the document has been altered (the document has become *dirty*), which causes the **Save** menu item to be enabled and the user to be warned if he/she tries to close the window without saving it:

```
    if (moveIndex == -1) {
      Circle newCircle(mousePoint, CircleRadius,
                       nextColor);
      circleList.push_back(newCircle);
      Invalidate(newCircle.Area());
      UpdateWindow();
      SetDirty(true);
    }
  }
}
```

The OnMouseMove method is called every time the user moves the mouse with at least one mouse button pressed. We first need to check whether the user is pressing the left mouse button and is clicking on a circle (whether the moveIndex method does not equal −1). If the user is, we calculate the distance from the previous mouse event (OnMouseDown or OnMouseMove) by comparing the previous and the current mouse position using the mousePoint method. We update the circle position, invalidate both the old and new area, forcing a redrawing of the invalidated areas with the UpdateWindow method, and set the dirty flag:

```
void CircleDocument::OnMouseMove
           (MouseButton mouseButtons, Point mousePoint,
            bool shiftPressed /* = false */,
            bool controlPressed /* = false */) {
  if ((mouseButtons == LeftButton)&&(moveIndex != -1)) {
    Size distanceSize = mousePoint - movePoint;
    movePoint = mousePoint;

    Circle& movedCircle = circleList[moveIndex];
    Invalidate(movedCircle.Area());
    movedCircle.Center() += distanceSize;
    Invalidate(movedCircle.Area());

    UpdateWindow();
    SetDirty(true);
  }
}
```

Strictly speaking, the OnMouseUp method could be excluded since the moveIndex method is set to minus one in the OnMouseDown method, which is always called before the OnMouseMove method. However, it has been included for the sake of completeness:

```
void CircleDocument::OnMouseUp
          (MouseButton mouseButtons, Point mousePoint,
           bool shiftPressed /* = false */,
           bool controlPressed /* = false */) {
  moveIndex = -1;
}
```

The OnDraw method is called every time the window needs to be (partly or completely) redrawn. The call can be initialized by the system as a response to an event (for instance, the window has been resized) or by an earlier call to the UpdateWindow method. The Graphics reference parameter has been created by the framework and can be considered as a toolbox for drawing lines, painting areas, and writing text. However, in this application, we do not write text.

We iterate through the circle list and, for each circle, call the Draw method. Note that we do not care about which circles are to be physically redrawn. We simple redraw all circles. However, only the circles located in an area that has been invalidated by a previous call to the Invalidate method will be physically redrawn.

The Draw method has a second parameter indicating the draw mode, which can be Paint or Print. The Paint method indicates that the OnDraw method is called by the OnPaint method in the Window class and that the painting is performed in the window's client area. The Print method indicates that the OnDraw method is called by the OnPrint method and that the painting is sent to a printer. However, in this application, we do not use that parameter:

```
void CircleDocument::OnDraw(Graphics& graphics,
                            DrawMode /* drawMode */) const {
  for (Circle circle : circleList) {
    circle.Draw(graphics);
  }
}
```

The RedRadio, GreenRadio, and BlueRadio methods are called before the menu items are shown, and the items will be marked with a radio button if they return true. The Red, Green, and Blue constants are defined in the Color class:

```
bool CircleDocument::RedRadio() const {
  return (nextColor == Red);
}
```

```
bool CircleDocument::GreenRadio() const {
  return (nextColor == Green);
}

bool CircleDocument::BlueRadio() const {
  return (nextColor == Blue);
}
```

The OnRed, OnGreen, and OnBlue methods are called when the user selects the corresponding menu item. They all set the nextColor field to an appropriate value:

```
void CircleDocument::OnRed() {
  nextColor = Red;
}

void CircleDocument::OnGreen() {
  nextColor = Green;
}

void CircleDocument::OnBlue() {
  nextColor = Blue;
}
```

The OnColorDialog method is called when the user selects the **Color** dialog menu item and displays the standard color dialog. If the user chooses a new color, the nextcolor method will be given the chosen color value:

```
void CircleDocument::OnColorDialog() {
  StandardDialog(this, nextColor);
}
```

The Circle class

Circle is a class holding the information about a single circle. The default constructor is used when reading a circle from a file. The second constructor is used when creating a new circle. The IsClick method returns true if the given point is located inside the circle (to check whether the user has clicked in the circle), the Area method returns the circle's surrounding rectangle (for invalidation), and the Draw method is called to redraw the circle:

Circle.h

```
class Circle {
  public:
    Circle();
    Circle(Point center, int radius, Color color);

    bool WriteCircle(ostream& outStream) const;
    bool ReadCircle(istream& inStream);

    bool IsClick(Point point) const;
    Rect Area() const;
    void Draw(Graphics& graphics) const;

    Point Center() const {return center;}
    Point& Center() {return center;}
    Color GetColor() {return color;}
```

As mentioned in the previous section, a circle is defined by its center position (`center`), radius (`radius`), and color (`color`):

```
  private:
    Point center;
    int radius;
    Color color;
};
```

The default constructor does not need to initialize the fields since it is called when the user opens a file and the values are read from the file. The second constructor, however, initializes the center point, radius, and color of the circle:

Circle.cpp

```
#include "..\\SmallWindows\\SmallWindows.h"
#include "Circle.h"

Circle::Circle() {
  // Empty.
}

Circle::Circle(Point center, int radius, Color color)
 :color(color),
  center(center),
  radius(radius) {
  // Empty.
}
```

The `WriteCircle` method writes the color, center point, and radius to the stream. Since `radius` is a regular integer, we simply use the C standard function `write`, while `Color` and `Point` have their own methods to write their values to a stream. In the `ReadCircle` method, we read the color, center point, and radius from the stream in a similar manner:

```
bool Circle::WriteCircle(ostream& outStream) const {
  color.WriteColorToStream(outStream);
  center.WritePointToStream(outStream);
  outStream.write((char*) &radius, sizeof radius);
  return ((bool) outStream);
}

bool Circle::ReadCircle(istream& inStream) {
  color.ReadColorFromStream(inStream);
  center.ReadPointFromStream(inStream);
  inStream.read((char*) &radius, sizeof radius);
  return ((bool) inStream);
}
```

The `IsClick` method uses Pythagoras' theorem to calculate the distance between the given point and the circle's center point and returns `true` if the point is located inside the circle (if the distance is less than or equal to the circle radius):

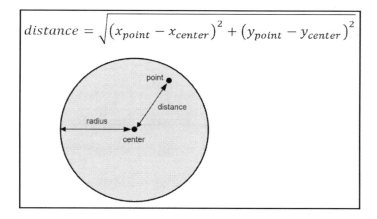

$$distance = \sqrt{\left(x_{point} - x_{center}\right)^2 + \left(y_{point} - y_{center}\right)^2}$$

```
Circle::IsClick(Point point) const {
  int width = point.X() - center.X(),
      height = point.Y() - center.Y();
  int distance = (int) sqrt((width * width) +
                            (height * height));
  return (distance <= radius);
}
```

The top-left corner of the resulting rectangle is the center point minus the radius and the bottom-right corner is the center point plus the radius:

```
Rect Circle::Area() const {
  Point topLeft = center - radius,
        bottomRight = center + radius;
  return Rect(topLeft, bottomRight);
}
```

We use the `FillEllipse` method (there is no `FillCircle` method) of the Small Windows Graphics class to draw the circle. The circle's border is always black, while its interior color is given by the `color` field:

```
void Circle::Draw(Graphics& graphics) const {
  Point topLeft = center - radius,
        bottomRight = center + radius;
  Rect circleRect(topLeft, bottomRight);
  graphics.FillEllipse(circleRect, Black, color);
}
```

Summary

In this chapter, you looked into two applications in Small Windows: a simple hello-world application and a slightly more advanced circle application, which introduced the framework. You also looked into menus, circle drawing, and mouse handling.

In Chapter 3, *Building a Tetris Application*, we will develop a classic Tetris game.

3

Building a Tetris Application

In this chapter, we develop a classic Tetris game. We look further into the `Window` class, including text writing and drawing figures that are more complex. We look also into timing, random numbers, and graphical updates such as falling figures and flash effects. An illustration of it is shown next:

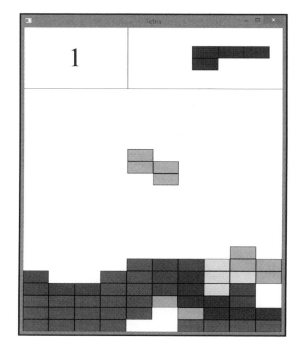

The MainWindow function

The `MainWindow` function is similar to the methods in Chapter 2, *Hello, Small World!*. It sets the application name and returns a pointer to the main window, which, in this case, is an instance of the `TetrisWindow` class. As stated in Chapter 2, *Hello, Small World!* the application name is used when accessing the registry, when opening or saving a file, and by the **About** menu item. However, none of that functionality is used in this application:

MainWindow.cpp

```
#include "..\\SmallWindows\\SmallWindows.h"
#include "GameGrid.h"
#include "TetrisFigure.h"
#include "RedFigure.h"
#include "BrownFigure.h"
#include "TurquoiseFigure.h"
#include "GreenFigure.h"
#include "YellowFigure.h"
#include "BlueFigure.h"
#include "PurpleFigure.h"
#include "TetrisWindow.h"

void MainWindow(vector<String> /* argumentList */,
                WindowShow windowShow) {
  Application::ApplicationName() = TEXT("Tetris");
  Application::MainWindowPtr() = new TetrisWindow(windowShow);
}
```

The Tetris window

In this application, we do not use the `StandardDocument` framework from the Chapter 2, *Hello, Small World!*. Instead, the `TetrisWindow` class extends the Small Windows root class `Window` directly. The reason is simply that we do not need the functionality of the `StandardDocument` framework or its base class `Document`. We do not use menus or accelerators, and we do not save or load files:

TetrisWindow.h

```
class TetrisWindow : public Window {
  public:
    TetrisWindow(WindowShow windowShow);
    ~TetrisWindow();
```

In this application, we ignore the mouse. Instead, we look into keyboard handling. The OnKeyDown method is called when the user presses or releases a key:

```
bool OnKeyDown(WORD key, bool shiftPressed,
               bool controlPressed);
```

Similar to the circle application, the OnDraw method is called every time the window's client area needs to be redrawn:

```
void OnDraw(Graphics& graphics, DrawMode drawMode) const;
```

The OnGainFocus and OnLoseFocus methods are called when the window gains or loses input focus, respectively. When the window loses input focus, it will not receive any keyboard input and the timer is turned off, preventing the falling figure from moving:

```
void OnGainFocus();
void OnLoseFocus();
```

The OnTimer method is called every second the window has focus. It tries to move the falling figure one step downward. It calls the NewFigure method if it fails to move the figure downward. The NewFigure method tries to introduce a new figure on the game board. If that fails, the GameOver method is called, which asks the user if they want a new game. The NewGame method is called if the user wants a new game. If the user does not want a new game, it exits the application:

```
void OnTimer(int timerId);
void EndOfFigure();
void GameOver();
void NewGame();
```

the DeleteFullRows examines each row by calling the IsRowFull method and calls the FlashRow and DeleteRow methods for each full row:

```
void DeleteFullRows();
bool IsRowFull(int row);
void FlashRow(int row);
void DeleteRow(int markedRow);
```

The TryClose method is called if the user tries to close the window by clicking on the cross in the top-right corner of the window. It displays a message box that asks the user if they really want to quit:

```
bool TryClose();
```

The gameGrid field holds the grid on which the figures are displayed (see the next section). The falling figure (fallingFigure) is falling down on the grid, and the next figure to fall down (nextFigure) is displayed in the top-right corner. Each time the player fills a row, the score (currScore) is increased. The timer identity (TimerId) is needed to keep track of the timer and is given the arbitrary value of 1000. Finally, the figure list (figureList) will be filled with seven figures, one of each color. Each time a new figure is needed, a randomly chosen figure from the list will be chosen and copied:

```
  private:
    GameGrid gameGrid;
    TetrisFigure fallingFigure, nextFigure;

    int currScore = 0;
    bool timerActive = true, inverse = false;

    static const int TimerId = 1000;
    vector<TetrisFigure> figureList;
};
```

The PreviewCoordinate parameter in the Window constructor call indicates that the window's size is fixed, and the second parameter indicates that the size is 100 * 100 units. This means that unlike the circle application, the size of figures and game boards will change when the user changes the window's size:

TetrisWindow.cpp

```
#include "..\\SmallWindows\\SmallWindows.h"
#include "GameGrid.h"
#include "TetrisFigure.h"
#include "RedFigure.h"
#include "BrownFigure.h"
#include "TurquoiseFigure.h"
#include "GreenFigure.h"
#include "YellowFigure.h"
#include "BlueFigure.h"
#include "PurpleFigure.h"
#include "TetrisWindow.h"

TetrisWindow::TetrisWindow(WindowShow windowShow)
 :Window(PreviewCoordinate, Rect(0, 0, 100, 100),
         nullptr, OverlappedWindow, NoStyle, Normal),
```

The upper 20 percent of the client area is reserved for the score and the next figure. The game grid covers the lower 80 percent of the client area (from height unit 20 to 100):

```
gameGrid(Rect(0, 20, 100, 100)) {
```

Since we extend the `Window` class, we need to set the window header manually:

```
SetHeader(TEXT("Tetris"));
```

The timer interval is set to `1000` milliseconds, which means that `OnTimer` will be called every second. The random generator is initialized by calling the C standard functions `srand` and `time`:

```
SetTimer(TimerId, 1000);
srand((unsigned int) time(nullptr));
```

The figure list is initialized with one figure of each color; the falling and next figure are randomly chosen from that list. One of the figures in the list will be copied every time we need a new figure:

```
figureList.push_back(RedFigure(this, &gameGrid));
figureList.push_back(BrownFigure(this, &gameGrid));
figureList.push_back(TurquoiseFigure(this, &gameGrid));
figureList.push_back(GreenFigure(this, &gameGrid));
figureList.push_back(YellowFigure(this, &gameGrid));
figureList.push_back(BlueFigure(this, &gameGrid));
figureList.push_back(PurpleFigure(this, &gameGrid));

fallingFigure = figureList[rand() % figureList.size()];
nextFigure = figureList[rand() % figureList.size()];
}
```

Strictly speaking, it is not necessary to drop the timer when closing the Tetris window. The destructor is included only for the sake of completeness:

```
TetrisWindow::~TetrisWindow() {
  DropTimer(TimerId);
}
```

Keyboard input

The `OnKeyDown` method overrides the method in the `Window` class and is called each time the user presses a key. We try to move the falling figure in accordance with the key pressed. We do not care whether the user has pressed the *Shift* or *Ctrl* key:

```
bool TetrisWindow::OnKeyDown(WORD key, bool /* shiftPressed */,
                             bool /* controlPressed */) {
  switch (key) {
    case KeyLeft:
      fallingFigure.TryMoveLeft();
      break;

    case KeyRight:
      fallingFigure.TryMoveRight();
      break;

    case KeyUp:
      fallingFigure.TryRotateAnticlockwise();
      break;

    case KeyDown:
      fallingFigure.TryRotateAnticlockwise();
      break;
```

When the user presses the Space key, the falling figure falls with visible speed to create the illusion of falling. We try to move the falling figure one step down every 10 milliseconds by calling the Win32 API function `Sleep`. The `TryMoveDown` method returns `false` when it is no longer possible to move the figure downward:

```
    case KeySpace:
      while (fallingFigure.TryMoveDown()) {
        ::Sleep(10);
      }
      break;
  }

  return true;
}
```

Drawing

The `OnDraw` method starts by drawing the game grid and two lines dividing the client area into three parts. The top-left corner displays the current score, the top-right corner displays the next figure, and the lower part displays the actual game grid:

```
void TetrisWindow::OnDraw(Graphics& graphics,
                          DrawMode /* drawMode */) const {
  gameGrid.DrawGameGrid(graphics, inverse);
  graphics.FillRectangle(Rect(Point(0, 0), Point(100,20)),
                         White, White);
  graphics.DrawLine(Point(40, 0), Point(40, 20), Black);
  graphics.DrawLine(Point(0, 20), Point(100, 20), Black);
```

Note that we add an offset when drawing the next figure in order to move from the game grid to the top-right corner. The value 25 moves the figure from the middle of the grid to the middle of its right half, and the value −18 moves from the grid up to the area preceding the grid:

```
  fallingFigure.DrawFigure(graphics);
  nextFigure.DrawFigure(graphics, Size(25, -18));
```

The score font is set to `Times New Roman`, size 10. Here, the size does not refer to typographical points, but to logical units. Since the call to the `Window` constructor states we gave the `PreviewCoordinate` coordinate system and the size 100 * 100, the height of the text will be 10 units, which is a tenth of the text client area's height. It is also half the height of the part of the client area where the score is written:

```
  Font scoreFont(TEXT("Times New Roman"), 10);
```

The final `false` parameter in the call to the `DrawText` method indicates that the size of the text won't be recalculated. In the next chapters, we will display text that maintains the same size, regardless of the window size and the screen resolution. In this chapter, however, the size of the text will be changed when the user changes the size of window:

```
  graphics.DrawText(Rect(0, 0, 40, 20), to_String(currScore),
                    scoreFont, Black, White, false);
}
```

Input focus

The `OnGainFocus` and `OnLoseFocus` methods start and stop the timer, respectively, so that the falling figure does not fall down when the window is out of focus:

```
void TetrisWindow::OnGainFocus() {
  SetTimer(TimerId, 1000);
}

void TetrisWindow::OnLoseFocus() {
  DropTimer(TimerId);
}
```

The timer

The timer is active when it has the input focus. When active, the `TryMoveDown` method will be called every time the `OnTimer` method is called (once every second). When the figure cannot fall down any more (the `TryMoveDown` method returns `false`), the `EndOfFigure` method is called:

```
void TetrisWindow::OnTimer(int /* timerId */) {
  if (timerActive) {
    if (!fallingFigure.TryMoveDown()) {
      EndOfFigure();
    }
  }
}
```

New figures

When it is not possible for the falling figure to move downward, the `OnTimer` method calls the `NewFigure` method. First, we need to store the falling figure to the game grid by calling the `AddToGrid` method. Then, we let the next figure become the new falling figure and we choose by random the new next figure from the figure list. We invalidate the area of the new falling figure and the area of the top-right corner where the next figure is drawn:

```
void TetrisWindow::NewFigure() {
  fallingFigure.AddToGrid();
  fallingFigure = nextFigure;
  fallingFigure.InvalidateFigure();
```

```
nextFigure = figureList[rand() % figureList.size()];
Rect nextArea(40, 0, 100, 20);
Invalidate(nextArea);
UpdateWindow();
```

We delete the possible full rows and update the window:

```
DeleteFullRows();
UpdateWindow();
```

If the new falling figure is not valid from the very beginning, the game is over and `GameOver` is called:

```
if (!fallingFigure.IsFigureValid()) {
  GameOver();
}
}
```

Game over

The `GameOver` method presents the score and lets the user decide whether they want a new game. If they want a new game, it is initialized by the `NewGame` call. If the user does not want a new game, the call to the Win32 API function `PostQuitMessage` terminates the execution of the application.

Note that we call another version of the `Invalidate` method, without parameters. It invalidates the whole client area:

```
void TetrisWindow::GameOver() {
  Invalidate();
  UpdateWindow();
```

The timer is inactive while the message is displayed:

```
timerActive = false;
String message = TEXT("Game Over.\nYou scored ") +
                 to_String(currScore) +
                 TEXT(" points.\nAnother game?");

if (MessageBox(message, TEXT("Tetris"), YesNo, Question)==Yes) {
  NewGame();
}
else {
  ::PostQuitMessage(0);
}
}
```

New game

The `NewGame` method initializes the randomly chosen new falling and next figures, resets the score, and clears the game grid before activating the timer, as well as invalidates and updates the window, which makes the new falling figure starting to fall and the new game to begin:

```
void TetrisWindow::NewGame() {
  fallingFigure = figureList[rand() % figureList.size()];
  nextFigure = figureList[rand() % figureList.size()];

  currScore = 0;
  gameGrid.ClearGameGrid();
  timerActive = true;
  Invalidate();
  UpdateWindow();
}
```

Deleting and flashing rows

When deleting full rows, we loop through the rows, flashing and removing each full row. We increase the score and update the area of the row. Note that the rows start at the top of the grid. This means that we have to loop from the highest row to the lowest row in order to delete the row in the right order.

Note that if the row becomes flashed and deleted, we do not update the `row` variable since the deleted row will be replaced by the row above, which also needs to be examined:

```
void TetrisWindow::DeleteFullRows() {
  int row = Rows - 1;
  while (row >= 0) {
    if (IsRowFull(row)) {
      FlashRow(row);
      DeleteRow(row);

      ++currScore;
      Rect scoreArea(0, 0, 40, 20);
      Invalidate(scoreArea);
      UpdateWindow();
    }
    else {
      --row;
    }
  }
}
```

A row is considered full if it does not contain a white square:

```
bool TetrisWindow::IsRowFull(int row) {
  for (int col = 0; col < Cols; ++col) {
    if (gameGrid[row][col] == White) {
      return false;
    }
  }

  return true;
}
```

The flash effect is executed by redrawing the row in normal and inversed color (the `inverse` method is set) three times with an interval of 50 milliseconds. While doing this, it is especially important that we only invalidate the area of the chosen row. Otherwise, the whole window client area will be flashed:

```
void TetrisWindow::FlashRow(int row) {
  Rect gridArea = gameGrid.GridArea();
  int colWidth = gridArea.Width() / Cols,
      rowHeight = gridArea.Height() / Rows;

  Rect rowArea(0, row * rowHeight, Cols * colWidth,
               (row + 1) * rowHeight);

  for (int count = 0; count < 3; ++count) {
    inverse = true;
    Invalidate(rowArea + gridArea.Top()Left());
    UpdateWindow();
    ::Sleep(50);

    inverse = false;
    Invalidate(rowArea + gridArea.Top()Left());
    UpdateWindow();
    ::Sleep(50);
  }
}
```

When deleting a row, we do not really delete it. Instead, we move each row above the deleted row one step downward and fill the top row with white squares. A complication is that we count rows from the top. This makes the lowest row on the screen the row with the highest index. This gives the appearance that we start from the bottom and remove every full row until we reach the top:

```
void TetrisWindow::DeleteRow(int markedRow) {
  for (int row = markedRow; row > 0; --row) {
    for (int col = 0; col < Cols; ++col) {
      gameGrid[row][col] = gameGrid[row - 1][col];
    }
  }

  for (int col = 0; col < Cols; ++col) {
    gameGrid[0][col] = White;
  }

  Invalidate(gameGrid.GridArea());
  Invalidate(g);
  UpdateWindow();
}
```

Closing the window

Finally, when the user wants to close the window by clicking in the cross on the top-right corner, we need to confirm that they really want to quit. If the `TryClose` method returns `true`, the window is closed:

```
bool TetrisWindow::TryClose() {
  timerActive = false;

  if (MessageBox(TEXT("Quit?"), TEXT("Tetris"),
                 YesNo, Question) == Yes) {
    return true;
  }

  timerActive = true;
  return false;
}
```

The TetrisFigure class

In this application, there is the root `figure` class and one subclass for each type of falling figure. All figures can be moved sideways or rotated as a response to the user's requests. They are also moved downward by the timer.

There are seven figures, one for each color: red, brown, turquoise, green, yellow, blue, and purple. Each of them also has a unique shape. However, they all contain four squares. They can further be divided into three groups based on their ability to rotate. The red figure is the simplest one. It is a square and does not rotate at all. The brown, turquoise, and green figure can be rotated in vertical and horizontal directions, while the yellow, blue, and purple figures can be rotated in north, east, south, and west directions. For the red figure, it does not really matter since it does not rotate.

The `row` and `col` fields of the `TetrisFigure` class hold the center of the figure, which is marked by a cross in the illustrations of this section. The `color` field holds the color of the figure, and `direction` holds the current direction of the figure.

Finally, the `direction` array holds the relative positions of the three squares surrounding the marked square. There are four directions at most. Each direction holds three squares, which are the three remaining squares that are not the center of the figure. Each square holds two integers: the relative position of the center row and column.

The default constructor is needed to initialize the `fallingFigure` and `nextFigure` methods in the `TetrisWindow` class. The second constructor is protected since it is only called by its sub classes. Each figure has its own `TetrisFigure` subclass. Their constructors take a pointer to the color grid and define its color, start position, and figure patterns:

TetrisFigure.h

```
class TetrisFigure {
  public:
    TetrisFigure();

  protected:
    TetrisFigure(Window* windowPtr, GameGrid* colorGridPtr,
            Color color, int row, int col, Direction direction,
            IntPair* northList, IntPair* eastList,
            IntPair* southList, IntPair* westList);

  public:
    TetrisFigure& operator=(const TetrisFigure& figure);
```

The TryMoveLeft, TryMoveRight, TryRotateClockwise, TryRotateClockwise, TryRotateAnticlockwise, and TryMoveDown methods all try to move the figure. They call the IsFigureValid method, which checks whether the new location is valid, that is, it is not located outside the game grid or at a location already occupied. The IsFigureValid method, in turn, calls the IsSquareValid method for each of its four squares:

```
void TryMoveLeft();
void TryMoveRight();
void TryRotateClockwise();
void TryRotateAnticlockwise();
bool TryMoveDown();
```

There are two versions of the IsFigureValid method, where the first version is called by the TetrisWindow method and the other version is called by the preceding try methods in order to test whether a new location of the falling figure is valid:

```
bool IsFigureValid();
static bool IsFigureValid(int direction, int row, int col,
            GameGrid* gameGridPtr, IntPair* figureInfo[]);
static bool IsSquareValid(int row, int col,
                        GameGrid* gameGridPtr);
```

The AddToGrid method adds the four squares of the figure to the game grid:

```
void AddToGrid();
```

The InvalidateFigure method invalidates the area occupied by the figure, and the DrawFigure method draws the figure:

```
void InvalidateFigure(Size offsetSize = ZeroSize);
void DrawFigure(Graphics& graphics,
                Size offsetSize = ZeroSize) const;
```

The gameGridPtr field is a pointer to the game grid, which we access when we try to move a figure in order to decide whether its new location is valid. The color field is the color of the figure (red, brown, turquoise, green, yellow, blue, or purple). The row, col, and direction fields hold the current location and direction of the figure.

The figureInfo field holds the shape of the figure. The figure can hold up to four directions: north, east, south, and west. Remember that row and col hold the location of the figures. More specifically, they hold the location of the center square of the four squares constituting the figure (marked by a cross in the following illustrations). The other three squares are defined by integer pairs holding their locations relative to the center square.

Technically, `figureInfo` is an array of four pointers (one each for the directions north, east, south, and west). Each pointer points at an array of three integer pairs, holding the locations of the three squares relative to the center square:

```
protected:
  Window* windowPtr;
  GameGrid* gameGridPtr;
  Color color;
  int row, col;
  Direction direction;
  IntPair* figureInfo[4];
};
```

The default constructor is necessary because `fallingFigure` and `nextFigure` are member objects of the `TetrisWindow` class. However, they do not need to be initialized since their values are assigned one of the seven figures in the `figureList` array:

TetrisFigure.cpp

```
#include "..\\SmallWindows\\SmallWindows.h"
#include "GameGrid.h"
#include "TetrisFigure.h"
#include "TetrisWindow.h"

TetrisFigure::TetrisFigure() {
  // Empty
}
```

The second constructor is called by the colored figure sub class constructor in order to initialize the figure. It takes a pointer to the main window and the game grid, the color of the figure, its start location and direction, and its location lists in the north, east, south, and west directions. Each of the lists holds three integer pairs representing the location of the squares relative to the center square:

```
TetrisFigure::TetrisFigure(Window*windowPtr, GameGrid*gameGridPtr,
                           Color color, int row, int col,
                           Direction direction,
                           IntPair* northList, IntPair* eastList,
                           IntPair* southList, IntPair* westList)
 :windowPtr(windowPtr),
  gameGridPtr(gameGridPtr),
  color(color),
  row(row),
  col(col),
  direction(direction) {
  figureInfo[North] = northList;
  figureInfo[East] = eastList;
```

```
      figureInfo[South] = southList;
      figureInfo[West] = westList;
}
```

The assignment operator is necessary because the `fallingFigure` and `nextFigure` methods in the `TetrisWindow` class are copied from the figure list:

```
TetrisFigure& TetrisFigure::operator=(const TetrisFigure& figure) {
   if (this != &figure) {
      windowPtr = figure.windowPtr;
      gameGridPtr = figure.gameGridPtr;
      color = figure.color;
      row = figure.row;
      col = figure.col;
      direction = figure.direction;
      figureInfo[North] = figure.figureInfo[North];
      figureInfo[East] = figure.figureInfo[East];
      figureInfo[South] = figure.figureInfo[South];
      figureInfo[West] = figure.figureInfo[West];
   }

   return *this;
}
```

The `TryMoveLeft, TryMoveRight, TryRotateClockwise,` and `TryRotateAnticlockwise` methods are called when the user presses the arrow keys. They try to move the figure and invalidate its previous and current area if they succeed:

```
void TetrisFigure::TryMoveLeft() {
   if (IsFigureValid(direction, row, col - 1
                     gameGridPtr, figureInfo)) {
      windowPtr->Invalidate(Area());
      --col;
      windowPtr->Invalidate(Area());
      windowPtr->UpdateWindow();
   }
}

void TetrisFigure::TryMoveRight() {
   if (IsFigureValid(direction, row, col + 1
                     gameGridPtr, figureInfo)) {
      windowPtr->Invalidate(Area());
      ++col;
      windowPtr->Invalidate(Area());
      windowPtr->UpdateWindow();
   }
}
```

```
void TetrisFigure::TryRotateClockwise() {
  Direction newDirection = (direction == West) ? North :
                           ((Direction) (direction + 1));

  if (IsFigureValid(newDirection, row, col,
                    gameGridPtr, figureInfo)) {
    InvalidateFigure();
    direction = newDirection;
    InvalidateFigure();
    windowPtr->UpdateWindow();
  }
}

void TetrisFigure::TryRotateAnticlockwise() {
  Direction newDirection = (this->direction == North) ? West :
                           ((Direction) (direction - 1));

  if (IsFigureValid(newDirection, row, col,
                    gameGridPtr, figureInfo)) {
    InvalidateFigure();
    direction = newDirection;
    InvalidateFigure();
    windowPtr->UpdateWindow();
  }
}
```

The TryMoveDown method is called by the timer when the player presses the Space key. It is also called by the OnTimer method in the TetrisWindow class; it returns a Boolean value indicating whether the movement succeeded:

```
bool TetrisFigure::TryMoveDown() {
  if (IsFigureValid(direction, row + 1, col
                    gameGridPtr, figureInfo)) {
    windowPtr->Invalidate(Area());
    ++row;
    windowPtr->Invalidate(Area());
    windowPtr->UpdateWindow();
    return true;
  }

  return false;
}
```

The first version of the IsFigureValid method is called by the TetrisWindow class and calls the second static version, with the current location and direction of the figure:

```
bool TetrisFigure::IsFigureValid() {
  return IsFigureValid(direction, row, col
                       gameGridPtr, figureInfo);
}
```

The second version of the IsFigureValid method is called by the preceding try methods and checks if the figure is valid by calling the IsSquareValid method for each square in the figure. In order to do so, it needs to look up the relative positions of the included squares in the figureInfo method. The first value of the integer pairs is the row, and the second value is the column:

```
bool TetrisFigure::IsFigureValid(int direction, int row, int col,
                                 GameGrid* gameGridPtr,
                                 IntPair* figureInfo[]) {
  int relRow0 = row + figureInfo[direction][0].first,
      relCol0 = col + figureInfo[direction][0].second,
      relRow1 = row + figureInfo[direction][1].first,
      relCol1 = col + figureInfo[direction][1].second,
      relRow2 = row + figureInfo[direction][2].first,
      relCol2 = col + figureInfo[direction][2].second;

  return IsSquareValid(row, col, gameGridPtr) &&
         IsSquareValid(relRow0, relCol0, gameGridPtr) &&
         IsSquareValid(relRow1, relCol1, gameGridPtr) &&
         IsSquareValid(relRow2, relCol2, gameGridPtr);
}
```

The IsSquareValid method returns true if the given square is located inside the game grid and not already occupied. A square on the game board is considered unoccupied if it is white:

```
bool TetrisFigure::IsSquareValid(int row, int col,
                                 GameGrid* gameGridPtr) {
  return (row >= 0) && (row < Rows) &&
         (col >= 0) && (col < Cols) &&
         ((*gameGridPtr)[row][col] == White);
}
```

When the falling figure has reached its final position, it is added to the game grid. It is performed by setting the figure's color to the squares in the game grid at its current location. A falling figure has reached its final position when it cannot fall any longer without colliding with an earlier figure or has reached the game grid's lower bound:

```
void TetrisFigure::AddToGrid() {
  (*gameGridPtr)[row][col] = color;
```

```
  { int relRow = row + figureInfo[direction][0].first,
      relCol = col + figureInfo[direction][0].second;
    (*gameGridPtr)[relRow][relCol] = color;
  }


  { int relRow = row + figureInfo[direction][1].first,
      relCol = col + figureInfo[direction][1].second;
    (*gameGridPtr)[relRow][relCol] = color;
  }

  { int relRow = row + figureInfo[direction][2].first,
      relCol = col + figureInfo[direction][2].second;
    (*gameGridPtr)[relRow][relCol] = color;
  }
}
```

When a figure has been moved, we need to redraw it. In order to avoid dazzle, we want to invalidate only its area, which is done by the `InvalidateFigure` method. We look up the rows and columns of the figure's four squares and call the `InvalidateSquare` method in the game grid for each of them:

```
void TetrisFigure::InvalidateFigure(Size offsetSize/*=ZeroSize*/){
  gameGridPtr->InvalidateSquare(windowPtr, row, col, offsetSize);

  { int relRow = row + figureInfo[direction][0].first,
      relCol = col + figureInfo[direction][0].second;
    gameGridPtr->InvalidateSquare(windowPtr, relRow,
                                  relCol, offsetSize);
  }
  { int relRow = row + figureInfo[direction][1].first,
      relCol = col + figureInfo[direction][1].second;
    gameGridPtr->InvalidateSquare(windowPtr, relRow,
                                  relCol, offsetSize);
  }
  { int relRow = row + figureInfo[direction][2].first,
      relCol = col + figureInfo[direction][2].second;
    gameGridPtr->InvalidateSquare(windowPtr, relRow,
                                  relCol, offsetSize);
  }
}
```

When drawing the figure, we need to look up the locations of the squares of the figure before we draw them in a way similar to the `InvalidateFigure` method:

```
void TetrisFigure::DrawFigure(Graphics& graphics,Size offsetSize)
                               const {
  gameGridPtr->DrawSquare(graphics, row, col,
                          Black, color, offsetSize);

  { int relRow = row + figureInfo[direction][0].first,
        relCol = col + figureInfo[direction][0].second;
    gameGridPtr->DrawSquare(graphics, relRow, relCol,
                            Black, color, offsetSize);
  }

  { int relRow = row + figureInfo[direction][1].first,
        relCol = col + figureInfo[direction][1].second;
    gameGridPtr->DrawSquare(graphics, relRow, relCol,
                            Black, color, offsetSize);
  }

  { int relRow = row + figureInfo[direction][2].first,
        relCol = col + figureInfo[direction][2].second;
    gameGridPtr->DrawSquare(graphics, relRow, relCol,
                            Black, color, offsetSize);
  }
}
```

The red figure

The red figure is one large square, built up by four smaller regular squares. It the simplest figure of the game since it does not change shape when rotating. This implies that we just need to look at one figure, shown as follows:

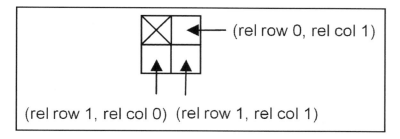

This also implies that it is enough to define the squares for one direction and this to define the shape of the figure in all four directions:

RedFigure.h

```
class RedFigure : public TetrisFigure {
  public:
    static IntPair GenericList[];
    RedFigure(Window* windowPtr, GameGrid* gameGridPtr);
};
```

RedFigure.cpp

```
#include "..\\SmallWindows\\SmallWindows.h"
#include "GameGrid.h"
#include "TetrisFigure.h"
#include "RedFigure.h"

IntPair RedFigure::GenericList[] =
                {IntPair(0,1), IntPair(1,0), IntPair(1,1)};

RedFigure::RedFigure(Window* windowPtr, GameGrid* gameGridPtr)
 :TetrisFigure(windowPtr, gameGridPtr, Red, 1, (Cols / 2) - 1,
               North, GenericList, GenericList, GenericList,
               GenericList) {
  // Empty.
}
```

The first integer pair (rel row 0, rel col 1) of the generic list represents the square to the right of the marked square, the second integer pair (rel row 1, rel col 0) represents the square below the marked square, and the third integer pair (rel row 1, rel col 1) represents the square below and to the right of the marked square. Note that the rows increase downward and the columns increase to the right.

The brown figure

The brown figure can be oriented in a horizontal or vertical direction. It is initialized to vertical mode, as it can only be rotated into two directions. The north and south arrays are initialized with the vertical array and the east and west arrays are initialized with the horizontal array, as shown in the following image:

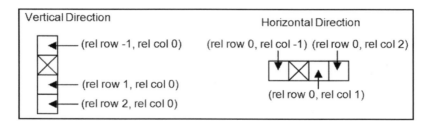

Since the row numbers increase downward and the column numbers increase to the right, the topmost square in the vertical direction (and the leftmost square in the horizontal direction) are represented by negative values:

BrownFigure.h

```
class BrownFigure : public TetrisFigure {
  public:
    static IntPair HorizontalList[], VerticalList[];
    BrownFigure(Window* windowPtr, GameGrid* gameGridPtr);
};
```

BrownFigure.cpp

```
#include "..\\SmallWindows\\SmallWindows.h"
#include "GameGrid.h"
#include "TetrisFigure.h"
#include "BrownFigure.h"

IntPair BrownFigure::HorizontalList[] =
                   {IntPair(-1,0), IntPair(1,0), IntPair(2,0)},
        BrownFigure::VerticalList[] =
                   {IntPair(0,-1), IntPair(0,1), IntPair(0,2)};

BrownFigure::BrownFigure(Window* windowPtr, GameGrid* gameGridPtr)
   :TetrisFigure(windowPtr, gameGridPtr, Brown, 1, (Cols / 2) - 1,
               North, HorizontalList, VerticalList,
               HorizontalList, VerticalList) {
  // Empty.
}
```

The turquoise figure

Similar to the brown figure, the turquoise figure can be rotated in a vertical and horizontal direction, as shown in the following figure:

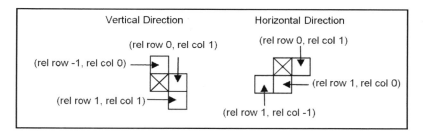

TurquoiseFigure.h

```
class TurquoiseFigure : public TetrisFigure {
  public:
    static IntPair HorizontalList[], VerticalList[];
    TurquoiseFigure(Window* windowPtr, GameGrid* gameGridPtr);
};
```

TurquoiseFigure cpp

```
#include "..\\SmallWindows\\SmallWindows.h"
#include "GameGrid.h"
#include "TetrisFigure.h"
#include "TurquoiseFigure.h"

IntPair TurquoiseFigure::HorizontalList[] =
               {IntPair(-1,0), IntPair(0,1), IntPair(1,1)},
       TurquoiseFigure::VerticalList[] =
               {IntPair(1,-1), IntPair(1,0), IntPair(0,1)};

TurquoiseFigure::TurquoiseFigure(Window* windowPtr,
                            GameGrid* gameGridPtr)
 :TetrisFigure(windowPtr, gameGridPtr, Turquoise, 1, (Cols/2) - 1,
            North, HorizontalList, VerticalList,
            HorizontalList, VerticalList) {
  // Empty.
}
```

The green figure

The green figure is mirrored in relation to the turquoise figure, shown as follows:

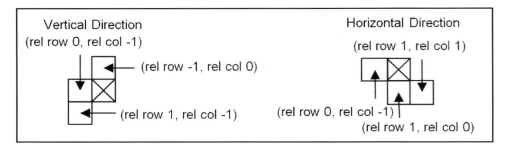

GreenFigure.h

```
class GreenFigure : public TetrisFigure {
  public:
    static IntPair HorizontalList[], VerticalList[];
    GreenFigure(Window* windowPtr, GameGrid* gameGridPtr);
};
```

GreenFigure.cpp

```
#include "..\\SmallWindows\\SmallWindows.h"
#include "GameGrid.h"
#include "TetrisFigure.h"
#include "GreenFigure.h"

IntPair GreenFigure::HorizontalList[] =
                {IntPair(1,-1), IntPair(0,-1), IntPair(-1,0)},
GreenFigure::VerticalList[] =
                {IntPair(0,-1), IntPair(1,0), IntPair(1,1)};

GreenFigure::GreenFigure(Window* windowPtr, GameGrid* gameGridPtr)
  :TetrisFigure(windowPtr, gameGridPtr, Green, 1, Cols / 2,
              North, HorizontalList, VerticalList,
              HorizontalList, VerticalList) {
  // Empty.
}
```

The yellow figure

The yellow figure can be rotated in a north, east, south, and west direction. It is initialized to the south, as shown in the following figure:

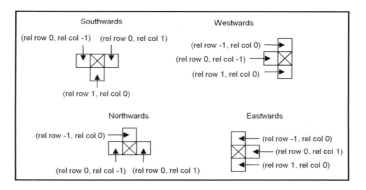

YellowFigure.h

```
class YellowFigure : public TetrisFigure {
  public:
    static IntPair NorthList[], EastList[],
                   SouthList[], WestList[];
    YellowFigure(Window* windowPtr, GameGrid* gameGridPtr);
};
```

YellowFigure.cpp

```
#include "..\\SmallWindows\\SmallWindows.h"
#include "GameGrid.h"
#include "TetrisFigure.h"
#include "YellowFigure.h"
IntPair YellowFigure::NorthList[] =
            {IntPair(0,-1), IntPair(-1,0), IntPair(0,1)},
        YellowFigure::EastList[] =
            {IntPair(-1,0),IntPair(0,1),IntPair(1,0)},
        YellowFigure::SouthList[] =
            {IntPair(0,-1),IntPair(1,0),IntPair(0,1)},
        YellowFigure::WestList[] =
            {IntPair(-1,0),IntPair(0,-1),IntPair(1,0)};
```

```
YellowFigure::YellowFigure(Window* windowPtr,
                           GameGrid* gameGridPtr)
 :TetrisFigure(windowPtr, gameGridPtr, Yellow, 1, (Cols / 2) - 1,
              South, NorthList, EastList, SouthList, WestList) {
  // Empty.
}
```

The blue figure

The blue figure can also be directed in all four directions. It is initialized to the south, as shown in the following figure:

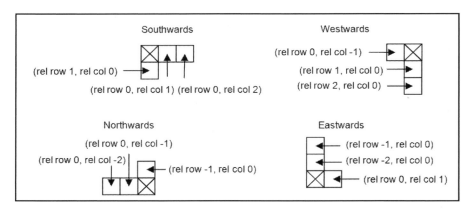

BlueFigure.h

```
class BlueFigure : public TetrisFigure {
  public:
    static IntPair NorthList[], EastList[],
          SouthList[], WestList[];
    BlueFigure(Window* windowPtr, GameGrid* gameGridPtr);
};
```

BlueFigure.cpp

```
#include "..\\SmallWindows\\SmallWindows.h"
#include "GameGrid.h"
#include "TetrisFigure.h"
#include "BlueFigure.h"
```

```
IntPair BlueFigure::NorthList[] =
                {IntPair(0,-2),IntPair(0,-1),IntPair(-1,0)},
        BlueFigure::EastList[] =
                {IntPair(-2,0), IntPair(-1,0), IntPair(0,1)},
        BlueFigure::SouthList[] =
                {IntPair(1,0), IntPair(0,1), IntPair(0,2)},
        BlueFigure::WestList[] =
                {IntPair(0,-1), IntPair(1,0), IntPair(2,0)};

BlueFigure::BlueFigure(Window* windowPtr, GameGrid* gameGridPtr)
 :TetrisFigure(windowPtr, gameGridPtr, Blue, 1, (Cols / 2) - 1,
            South, NorthList, EastList, SouthList, WestList) {
  // Empty.
}
```

The purple figure

Finally, the purple figure is mirrored in relation to the blue figure and also initialized to the south, as shown in the following image:

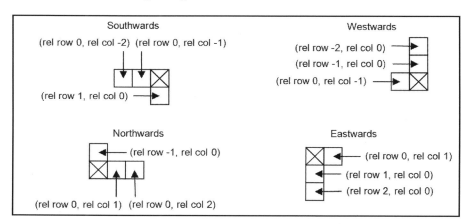

PurpleFigure.h

```
class PurpleFigure : public TetrisFigure {
  public:
    static IntPair NorthList[], EastList[],
                SouthList[], WestList[];
    PurpleFigure(Window* windowPtr, GameGrid* gameGridPtr);
};
```

PurpleFigure.cpp

```
#include "..\\SmallWindows\\SmallWindows.h"
#include "GameGrid.h"
#include "TetrisFigure.h"
#include "PurpleFigure.h"

IntPair PurpleFigure::NorthList[] =
             {IntPair(-1,0),IntPair(0,1),IntPair(0,2)},
        PurpleFigure::EastList[] =
             {IntPair(1,0), IntPair(2,0), IntPair(0,1)},
        PurpleFigure::SouthList[] =
             {IntPair(0,-2),IntPair(0,-1),IntPair(1,0)},
        PurpleFigure::WestList[] =
             {IntPair(0,-1),IntPair(-2,0),IntPair(-1,0)};



PurpleFigure::PurpleFigure(Window* windowPtr,
                           GameGrid* gameGridPtr)
 :TetrisFigure(windowPtr, gameGridPtr, Purple, 1, Cols / 2, South,
              NorthList, EastList, SouthList, WestList) {
  // Empty.
}
```

The GameGrid class

Finally, the GameGrid class is quite simple. It keeps track of the squares on the game board. The gridArea field is the portion of the total client area that is occupied by the grid:

GameGrid.h

```
const int Rows = 20, Cols = 10;

class GameGrid {
  public:
    GameGrid(Rect gridArea);
    void ClearGameGrid();

    Color* operator[](int row) {return gameGrid[row];}
    void InvalidateSquare(Window* windowPtr, int row,
                          int col, Size offsetSize);
    void DrawGameGrid(Graphics& graphics, bool inverse) const;
```

```
void DrawSquare(Graphics& graphics, int row, int col,
                Color penColor, Color brushColor,
                Size offsetSize = ZeroSize) const;

    Rect GridArea() const {return gridArea;}

  private:
    Rect gridArea;
    Color gameGrid[Rows][Cols];
};
```

When called by the `TetrisWindow` constructor, the grid area will be set to (0, 20, 100, 100) units, placing it in the lower 80 percent of the client area of the window:

GameGrid.cpp

```
#include "..\\SmallWindows\\SmallWindows.h"
#include "GameGrid.h"



GameGrid::GameGrid(Rect gridArea)
 :gridArea(gridArea) {
  ClearGameGrid();
}
```

When clearing the grid, we actually set every square to white:

```
void GameGrid::ClearGameGrid () {
  for (int row = 0; row < Rows; ++row) {
    for (int col = 0; col < Cols; ++col) {
      gameGrid[row][col] = White;
    }
  }
}
```

Invalidating and drawing squares

The `DrawGameGrid` iterates through the squares of the grid. White squares are surrounded by white borders, while squares of every other color are surrounded by black borders. If the `inverseColor` parameter is true, the square color is inversed before drawn. This is useful when flashing rows:

```
void GameGrid::DrawGameGrid(Graphics& graphics, bool inverse)
                              const {
  for (int row = 0; row < Rows; ++row) {
    for (int col = 0; col < Cols; ++col) {
      Color squareColor = gameGrid[row][col];
      Color penColor = (squareColor == White) ? White : Black;
      Color brushColor = inverse ? squareColor.Inverse()
                                 : squareColor;
      DrawSquare(graphics, row, col, penColor, brushColor);
    }
  }
}
```

Note that the InvalidateSquare and DrawSquare methods add an offset. It is zero in all cases except when invalidating or drawing the next figure in the TetrisWindow class. Both methods calculate the size of the rows and columns of the grid and define the area of the square invalidated or drawn:

```
void GameGrid::InvalidateSquare(Window* windowPtr, int row,
                                int col, Size offsetSize) {
  int colWidth = gridArea.Width() / Cols,
      rowHeight = gridArea.Height() / Rows;

  Rect squareArea(col * colWidth, row * rowHeight,
                  (col + 1) * colWidth, (row + 1) * rowHeight);
  windowPtr->Invalidate(gridArea.TopLeft() + squareArea +
                        offsetSize);
}

void GameGrid::DrawSquare(Graphics& graphics, int row, int col,
                          Color penColor, Color brushColor,
                          Size offsetSize /* = ZeroSize */) const{
  int colWidth = gridArea.Width() / Cols,
      rowHeight = gridArea.Height() / Rows;

  Rect squareArea (col * colWidth, row * rowHeight,
                   (col + 1) * colWidth, (row + 1) * rowHeight);
  graphics.FillRectangle(gridArea.TopLeft() + squareArea +
                         offsetSize, penColor, brushColor);
}
```

Summary

In this chapter, we developed a Tetris game. You looked into timing and randomization, as well as a new coordinate system, more advanced drawing, how to catch keyboard events, and how to write text.

In Chapter 4, *Working with Shapes and Figures*, we will develop a drawing program capable of drawing lines, arrows, rectangles, and ellipses.

4

Working with Shapes and Figures

In this chapter, we develop a program capable of drawing lines, arrows, rectangles, and ellipses. The application can be viewed as a more advanced version of the circle application. Similar to the circle application, we have a list of figures and we catch the user's mouse actions. However, there are four different kinds of figures: lines, arrows, rectangles, and ellipses. They are defined in a class hierarchy that is similar to but more advanced than the hierarchy in the Tetris game. Moreover, we also introduce cut, copy, paste, cursor control, and registry handling:

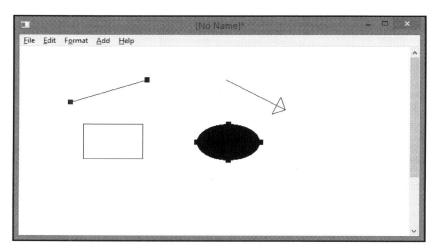

The user can add new figures, move one or several figures, modify figures by grabbing their endpoints, mark and unmark figures by pressing the mouse button and the *Ctrl* key, and mark several figures by enclosing them by a rectangle. When a figure is marked, it becomes annotated with small black squares. The user can modify the shape of a figure by grabbing one of the squares. The user can also move a figure by grabbing some other part of the figure.

The MainWindow function

The MainWindow function in this application is very similar to that in Chapter 3, *Building a Tetris Application*; it sets the application name and creates the main document window:

```
#include "..\\SmallWindows\\SmallWindows.h"
#include "DrawFigure.h"
#include "LineFigure.h"
#include "ArrowFigure.h"
#include "RectangleFigure.h"
#include "EllipseFigure.h"
#include "TextFigure.h"
#include "DrawDocument.h"

void MainWindow(vector<String> /* argumentList */,
                WindowShow windowShow) {
  Application::ApplicationName() = TEXT("DrawFigure");
  Application::MainWindowPtr() = new DrawDocument(windowShow);
}
```

The DrawDocument class

The DrawDocument class extends the StandardDocument framework, similar to the circle application. It catches the mouse events, overrides the file methods, implements cut, copy, and paste, as well as cursor handling:

DrawDocument.h

```
class DrawDocument : public StandardDocument {
  public:
    DrawDocument(WindowShow windowShow);
    ~DrawDocument();
```

Similar to the circle application, we catch mouse action with the `OnMouseDown`, `OnMouseMove`, and `OnMouseUp` methods. However, in this application, we also catch double-clicks with the `OnDoubleClick` method. When the user double-clicks on a figure, it takes individual actions:

```
void OnMouseDown(MouseButton mouseButtons, Point mousePoint,
                 bool shiftPressed, bool controlPressed);
void OnMouseMove(MouseButton mouseButtons, Point mousePoint,
                 bool shiftPressed, bool controlPressed);
void OnDoubleClick(MouseButton mouseButtons, Point mousePoint,
                   bool shiftPressed, bool controlPressed);
void OnMouseUp(MouseButton mouseButtons, Point mousePoint,
               bool shiftPressed, bool controlPressed);
```

The `OnDraw` method is called when the window's client area needs to be redrawn. It draws the figures, and the rectangle enclosing the figures, if the user is in the process of marking figures with a rectangle:

```
void OnDraw(Graphics& graphics, DrawMode drawMode) const;
```

The `ClearDocument` method is called when the user selects the **New** menu item, the `ReadDocumentFromStream` method is called when they select the **Open** menu item, and the `WriteDocumentToStream` method is called when they select the **Save** or **Save As** menu item:

```
void ClearDocument();
bool WriteDocumentToStream(String name, ostream& outstream)
                           const;
```

Each figure has an integer identity value that is written by the `WriteDocumentToStream` method and read by the `ReadDocumentFromStream` method to decide which figure has to be created. Given the identity value, the `CreateFigure` method creates the new figure:

```
bool ReadDocumentFromStream(String name, istream& instream);
DrawFigure* CreateFigure(FigureId figureId) const;
```

In this application, we introduce functionality for cut, copy, and paste. The `CopyGeneric` method is called when the user selects the **Cut** or **Copy** menu item in the **Edit** menu and the `PasteGeneric` method is called when the user selects the **Paste** menu item. In the `StandardDocument` framework, there are methods for cutting, copying, and pasting ASCII and Unicode text as well. However, we do not use them in this application:

```
bool IsCopyGenericReady(int /* format */) const;
void CopyGeneric(int format, InfoList& infoList) const;
void PasteGeneric(int format, InfoList& infoList);
```

The CopyEnable method returns true if information is ready to be copied. In that case, the **Cut**, **Copy**, and **Delete** menu items are enabled. In this application, we do not override the PasteEnable method, since the StandardDocument framework looks up whether there is a memory buffer in the global clipboard suitable to paste. The OnDelete method is called when the user selects the **Delete** menu item:

```
bool CopyEnable() const;
void OnDelete();
```

Similar to the circle application, we have a set of listeners, even though the set is larger in this case. Each listener is added to the menus in the constructor. Unlike the circle application, we also use enable methods: methods that are called before the menu item becomes visible. If the methods return false, the menu items become disabled and grayed. If the menu item is connected to an accelerator, the accelerator also becomes disabled. We place the **Modify**, **Color**, and **Fill** items in the **Modify** menu, and the **Line**, **Arrow**, **Rectangle**, and **Ellipse** items in the **Add** menu:

```
DEFINE_BOOL_LISTENER(DrawDocument, ModifyEnable)
DEFINE_BOOL_LISTENER(DrawDocument, ModifyRadio)
DEFINE_VOID_LISTENER(DrawDocument, OnModify)

DEFINE_BOOL_LISTENER(DrawDocument, ColorEnable)
DEFINE_VOID_LISTENER(DrawDocument, OnColor)

DEFINE_BOOL_LISTENER(DrawDocument, FillEnable)
DEFINE_BOOL_LISTENER(DrawDocument, FillCheck)
DEFINE_VOID_LISTENER(DrawDocument, OnFill)

DEFINE_BOOL_LISTENER(DrawDocument, LineEnable);
DEFINE_BOOL_LISTENER(DrawDocument, ArrowEnable);
DEFINE_BOOL_LISTENER(DrawDocument, RectangleEnable);
DEFINE_BOOL_LISTENER(DrawDocument, EllipseEnable);

DEFINE_BOOL_LISTENER(DrawDocument, LineRadio);
DEFINE_BOOL_LISTENER(DrawDocument, ArrowRadio);
DEFINE_BOOL_LISTENER(DrawDocument, RectangleRadio);
DEFINE_BOOL_LISTENER(DrawDocument, EllipseRadio);

DEFINE_VOID_LISTENER(DrawDocument, OnLine);
DEFINE_VOID_LISTENER(DrawDocument, OnArrow);
DEFINE_VOID_LISTENER(DrawDocument, OnRectangle);
DEFINE_VOID_LISTENER(DrawDocument, OnEllipse);
```

In this application, we also introduce cursor control. The UpdateCursor method sets the cursor to an appropriate appearance depending on whether the user is creating, modifying, or moving figures:

```
void UpdateCursor();
```

One central point of this application is its mode: the `applicationMode` method keeps track of the actions when the user presses the left mouse button. It holds the following modes:

- `Idle`: The application waits for input from the user. This is always the mode as long as the user does not press the left mouse button. However, when the user presses the mouse button, until they release it, the `applicationMode` method holds one value. The user presses the *Ctrl* key and clicks on an already marked figure. The figure becomes unmarked, nothing more happens.
- `ModifySingle`: The user grabs one single figure that is being modified (if the user clicks on one of its endpoints) or moved (if the user clicks on any other part of the figure).
- `ModifyRectangle`: The user has clicked on the client area without hitting a figure, resulting in a rectangle being drawn. When the user releases the mouse button, every figure completely enclosed by the rectangle is marked.
- `MoveMultiple`: The user presses the *Ctrl* key and clicks on an unmarked figure. It is not possible to modify more than one figure at the same time.

Note that the `applicationMode` method is relevant only as long as the user presses the left mouse button. As soon as they release the mouse button, the `applicationMode` method is always `Idle`:

```
private:
  enum ApplicationMode {Idle, ModifySingle,
                        MoveMultiple, ModifyRectangle};
  ApplicationMode applicationMode = Idle;
```

When the `applicationMode` method holds the `Idle` mode, the application waits for further input from the user. The `actionMode` field defines the next action, which may hold the following values:

- `Modify`: When the user presses the mouse button, the `applicationMode` method is set to the `ModifySingle` mode if they click on a figure, the `MoveMultiple` mode if they click on an unmarked figure while pressing the *Ctrl* key, the `Idle` mode if the figure is already marked, or the `ModifyRectangle` mode if they click on the client area without hitting a figure.
- `Add`: When the user presses the left mouse button, a new figure is created at the location, regardless of whether there already is a figure at the location. The value of the `addFigureId` method decides which kind of figure should be added; it can hold any of the values `LineId`, `ArrowId`, `RectangleId`, or `EllipseId`.

```
enum ActionMode {Modify, Add};
ActionMode actionMode = Add;
FigureId addFigureId = LineId;
```

Later in the chapter, we will encounter expressions such as **in Modify mode** and **in Add mode**, which refer to the value of the `actionMode` variable: `Modify` or `Add`.

The `nextColor` and `nextFill` fields hold the figure's color and fill status (in the case of a rectangle or ellipse), respectively, of the next figure to be added:

```
Color nextColor;
bool nextFill;
```

Similar to the circle application, when the user adds or modifies a figure, we need to store the previous mouse position in the `prevMousePoint` method in order to keep track of the distance the mouse has been moved since the last mouse action:

```
Point prevMousePoint;
```

When the `applicationMode` method holds the `ModifySingle` value, the figure being modified is always placed at the beginning of the figure pointer list (`figurePtrList[0]`) in order for it to appear on top of the figures. When the `applicationMode` method holds the `ModifyRectangle` mode, the `insideRectangle` method keeps track of the rectangle enclosing the figures:

```
Rect insideRectangle;
```

The `static DrawFormat` constant is used to identify data to be cut, copied, or pasted in the global clipboard. It is arbitrarily set to 1000:

```
static const unsigned int DrawFormat = 1000;
```

As the user adds and removes figures from the drawing, the figures are dynamically created and deleted; their addresses are stored in the `figurePtrList` list. The `DynamicList` class is a Small Windows class that is a more advanced version of the C++ standard classes `list` and `vector`.

The values of the figure list are pointers to the `DrawFigure` class, which is the root class of the figure hierarchy used in this application (described in Chapter 5, *The Figure Hierarchy*). Unlike the circle and Tetris applications in the previous chapters, we do not store the figure objects directly in the list, but rather their pointers. This is necessary, since we use class hierarchy holds with pure virtual methods, which makes the `DrawWindow` class abstract and not possible to store directly in the list. It is also necessary in order to take advantage of dynamic binding of the class hierarchy:

```
    DynamicList<DrawFigure*> figurePtrList;
};
```

The application modes

This section holds a further description of the `applicationMode` field. It is closely connected to the mouse input cycle. When the user is not pressing the left mouse button, the `applicationMode` method is always in the `Idle` mode. When the user presses the left mouse button in modify mode, they can choose to press the *Ctrl* key at the same time:

- If they do not press the *Ctrl* key, the `applicationMode` method is set to the `ModifySingle` mode if they hit a figure. That figure becomes marked and other figures become unmarked.
- If they do press the *Ctrl* key, the `applicationMode` method is set to the `MoveMultiple` mode if they hit a figure that is not marked and to the `Idle` mode if it is marked. The figure becomes marked if it is unmarked and unmarked if it is marked. The rest of the figures are unaffected.
- If they do not hit a figure, the `applicationMode` method is set to the `ModifyRectangle` mode regardless of whether they pressed the *Ctrl* key and the inside rectangle (`insideRectangle`) is being initialized. All figures become unmarked. All figures that are completely enclosed by the rectangle when the user releases the left button are marked.

When the user moves the mouse with the left button pressed in modify mode, there are four possible values of the `applicationMode` method to consider:

- `Idle`: We do nothing.
- `ModifySingle`: We call the `Modify` method on the single figure. This may result in the single hit figure being modified or moved, depending on where the user hit the figure.
- `MoveMultiple`: We call the `Move` method on all marked figures. This always results in the marked figures being moved, not modified.
- `ModifyRectangle`: We modify the inside rectangle.

Finally, when the user releases the left mouse button, we again look into the four modes of the `applicationMode` method:

- `Idle`, `ModifySingle`, or `MoveMultiple`: We do nothing since everything has already been done when the user moved the mouse. The marked figures have been moved or modified.

- `ModifyRectangle`: We mark all figures completely enclosed by the rectangle.

The DynamicList class

In this chapter, we use a subset of the methods of the auxiliary `DynamicList` class. It holds a set of methods that take callback functions, that is, functions that are sent as parameters to methods and called by the methods:

```
template <class Type>
class DynamicList {
  public:
```

`IfFuncPtr` and `DoFuncPtr` are pointers to callback functions. The difference between them is that the `IfFuncPtr` pointer is intended for methods that only inspect the values of the list. Therefore, the `value` parameter is constant. The `DoFuncPtr` pointer is intended for methods that modify the values. Consequently, the `value` parameter is not constant:

```
typedef bool (*IfFuncPtr) (const Type& value, void* voidPtr);
typedef void (*DoFuncPtr) (Type& value, void* voidPtr);
```

The `AnyOf` method takes the `ifFuncPtr` pointer and applies it to each value of the array. The methods return `true` if at least one of the values satisfies the `ifFunctPtr` pointer (if the `ifFuncPtr` pointer returns `true` for the value). The `ifVoidPtr` parameter is sent as the second parameter to the `ifFuncPtr` pointer:

```
bool AnyOf(IfFuncPtr ifFuncPtr, void* ifVoidPtr = nullptr)
          const;
```

The `FirstOf` method also returns `true` if at least one value satisfies the `ifFuncPtr` pointer. In that case, the first satisfied value is copied to the `value` parameter:

```
bool FirstOf(IfFuncPtr ifFuncPtr,Type& value,
          void* ifVoidPtr = nullptr) const;
```

The `Apply` method calls the `doFunctPtr` pointer to every value of the list. The `ApplyIf` method calls the `doFuncPtr` pointer to all values that satisfy the `ifFuncPtr` pointer:

```
void Apply(DoFuncPtr doFuncPtr, void* ifVoidPtr = nullptr);
void ApplyIf(IfFuncPtr ifFuncPtr, DoFuncPtr doFuncPtr,
          void* ifVoidPtr = nullptr,
          void* doVoidPtr = nullptr);
```

The `CopyIf` method copies the values satisfying the `ifFuncPtr` pointer into the `copyArray` method. The `RemoveIf` method removes every value satisfying the `ifFuncPtr` pointer:

```
void CopyIf(IfFuncPtr ifFuncPtr, DynamicList& copyArray,
            void* ifVoidPtr = nullptr) const;
void RemoveIf(IfFuncPtr ifFuncPtr, void* ifVoidPtr = nullptr);
```

The `ApplyRemoveIf` method calls the `doFuncPtr` pointer and then removes every value satisfying the `ifFuncPtr` pointer, which comes in handy when we want to deallocate and remove pointers from the list:

```
void ApplyRemoveIf(IfFuncPtr ifFuncPtr, DoFuncPtr doFuncPtr,
            void* ifVoidPtr = nullptr, void* doVoidPtr=nullptr);
};
```

Initialization

The constructor of the `DrawDocument` class is similar to the constructor of the `CircleDocument` class. We use the `LogicalWithScroll` coordinate system with US letter size. The file description `Draw Files` and the suffix `drw` are used to filter drawing files in the open and save dialogs. The null pointer indicates that the document does not have a parent window, and the `false` parameter indicates that the **Print** and **Print Preview** items in the **File** menu are omitted. Finally, the initiation lists holding the `DrawFormat` parameter indicates the format used to identify data to be copied and pasted. In this case, we use the same format for both copying and pasting:

DrawDocument.cpp

```
#include "..\\SmallWindows\\SmallWindows.h"
#include "DrawFigure.h"
#include "LineFigure.h"
#include "ArrowFigure.h"
#include "RectangleFigure.h"
#include "EllipseFigure.h"
#include "TextFigure.h"
#include "DrawDocument.h"

DrawDocument::DrawDocument(WindowShow windowShow)
 :StandardDocument(LogicalWithScroll, USLetterPortrait,
                TEXT("Draw Files, drw"), nullptr,
                OverlappedWindow, windowShow,
                {DrawFormat}, {DrawFormat}) {
```

Since we extend the `StandardDocument` framework, the window has a standard menu bar with the **File** menu holding **New**, **Open**, **Save**, **Save As**, and **Exit** (the **Print** and **Print**

Preview items are omitted due to the `false` parameter in the constructor call) items, the **Edit** menu holding **Cut**, **Copy**, **Paste**, and **Delete**, and the **Help** items, and **About**.

We also add two application-specific menus: **Format** and **Add**. The **Format** menu holds the menu items **Modify**, **Color**, and **Fill**. Similar to the circle application, we mark the menu items with mnemonics and accelerators. However, we also use the enable parameters; the `ModifyEnable`, `ColorEnable`, and `FillEnable` methods are called before the menu items become visible. If they return `false`, the menu item is disabled and grayed:

```
Menu menuBar(this);
menuBar.AddMenu(StandardFileMenu(false));
menuBar.AddMenu(StandardEditMenu());

Menu formatMenu(this, TEXT("F&ormat"));
formatMenu.AddItem(TEXT("&Modify\tCtrl+M"), OnModify,
                   ModifyEnable, nullptr, ModifyRadio);
formatMenu.AddItem(TEXT("&Color\tAlt+C"), OnColor, ColorEnable);
formatMenu.AddItem(TEXT("F&ill\tCtrl+I"), OnFill, FillEnable
                   FillCheck, nullptr);
menuBar.AddMenu(formatMenu);
```

The **Add** menu holds one item for each kind of figure to be added:

```
Menu addMenu(this, TEXT("&Add"));
addMenu.AddItem(TEXT("&Line\tCtrl+L"), OnLine,
                LineEnable, nullptr, LineRadio);
addMenu.AddItem(TEXT("&Arrow\tAlt+A"), OnArrow,
                ArrowEnable, nullptr, ArrowRadio);
addMenu.AddItem(TEXT("&Rectangle\tCtrl+R"), OnRectangle,
                RectangleEnable, nullptr, RectangleRadio);
addMenu.AddItem(TEXT("&Ellipse\tCtrl+E"), OnEllipse,
                EllipseEnable, nullptr, EllipseRadio);
menuBar.AddMenu(addMenu);

menuBar.AddMenu(StandardHelpMenu());
SetMenuBar(menuBar);
```

Finally, we read values from the **Windows Registry**, which is a database in the Windows system that we can use to store values between the executions of our applications. The Small Windows auxiliary classes `Color`, `Font`, `Point`, `Size`, and `Rect` have their own registry methods. The Small Windows `Registry` class holds static methods for reading and writing text as well as numerical and integer values:

```
actionMode = (ActionMode)
            Registry::ReadInteger(TEXT("actionMode"), Modify);
addFigureId = (FigureId)
            Registry::ReadInteger(TEXT("addFigureId"), LineId);
```

```
  nextColor.ReadColorFromRegistry(TEXT("nextColor"));
  nextFill = Registry::ReadBoolean(TEXT("nextFill"), false);
}
```

The destructor writes the values to the registry. In this application, it is not necessary to provide any common destructor actions such as deallocating memory or closing files:

```
DrawDocument::~DrawDocument() {
  Registry::WriteInteger(TEXT("actionMode"), actionMode);
  Registry::WriteInteger(TEXT("addFigureId "), addFigureId);
  nextColor.WriteColorToRegistry(TEXT("nextColor"));
  Registry::WriteBoolean(TEXT("nextFill"), nextFill);
}
```

Mouse input

IsFigureMarked, IsFigureClicked, and UnmarkFigure are callback functions that are called by the DynamicList methods AnyOf, FirstOf, CopyIf, ApplyIf, and ApplyRemoveIf. These methods take the pointer to a figure and an optional void pointer that holds additional information.

The IsFigureMarked function returnstrue if the figure is marked, the IsFigureClicked function returns true if the mouse point given in the voidPtr pointer hits the figure, and the IsFigureClicked function unmarks the figure if it is marked. As you can see, the IsFigureMarked function is defined as a lambda function, while the IsFigureClicked function is defined as a regular function.

There is no rational reason for this, other than that I would like to demonstrate both ways to define functions:

```
auto IsFigureMarked = [](DrawFigure* const& figurePtr,
                         void* /* voidPtr */) {
  return figurePtr->IsMarked();
};

bool IsFigureClicked(DrawFigure* const& figurePtr, void* voidPtr) {
  Point* mousePointPtr = (Point*) voidPtr;
  return figurePtr->IsClick(*mousePointPtr);
}

void UnmarkFigure(DrawFigure*& figurePtr, void* /* voidPtr */) {
  if (figurePtr->IsMarked()) {
    figurePtr->Mark(false);
  }
}
```

In the `OnMouseDown` method, we first check that the user presses the left mouse button. If so, we save the mouse position in the `prevMousePoint` field so that we can calculate the distance the figure has moved in subsequent calls to the `OnMouseMove` method:

```
void DrawDocument::OnMouseDown(MouseButton mouseButtons,
                   Point mousePoint, bool shiftPressed,
                   bool controlPressed) {
  if (mouseButtons == LeftButton) {
    prevMousePoint = mousePoint;
```

As mentioned earlier, the mouse click will result in different actions depending on the value of the `actionMode` method. In case of the `Modify` method, we call the `FirstOf` parameter on the figure pointer list to extract the first clicked figure. The figures can overlap, and the click may hit more than one figure. In that case, we want the topmost figure located at the beginning of the list. The `FirstOf` method returns `true` if there is at least one clicked figure, which is copied into the `topClickedFigurePtr` reference parameter. The address of the `mousePoint` method is given as the second parameter to the `FirstOf` method and is, in turn, given to the `IsFigureClicked` function as its second parameter:

```
switch (actionMode) {
  case Modify: {
      DrawFigure* topClickedFigurePtr;
      if (figurePtrList.FirstOf(IsFigureClicked,
                   topClickedFigurePtr, &mousePoint)) {
```

We have two cases to consider, depending on whether the user presses the *Ctrl* key. If they do so, the figure will be marked if it is unmarked and vice versa, and other marked figures will remain marked.

However, in the other case, when the user does not press the *Ctrl* key, the figure becomes marked regardless of whether it is already marked, all other marked figures become unmarked, and the application is set to the `ModifySingle` mode. The figures are removed from the list and inserted at the beginning (front) in order to appear on top of the drawing:

```
if (!controlPressed) {
  figurePtrList.ApplyIf(IsFigureMarked, UnmarkFigure);
  topClickedFigurePtr->Mark(true);
  applicationMode = ModifySingle;
  int topFigureIndex =
    figurePtrList.IndexOf(topClickedFigurePtr);
  figurePtrList.Erase(topFigureIndex);
  figurePtrList.PushFront(topClickedFigurePtr);
}
```

If the user presses the *Ctrl* key, we have another two cases. If the clicked figure is already marked, we unmark it and set the applicationMode method to the Idle mode. If the clicked figure is not already marked, we mark it and set the applicationMode method to the MoveMultiple mode. In this way, we have at least one marked figure to be moved in the OnMouseMove method when the user moves the mouse. Note that if the user presses the *Ctrl* key, one or several figures can be moved but not modified. It would be illogical to modify more than one figure at the same time:

```
else {
  if (topClickedFigurePtr->IsMarked()) {
    applicationMode = Idle;
    topClickedFigurePtr->Mark(false);
  }
  else {
    applicationMode = MoveMultiple;
    topClickedFigurePtr->Mark(true);
  }
}
}
```

If the user hits a point where no figure is located (the figurePtrList.FirstOf method returns false), we unmark all marked figures, initialize the insideRectangle method, and set the applicationMode method to the ModifyRectangle mode.

```
else {
  figurePtrList.ApplyIf(IsFigureMarked, UnmarkFigure);
  insideRectangle = Rect(mousePoint, mousePoint);
  applicationMode = ModifyRectangle;
}
}
break;
```

All the aforementioned cases in this method takes place when the actionMode method is Modify. However, it can also be Add, in which case a new figure will be added to the drawing. We use the addFigureId method to decide which kind of figure to add when calling the CreateFigure method. We set the dirty flag, since we have added a figure and the document has been modified. Finally, we add the address of the new figure to the beginning of the figure list (so that it appears on top) and set the applicationMode method to the ModifySingle mode:

```
case Add: {
    DrawFigure* newFigurePtr = CreateFigure(addFigureId);
    newFigurePtr->SetColor(nextColor);
    newFigurePtr->Fill(nextFill);
    newFigurePtr->SetFirstPoint(mousePoint);
```

```
            SetDirty(true);
            figurePtrList.PushFront(newFigurePtr);
            applicationMode = ModifySingle;
        }
        break;
    }
}
```

Depending on the action and modes, the window and cursor may need to be updated:

```
        UpdateWindow();
        UpdateCursor();
    }
}
```

The `MoveMarkFigure` method is a callback function that is called by the `Apply` method on `figurePtrList` in the `OnMouseMove` method. It moves the figure that is marked. The address of the moving distance is given in the `voidPtr` parameter:

```
void MoveMarkedFigure(DrawFigure*& figurePtr, void* voidPtr) {
  if (figurePtr->IsMarked()) {
    figurePtr->Invalidate();
    Size* distanzeSizePtr = (Size*) voidPtr;
    figurePtr->Move(*distanzeSizePtr);
    figurePtr->Invalidate();
  }
}
```

In the `OnMouseMove` method, we start by calculating the distance since the previous call to the `OnMouseDown` or `OnMouseMove` method. We also set the `prevMousePoint` method to the mouse position:

```
void DrawDocument::OnMouseMove(MouseButton mouseButtons,
                               Point mousePoint,bool shiftPressed,
                               bool controlPressed) {
  if (mouseButtons == LeftButton) {
    Size distanceSize = mousePoint - prevMousePoint;
    prevMousePoint = mousePoint;
```

Depending on the `applicationMode` method, we perform different tasks. In case of the `Modify` method on a single figure, we call the `MoveOrModify` method on that figure. The figure is placed at the beginning of the figure pointer list (`figurePtrList[0]`), since we placed it there in the `OnMouseDown` method. The idea is that the figure itself, depending on where the user clicked, decides whether it is moved or modified. The state of the figure is set when the user clicks on it, and depends on whether they click on any of the endpoints of the figure:

```
switch (applicationMode) {
  case ModifySingle:
    figurePtrList[0]->Modify(distanceSize);
    SetDirty(true);
    break;
```

In case of multiple movements, we move every marked figure the distance since the last mouse message. Note that we do not modify the figures in the multiple cases as we do in the single case:

```
  case MoveMultiple:
    figurePtrList.Apply(MoveMarkedFigure, &distanceSize);
    SetDirty(true);
    break;
```

In the rectangle case, we set its bottom-right corner and redraw it:

```
  case ModifyRectangle:
    Invalidate(insideRectangle);
    insideRectangle.SetBottomRight(mousePoint);
    Invalidate(insideRectangle);
    UpdateWindow();
    break;
  }

  UpdateWindow();
  UpdateCursor();
  }
}
```

The `IsFigureInside` and `MarkFigure` methods are callback functions that are called by the `DynamicList` methods `CopyIf`, `RemoveIf`, and `Apply` on `figurePtrList` in the `OnMouseUp` method. The `IsFigureInside` method returns `true` if the figure is located inside the given rectangle, while the `MarkFigure` method simply marks the figure:

```
bool IsFigureInside(DrawFigure* const& figurePtr, void* voidPtr) {
  Rect* insideRectanglePtr = (Rect*) voidPtr;
  return figurePtr->IsInside(*insideRectanglePtr);
}

void MarkFigure(DrawFigure*& figurePtr, void* /* voidPtr */) {
  figurePtr->Mark(true);
}
```

In the `OnMouseUp` method, we only need to take the `ModifyRectangle` case into consideration. We need to decide which figures are totally enclosed by the rectangle. In order for them to appear on top of the drawing, we first call the `CopyIf` method on the `figurePtrList` list to temporarily copy the figures located completely inside the rectangle to the `insideList` list.

Then we remove the figures from the `figurePtrList` list and insert them from the `insideList` list at the beginning of the `figurePtrList` list. This makes them appear at the top of the drawing. Finally, we mark the figure inside the rectangle by calling `Apply` on the `insideList` list:

```
void DrawDocument::OnMouseUp(MouseButton mouseButtons,
                             Point mousePoint, bool shiftPressed,
                             bool controlPressed) {
  if (mouseButtons == LeftButton) {
    switch (applicationMode) {
      case ModifyRectangle: {
          insideRectangle.Normalize();
          DynamicList<DrawFigure*> insideList;
          figurePtrList.CopyIf(IsFigureInside, insideList,
                               &insideRectangle);
          figurePtrList.RemoveIf(IsFigureInside,
                               &insideRectangle);
          figurePtrList.PushFront(insideList);
          insideList.Apply(MarkFigure);
          Invalidate(insideRectangle);
          insideRectangle.Clear();
          UpdateWindow();
        }
        break;
    }
```

After the user has released the left mouse button, the application holds the `Idle` mode, which it always holds as long as the user does not press the left mouse button:

```
    applicationMode = Idle;
  }
}
```

The `OnDoubleClick` method is called when the user double-clicks on the mouse button. The difference between a double-click and two consecutive clicks is decided by the Windows system, and can be adjusted in the Windows control panel. In case of a double-click, the `OnMouseDown` and `OnMouseUp` methods are called before the `OnDoubleClick` method. We extract the topmost clicked figure, if any, and call the `DoubleClick` method. The result depends on the type of figure: the head of an arrow is reversed, a rectangle or ellipse is filled if unfilled and vice versa, and a line is not affected at all:

```
void DrawDocument::OnDoubleClick(MouseButton mouseButtons,
                        Point mousePoint, bool shiftPressed,
                        bool controlPressed) {
  if ((mouseButtons == LeftButton) && !controlPressed) {
    DrawFigure* topClickedFigurePtr;

    if (figurePtrList.FirstOf(IsFigureClicked,topClickedFigurePtr,
                        &mousePoint)) {
      topClickedFigurePtr->DoubleClick(mousePoint);
    }
  }
}
```

Painting

In Small Windows, there are three general painting methods: OnPaint, OnPrint, and OnDraw. The Windows system indirectly calls the OnPaint and OnPrint methods for painting a window or printing a paper, respectively. Their default behavior is to call the OnDraw method. Remember that we do not take any initiatives to paint the window, we just wait for the right message. The idea is that in cases when we need to distinguish between painting and printing, we override the OnPaint and OnPrint methods, and when we do not need that distinction, we override the OnDraw method instead.

In the word processor, which is discussed later in this book, we will look into the difference between painting and printing. However, in this application, we just override the OnDraw method. As mentioned in Chapter 3, *Building a Tetris Application*, the Graphics class reference is created by the framework and can be considered a toolbox equipped with pens and brushes. In this case, we just call the DrawFigure method for each figure with the Graphics reference as a parameter. In case of the ModifyRectangle mode, we also draw the rectangle:

```
void DrawDocument::OnDraw(Graphics& graphics,
                        DrawMode /* drawMode */) const {
  int size = figurePtrList.Size();
  for (int index = (size - 1); index >= 0; --index) {
    DrawFigure* figurePtr := figurePtrList) {[index];
    figurePtr->Draw(graphics);
  }

  if (applicationMode == ModifyRectangle) {
    graphics.DrawRectangle(insideRectangle, Gray);
  }
}
```

The File menu

Thanks to the framework in the `StandardDocument` class, the file management is quite easy. The `ClearDocument` method is called when the user selects the **New** menu item, we just delete the figures and clear the figure list:

```
void DrawDocument::ClearDocument() {
  for (DrawFigure* figurePtr : figurePtrList) {
    delete figurePtr;
  }

  figurePtrList.Clear();
}
```

The `WriteDocumentToStream` method is called when the user selects the **Save** or **Save As** menu item. It first writes the size of the figure list, and for each figure it writes its identity number (which is necessary when reading the figure in the `ReadDocumentFromStream` method shown as follows), and then writes the figure itself by calling its `WriteFigureToStream` method:

```
bool DrawDocument::WriteDocumentToStream(String name,
                                         ostream& outStream)const{
  int listSize = figurePtrList.Size();
  outStream.write((char*) &listSize, sizeof listSize);

  for (DrawFigure* figurePtr : figurePtrList) {
    FigureId figureId = figurePtr->GetId();
    outStream.write((char*) &figureId, sizeof figureId);
    figurePtr->WriteFigureToStream(outStream);
  }

  return ((bool) outStream);
}
```

The `ReadDocumentFromStream` method is called when the user selects the **Open** menu item. It starts by reading the number of figures in the figure list. We need to read the identity number for the next figure and call the `CreateFigure` method to receive a pointer to the created figure. Then we just call the `ReadFigureFromStream` method for the figure and add the figure's address to the figure pointer list:

```
bool DrawDocument::ReadDocumentFromStream(String name,
                                          istream& inStream) {
  int listSize;
  inStream.read((char*) &listSize, sizeof listSize);
```

```
for (int index = 0; index < listSize; ++index) {
  FigureId figureId;
  inStream.read((char*) &figureId, sizeof figureId);

  DrawFigure* figurePtr = CreateFigure(figureId);
  figurePtr->ReadFigureFromStream(inStream);

  figurePtrList.PushBack(figurePtr);
}

return ((bool) inStream);
}
```

The `CreateFigure` method is called by the `ReadFigureFromStream` and `ReadFigureFromClipboard` method and creates a figure of the given type:

```
DrawFigure* DrawDocument::CreateFigure(FigureId figureId) const {
  switch (figureId) {
    case LineId:
      return (new LineFigure(this));

    case ArrowId:
      return (new ArrowFigure(this));

    case RectangleId:
      return (new RectangleFigure(this));

    case EllipseId:
      return (new EllipseFigure(this));
  }

  return nullptr;
}
```

Cut, copy, and paste

Similar to the aforementioned file management case, the framework also takes care of the details of cut, copy, and paste. First, we do need to decide when the cut and copy menu items and accelerators will be enabled. In `Modify` mode, it is enough that at least one figure is marked. We use the `DynamicList` method `AnyOf` to decide whether at least one figure is marked. In `Add` mode, cut or copy is never allowed. We do not need to override the `CutEnable` method, since its default behavior in the `StandardDocument` framework is to call the `CopyEnable` method:

```
bool DrawDocument::CopyEnable() const {
  if (applicationMode == Idle) {
    switch (actionMode) {
      case Modify:
        return figurePtrList.AnyOf(IsFigureMarked);

      case Add:
        return false;
    }
  }

  return false;
}
```

There is a `PasteEnable` method in the `StandardDocument` framework. However, in this application we do not need to override it, since the framework decides when to enable pasting or, more specifically, when there is data on the global clipboard with the format code given in the `StandardDocument` constructor, in this case the `DrawFormat` field. The global clipboard is a Windows resource intended for short-term storing of information that has been copied.

The `CopyGeneric` method takes a list of characters that are intended to be filled with application-specific information. We save the number of marked figures, and for each marked figure, we write its identity number and call the `WriteFigureToClipboard` method, which writes the figure-specific information to the `infoList` parameter:

```
bool DrawDocument::IsCopyGenericReady(int /* format */) const {
  return true;
}

void DrawDocument::CopyGeneric(int format, InfoList& infoList)
                              const {
  DynamicList<DrawFigure*> markedList;
  figurePtrList.CopyIf(IsFigureMarked, markedList);
  infoList.AddValue<int>(markedList.Size());

  for (DrawFigure* figurePtr : markedList) {
    infoList.AddValue<FigureId>(figurePtr->GetId());
    figurePtr->WriteFigureToClipboard(infoList);
  }
}
```

The `PasteGeneric` method pastes the figures in a way similar to the aforementioned the `ReadDocumentFromStream` method:

```
void DrawDocument::PasteGeneric(int format, InfoList& infoList) {
  figurePtrList.ApplyIf(IsFigureMarked, UnmarkFigure);

  int pasteSize;
  infoList.GetValue<int>(pasteSize);

  for (int count = 0; count < pasteSize; ++count) {
    FigureId figureId;
    infoList.GetValue<FigureId>(figureId);

    DrawFigure* figurePtr = CreateFigure(figureId);
    figurePtr->ReadFigureFromClipboard(infoList);
    figurePtr->Move(Size(1000, 1000));
    figurePtrList.PushBack(figurePtr);

    figurePtr->Mark(true);
  }

  UpdateWindow();
}
```

There is a `DeleteEnable` method in the `StandardDocument` framework, which we do not need to override since its default behavior is to call the `CopyEnable` method. The `OnDelete` method goes through the figure list, invalidating and deleting the marked figures. We use the `DynamicList` method `ApplyRemoveIf` to remove and delete marked figures.

We cannot simply use the `ApplyIf` and `RemoveIf` methods to deallocate and remove the figures, since it would result in memory errors (dangling pointers):

```
void DeleteFigure(DrawFigure*& figurePtr, void* /* voidPtr */) {
  figurePtr->Invalidate();
  delete figurePtr;
}

void DrawDocument::OnDelete() {
  figurePtrList.ApplyRemoveIf(IsFigureMarked, DeleteFigure,
                              nullptr, this);
  UpdateWindow();
  SetDirty(true);
}
```

The Modify menu

The **Modify** menu item is quite easy to handle. It is enabled in case the application is in the `Idle` mode, which it is in when the user does not press the left mouse button. The radio button is also present if the `actionMode` method is `Modify`, and the menu item listener just sets the `actionMode` method to `Modify`:

```
bool DrawDocument::ModifyEnable() const {
  return (applicationMode == Idle);
}

bool DrawDocument::ModifyRadio() const {
  return ((applicationMode == Idle) && (actionMode == Modify));
}

void DrawDocument::OnModify() {
  actionMode = Modify;
}
```

For the **Color** and **Fill** menu items, there are enable methods that are rather easy and listeners that are a little bit more complicated. It is possible to change the color in `Modify` mode if at least one figure is marked. In `Add` mode, it is always possible to change the color:

```
bool DrawDocument::ColorEnable() const {
  if (applicationMode == Idle) {
    switch (actionMode) {
      case Modify:
        return figurePtrList.AnyOf(IsFigureMarked);
      case Add:
        return true;
    }
  }
  return false;
}
```

The `SetFigureColor` method is a callback function that is called by the `ApplyIf` method on the `figurePtrList` list in the `OnColor` method:

```
void SetFigureColor(DrawFigure*& figurePtr, void* voidPtr) {
  Color* colorPtr = (Color*) voidPtr;

  if (figurePtr->IsMarked() &&
      (figurePtr->GetColor() != *colorPtr)) {
    figurePtr->SetColor(*colorPtr);
  }
}
```

The `OnColor` method is called when the user selects the **Color** menu item. In `Modify` mode, we extract the marked figures and choose the color of the topmost of them. We know that at least one figure is marked, otherwise the preceding `ColorEnable` method would return `false` and the **Color** menu item would be disabled. If the `ColorDialog` call returns `true`, we set the new color of all marked figures by calling the `ApplyIf` method on the `figurePtrList` list:

```
void DrawDocument::OnColor() {
  switch (actionMode) {
    case Modify: {
        DynamicList<DrawFigure*> markedList;
        figurePtrList.CopyIf(IsFigureMarked, markedList);
        DrawFigure* topFigurePtr = markedList[0];
        Color topColor = topFigurePtr->GetColor();

        if (StandardDialog::ColorDialog(this, topColor)) {
          nextColor = topColor;
          figurePtrList.ApplyIf(IsFigureMarked, SetFigureColor,
                                nullptr, &topColor);
          UpdateWindow();
          SetDirty(true);
        }
      }
      break;
```

If the `actionMode` method is `Add`, we just display a color dialog to set the next color:

```
    case Add:
      StandardDialog::ColorDialog(this, nextColor);
      break;
  }
}
```

The `IsFigureMarkedAndFilled` method is a callback function that is called by the `AnyOf` method on the `figurePtrList` list in the `FillCheck` method. The **Fill** menu item is checked with a radio mark if at least one figure is marked and filled:

```
bool IsFigureMarkedAndFilled(DrawFigure* const& figurePtr,
                             void* /* voidPtr */) {
  return (figurePtr->IsMarked() && figurePtr->IsFilled());
}

bool DrawDocument::FillCheck() const {
  if (applicationMode == Idle) {
    switch (actionMode) {
      case Modify:
        return figurePtrList.AnyOf(IsFigureMarkedAndFilled);
```

```
        case Add:
          return nextFill;
      }
   }

   return false;
}
```

The `IsFigureMarkedAndFillable` method is a callback function that is called by the `AnyOf` method on the `figurePtrList` list in the `FillEnable` method. The **Fill** menu item is enabled if at least one fillable figure (rectangle or ellipse) is marked, or if the user is about to add a rectangle or ellipse:

```
bool IsFigureMarkedAndFillable(DrawFigure* const& figurePtr,
                               void* /* voidPtr */){
   return (figurePtr->IsMarked() && figurePtr->IsFillable());
}

bool DrawDocument::FillEnable() const {
   if (applicationMode == Idle) {
     switch (actionMode) {
       case Modify:
         return figurePtrList.AnyOf(IsFigureMarkedAndFillable);
```

In order to test whether the figure type of the next figure to be added is fillable, we create and delete such a figure:

```
        case Add: {
            DrawFigure* addFigurePtr = CreateFigure(addFigureId);
            bool fillable = addFigurePtr->IsFillable();
            delete addFigurePtr;
            return fillable;
          }
      }
   }
   return false;
}
```

The `InverseFill` method is a callback function that is called by the `AnyOf` method on the `figurePtrList` list in the `OnFill` method, which is called when the user selects the **Fill** menu item. The `OnFill` method inverts the fill status of all marked figures in `Modify` mode. In `Add` mode, it just inverts the value of `nextFill`, indicating that the next figure to be added will have the inverted fill status:

```
void InverseFill(DrawFigure*& figurePtr, void* /* voidPtr */) {
  if (figurePtr->IsMarked()) {
    figurePtr->Fill(!figurePtr->IsFilled());
  }
}

void DrawDocument::OnFill() {
  switch (actionMode) {
    case Modify:
      figurePtrList.ApplyIf(IsFigureMarked, InverseFill);
      UpdateWindow();
      break;

    case Add:
      nextFill = !nextFill;
      break;
  }
}
```

The Add menu

The listeners for the items of the Add menu are rather straightforward. The enable methods are simple, for the menu item to be enabled it is enough if the applicationMode method is in the Idle mode:

```
bool DrawDocument::LineEnable() const {
  return (applicationMode == Idle);
}
bool DrawDocument::ArrowEnable() const {
  return (applicationMode == Idle);
}

bool DrawDocument::RectangleEnable() const {
  return (applicationMode == Idle);
}

bool DrawDocument::EllipseEnable() const {
  return (applicationMode == Idle);
}
```

The radio methods return true in Add mode if the figure to be added matches the figure of the radio method:

```
bool DrawDocument::LineRadio() const {
  return ((actionMode == Add) && (addFigureId == LineId));
}
```

```
bool DrawDocument::ArrowRadio() const {
  return ((actionMode == Add) && (addFigureId == ArrowId));
}

bool DrawDocument::RectangleRadio() const {
  return ((actionMode == Add) && (addFigureId == RectangleId));
}

bool DrawDocument::EllipseRadio() const {
  return ((actionMode == Add) && (addFigureId == EllipseId));
}
```

Finally, the methods responding to the menu item and accelerator selections sets the `actionMode` to `Add` and the figure to be added:

```
void DrawDocument::OnLine() {
  actionMode = Add;
  addFigureId = LineId;
}

void DrawDocument::OnArrow() {
  actionMode = Add;
  addFigureId = ArrowId;
}
void DrawDocument::OnRectangle() {
  actionMode = Add;
  addFigureId = RectangleId;
}

void DrawDocument::OnEllipse() {
  actionMode = Add;
  addFigureId = EllipseId;
}
```

The cursor

The `Set` method in the `Cursor` class sets the cursor to an appropriate value. If the application mode is `Idle` mode, we wait for the user to press the mouse button. In that case, we use the well-known arrow cursor image. If the user is in the process of enclosing figures with a rectangle, we use the cross-hair. If the user is in the process of moving several figures, we use the cursor with four arrows (size all). Finally, if they are in the process of modifying a single figure, the figure (whose address is located in the `figurePtrList[0]` list) itself is deciding which cursor to use:

```
void DrawDocument::UpdateCursor() {
  switch (applicationMode) {
    case Idle:
      Cursor::Set(Cursor::Arrow);
      break;

    case ModifyRectangle:
      Cursor::Set(Cursor::Crosshair);
      break;

    case MoveMultiple:
      Cursor::Set(Cursor::SizeAll);
      break;

    case ModifySingle:
      Cursor::Set(figurePtrList[0]->GetCursor());
      break;
  }
}
```

Summary

In this chapter, you started the development of a drawing program capable of drawing lines, arrows, rectangles, and ellipses. In Chapter 5, *The Figure Hierarchy*, we will look into the figure hierarchy.

5

The Figure Hierarchy

This chapter introduces the figure classes of the drawing program. Each figure is responsible for deciding whether it is hit by a mouse click or if it is enclosed by a rectangle. It is also responsible for moving or modifying, as well as drawing and communicating with a file stream and the clipboard.

The drawing figure hierarchy is made up of the `Draw`, `LineFigure`, `ArrowFigure`, `RectangleFigure`, and `EllipseFigure` classes, as shown in the following image:

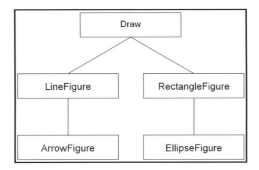

The DrawFigure class

The `Draw` class is the root class of the hierarchy and is mostly made up of virtual and pure virtual methods intended to be overridden by the subclasses.

The difference between a virtual method and a pure virtual method is that the virtual method has a body and it may be overridden by a subclass. If the subclass overrides the method, its version of the method is called.

If the subclass does not override the method, the method of the base class is called instead. A pure virtual method does not usually have a body, and a class holding at least one pure virtual method becomes abstract. The subclass can either override all the pure virtual methods of its base class or become abstract itself:

Draw.h

```
enum FigureId {LineId, ArrowId, RectangleId, EllipseId};
class DrawDocument;

class Draw {
  public:
    Draw(const Window* windowPtr);
```

Each figure has its own identity number, returned by the GetId method:

```
virtual FigureId GetId() const = 0;
virtual void SetFirstPoint(Point point) = 0;
```

The IsClick method returns True if the mouse point hits the figure, and the IsInside method returns True if the figure is completely enclosed by the area. The DoubleClick method gives the figure a possibility to perform a figure-specific action:

```
virtual bool IsClick(Point mousePoint) = 0;
virtual bool IsInside(Rect area) = 0;
virtual void DoubleClick(Point mousePoint) = 0;
```

The Modify and Move methods simply move the figure. However, the Modify method performs figure-specific actions defined by the IsClick method. If the user clicked on one of the figure endpoints, it will be modified, and if they clicked on any other part of the figure, it will be moved:

```
virtual void Modify(Size distanceSize) = 0;
virtual void Move(Size distanceSize) = 0;
```

The Invalidate method invalidates the figure by calling the Area method, which returns the area occupied by the figure. The Draw method draws the figure with the given Graphics class's reference:

```
virtual Rect Area() const = 0;
virtual void Draw(Graphics& graphics) const = 0;
void Invalidate() const {windowPtr->Invalidate(Area());}
```

The `IsFillable`, `IsFilled`, and `Fill` methods are only overridden by the `Rectangle` and `Ellipse` methods:

```
virtual bool IsFillable() const {return false;}
virtual bool IsFilled() const {return false;}
virtual void Fill(bool fill) {/* Empty. */}
```

The `WriteFigureToStream` and `ReadFigureFromStream` methods are called when the user opens or saves a document. They write or read the information of the figure to and from the streams:

```
virtual bool WriteFigureToStream(ostream& outStream) const;
virtual bool ReadFigureFromStream(istream& inStream);
```

The `WriteFigureToClipboard` and `ReadFigureFromClipboard` methods are called when the user copies or pastes figures. They write information to a character list and read information to a character buffer:

```
virtual void WriteFigureToClipboard(InfoList& infoList) const;
virtual void ReadFigureFromClipboard(InfoList& infoList);
```

The `color` and `marked` fields have their own get and set methods:

```
bool IsMarked() const {return marked;}
void Mark(bool mark);

Color GetColor() const {return color;}
void SetColor(Color color);
```

The `GetCursor` method returns the correct cursor for the figure:

```
virtual CursoTyper GetCursor() const = 0;
```

The `MarkRadius` method is the size of the small squares showing that the figure is marked:

```
static const Size MarkRadius;
```

The `windowPtr` pointer is used when invalidating the figure:

```
private:
  const Window* windowPtr;
```

Each figure, regardless of its type, has a color and is marked or unmarked:

```
    Color color;
    bool marked = false;
};
```

Draw.cpp

```
#include "..\\SmallWindows\\SmallWindows.h"
#include "Draw.h"
```

The `MarkRadius` parameter is set to 100 * 100 units, which is 1 * 1 millimeters:

```
const Size DrawFigure::MarkRadius(100, 100);
```

When a figure is created, it is always unmarked.

```
DrawFigure::Draw(const Window* windowPtr)
 :windowPtr(windowPtr) {
    // Empty.
}
```

We redraw when the user toggles the figure's marked state. You may notice the different order in the `if...else` statements. The reason is that when we mark a figure, it becomes larger; that is why we first set the `marked` parameter to `True` and then invalidate the figure to catch its area including its markings. On the other hand, when we unmark a figure it becomes smaller; that is why we first invalidate it to catch its area, including the markings, and then set the `marked` parameter to `False`.

```
void DrawFigure::Mark(bool mark) {
  if (!marked && mark) {
    marked = true;
    Invalidate();
  }
  else if (marked && !mark) {
    Invalidate();
    marked = false;
  }
}
```

The color is the only field written or read in file handling and in communication with the clipboard. The subclasses of the `DrawFigure` class call these methods and then write and read figure-specific information. The `WriteFigureToStream` and `ReadFigureFromStream` methods return the Boolean value of the stream to indicate whether the file operation succeeded.

```
bool DrawFigure::WriteFigureToStream(ostream& outStream) const {
  color.WriteColorToStream(outStream);
  return ((bool) outStream);
}

bool DrawFigure::ReadFigureFromStream(istream& inStream) {
  color.ReadColorFromStream(inStream);
  return ((bool) inStream);
}

void DrawFigure::WriteFigureToClipboard(InfoList& infoList) const{
  color.WriteColorToClipboard(charList);
}

void DrawFigure::ReadFigureFromClipboard(InfoList& infoList) {
  color.ReadColorFromClipboard(infoList);
}
```

The LineFigure class

A line is drawn between two points, represented by the `firstPoint` field to the `lastPoint` field in the `LineFigure` class, as shown in the following image:

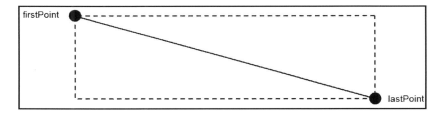

The `header` file overrides some of the methods of its `DrawFigure` base class. The `DoubleClick` method does nothing. As I see it, there is no really meaningful response to a double-click on a line. However, we still need to override the `DoubleClick` method, since it is a pure virtual method in the `DrawFigure` base class. If we do not override it, the `LineFigure` class will be abstract.

LineFigure.h

```
class LineFigure : public DrawFigure {
  public:
    LineFigure(const Window* windowPtr);
    virtual FigureId GetId() const {return LineId;}
    virtual void SetFirstPoint(Point point);

    virtual bool IsClick(Point mousePoint);
    virtual bool IsInside(Rect rectangleArea);
    virtual void DoubleClick(Point mousePoint) {/* Empty. */}

    virtual void Modify(Size distanceSize);
    virtual void Move(Size distanceSize);

    virtual Rect Area() const;
    virtual void Draw(Graphics& graphics) const;
    virtual CursorType GetCursor() const;

    virtual bool WriteFigureToStream(ostream& outStream) const;
    virtual bool ReadFigureFromStream(istream& inStream);

    virtual void WriteFigureToClipboard(InfoList& infoList) const;
    virtual void ReadFigureFromClipboard(InfoList& infoList);

  protected:
    enum {CreateLine, FirstPoint, LastPoint, MoveLine} lineMode;
    Point firstPoint, lastPoint;
    static bool IsPointInLine(Point firstPoint, Point lastPoint,
                              Point point);
};
```

LineFigure.cpp

```
#include "..\\SmallWindows\\SmallWindows.h"
#include "Draw.h"
#include "LineFigure.h"

LineFigure::LineFigure(const Window* windowPtr)
 :Draw(windowPtr), lineMode(CreateLine) {
 // Empty.
}
```

The `SetFirstPoint` method is called when the line is created and sets both the first and last points.

```
void LineFigure::SetFirstPoint(Point point) {
  firstPoint = point;
  lastPoint = point;
}
```

The `IsClick` method has two cases: the user has to hit either one of the endpoints or the line itself. We define two squares (`firstSquare` and `lastSquare`) covering the endpoints, and test whether the mouse hits one of them. If not, we test whether the mouse hits the line itself by calling the `IsPointInLine` method.

```
bool LineFigure::IsClick(Point mousePoint) {
  Rect firstSquare(firstPoint - MarkRadius,
                   firstPoint + MarkRadius);
  firstSquare.Normalize();

  if (firstSquare.PointInside(mousePoint)) {
    lineMode = FirstPoint;
    return true;
  }

  Rect lastSquare(lastPoint - MarkRadius, lastPoint + MarkRadius);
  lastSquare.Normalize();

  if (lastSquare.PointInside(mousePoint)) {
    lineMode = LastPoint;
    return true;
  }

  if (IsPointInLine(firstPoint, lastPoint, mousePoint)) {
    lineMode = MoveLine;
    return true;
  }

  return false;
}
```

The `IsPointInLine` method checks whether the point is located on the line, with some tolerance. We use trigonometric functions to calculate the position of the point relative to the line. However, if the line is completely vertical and the points have the same x coordinate, we have a special case.

Applying the trigonometric functions would result in division by zero. Instead, we create a small rectangle surrounding the line and check if the point is located in the rectangle, as shown in the following image:

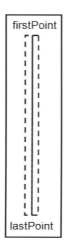

```
bool LineFigure::IsPointInLine(Point firstPoint, Point lastPoint,
                               Point point) {
   if (firstPoint.X() == lastPoint.X()) {
      Rect lineRect(firstPoint - MarkRadius,
                    lastPoint + MarkRadius);
      lineRect.Normalize();
      return lineRect.PointInside(point);
   }
```

If the line is not vertical, we start by creating an enclosing rectangle and test if the mouse point is in it. If it is, we let the leftmost point of the firstPoint and lastPoint fields equal to the minPoint field and the rightmost point equal to the maxPoint field. Then we calculate the width (lineWidth) and height (lineHeight) of the enclosing rectangle, as well as the distance between the minPoint and mousePoint fields in x and y directions (diffWidth and diffHeight), as shown in the following image:

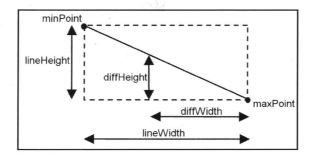

Due to uniformity, the following equation is true if the mouse point hits the line:

$$\frac{diffWidth}{diffHeight} = \frac{lineWidth}{lineHeight}$$

This implies that:

$$\frac{lineHeight}{lineWidth}\, diffWidth = diffHeight$$

And this also implies that:

$$diffHeight - \frac{lineHeight}{lineWidth}\, diffWidth = 0.$$

Let us allow for a small tolerance; let us say that the user is allowed to miss the line by a millimeter (100 units). This changes the last equation to the following:

$$delta = \left| diffHeight - \frac{lineHeight}{lineWidth}\, diffWidth \right|$$

$$delta \leq 100 \Rightarrow Hit$$

```
    else {
      Point minPoint = Min(firstPoint, lastPoint),
            maxPoint = Max(firstPoint, lastPoint);

      if ((minPoint.X() <= point.X()) &&
          (point.X() <= maxPoint.X())) {
        int lineWidth = maxPoint.X() - minPoint.X(),
            lineHeight = maxPoint.Y() - minPoint.Y();

        int diffWidth = point.X() - minPoint.X(),
            diffHeight = point.Y() - minPoint.Y();

        double delta = fabs(diffHeight - (diffWidth *
                               ((double) lineHeight) / lineWidth));
        return (delta <= 100);
      }

      return false;
    }
  }
```

The `IsInside` method is easier than the `IsClick` method. We just check whether both endpoints are enclosed by the given rectangle.

```
bool LineFigure::IsInside(Rect rect) {
  return (rect.PointInside(firstPoint) &&
          rect.PointInside(lastPoint));
}
```

In the `Modify` mode, we move one of the endpoints or the line depending on the value of the `lineMode` parameter set by the `IsClick` method. If the user has hit the first point, we move it. If they have hit the last point, or if the line is in the process of being created, we move the last point. If they have hit the line, we move the line. That is, we move both the first and last points.

```
void LineFigure::Modify(Size distanceSize) {
  Invalidate();
  switch (lineMode) {
    case FirstPoint:
      firstPoint += distanceSize;
      break;

    case CreateLine:
    case LastPoint:
      lastPoint += distanceSize;
      break;
```

```
    case MoveLine:
      Move(distanceSize);
      break;
  }

  Invalidate();
}
```

The `Move` method is also easy; we just move the two endpoints.

```
void LineFigure::Move(Size distanceSize) {
  Invalidate();
  firstPoint += distanceSize;
  lastPoint += distanceSize;
  Invalidate();
}
```

In the `Draw` method, we draw the line and, if the line is marked, its two endpoints are always black.

```
void LineFigure::Draw(Graphics& graphics) const {
  graphics.DrawLine(firstPoint, lastPoint, GetColor());

  if (IsMarked()) {
    graphics.FillRectangle(Rect(firstPoint - MarkRadius,
                           firstPoint + MarkRadius), Black,Black);
    graphics.FillRectangle(Rect(lastPoint - MarkRadius,
                           lastPoint + MarkRadius), Black, Black);
  }
}
```

The area occupied by the line is a rectangle with the endpoints as corners. If the line is marked, the mark radius is added.

```
Rect LineFigure::Area() const {
  Rect lineArea(firstPoint.X(), firstPoint.Y(),
                lastPoint.X(), lastPoint.Y());
  lineArea.Normalize();

  if (IsMarked()) {
    lineArea -= MarkRadius;
    lineArea += MarkRadius;
  }

  return lineArea;
}
```

If the line is being modified, the `Crosshair` cursor is returned. If it is being moved, the size-all cursor (four arrows in the compass directions) is returned. If none of these cases apply, then we just return the normal arrow cursor.

```
CursorType LineFigure::GetCursor() const {
  switch (lineMode) {
    case CreateLine:
    case FirstPoint:
    case LastPoint:
      return Cursor::Crosshair;

    case MoveLine:
      return Cursor::SizeAll;

    default:
      return Cursor::Normal;
  }
}
```

The `WriteFigureToStream`, `ReadFigureFromStream`, `WriteFigureToClipboard`, and `ReadFigureFromClipboard` methods write and read the first and last endpoints of the line after calling the corresponding methods in the `DrawFigure` class.

```
bool LineFigure::WriteFigureToStream(ostream& outStream) const {
  DrawFigure::WriteFigureToStream(outStream);
  firstPoint.WritePointToStream(outStream);
  lastPoint.WritePointToStream(outStream);
  return ((bool) outStream);
}

bool LineFigure::ReadFigureFromStream (istream& inStream) {
  DrawFigure::ReadFigureFromStream(inStream);
  firstPoint.ReadPointFromStream(inStream);
  lastPoint.ReadPointFromStream(inStream);
  return ((bool) inStream);
}

void LineFigure::WriteFigureToClipboard(InfoList& infoList) const{
  DrawFigure::WriteFigureToClipboard(charList);
  firstPoint.WritePointToClipboard(charList);
  lastPoint.WritePointToClipboard(charList);
}
```

```
void LineFigure::ReadFigureFromClipboard(InfoList& infoList) {
  DrawFigure::ReadFigureFromClipboard(infoList);
  firstPoint.ReadPointFromClipboard(infoList);
  lastPoint.ReadPointFromClipboard(infoList);
}
```

The ArrowFigure class

The ArrowFigure is a subclass of the LineFigure class and reuses the firstPoint and lastPoint fields and some of its functionality. The endpoints of the arrowhead are stored in the leftPoint and rightPoint fields, as shown in the following image. The lengths of the sides are defined by the ArrowLength constant to 500 units, which is 5 millimeters.

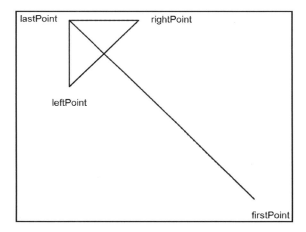

The ArrowFigure class overrides some of the methods of the LineFigure class. Mostly, it calls the methods of the LineFigure class and then adds functionality of its own.

ArrowFigure.h

```
class ArrowFigure : public LineFigure {
  public:
    ArrowFigure(const Window* windowPtr);
    FigureId GetId() const {return ArrowId;};

    bool IsClick(Point mousePoint);
    bool IsInside(Rect area);
    void DoubleClick(Point mousePoint);
```

```
      void Modify(Size distanceSize);
      void Move(Size distanceSize);
      Rect Area() const;
      void Draw(Graphics& graphics) const;

      bool WriteFigureToStream(ostream& outStream) const;
      bool ReadFigureFromStream(istream& inStream);

      void WriteFigureToClipboard(InfoList& infoList) const;
      void ReadFigureFromClipboard(InfoList& infoList);

   private:
      static const int ArrowLength = 500;
      Point leftPoint, rightPoint;
      void CalculateArrowHead();
};
```

The constructors let the `LineFigure` constructors initialize the arrow's endpoints, and then call the `CalculateArrowHead` method to calculate the endpoints of the arrowhead.

ArrowFigure.cpp

```
#include "..\\SmallWindows\\SmallWindows.h"
#include "Draw.h"
#include "LineFigure.h"
#include "ArrowFigure.h"

ArrowFigure::ArrowFigure(const Window* windowPtr)
 :LineFigure(windowPtr) {
  CalculateArrowHead();
}
```

The `IsClick` method returns `True` if the user clicks on the line or any part of the arrowhead.

```
bool ArrowFigure::IsClick(Point mousePoint) {
   return LineFigure::IsClick(mousePoint) ||
          IsPointInLine(firstPoint, leftPoint, mousePoint) ||
          IsPointInLine(firstPoint, rightPoint, mousePoint) ||
          IsPointInLine(leftPoint, rightPoint, mousePoint);
}
```

The `IsInside` method returns `True` if all the endpoints of the line and arrowhead are inside the area.

```
bool ArrowFigure::IsInside(Rect area) {
  return area.PointInside(firstPoint) &&
         area.PointInside(lastPoint) &&
         area.PointInside(leftPoint) &&
         area.PointInside(rightPoint);
}
```

The `Modify` method modifies the line and recalculates the arrowhead.

```
void ArrowFigure::Modify(Size distanceSize) {
  LineFigure::Modify(distanceSize);
  CalculateArrowHead();
}
```

The `Move` method moves the line and the arrowhead.

```
void ArrowFigure::Move(Size distanceSize) {
  LineFigure::Move(distanceSize);
  leftPoint += distanceSize;
  rightPoint += distanceSize;
}
```

When the user double-clicks on the arrow, its head and tail are swapped.

```
void ArrowFigure::DoubleClick(Point mousePoint) {
  if (IsClick(mousePoint)) {
    Invalidate();
    Point tempPoint = firstPoint;
    firstPoint = lastPoint;
    lastPoint = tempPoint;
    CalculateArrowHead();
    Invalidate();
  }
}
```

The `Area` method calculates the minimum and maximum of the line's and arrowhead's endpoints and returns an area with its top-left and bottom-right corners. If the arrow is marked, the mark radius is added to the area.

```
Rect ArrowFigure::Area() const {
  Point topLeft(min(firstPoint.X(), min(lastPoint.X(),
                min(leftPoint.X(), rightPoint.X()))),
                min(firstPoint.Y(), min(lastPoint.Y(),
                min(leftPoint.Y(), rightPoint.Y())))),
        bottomRight(max(firstPoint.X(), max(lastPoint.X(),
                    max(leftPoint.X(), rightPoint.X()))),
                    max(firstPoint.Y(), max(lastPoint.Y(),
                    max(leftPoint.Y(), rightPoint.Y()))));
```

```
  if (IsMarked()) {
    topLeft -= MarkRadius;
    bottomRight += MarkRadius;
  }

  return Rect(topLeft, bottomRight);
}
```

The `Draw` method draws the line and the arrowhead. If the arrow is marked, the arrow's endpoints are also marked with squares.

```
void ArrowFigure::Draw(Graphics& graphics) const {
  LineFigure::Draw(graphics);

  graphics.DrawLine(lastPoint, leftPoint, GetColor());
  graphics.DrawLine(lastPoint, rightPoint, GetColor());
  graphics.DrawLine(leftPoint, rightPoint, GetColor());
  if (IsMarked()) {
    graphics.FillRectangle(Rect(leftPoint - MarkRadius,
                           leftPoint + MarkRadius), Black, Black);
    graphics.FillRectangle(Rect(rightPoint - MarkRadius,
                           rightPoint + MarkRadius), Black,Black);
  }
}
```

The `WriteFigureToStream`, `ReadFigureFromStream`, `WriteFigureToClipboard`, and `ReadFigureFromClipboard` methods let the `LineFigure` class write and read the line's endpoints. Then it writes and reads the arrowhead's endpoints.

```
bool ArrowFigure::WriteFigureToStream(ostream& outStream) const {
  LineFigure::WriteFigureToStream(outStream);
  leftPoint.WritePointToStream(outStream);
  rightPoint.WritePointToStream(outStream);
  return ((bool) outStream);
}

bool ArrowFigure::ReadFigureFromStream(istream& inStream) {
  LineFigure::ReadFigureFromStream(inStream);
  leftPoint.ReadPointFromStream(inStream);
  rightPoint.ReadPointFromStream(inStream);
  return ((bool) inStream);
}

void ArrowFigure::WriteFigureToClipboard(InfoList& infoList)const{
  LineFigure::WriteFigureToClipboard(charList);
  leftPoint.WritePointToClipboard(charList);
  rightPoint.WritePointToClipboard(charList);
}
```

```
void ArrowFigure::ReadFigureFromClipboard(InfoList& infoList) {
  LineFigure::ReadFigureFromClipboard(infoList);
  leftPoint.ReadPointFromClipboard(infoList);
  rightPoint.ReadPointFromClipboard(infoList);
}
```

The `CalculateArrowHead` method is a private auxiliary method that calculates the endpoints of the arrowhead. We will use the following relations to calculate the `leftPoint` and `rightPoint` fields.

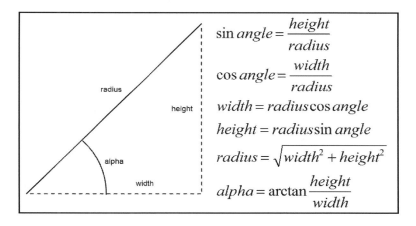

$$\sin angle = \frac{height}{radius}$$

$$\cos angle = \frac{width}{radius}$$

$$width = radius \cos angle$$

$$height = radius \sin angle$$

$$radius = \sqrt{width^2 + height^2}$$

$$alpha = \arctan \frac{height}{width}$$

The calculation is performed in three steps; first we calculate `alpha` and `beta`. See the following illustration for the definition of the angles:

$$width = lastPoint.X - firstPoint.X$$

$$height = lastPoint.Y - firstPoint.Y$$

$$alpha = \arctan \frac{height}{Width}$$

$$beta = alpha + \pi$$

Then we calculate `leftAngle` and `rightAngle` and use their values to calculate the value of `leftPoint` and `rightPoint`. The angle between the line and the arrowhead parts is 45 degrees, which is equivialent to Π/4 radians. So, in order to determine the angles for the arrowhead parts, we simply subtract Π/4 from `beta` and add Π/4 to `beta`:

$$leftAngle = beta - \frac{\pi}{4}$$

$$rightAngle = beta + \frac{\pi}{4}$$

Then we use the following formulas to finally determine `leftPoint` and `rightPoint`:

$$leftPoint.X = lastPoint.X + ArrowLenght\, \cos leftAngle$$
$$leftPoint.Y = lastPoint.Y + ArrowLenght\, \sin leftAngle$$
$$rightPoint.X = lastPoint.X + ArrowLenght\, \cos rightAngle$$
$$rightPoint.Y = lastPoint.Y + ArrowLenght\, \sin rightAngle$$

The trigonometric functions are available in the C standard library. However, we need to define our value for Π. The `atan2` function calculates the tangent value for the quota of `height` and `width` and takes into consideration the possibility that `width` might be zero.

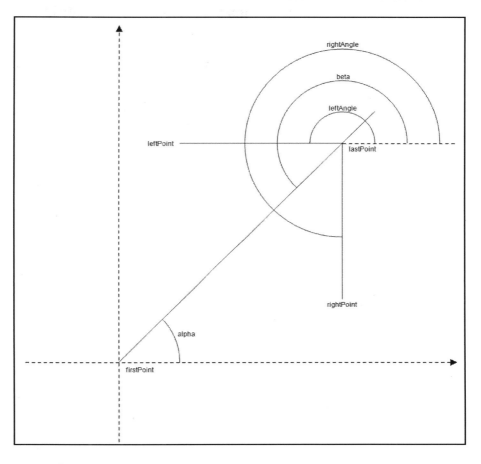

```
void ArrowFigure::CalculateArrowHead() {
  int height = lastPoint.Y() - firstPoint.Y();
  int width = lastPoint.X() - firstPoint.X();

  const double Pi = 3.14159265;
  double alpha = atan2((double) height, (double) width);
  double beta = alpha + Pi;

  double leftAngle = beta - (Pi / 4);
  double rightAngle = beta + (Pi / 4);

  leftPoint.X() = lastPoint.X() +
                  (int) (ArrowLength * cos(leftAngle));
  leftPoint.Y() = lastPoint.Y() +
                  (int) (ArrowLength * sin(leftAngle));
```

```
    rightPoint.X() = lastPoint.X() +
                      (int) (ArrowLength * cos(rightAngle));
    rightPoint.Y() = lastPoint.Y() +
                      (int) (ArrowLength * sin(rightAngle));
}
```

The RectangleFigure class

The RectangleFigure class holds a rectangle, which can be filled or unfilled. The user can modify it by grabbing one of its four corners. The DrawRectangle class overrides most of the methods of the DrawFigure class.

One difference compared to the line and arrow cases is that a rectangle is two-dimensional and can be filled or unfilled. The Fillable method returns True and the IsFilled and Fill methods are overridden. When the user double-clicks on a rectangle it will be toggled between the filled and unfilled states.

RectangleFigure.h

```
class RectangleFigure : public DrawFigure {
  public:
    RectangleFigure(const Window* windowPtr);

    virtual void SetFirstPoint(Point point);
    virtual FigureId GetId() const {return RectangleId;}

    virtual bool IsClick(Point mousePoint);
    virtual bool IsInside(Rect rectangleArea);
    virtual void DoubleClick(Point mousePoint);

    virtual void Modify(Size distanceSize);
    virtual void Move(Size distanceSize);

    virtual Rect Area() const;
    virtual void Draw(Graphics& graphics) const;
    virtual CursorType GetCursor() const;

    bool IsFillable() const {return true;}
    bool IsFilled() const {return filled;}
    void Fill(bool fill) {filled = fill; Invalidate();}

    virtual bool WriteFigureToStream(ostream& outStream) const;
    virtual bool ReadFigureFromStream(istream& inStream);
```

```
    virtual void WriteFigureToClipboard(InfoList& infoList) const;
    virtual void ReadFigureFromClipboard(InfoList& infoList);

  private:
    enum {CreateRectangle, TopLeftPoint, TopRightPoint,
        BottomRightPoint, BottomLeftPoint, MoveRectangle}
        rectangleMode;

  protected:
    bool filled = false;
    Point topLeft, bottomRight;
};
```

RectangleFigure.cpp

```
#include "..\\SmallWindows\\SmallWindows.h"
#include "Draw.h"
#include "RectangleFigure.h"
RectangleFigure::RectangleFigure(const Window* windowPtr)
:Draw(windowPtr), rectangleMode(CreateRectangle) { /* Empty. */ }
void RectangleFigure::SetFirstPoint(Point point) { topLeft = point;
bottomRight = point; }
```

When the user clicks on the rectangle, they may hit one of its four corners, the borders of the rectangle, or (if it is filled) its interior. First, we check the corners and then the rectangle itself. If it is filled, we just test whether the mouse point is enclosed in the rectangle. If the rectangle is unfilled, we test whether any of its four borders has been hit by constructing a slightly smaller rectangle and a slightly larger one. If the mouse position is included in the larger rectangle, but not in the smaller one, the user has hit one of the rectangle borders.

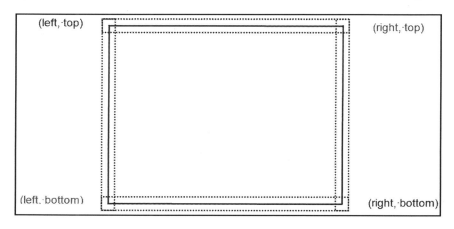

```
bool RectangleFigure::IsClick(Point mousePoint) {
  Rect topLeftRect(topLeft - MarkRadius, topLeft + MarkRadius);

  if (topLeftRect.PointInside(mousePoint)) {
    rectangleMode = TopLeftPoint;
    return true;
  }

  Point topRightPoint(bottomRight.X(), topLeft.Y());
  Rect topRectRight(topRightPoint - MarkRadius,
                    topRightPoint + MarkRadius);

  if (topRectRight.PointInside(mousePoint)) {
    rectangleMode = TopRightPoint;
    return true;
  }

  Rect bottomRightRect(bottomRight - MarkRadius,
                       bottomRight + MarkRadius);

  if (bottomRightRect.PointInside(mousePoint)) {
    rectangleMode = BottomRightPoint;
    return true;
  }

  Point bottomLeftPoint(topLeft.X(), bottomRight.Y());
  Rect bottomLeftRect(bottomLeftPoint - MarkRadius,
                      bottomLeftPoint + MarkRadius);

  if (bottomLeftRect.PointInside(mousePoint)) {
    rectangleMode = BottomLeftPoint;
    return true;
  }

  Rect areaRect(topLeft, bottomRight);
  areaRect.Normalize();

  if (IsFilled()) {
    areaRect.PointInside(mousePoint);

    if (areaRect.PointInside(mousePoint)) {
      rectangleMode = MoveRectangle;
      return true;
    }
  }
```

```
    else {
      Rect largeAreaRect(areaRect.TopLeft() - MarkRadius,
                         areaRect.BottomRight() + MarkRadius),
           smallAreaRect(areaRect.TopLeft() + MarkRadius,
                         areaRect.BottomRight() - MarkRadius);
      if (largeAreaRect.PointInside(mousePoint) &&
          !smallAreaRect.PointInside(mousePoint)) {
        rectangleMode = MoveRectangle;
        return true;
      }
    }

    return false;
  }
```

The IsInside method returns true if the top-left and bottom-right corners are enclosed by the rectangle area.

```
  bool RectangleFigure::IsInside(Rect area) {
    return area.PointInside(topLeft) &&
           area.PointInside(bottomRight);
  }
```

The DoubleClick method fills the rectangle if it is unfilled and vice versa.

```
  void RectangleFigure::DoubleClick(Point mousePoint) {
    if (IsClick(mousePoint)) {
      filled = !filled;
      Invalidate();
    }
  }
```

The Modify method modifies or moves the rectangle in accordance with the setting of the rectangleMode parameter in the IsClick method.

```
  void RectangleFigure::Modify(Size distanceSize) {
    Invalidate();

    switch (rectangleMode) {
      case TopLeftPoint:
        topLeft += distanceSize;
        break;

      case TopRightPoint:
        topLeft.Y() += distanceSize.Height();
        bottomRight.X() += distanceSize.Width();
        break;
```

```
    case CreateRectangle:
    case BottomRightPoint:
      bottomRight += distanceSize;
      break;

    case BottomLeftPoint:
      topLeft.X() += distanceSize.Width();
      bottomRight.Y() += distanceSize.Height();
      break;

    case MoveRectangle:
      Move(distanceSize);
      break;
  }

  Invalidate();
}
```

The `Move` method moves the rectangle's corners.

```
void RectangleFigure::Move(Size distanceSize) {
  Invalidate();
  topLeft += distanceSize;
  bottomRight += distanceSize;
  Invalidate();
}
```

The area of the rectangle is simply that of the rectangle. However, if it is marked, we increase it in order to include the corner squares.

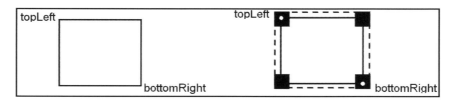

```
Rect RectangleFigure::Area() const {
  Rect areaRect(topLeft, bottomRight);
  areaRect.Normalize();

  if (IsMarked()) {
    areaRect -= MarkRadius;
    areaRect += MarkRadius;
  }
  return areaRect;
}
```

The `Draw` method draws or fills the rectangle. It also fills the squares if it is marked.

```
void RectangleFigure::Draw(Graphics& graphics) const {
  if (filled) {
    graphics.FillRectangle(Rect(topLeft, bottomRight),
                           GetColor(), GetColor());
  }
  else {
    graphics.DrawRectangle(Rect(topLeft, bottomRight),
                           GetColor());
  }

  if (IsMarked()) {
    graphics.FillRectangle(Rect(topLeft - MarkRadius,
                                topLeft + MarkRadius), Black, Black);

    Point topRight(bottomRight.X(), topLeft.Y());
    graphics.FillRectangle(Rect(topRight - MarkRadius,
                                topRight + MarkRadius), Black, Black);

    graphics.FillRectangle(Rect(bottomRight - MarkRadius,
                                bottomRight + MarkRadius),Black,Black);

    Point bottomLeft(topLeft.X(), bottomRight.Y());
    graphics.FillRectangle(Rect(bottomLeft - MarkRadius,
                bottomLeft + MarkRadius.Height()), Black, Black);
  }
}
```

The cursor of the rectangle is the size-all cursor (arrows in the four compass directions) when the figure is being moved. It is a cursor with arrows in accordance with the grabbed corner while being modified: north-west and south-east arrows in the case of the top-left or bottom-right corner, and north-east and south-west arrows in the case of the top-right or bottom-left corner.

```
CursorType RectangleFigure::GetCursor() const {
  switch (rectangleMode) {
    case TopLeftPoint:
    case BottomRightPoint:
      return Cursor::SizeNorthWestSouthEast;

    case TopRightPoint:
    case BottomLeftPoint:
      return Cursor::SizeNorthEastSouthWest;

    case MoveRectangle:
      return Cursor::SizeAll;
```

```
        default:
          return Cursor::Normal;
    }
  }
```

The WriteFigureToStream, ReadFigureFromStream, WriteFigureToClipboard, and ReadFigureFromClipboard methods call the corresponding methods in the DrawFigure class. Then they write and read the four corners of the rectangle, and whether it is filled or not.

```
bool RectangleFigure::WriteFigureToStream(ostream& outStream)
                                                  const {
  DrawFigure::WriteFigureToStream(outStream);
  topLeft.WritePointToStream(outStream);
  bottomRight.WritePointToStream(outStream);
  outStream.write((char*) &filled, sizeof filled);
  return ((bool) outStream);
}

bool RectangleFigure::ReadFigureFromStream (istream& inStream) {
  DrawFigure::ReadFigureFromStream(inStream);
  topLeft.ReadPointFromStream(inStream);
  bottomRight.ReadPointFromStream(inStream);
  inStream.read((char*) &filled, sizeof filled);
  return ((bool) inStream);
}

void RectangleFigure::WriteFigureToClipboard(InfoList& infoList)
                                                 const {
  DrawFigure::WriteFigureToClipboard(infoList);
  topLeft.WritePointToClipboard(infoList);
  bottomRight.WritePointToClipboard(infoList);
  infoList.AddValue<bool>(filled);
}

void RectangleFigure::ReadFigureFromClipboard(InfoList& infoList) {
  DrawFigure::ReadFigureFromClipboard(infoList);
  topLeft.ReadPointFromClipboard(infoList);
  bottomRight.ReadPointFromClipboard(infoList);
  infoList.GetValue<bool>(filled);
}
```

The EllipseFigure class

The `EllipseFigure` class is a subclass of the `RectangleFigure` class. The ellipse can be moved or reshaped by the horizontal or vertical corners. Most of the methods from the `RectangleFigure` class are not overridden by the `Ellipse` class.

Ellipse.h

```
class EllipseFigure : public RectangleFigure {
  public:
    EllipseFigure(const Window* windowPtr);
    FigureId GetId() const {return EllipseId;}

    bool IsClick(Point mousePoint);
    void Modify(Size distanceSize);
    void Draw(Graphics& graphics) const;
    CursoTyper GetCursor() const;

  private:
    enum {CreateEllipse, LeftPoint, TopPoint, RightPoint,
          BottomPoint, MoveEllipse} ellipseMode;
};
```

Ellipse.cpp

```
#include "..\\SmallWindows\\SmallWindows.h"
#include "Draw.h"
#include "RectangleFigure.h"
#include "EllipseFigure.h"
EllipseFigure::EllipseFigure(const Window* windowPtr)
 :RectangleFigure(windowPtr),
  ellipseMode(CreateEllipse) {
  // Empty.
}
```

Just as in the rectangle case, the `IsClick` method first decides if the user has clicked on one of the four endpoints; however, the positions are different compared to the rectangle corners.

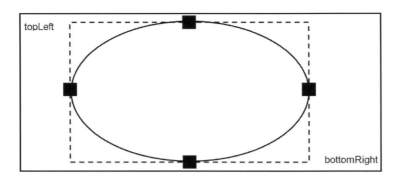

```
bool EllipseFigure::IsClick(Point mousePoint) {
  Point leftPoint(topLeft.X(), (topLeft.Y() + bottomRight.Y())/2);
  Rect leftRect(leftPoint - MarkRadius, leftPoint + MarkRadius);

  if (leftRect.PointInside(mousePoint)) {
    ellipseMode = LeftPoint;
    return true;
  }

  Point topPoint((topLeft.X() + bottomRight.X()) / 2,topLeft.Y());
  Rect topRect(topPoint - MarkRadius, topPoint + MarkRadius);

  if (topRect.PointInside(mousePoint)) {
    ellipseMode = TopPoint;
    return true;
  }

  Point rightPoint(bottomRight.X(),
                   (topLeft.Y() + bottomRight.Y()) / 2);
  Rect rightRect(rightPoint - MarkRadius,
                 rightPoint + MarkRadius);

  if (rightRect.PointInside(mousePoint)) {
    ellipseMode = RightPoint;
    return true;
  }
  Point bottomPoint((topLeft.X() + bottomRight.X()) / 2,
                    bottomRight.Y());
  Rect bottomRect(bottomPoint - MarkRadius,
                  bottomPoint + MarkRadius);

  if (bottomRect.PointInside(mousePoint)) {
    ellipseMode = BottomPoint;
    return true;
  }
```

If the user has not clicked on one of the modifying positions, we have to decide if the user has clicked on the ellipse itself. It is rather easy if the ellipse is not filled. We create an elliptic region by using the Win32 API function CreateEllipticRgn and test if the mouse position is in it. If the ellipse is not filled, we create two regions, one slightly smaller and one slightly larger. If the mouse position is included in the larger region, but not in the smaller one, we have a hit.

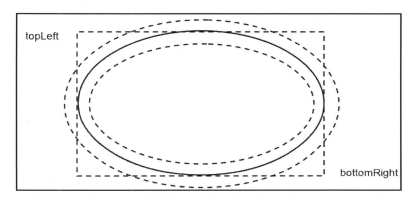

```
ellipseMode = MoveEllipse;
Point minPoint = Min(topLeft, bottomRight),
      maxPoint = Max(topLeft, bottomRight);
if (IsFilled()) {
  HRGN ellipseRegion =
    CreateEllipticRgn(minPoint.X(), minPoint.Y(),
                      maxPoint.X(), maxPoint.Y());
  return (PtInRegion(ellipseRegion, mousePoint.X(),
                     mousePoint.Y()) != 0);
}
else {
  HRGN smallRegion =
    CreateEllipticRgn(minPoint.X() + MarkRadius.Width(),
                      minPoint.Y() + MarkRadius.Height(),
                      maxPoint.X() - MarkRadius.Width(),
                      maxPoint.Y() - MarkRadius.Height());
  HRGN largeRegion =
    CreateEllipticRgn(minPoint.X() - MarkRadius.Width(),
                      minPoint.Y() - MarkRadius.Height(),
                      maxPoint.X() + MarkRadius.Width(),
                      maxPoint.Y() + MarkRadius.Height());
  return ((PtInRegion(largeRegion, mousePoint.X(),
                      mousePoint.Y()) != 0) &&
          (PtInRegion(smallRegion, mousePoint.X(),
                      mousePoint.Y()) == 0));
}
```

```
    return false;
  }
```

The `Modify` method moves the corner in accordance with the setting of the `ellipseMode` parameter in the `IsClick` method.

```
void EllipseFigure::Modify(Size distanceSize) {
  Invalidate();

  switch (ellipseMode) {
    case CreateEllipse:
      bottomRight += distanceSize;
      break;

    case LeftPoint:
      topLeft.X() += distanceSize.Width();
      break;

    case RightPoint:
      bottomRight.X() += distanceSize.Width();
      break;

    case TopPoint:
      topLeft.Y() += distanceSize.Height();
      break;

    case BottomPoint:
      bottomRight.Y() += distanceSize.Height();
      break;

    case MoveEllipse:
      Move(distanceSize);
      break;
  }

  Invalidate();
}
```

The `Draw` method fills or draws the ellipse, and the four squares if the ellipse is marked.

```
void EllipseFigure::Draw(Graphics& graphics) const {
  if (filled) {
    graphics.FillEllipse(Rect(topLeft, bottomRight),
                         GetColor(), GetColor());
  }
  else {
    graphics.DrawEllipse(Rect(topLeft, bottomRight), GetColor());
  }

  if (IsMarked()) {
    Point leftPoint(topLeft.X(), (topLeft.Y()+bottomRight.Y())/2);
    graphics.FillRectangle(Rect(leftPoint - MarkRadius,
                           leftPoint + MarkRadius), Black, Black);

    Point topPoint((topLeft.X() + bottomRight.X())/2,topLeft.Y());
    graphics.FillRectangle(Rect(topPoint - MarkRadius,
                           topPoint + MarkRadius),Black, Black);

    Point rightPoint(bottomRight.X(),
                     (topLeft.Y() + bottomRight.Y()) / 2);
    graphics.FillRectangle(Rect(rightPoint - MarkRadius,
                           rightPoint + MarkRadius), Black,Black);

    Point bottomPoint((topLeft.X() + bottomRight.X()) / 2,
                      bottomRight.Y());
    graphics.FillRectangle(Rect(bottomPoint - MarkRadius,
                           bottomPoint + MarkRadius),Black,Black);
  }
}
```

Finally, when it comes to the cursor, we have the following five different cases:

- When the ellipse is being created, the crosshair is returned
- When the user grabs the left or right endpoint of the ellipse, the west-east (left-right) arrow is returned
- When the user grabs the top or bottom endpoint, the top-bottom (up-down) arrow is returned
- When the user moves the ellipse, the size-all arrow (four arrows that point left, right, up, and down) is returned
- Finally, when the user neither moves nor modifies the ellipse, the normal arrow cursor is returned

```
CursorType EllipseFigure::GetCursor() const {
  switch (ellipseMode) {
    case CreateEllipse:
      return Cursor::Crosshair;

    case LeftPoint:
    case RightPoint:
      return Cursor::SizeWestEast;

    case TopPoint:
    case BottomPoint:
      return Cursor::SizeNorthSouth;

    case MoveEllipse:
      return Cursor::SizeAll;

    default:
      return Cursor::Normal;
  }
}
```

Summary

In this chapter, you studied the figure class hierarchy for the drawing program of Chapter 4, *Working with Shapes and Figures*. You covered the following topics:

- Testing whether the figure has been hit by a mouse click or if it is enclosed by a rectangle
- Modification and movement of the figure
- Drawing the figure and calculating the area of the figure
- Writing and reading the figure to and from a file stream or the clipboard
- Cursor handling with different cursors depending on the current state of figure

In Chapter 6, *Building a Word Processor*, you will start developing a word processor.

6

Building a Word Processor

In this chapter, we build a word processor that is capable of handling text on character level: that is, a single character that has its own font, color, size, and style. We also introduce caret handling, printing and print previewing, and file dropping, as well as clipboard handling with ASCII and Unicode text, which means that we can cut and paste between this application and, for instance, a text editor.

Auxiliary classes

A document in this application is made up of pages, paragraphs, lines, and characters. Let me try to explain how it all hangs together:

- First of all, the document is made up of a list of characters. Each character has its own font and pointers to the paragraph and line it belongs to. The character information is stored in objects of the CharInfo class. The charList field in the WordDocument class is a list of CharInfo objects.

- The characters are divided into paragraphs. A paragraph does not hold its own character list. Instead, it holds the indexes in the character list of its first and last characters. The `paragraphList` field in `WordDocument` is a list of `Paragraph` objects. The last character of each paragraph is always a newline.
- Each paragraph is divided into a list of lines. The `Paragraph` class below holds a list of `Line` objects. A line holds the indexes of its first and last characters relative to the beginning of the paragraph.
- Finally, the document is also divided into pages. A page holds as many whole paragraphs as possible.

Every time something is changed in the document, the current line and paragraph are recalculated. The page list is also recalculated.

Let's continue to look into the `CharInfo`, `LineInfo`, and `Paragraph` classes.

Character information

The `CharInfo` class is a structure that holds the following:

- A character and its font
- Its enclosing rectangle, which is used when drawing the character
- Pointers to the line and the paragraph it belongs to

CharInfo.h

```
class LineInfo;
class Paragraph;

class CharInfo {
  public:
    CharInfo(Paragraph* paragraphPtr = nullptr,
             TCHAR tChar = TEXT('\0'),
             Font font = SystemFont, Rect rect = ZeroRect);

    CharInfo(const CharInfo& charInfo);
    CharInfo& operator=(const CharInfo& charInfo);

    bool WriteCharInfoToStream(ostream& outStream) const;
    bool ReadCharInfoFromStream(istream& inStream);

    void WriteCharInfoToClipboard(InfoList& infoList) const;
    void ReadCharInfoFromClipboard(InfoList& infoList);
```

Each of the private fields in this class has its own method for getting and setting the value. The first set of methods is constant and returns the value itself, which means that the value of the field cannot be changed by these methods. The second set of methods is nonconstant and returns a reference to the field, which means that the value can be changed. However, they cannot be called from a constant object.

```
TCHAR Char() const {return tChar;}
Font CharFont() const {return charFont;}
Rect CharRect() const {return charRect;}
LineInfo* LineInfoPtr() const {return lineInfoPtr;}
Paragraph* ParagraphPtr() const {return paragraphPtr;}

TCHAR& Char() {return tChar;}
Font& CharFont() {return charFont;}
Rect& CharRect() {return charRect;}
LineInfo*& LineInfoPtr() {return lineInfoPtr;}
Paragraph*& ParagraphPtr() {return paragraphPtr;}
```

The `tChar` and `charFont` fields hold the character itself and its font, and the `charRect` coordinates are relative to the top-left position of the paragraph the character belongs to. Each character belongs to a paragraph and one of the lines of that paragraph, which `paragraphPtr` and `lineInfoPtr` point at.

```
private:
    TCHAR tChar;
    Font charFont;
    Rect charRect;
    Paragraph* paragraphPtr;
    LineInfo* lineInfoPtr;
};
```

CharInfo.cpp

```
#include "..\\SmallWindows\\SmallWindows.h"
#include "CharInfo.h"
```

The default value of the `font` parameter is the system font that gives the default font. It is often 10 point Arial.

```
CharInfo::CharInfo(Paragraph* paragraphPtr /* = nullptr */,
                   TCHAR tChar /* = TEXT('\0') */,
                   Font font/* = SystemFont */,
                   Rect rect /* = ZeroRect */)
 :lineInfoPtr(nullptr),
  paragraphPtr(paragraphPtr),
  tChar(tChar),
  charFont(font),
```

```
    charRect(rect) {
    // Empty.
}
```

The copy constructor and assignment operator copies the fields. They are called on several occasions when the characters are written to and read from file streams, or when they are cut, copied, or pasted.

```
CharInfo::CharInfo(const CharInfo& charInfo)
 :lineInfoPtr(charInfo.lineInfoPtr),
  paragraphPtr(charInfo.paragraphPtr),
  tChar(charInfo.tChar),
  charFont(charInfo.charFont),
  charRect(charInfo.charRect) {
  // Empty.
}

CharInfo& CharInfo::operator=(const CharInfo& charInfo) {
  lineInfoPtr = charInfo.lineInfoPtr;
  paragraphPtr = charInfo.paragraphPtr;
  tChar = charInfo.tChar;
  charFont = charInfo.charFont;
  charRect = charInfo.charRect;
  return *this;
}
```

The `WriteCharInfoToStream` method writes and the `ReadCharInfoFromStream` method reads the values of the class to and from a file stream and the clipboard. Note that we omit the `paragraphPtr` and `lineInfoPtr` pointers since it would be meaningless to save pointer addresses to a stream. Instead, their values are set by the `ReadDocumentFromStream` method in the `WordDocument` class after calling the `ReadCharInfoFromStream` method.

```
bool CharInfo::WriteCharInfoToStream(ostream& outStream) const {
  outStream.write((char*) &tChar, sizeof tChar);
  charFont.WriteFontToStream(outStream);
  charRect.WriteRectToStream(outStream);
  return ((bool) outStream);
}

bool CharInfo::ReadCharInfoFromStream(istream& inStream) {
  inStream.read((char*) &tChar, sizeof tChar);
  charFont.ReadFontFromStream(inStream);
  charRect.ReadRectFromStream(inStream);
  return ((bool) inStream);
}
```

The `WriteCharInfoToClipboard` method writes and the `ReadCharInfoFromClipboard` method reads the values to and from the clipboard. Also, in this case, we omit the `paragraphPtr` and `lineInfoPtr` pointers. These pointers are set by the `PasteGeneric` method in the `WordDocument` class after the call to the `ReadCharInfoFromClipboard` method.

```
void CharInfo::WriteCharInfoToClipboard(InfoList& infoList) const{
  infoList.AddValue<TCHAR>(tChar);
  charFont.WriteFontToClipboard(infoList);
}

void CharInfo::ReadCharInfoFromClipboard(InfoList& infoList) {
  infoList.GetValue<TCHAR>(tChar);
  charFont.ReadFontFromClipboard(infoList);
}
```

Line information

The `LineInfo` method is a small structure holding information about a line in a paragraph:

- The integer index of its first and last characters
- Its height and ascent, that is, the height and ascent of the largest character on the line.
- The top position of the line relative to its paragraph top position

LineInfo.h

```
class LineInfo {
  public:
    LineInfo();
    LineInfo(int first, int last, int top,
             int height, int ascent);

    bool WriteLineInfoToStream(ostream& outStream) const;
    bool ReadLineInfoFromStream(istream& inStream);
```

Similar to the `CharInfo` method mentioned previously, the `LineInfo` method holds a set of constant methods for inspecting the class fields and a set of nonconstant methods for modifying them.

```
    int First() const {return first;}
    int Last() const {return last;}
    int Top() const {return top;}
    int Height() const {return height;}
```

```
int Ascent() const {return ascent;}
int& First() {return first;}
int& Last() {return last;}
int& Top() {return top;}
int& Height() {return height;}
int& Ascent() {return ascent;}
```

The fields of this class are four integer values; the `first` and `last` fields refer to the first and last characters on the line, respectively. The `top`, `height`, and `ascent` fields are the top position of the line relative to the top position of the paragraph, the maximum height, and ascent of the line.

```
    private:
        int first, last, top, height, ascent;
};
```

LineInfo.cpp

```
#include "..\\SmallWindows\\SmallWindows.h"
#include "LineInfo.h"
```

The default construct is called when the user reads a document from a stream, while the second constructor is called when new lines of a paragraph are being generated.

```
LineInfo::LineInfo() {
  // Empty.
}

LineInfo::LineInfo(int first, int last, int top,
                   int height, int ascent)
 :first(first),
  last(last),
  top(top),
  height(height),
  ascent(ascent) {
  // Empty.
}
```

The `WriteLineInfoToStream` and `ReadLineInfoFromStream` methods simply write and read, respectively, the field value. Note that there are no corresponding methods for cut, copy, and paste since the line list of a paragraph is regenerated each time the paragraph is pasted.

```
bool LineInfo::WriteLineInfoToStream(ostream& outStream) const {
  outStream.write((char*) &first, sizeof first);
  outStream.write((char*) &last, sizeof last);
  outStream.write((char*) &ascent, sizeof ascent);
```

```
    outStream.write((char*) &top, sizeof top);
    outStream.write((char*) &height, sizeof height);
    return ((bool) outStream);
  }

  bool LineInfo::ReadLineInfoFromStream(istream& inStream) {
    inStream.read((char*) &first, sizeof first);
    inStream.read((char*) &last, sizeof last);
    inStream.read((char*) &ascent, sizeof ascent);
    inStream.read((char*) &top, sizeof top);
    inStream.read((char*) &height, sizeof height);
    return ((bool) inStream);
  }
```

The Paragraph class

A document is made up of a sequence of paragraphs. The `Paragraph` structure holds the following:

- The index of its first and last characters
- Its top position relative to the beginning of the document, and its height
- Its index in the document paragraph pointer list
- Its alignment–a paragraph can be left, center, justified, or right aligned
- Whether it holds a page break, that is, whether this paragraph will be located at the beginning of the next page

Paragraph.h

```
    enum Alignment {Left, Center, Right, Justified};
    class WordDocument:

    class Paragraph {
      public:
        Paragraph();
        Paragraph(int first, int last,
                  Alignment alignment, int index);

        bool WriteParagraphToStream(ostream& outStream) const;
        bool ReadParagraphFromStream(WordDocument* wordDocumentPtr,
                                     istream& inStream);

        void WriteParagraphToClipboard(InfoList& infoList) const;
        void ReadParagraphFromClipboard(InfoList& infoList);
```

```
int& First() {return first;}
int& Last() {return last;}
int& Top() {return top;}
int& Index() {return index;}
int& Height() {return height;}
bool& PageBreak() {return pageBreak;}
```

As you can see, we name the `AlignmentField` method instead of just the `Alignment` method. The reason for this is that there already is a class named `Alignment`. We cannot give the same name to both the class and method. Therefore, we add the `Field` suffix to the method name.

```
Alignment& AlignmentField() {return alignment;}
DynamicList<LineInfo*>& LinePtrList() {return linePtrList;}
```

The `first` and `last` fields are the index in the document character list of the first and last characters in the paragraph, respectively; the last character of the paragraph is always a newline. The `top` field is the top position of the paragraph relative to the beginning of the document, which is always zero for the first paragraph of the document and positive for the other paragraphs. The `height` is the height of the paragraph, and `index` refers to the index of the paragraph in the document paragraph pointer list. If `pageBreak` is `true`, the paragraph will always be located at the beginning of a page.

```
int first, last, top, height, index;
bool pageBreak;
```

A paragraph can be left, right, centered, and justified aligned. In the justified case, the spaces are extended in order for the words to be distributed over the whole width of the page.

```
Alignment alignment;
```

A paragraph is made up of at least one line. The indexes of the `linePtrList` list are relative to the index of the first character in the paragraph (not the document), and the coordinates are relative to the top of the paragraph (again, not the document).

```
DynamicList<LineInfo*> linePtrList;
};
```

Paragraph.cpp

```
#include "..\\SmallWindows\\SmallWindows.h"
#include "CharInfo.h"
#include "LineInfo.h"
#include "Paragraph.h"
#include "WordDocument.h"
Paragraph::Paragraph() { /* Empty. */ }
Paragraph::Paragraph(int first, int last, Alignment alignment, int index)
:top(-1), first(first), last(last), index(index), pageBreak(false),
alignment(alignment) { /* Empty. */ }
```

The idea is that the `WriteParagraphToStream` and `ReadParagraphFromStream` methods write and read, respectively, all information about the paragraph. Remember that all coordinates are given in logical units (hundredths of millimeters), which means that works to save and open the file on screens with different resolutions.

```
bool Paragraph::WriteParagraphToStream(ostream& outStream) const {
   outStream.write((char*) &first, sizeof first);
   outStream.write((char*) &last, sizeof last);
   outStream.write((char*) &top, sizeof top);
   outStream.write((char*) &height, sizeof height);
   outStream.write((char*) &index, sizeof index);
   outStream.write((char*) &pageBreak, sizeof pageBreak);
   outStream.write((char*) &alignment, sizeof alignment);

   { int linePtrListSize = linePtrList.Size();
     outStream.write((char*) &linePtrListSize,
                   sizeof linePtrListSize);

     for (const LineInfo* lineInfoPtr : linePtrList) {
       lineInfoPtr->WriteLineInfoToStream(outStream);
     }
   }

   return ((bool) outStream);
}

bool Paragraph::ReadParagraphFromStream
                (WordDocument* wordDocumentPtr, istream& inStream){
   inStream.read((char*) &first, sizeof first);
   inStream.read((char*) &last, sizeof last);
   inStream.read((char*) &top, sizeof top);
   inStream.read((char*) &height, sizeof height);
   inStream.read((char*) &index, sizeof index);
   inStream.read((char*) &pageBreak, sizeof pageBreak);
   inStream.read((char*) &alignment, sizeof alignment);
```

When we have read indexes of the first and last character of the paragraph, we need to set the paragraph pointer of each character.

```
for (int charIndex = first; charIndex <= last; ++charIndex) {
  wordDocumentPtr->CharList()[charIndex].ParagraphPtr() = this;
}

{ int linePtrListSize = linePtrList.Size();
  inStream.read((char*) &linePtrListSize,
              sizeof linePtrListSize);

  for (int count = 0; count < linePtrListSize; ++count) {
    LineInfo* lineInfoPtr = new LineInfo();
    assert(lineInfoPtr != nullptr);
    lineInfoPtr->ReadLineInfoFromStream(inStream);
    linePtrList.PushBack(lineInfoPtr);
```

In the same way as in the paragraph pointer case above, we need to set the line pointer of each character.

```
    for (int charIndex = lineInfoPtr->First();
         charIndex <= lineInfoPtr->Last(); ++charIndex) {
      wordDocumentPtr->CharList()[first + charIndex].
        LineInfoPtr() = lineInfoPtr;
    }
  }
}

return ((bool) inStream);
}
```

On the other hand, the `WriteParagraphToClipboard` and `ReadParagraphFromClipboard` methods only write and read, respectively, the essential information. After the paragraph has been read, the `CalaulateParagraph` method is then called, which calculates the character rectangles and the height of the paragraph and generates its line pointer list.

```
void Paragraph::WriteParagraphToClipboard(InfoList& infoList) const {
  infoList.AddValue<int>(first);
  infoList.AddValue<int>(last);
  infoList.AddValue<int>(top);
  infoList.AddValue<int>(index);
  infoList.AddValue<bool>(pageBreak);
  infoList.AddValue<Alignment>(alignment);
}
```

```
void Paragraph::ReadParagraphFromClipboard(InfoList& infoList) {
  infoList.GetValue<int>(first);
  infoList.GetValue<int>(last);
  infoList.GetValue<int>(top);
  infoList.GetValue<int>(index);
  infoList.GetValue<bool>(pageBreak);
  infoList.GetValue<Alignment>(alignment);
}
```

The MainWindow class

The `MainWindow` class is nearly identical to the versions of the previous chapters. It sets the application name to `Word` and returns the address of a `WordDocument` instance:

```
#include "..\\SmallWindows\\SmallWindows.h"
#include "CharInfo.h"
#include "LineInfo.h"
#include "Paragraph.h"
#include "WordDocument.h"

void MainWindow(vector<String> /* argumentList */,
                WindowShow windowShow) {
  Application::ApplicationName() = TEXT("Word");
  Application::MainWindowPtr() = new WordDocument(windowShow);
}
```

The WordDocument class

The `WordDocument` class is the main class of the application. It extends the `StandardDocument` class and takes advantage of its document-based functionality.

WordDocument.h

```
class WordDocument : public StandardDocument {
  public:
    WordDocument(WindowShow windowShow);
```

The `InitDocument` class is called by the constructor, the `ClearDocument`, and `Delete` classes.

```
    void InitDocument();
```

The `OnKeyboardMode` method is called every time the user presses the *Insert* key. The `UpdateCaret` method sets the caret to a vertical bar in `insert` mode and a block in `overwrite` mode. When the user marks one or several characters, the caret is cleared.

```
void OnKeyboardMode(KeyboardMode keyboardMode);
void UpdateCaret();
```

When the user presses, moves, and releases the mouse, we need to find the index of the character located at the mouse position. The `MousePointToIndex` method finds the paragraph, and the `MousePointToParagraphIndex` method finds the character in the paragraph. The `InvalidateBlock` method invalidates the characters from the smallest index, inclusive, to the largest index, exclusive.

```
void OnMouseDown(MouseButton mouseButtons, Point mousePoint,
                 bool shiftPressed,
                 bool controlPressed);
void OnMouseMove(MouseButton mouseButtons, Point mousePoint,
                 bool shiftPressed,
                 bool controlPressed);
void OnMouseUp(MouseButton mouseButtons, Point mousePoint,
               bool shiftPressed,
               bool controlPressed);
int MousePointToIndex(Point mousePoint) const;
int MousePointToParagraphIndex(Paragraph* paragraphPtr,
                               Point mousePoint) const;
void InvalidateBlock(int firstIndex, int lastIndex);
```

When the user double-clicks on a word, it will be marked. The `GetFirstWordIndex` and `GetLastWordIndex` methods find the first and last index of the word, respectively, if in fact the user double-clicks on a word (rather than a space, period, comma, or question mark).

```
void OnDoubleClick(MouseButton mouseButtons, Point mousePoint,
                   bool shiftPressed, bool controlPressed);
int GetFirstWordIndex(int charIndex) const;
int GetLastWordIndex(int charIndex) const;
```

In this application, we introduce touchscreen handling. Unlike mouse clicks, it is possible to touch the screen in several locations at the same time. Therefore, the parameter is a list of points rather that one individual point.

```
void OnTouchDown(vector<Point> pointList);
void OnTouchMove(vector<Point> pointList);
```

The `OnPageSetup` method is called when the user has changed the page setting by selecting the **Page Setup** menu item in the **File** menu, which allows the user to modify the page and paragraphs settings. The `CalculateDocument` method distributes the paragraphs on the pages. If a paragraph is marked with a page break, or if it does not completely fit on the rest of the current page, it is placed at the beginning of the next page.

```
void OnPageSetup(PageSetupInfo pageSetupInfo);
void CalculateDocument();
```

Unlike the applications in the previous chapters, we override both the OnPaint and OnDraw methods. The OnPaint method is called when the client area needs to be redrawn. It performs paint-specific actions, that is, actions that will be performed only when the document is drawn in a window, but not when it is sent to the printer. More specifically, we add page break markers in the client area, but not in the printer text.

The OnPaint method then calls the OnDraw method that performs the actual drawing of the document. There is also a method OnPrint in the StandardDocument class (which we do not override) that calls the OnDraw method when printing the document.

```
void OnPaint(Graphics& graphics) const;
void OnDraw(Graphics& graphics, DrawMode drawMode) const;
```

Similar to the applications in the previous chapters, the ClearDocument, WriteDocumentToStream, and ReadDocumentFromStream methods are called when the user selects the **New, Save, Save As**, or **Open** menu items in the **File** menu.

```
void ClearDocument();
bool WriteDocumentToStream(String name, ostream& outStream)
                              const;
bool ReadDocumentFromStream(String name, istream& inStream);
```

The CopyEnable method returns true when text is ready to be copied, that is, when the user has marked a part of the text. The CopyAscii and CopyUnicode methods are called when the user selects the **Cut** or **Copy** menu item and copies the marked text into a string list. The CopyGeneric method is also called when the user selects the **Cut** or **Copy** menu item and copies the marked text in an application-specific format that also copies the font and style of the characters.

```
bool CopyEnable() const;
bool IsCopyAsciiReady() const;
bool IsCopyUnicodeReady() const;
bool IsCopyGenericReady(int format) const;

void CopyAscii(vector<String>& textList) const;
void CopyUnicode(vector<String>& textList) const;
void CopyGeneric(int format, InfoList& infoList) const;
```

The `PasteAscii`, `PasteUnicode`, and `PasteGeneric` methods are called when the user selects the **Paste** menu item. One difference between copying and pasting is that all the three aforementioned methods are called when copying, but only one method when pasting, in the order the format is given in the `StandardDocument` constructor call.

```
void PasteAscii(const vector<String>& textList);
void PasteUnicode(const vector<String>& textList);
void PasteGeneric(int format, InfoList& infoList);
```

We do not override the `CutEnable` or `OnCut` methods, since the `CutEnable` method in the `StandardDocument` class calls the `CopyEnable` method, and the `OnCut` method calls the `OnDelete` method followed by the `OnCopy` method.

The **Delete** menu item is enabled unless the input position is at the end of the document, in which case there is nothing to delete. The `Delete` method is a general method for deleting text and is called when the user presses the *Delete* or *Backspace* keys or when a marked text block is being overwritten.

```
bool DeleteEnable() const;
void OnDelete();
void Delete(int firstIndex, int lastIndex);
```

The `OnPageBreak` method sets the page break status of the edit paragraph. In case of a page break, the paragraph will be placed at the beginning of the next page. The `OnFont` method displays the standard font dialog that sets the font and color of the next character to be input or the font of the marked block.

```
DEFINE_BOOL_LISTENER(WordDocument, PageBreakEnable)
DEFINE_VOID_LISTENER(WordDocument, OnPageBreak)
DEFINE_VOID_LISTENER(WordDocument, OnFont)
```

A paragraph can be left, center, right, or justified aligned. The radio mark is present if the paragraph currently edited or all paragraphs currently marked have the alignment in question. All the listeners call the `IsAlignment` and `SetAlignment` methods, which returns the current alignment and sets the alignment, respectively, for the edited paragraph or all marked paragraphs.

```
DEFINE_BOOL_LISTENER(WordDocument, LeftRadio)
DEFINE_VOID_LISTENER(WordDocument, OnLeft)
DEFINE_BOOL_LISTENER(WordDocument, CenterRadio)
DEFINE_VOID_LISTENER(WordDocument, OnCenter)
DEFINE_BOOL_LISTENER(WordDocument, RightRadio)
DEFINE_VOID_LISTENER(WordDocument, OnRight)
DEFINE_BOOL_LISTENER(WordDocument, JustifiedRadio)
DEFINE_VOID_LISTENER(WordDocument, OnJustified)
```

```
bool IsAlignment(Alignment alignment) const;
void SetAlignment(Alignment alignment);
```

The `OnChar` method is called every time the user presses a graphical character; it calls the `InsertChar` or `OverwriteChar` method, depending on whether the keyboard holds `insert` or `overwrite` mode. When the text is marked and the user changes the font, the font is set on all marked characters. However, when editing text, the font of the next character to be input is set.

When the user does anything else than input the next character, such as clicking the mouse or pressing any of the arrow keys, the `ClearNextFont` method is called, which clears the next font by setting it to the `SystemFont` method.

```
void OnChar(TCHAR tChar);
void InsertChar(TCHAR tChar, Paragraph* paragraphPtr);
void OverwriteChar(TCHAR tChar, Paragraph* paragraphPtr);
void ClearNextFont();
```

The `OnKeyDown` method is called every time the user presses a key, such as the arrow keys, *Page Up* and *Page Down*, *Home* and *End*, *Delete*, or *Backspace*:

```
bool OnKeyDown(WORD key, bool shiftPressed,
               bool controlPressed);
void OnRegularKey(WORD key);
void EnsureEditStatus();
void OnLeftArrowKey();
void OnRightArrowKey();
void OnUpArrowKey();
void OnDownArrowKey();
int MousePointToIndexDown(Point mousePoint) const;
void OnPageUpKey();
void OnPageDownKey();
void OnHomeKey();
void OnEndKey();
```

When the user presses the key without pressing the *Shift* key at the same time, the caret is moved. However, when they press the *Shift* key, the marking of the text is changed.

```
void OnShiftKey(WORD key);
void EnsureMarkStatus();
void OnShiftLeftArrowKey();
void OnShiftRightArrowKey();
void OnShiftUpArrowKey();
void OnShiftDownArrowKey();
void OnShiftPageUpKey();
void OnShiftPageDownKey();
void OnShiftHomeKey();
```

```
void OnShiftEndKey();
```

When the user presses the *Home* or *End* key together with the *Ctrl* key, the caret is placed at the beginning or end of the document. If they also press the *Shift* key, the text is marked.

The reason we use listener instead of regular methods is that all actions involving the *Ctrl* key are interpreted as accelerators by Small Windows. The listeners are also added to a menu in the following constructor.

```
DEFINE_VOID_LISTENER(WordDocument, OnControlHomeKey);
DEFINE_VOID_LISTENER(WordDocument, OnControlEndKey);
DEFINE_VOID_LISTENER(WordDocument, OnShiftControlHomeKey);
DEFINE_VOID_LISTENER(WordDocument, OnShiftControlEndKey);
```

There are also the *Return, Backspace*, and *Delete* keys, in which case we do not care whether the *Shift* or *Ctrl* key is pressed. The *Delete* key is handled by the **Delete** menu item accelerator.

```
void OnNeutralKey(WORD key);
void OnReturnKey();
void OnBackspaceKey();
```

When the user moves the caret with the keyboard, the edit character will be visible. The `MakeVisible` method makes sure it is visible, even if it means scrolling the document.

```
void MakeVisible();
```

When something happens to the paragraph (characters are added or deleted, the font or alignment is changed, or the page setup), the positions of the characters need to be calculated. The `GenerateParagraph` method calculates the surrounding rectangle for each of its character and generates its line list by calling the `GenerateSizeAndAscentList` method to calculate the size and ascent line for the characters, the `GenerateLineList` method to divide the paragraph into lines, the `GenerateRegularLineRectList` method to generate the character rectangles for left, center, or right aligned paragraphs or the `GenerateJustifiedLineRectList` method for justified paragraphs, and the `GenerateRepaintSet` method to invalidate the changed characters.

```
void GenerateParagraph(Paragraph* paragraphPtr);
void GenerateSizeAndAscentList(Paragraph* paragraphPtr,
                               DynamicList<Size>& sizeList,
                               DynamicList<int>& ascentList);
void GenerateLineList(Paragraph* paragraphPtr,
                      DynamicList<Size>& sizeList,
                      DynamicList<int>& ascentList);
```

```
void GenerateRegularLineRectList(Paragraph* paragraphPtr,
                        LineInfo* lineInfoPtr,
                        DynamicList<Size>& sizeList,
                        DynamicList<int>&ascentList);
void GenerateJustifiedLineRectList(Paragraph* paragraphPtr,
                        LineInfo* lineInfoPtr,
                        DynamicList<Size>& sizeList,
                        DynamicList<int>& ascentList);
void InvalidateRepaintSet(Paragraph* paragraphPtr,
                        DynamicList<CharInfo>& prevRectList);
DynamicList<CharInfo>& CharList() {return charList;}
```

One central part of this application is the `wordMode` method. At a certain time, the application can be set to `edit` mode (the caret is visible), in which case `wordMode` is the `WordEdit` method, or `mark` mode (a part of the text is marked), in which case `wordMode` is the `WordMark` method. Later in the chapter, we will encounter expressions such as **in edit mode** and **in mark mode**, which refer to the value of `wordMode`: `WordEdit` or `WordMark`.

We will also encounter the expressions **in insert mode** and **in overwrite mode**, which refer to the `input` mode of the keyboard, the `InsertKeyboard` or `OverwriteKeyboard` method, which is returned by the `GetKeyboardMode` method in the Small Windows class `Document`.

The `totalPages` field holds the number of pages, which is used when printing and when setting the vertical scroll bar. The list of characters is stored in the `charList` list, and the list of paragraph pointers is stored in the `paragraphList` list. Note that the paragraphs are dynamically created and deleted `Paragraph` objects while the characters are static `CharInfo` objects. Also note that each paragraph does not hold a character list. There is only one `charList`, which is common to all paragraphs. However, each paragraph holds its own list of `Line` pointers that are local to the paragraph.

In this chapter, we will also encounter expressions such as **the edit character**, which refers to the character with index `editIndex` in the `charList` list. As mentioned at the beginning of this chapter, each character has pointers to its paragraph and line. The expressions **the edit paragraph** and **the edit line** refer to the paragraph and line pointed at by the edit character.

The `firstMarkIndex` and `lastMarkIndex` fields hold the indexes of the first and last marked characters in `mark` mode. They are also referred to in expressions such as **the first marked character**, **the first marked paragraph**, and **the first marked line** as well as **the last marked character**, **the last marked paragraph**, and **the last marked line**. Note that the two fields refer to the chronological order, not necessarily their physical order. When needed, we will define the `minIndex` and `maxIndex` methods to refer to the first and last markings in the document in physical order.

When the user sets the font in edit mode, it is stored in the nextFont font, which is then used when the user inputs the next character. The caret takes into consideration the status of the nextFont font, that is, if the nextFont font is not equal to the ZeroFont font, it is used to set the caret. However, the nextFont font is cleared as soon as the user does anything else.

The user can zoom the document by menu items or by touching the screen. In that case, we need the initZoom and initDistance fields to keep track of the zooming. Finally, we need the WordFormat field to identify cut, copied, and pasted application-specific information. It is given the arbitrary value of 1002.

```cpp
private:
    enum {WordEdit, WordMark} wordMode;

    int totalPages;
    DynamicList<CharInfo> charList;
    DynamicList<Paragraph*> paragraphList;

    int editIndex, firstMarkIndex, lastMarkIndex;
    Font nextFont;

    double initZoom, initDistance;
    static const unsigned int WordFormat = 1002;
};
```

WordDocument.cpp

```cpp
#include "..\\SmallWindows\\SmallWindows.h"
#include "CharInfo.h"
#include "LineInfo.h"
#include "Paragraph.h"
#include "WordDocument.h"
```

The WordDocument constructor calls the StandardDocument constructor. The UnicodeFormat and AsciiFormat methods are general formats defined by Small Windows, while the WordFormat method is specific to this application.

```cpp
WordDocument::WordDocument(WindowShow windowShow)
  :StandardDocument(LogicalWithScroll, USLetterPortrait,
                    TEXT("Word Files, wrd; Text Files, txt"),
                    nullptr, OverlappedWindow, windowShow,
                    {WordFormat, UnicodeFormat, AsciiFormat},
                    {WordFormat, UnicodeFormat, AsciiFormat}) {
```

The **Format** menu holds the **Font** and **Page Break** menu items. Unlike the earlier applications in this book, we send `true` to `StandardFileMenu`. It indicates that we want to include the **Page Setup**, **Print Preview**, and **Print** menu items in the **File** menu.

```
Menu menuBar(this);
menuBar.AddMenu(StandardFileMenu(true));
menuBar.AddMenu(StandardEditMenu());

Menu formatMenu(this, TEXT("F&ormat"));
formatMenu.AddItem(TEXT("&Font\tCtrl+F"), OnFont);
formatMenu.AddItem(TEXT("&Page Break\tCtrl+B"),
                   OnPageBreak, PageBreakEnable);
menuBar.AddMenu(formatMenu);
```

The **Alignment** menu holds items for the left, center, right, and justified alignment:

```
Menu alignmentMenu(this, TEXT("&Alignment"));
alignmentMenu.AddItem(TEXT("&Left\tCtrl+L"), OnLeft,
                      nullptr, nullptr, LeftRadio);
alignmentMenu.AddItem(TEXT("&Center\tCtrl+E"), OnCenter,
                      nullptr, nullptr, CenterRadio);
alignmentMenu.AddItem(TEXT("&Right\tCtrl+R"), OnRight,
                      nullptr, nullptr, RightRadio);
alignmentMenu.AddItem(TEXT("&Justified\tCtrl+J"), OnJustified,
                      nullptr, nullptr, JustifiedRadio);
menuBar.AddMenu(alignmentMenu);

menuBar.AddMenu(StandardHelpMenu());
SetMenuBar(menuBar);
```

The `extraMenu` menu is only added for the accelerators; note that we do not add it to the menu bar. The text of the menu, or its items, does not matter either. We only want to allow the user to jump to the beginning or end of the document by pressing the *Ctrl* key with *Home* or *End*, and possibly *Shift*.

```
Menu extraMenu(this);
extraMenu.AddItem(TEXT("&A\tCtrl+Home"), OnControlHomeKey);
extraMenu.AddItem(TEXT("&B\tCtrl+End"), OnControlEndKey);
extraMenu.AddItem(TEXT("&C\tShift+Ctrl+Home"),
                  OnShiftControlHomeKey);
extraMenu.AddItem(TEXT("&D\tShift+Ctrl+End"),
                  OnShiftControlEndKey);
```

Finally, we call the `InitDocument` method that initializes the empty document. The `InitDocument` method is also called by the `ClearDocument` and `Delete` classes as follows, when the initialization code is placed in its own method.

```
    InitDocument();
}
```

A document always holds at least one paragraph, which, in turn, holds at least a newline. We create the first character and the first left-justified paragraph. The paragraph and character are added to the paragraphList and charList lists.

Then, the paragraph is calculated by the GenerateParagraph method and distributed on the document by the CalculateDocument method. Finally, the caret is updated by the UpdateCaret method.

```
void WordDocument::InitDocument() {
  wordMode = WordEdit;
  editIndex = 0;
  Paragraph* firstParagraphPtr = new Paragraph(0, 0, Left, 0);
  assert(firstParagraphPtr != nullptr);
  Font font(TEXT("Times New Roman"), 36, false, true);
  charList.PushBack(CharInfo(firstParagraphPtr, NewLine, font));
  GenerateParagraph(firstParagraphPtr);
  paragraphList.PushBack(firstParagraphPtr);
  CalculateDocument();
  UpdateCaret();
}
```

The caret

Since in this chapter we introduce text handling, we need to keep track of the caret: the blinking vertical bar (in insert mode) or block (in overwrite mode) indicating where to input the character. The UpdateCaret method is called by the OnKeyboardMode method (which is called when the user presses the *Insert* key) as well as other methods when the input position is being modified.

```
void WordDocument::OnKeyboardMode(KeyboardMode/*=KeyboardMode*/) {
  UpdateCaret();
}

void WordDocument::UpdateCaret() {
  switch (wordMode) {
    case WordEdit: {
        CharInfo charInfo = charList[editIndex];
        Rect caretRect = charList[editIndex].CharRect();
```

In edit mode, the caret will be visible, and we obtain the area from the edit character. However, if the nextFont font is active (does not equal the SystemFont font), the user has changed the font, which we must take into consideration. In that case, we set the width and height of the caret in accordance with the size of an average character of the nextFont font.

```
if (nextFont != SystemFont) {
  int width = GetCharacterAverageWidth(nextFont),
      height = GetCharacterHeight(nextFont);
  caretRect.Right() = caretRect.Left() + width;
  caretRect.Top() = caretRect.Bottom() - height;
}
```

If the nextFont font is not active, we check whether the keyboard holds insert mode and the caret is not located at the beginning of the paragraph. In that case, the caret's vertical coordinates will reflect the font size of the preceding character, since the next character to be input will be given its font.

```
else if ((GetKeyboardMode() == InsertKeyboard) &&
         (charInfo.ParagraphPtr()->First() < editIndex)) {
  Rect prevCharRect = charList[editIndex - 1].CharRect();
  caretRect.Top() = caretRect.Bottom() - prevCharRect.Height();
}
```

If the keyboard holds the insert mode, the caret will be a vertical bar, regardless of whether the nextFont font is active. It is given the width of one unit (which is later rounded to the width of one physical pixel).

```
if (GetKeyboardMode() == InsertKeyboard) {
  caretRect.Right() = caretRect.Left() + 1;
}
```

The caret will not extend outside the page. If it does, its right border is set to the page's border.

```
if (caretRect.Right() >= PageInnerWidth()) {
  caretRect.Right() = PageInnerWidth() - 1;
}
```

Finally, we need the top position of the edit paragraph, since the caret so far is calculated relative to its top position.

```
Paragraph* paragraphPtr =
  charList[editIndex].ParagraphPtr();
Point topLeft = Point(0, paragraphPtr->Top());
SetCaret(topLeft + caretRect);
      }
      break;
```

In `mark` mode, the caret will be invisible. Therefore, we call `ClearCaret` as follows:

```
      case WordMark:
         ClearCaret();
         break;
   }
}
```

Mouse input

The `OnMouseDown`, `OnMouseMove`, `OnMouseUp`, and `OnDoubleClick` methods take the pressed buttons and the mouse coordinates. In all four cases, we check that the left mouse button is pressed. The `OnMouseDown` method first calls the `EnsureEditStatus` method in order to clear any potential marked area. Then it sets the application to `mark` mode (which may later be changed by the `OnMouseUp` method) and looks up the index of the character pointed at by calling the `MousePointToIndex` method. The `nextFont` field is cleared by a call to the `ClearNextFont` method. We also call the `UpdateCaret` method, since the caret will be cleared while the user drags the mouse.

```
void WordDocument::OnMouseDown(MouseButton mouseButtons,
                     Point mousePoint, bool shiftPressed,
                     bool controlPressed) {
   if (mouseButtons == LeftButton) {
     EnsureEditStatus();
     ClearNextFont();
     wordMode = WordMark;
     firstMarkIndex = lastMarkIndex =
       MousePointToIndex(mousePoint);
     UpdateCaret();
   }
}
```

In the `OnMouseMove` method, we retrieve the paragraph and character of the mouse by calling the `MousePointToIndex` method. If the mouse has been moved to a new character since the last call to the `OnMouseDown` or `OnMouseMove` method, we update the marked text by calling the `InvalidateBlock` method with the current and new mouse position, which invalidates the part of the text between the current and previous mouse event. Note that we do not invalidate the whole marked block. We only invalidate the block between the previous and current mouse positions in order to avoid dazzles.

```
void WordDocument::OnMouseMove(MouseButton mouseButtons,
                        Point mousePoint, bool shiftPressed,
                        bool controlPressed) {
  if (mouseButtons == LeftButton) {
    int newLastMarkIndex = MousePointToIndex(mousePoint);

    if (lastMarkIndex != newLastMarkIndex) {
      InvalidateBlock(lastMarkIndex, newLastMarkIndex);
      lastMarkIndex = newLastMarkIndex;
    }
  }
}
```

In the `OnMouseUp` method, we just have to check the last position. If it is the same as the first position (the user pressed and released the mouse at the same character), we change the application to `edit` mode and call the `UpdateCaret` method to make the caret visible.

```
void WordDocument::OnMouseUp(MouseButton mouseButtons,
                        Point mousePoint, bool shiftPressed,
                        bool controlPressed) {
  if (mouseButtons == LeftButton) {
    if (firstMarkIndex == lastMarkIndex) {
      wordMode = WordEdit;
      editIndex = min(firstMarkIndex, charList.Size() - 1);
      UpdateCaret();
    }
  }
}
```

The `MousePointToIndex` method finds the paragraph that the user has clicked on and calls the `MousePointToParagraphIndex` method to find the character in the paragraph. The reason we divide the functionality into two methods is that the `MousePointToIndexDown` method in Chapter 7, *Keyboard Input and Character Calculation*, also calls the `MousePointToParagraphIndex` method, which iterates through the paragraph list. If the vertical position is less than the top position of a paragraph, the correct paragraph is the previous one.

This somewhat cumbersome way of finding the correct paragraph is due to the fact that paragraphs are distributed over the pages in such manner that when a paragraph does not fit on the rest of the page, or if it is marked with a page break, it is placed at the beginning of the next page. This may result in parts of the document where no paragraph is located. If the user clicks on such an area, we want the paragraph located before that area to be the correct one. In the same way, if the user clicks below the last paragraph of the document, it becomes the correct one.

```
int WordDocument::MousePointToIndex(Point mousePoint) const{
  for (int parIndex = 1; parIndex < paragraphList.Size();
       ++parIndex) {
    Paragraph* paragraphPtr = paragraphList[parIndex];

    if (mousePoint.Y() < paragraphPtr->Top()) {
      return MousePointToParagraphIndex
            (paragraphList[parIndex - 1], mousePoint);
    }
  }

  return MousePointToParagraphIndex
        (paragraphList[paragraphList.Size() - 1], mousePoint);
}
```

The `MousePointToParagraphIndex` method finds the clicked character in the paragraph. First, we subtract the paragraph's top position from the mouse position, since the paragraph's line coordinates are relative to the paragraph's top position.

```
int WordDocument::MousePointToParagraphIndex
                    (Paragraph* paragraphPtr,Point mousePoint) const{
  mousePoint.Y() -= paragraphPtr->Top();
```

As mentioned previously, the user may click on a position below the paragraph's area. In that case, we set the mouse position to its height, −1, which is equivalent to the user clicking on the last line of the paragraph.

```
  if (mousePoint.Y() >= paragraphPtr->Height()) {
    mousePoint.Y() = paragraphPtr->Height() - 1;
  }
```

First, we need to find the correct line in the paragraph. We check every line and test if the mouse position is located within the line by comparing it to the sum of the line's top position and its height. Compared to the paragraph search in the `MousePointToIndex` method, as mentioned previously, this search is a bit simpler, since there is no space between the lines in the paragraph as there may be between the paragraphs in the document.

```
  int firstChar = paragraphPtr->First();
  for (LineInfo* lineInfoPtr : paragraphPtr->LinePtrList()) {
    if (mousePoint.Y() < (lineInfoPtr->Top() +
                          lineInfoPtr->Height())) {
      Rect firstRect =
            charList[firstChar +lineInfoPtr->First()].CharRect(),
          lastRect =
            charList[firstChar + lineInfoPtr->Last()].CharRect();
```

When we have found the correct line, we have three cases to consider: the user may have clicked on the left of the text (if the paragraph is center or right aligned), to its right (if it is left or center aligned), or on the text itself. If they have clicked on the left or right of the line, we return the index of the first or last character of the line. Note that we add the index of the first character of the paragraph, since the indexes of the lines are relative to the paragraph's first index.

```
if (mousePoint.X() < firstRect.Left()) {
  return paragraphPtr->First() + lineInfoPtr->First();
}
else if (lastRect.Right() <= mousePoint.X()) {
  return paragraphPtr->First() + lineInfoPtr->Last();
}
```

If the user has clicked on the text, we need to find the correct character. We iterate through the characters of the line and compare the mouse position to the right-hand border of the character. When we have found the correct character, we need to decide whether the user has clicked near the character's left or right border. In case of the right border, we add one to the character index.

```
else {
  for (int charIndex = lineInfoPtr->First();
       charIndex <= lineInfoPtr->Last(); ++charIndex) {
    Rect charRect = charList[charIndex].CharRect();

    if (mousePoint.X() < charRect.Right()) {
      int leftSize = mousePoint.X() - charRect.Left(),
          rightSide = charRect.Right() - mousePoint.X();

      return paragraphPtr->First() +
        ((leftSize < rightSide) ? charIndex
                                : (charIndex + 1));
    }
  }
}
```

As mentioned previously, there is no space between the lines in a paragraph. Therefore, we will always find the correct line and never reach this point. However, in order to avoid compiler errors, we still have to return a value. In this book, we will on a few occasions use the following notation:

```
  assert(false);
  return 0;
}
```

```
void WordDocument::InvalidateBlock(int firstIndex, int lastIndex){
  int minIndex = min(firstIndex, lastIndex),
      maxIndex = min(max(firstIndex, lastIndex).
                     charList.Size() - 1);

  for (int charIndex = minIndex; charIndex <= maxIndex;
       ++charIndex) {
    CharInfo charInfo = charList[charIndex];
    Point topLeft(0, charInfo.ParagraphPtr()->Top());
    Invalidate(topLeft + charInfo.CharRect());
  }
}
```

When the user double-clicks the left mouse button, the word hit by the mouse will be marked. The application has been set to `edit` mode and the `editIndex` method has been properly set, because the call to the `OnDoubleClick` method is always preceded by calls to the `OnMouseDown` and `OnMouseUp` methods. If the mouse hits a word, we mark the word and set the application to `mark` mode.

We find the indexes of the first and last characters in a word by calling the `GetFirstWordIndex` and `GetLastWordIndex` methods. If the first index is less than the last index, the user has double-clicked on an actual word, which we mark. If the first index is not less than the last index, the user has double-clicked on a space or a delimiter, in which case the double-click has no effect.

```
void WordDocument::OnDoubleClick(MouseButton mouseButtons,
                    Point mousePoint, bool shiftPressed,
                    bool controlPressed) {
  int firstIndex = GetFirstWordIndex(editIndex),
      lastIndex = GetLastWordIndex(editIndex);

  if (firstIndex < lastIndex) {
    wordMode = WordMark;
    firstMarkIndex = firstIndex;
    lastMarkIndex = lastIndex;

    UpdateCaret();
    InvalidateBlock(firstMarkIndex, lastMarkIndex);
    UpdateWindow();
  }
}
```

In the `GetFirstWordIndex` method, we find the index of the first character of the word by going backward in the character list until we reach the beginning of the document or a character that is not a letter.

```
int WordDocument::GetFirstWordIndex(int charIndex) const{
  while ((charIndex >= 0) &&
         (isalpha(charList[charIndex].Char()))) {
    --charIndex;
  }
  return (charIndex + 1);
}
```

In the `GetLastWordIndex` method, we do not need to check the end of the character list, since the last character always is a newline, which is not a letter. Note that in this case we return the index of the character after the last character of the word, since the marking of text is valid up to, but not inclusive of, the last character.

```
int WordDocument::GetLastWordIndex(int charIndex) const{
  while (isalpha(charList[charIndex].Char())) {
    ++charIndex;
  }
  return charIndex;
}
```

Touchscreen

On a touchscreen, the user can zoom the document by dragging two fingers on the screen. The `OnTouchDown` method is called when the user touches the screen, and the `OnTouchMove` method is called when they move their fingers. Unlike the mouse input methods mentioned previously, the user can touch several points on the screen at the same time. The points are stored in the `pointList` list.

If the list does not hold two points, we just let the `Window` class perform the default action, which is to convert each touch action to a mouse action.

```
void WordDocument::OnTouchDown(vector<Point> pointList) {
  if (pointList.size() == 2) {
    initZoom = GetZoom();
    Point firstInitPoint = pointList[0],
          secondInitPoint = pointList[1];
    double width = firstInitPoint.X() - secondInitPoint.X(),
           height = firstInitPoint.Y() - secondInitPoint.Y(),
    initDistance = sqrt((width * width) + (height * height));
  }
  else {
    Window::OnTouchDown(pointList);
  }
}
```

When the user moves their fingers on the screen, the distance between the fingers is calculated and the zoom is set with regard to the initial distance. The zooming is allowed to range between 10% (factor 0.1) and 1,000% (factor 10.0):

```
void WordDocument::OnTouchMove(vector<Point> pointList) {
  if (pointList.size() == 2) {
    Point firstPoint = pointList[0], secondPoint = pointList[1];

    int width = firstPoint.X() - secondPoint.X(),
        height = firstPoint.Y() - secondPoint.Y();
    double distance = sqrt((width * width) + (height * height));

    double factor = distance / initDistance;
    double newZoom = factor * initZoom;
    SetZoom(min(max(newZoom, 0.1), 10.0));

    UpdateCaret();
    Invalidate();
    UpdateWindow();
  }
  else {
    Window::OnTouchMove(pointList);
  }
}
```

Page setup and calculation

The OnPageSetup method is called when the user selects the standard **Page Setup** menu item in the **File** menu. Since the page settings have been altered, we need to recalculate each paragraph as well as the whole document.

```
void WordDocument::OnPageSetup(PageSetupInfo pageSetupInfo) {
  ClearNextFont();

  for (Paragraph* paragraphPtr : paragraphList) {
    GenerateParagraph(paragraphPtr);
  }

  CalculateDocument();
  UpdateCaret();
  UpdateWindow();
}
```

A small change may affect the whole document, and we need to calculate the paragraphs and distribute them on the pages in the document.

```
void WordDocument::CalculateDocument() {
  int pageInnerWidth = PageInnerWidth(),
      pageInnerHeight = PageInnerHeight(),
      documentHeight = 0, newTotalPages = 1;
```

We iterate through the paragraph list, and in case the current document height differs from the paragraph's top position, we update its top position and invalidate it.

```
  for (int parIndex = 0; parIndex < paragraphList.Size();
      ++parIndex) {
    Paragraph* paragraphPtr = paragraphList[parIndex];

    if (paragraphPtr->Top() != documentHeight) {
      paragraphPtr->Top() = documentHeight;
      Invalidate(Rect(0, paragraphPtr->Top(), pageInnerWidth,
              paragraphPtr->Top() + paragraphPtr->Height()));
    }
```

We have a page break if the paragraph is marked with a page break and if it is not already located at the top of a page.

```
    bool pageBreak = paragraphPtr->PageBreak() &&
                  ((paragraphPtr->Top() % pageInnerHeight) != 0);
```

The paragraph does not fit on the rest of the page if its top position plus its height is greater than the page height.

```
    bool notFitOnPage =
      (documentHeight > 0) &&
      ((paragraphPtr->Top() + paragraphPtr->Height()) >
      (newTotalPages * pageInnerHeight));
```

If we have a page break, or if the paragraph does not fit on the rest of the page, we invalidate the rest of the page and place the paragraph at the top of the next page.

```
    if (pageBreak || notFitOnPage) {
      Rect restOfPage(0, documentHeight, pageInnerWidth,
                  newTotalPages * pageInnerHeight);
      Invalidate(restOfPage);
      paragraphPtr->Top() = (newTotalPages++) * pageInnerHeight;
```

Since the paragraph has been moved to a new position, we need to invalidate its new area.

```
      Invalidate(Rect(0, paragraphPtr->Top(), pageInnerWidth,
              paragraphPtr->Top() + paragraphPtr->Height()));
      documentHeight = paragraphPtr->Top() +
                    paragraphPtr->Height();
    }
```

If the paragraph fits on the rest of the document, we just increase the document height.

```
  else {
    documentHeight += paragraphPtr->Height();
  }
}
```

After the last paragraph, we need to invalidate the rest of the last page.

```
Rect restOfPage(0, documentHeight, pageInnerWidth,
                newTotalPages * pageInnerHeight);
Invalidate(restOfPage);
```

If the number of pages has changed, we invalidate the pages that differ.

```
if (totalPages != newTotalPages) {
  int minTotalPages = min(totalPages, newTotalPages),
      maxTotalPages = max(totalPages, newTotalPages);
  Invalidate(Rect(0, minTotalPages * pageInnerHeight,
                  pageInnerWidth, maxTotalPages * pageInnerHeight));
  totalPages = newTotalPages;
  SetVerticalScrollTotalHeight(totalPages * pageInnerHeight);
}
}
```

Painting and drawing

The OnPaint method performs the action that is specific to drawing the client area, while the OnPrint method performs the action specific to printing. The default behavior for both the OnPaint and OnPrint methods in the StandardDocument class is to call the OnDraw method.

In the application of the previous chapters, we have overridden only the OnDraw method, resulting in the same drawing regardless of whether the drawing occurs in the client area or is sent to a printer. However, in this application, we also override the OnPaint method, which fills the parts of the client area outside the document with a light gray color and places the text **Page Break** between every pair of pages, and finally calls the OnDraw method that performs the actual drawing of the document.

```
void WordDocument::OnPaint(Graphics& graphics) const {
  int pageInnerWidth = PageInnerWidth(),
      pageInnerHeight = PageInnerHeight();

  int documentInnerHeight = totalPages * pageInnerHeight;
  Size clientSize = GetClientSize();
```

```
if (pageInnerWidth() < clientSize.Width()) {
  int maxHeight = max(documentInnerHeight, clientSize.Height());
  Rect rightRect(pageInnerWidth, 0,
                 clientSize.Width(), maxHeight);
  graphics.FillRectangle(rightRect, LightGray, LightGray);
}

if (documentInnerHeight() < clientSize.Height()) {
  Rect bottomRect(0, documentInnerHeight(),
                  pageInnerWidth(), clientSize.Height());
  graphics.FillRectangle(bottomRect, LightGray, LightGray);
}

OnDraw(graphics, Paint);

int breakWidth = min(clientSize.Width()),
    breakHeight = GetCharacterHeight(SystemFont);
Size breakSize(breakWidth, breakHeight);

for (int pageIndex = 1; pageIndex < totalPages; ++pageIndex) {
  int line = pageIndex * pageInnerHeight;
  graphics.DrawLine(Point(0, line), Point(pageInnerWidth, line),
                    Black);

  Point topLeft(0, line - (breakHeight / 2));
  graphics.DrawText(Rect(topLeft, breakSize),
                    TEXT("Page Break"), SystemFont,Black,White);
}
}
```

The `OnDraw` method draws every character in the `charList` list. The `drawMode` parameter is `Paint` if the `OnDraw` method is called by the `OnPaint` method, and `Print` if it is called by the `OnPrint` method. In the previous applications, we have ignored the `drawMode` method. However, in this application, we draw a small square at every paragraph marked with a page break, if called by the `OnPaint` method.

```
void WordDocument::OnDraw(Graphics& graphics, DrawMode drawMode) const {
  minCharIndex = min(firstMarkIndex, lastMarkIndex),
  maxCharIndex = max(firstMarkIndex, lastMarkIndex);

  for (int charIndex = 0; charIndex <= charList.Size() - 1;
       ++charIndex) {
    CharInfo charInfo = charList[charIndex];
    Point topLeft(0, charInfo.ParagraphPtr()->Top());

    Color textColor = charInfo.CharFont().GetColor();
    Color backColor = textColor.Inverse();
```

If the character is marked, its text and background colors are inverted.

```
if ((wordMode == WordMark) &&
    (minCharIndex <= charIndex)&&(charIndex < maxCharIndex)) {
  swap(textColor, backColor);
}
```

If the character is newline, a space is drawn instead.

```
TCHAR tChar = (charInfo.Char() == NewLine)
              ? Space: charInfo.Char();
TCHAR text[] = {tChar, TEXT('\0')};
```

If the character's rectangle is located outside the page, its right border is set to the page right border.

```
Rect charRect = charList[charIndex].CharRect();
if (charRect.Right() >= pageWidth) {
  charRect.Right() = pageWidth - 1;
}
```

Finally, the character is drawn:

```
graphics.DrawText(topLeft + charRect, text,
                  charInfo.CharFont(), textColor, backColor);
    }
```

Actually, there is one more thing: if the OnDraw method has been called by the OnPaint method, we draw a small red square (2 × 2 millimeters) at its top-left position for every paragraph marked with a page break.

```
if (drawMode == Paint) {
  for (Paragraph* paragraphPtr : paragraphList) {
    if (paragraphPtr->PageBreak()) {
      Point topLeft(0, paragraphPtr->Top());
      graphics.FillRectangle(Rect(topLeft, topLeft +
                             Size(200, 200)), Red, Red);
    }
  }
}
```

File management

The `ClearDocument` method is called by the `StandardDocument` class when the user selects the **New** menu item in the **File** menu; the `WriteDocumentToStream` method is called when they select the **Save** or **Save As** menu items in the **File** menu, and the `ReadDocumentFromStream` method is called when they select the **Open** menu item.

The `ClearDocument` method deletes every paragraph in the `paragraphList` list by calling the `DeleteParagraph` method, which, in turn, deletes each line of the paragraph. This is actually the only memory we need to delete, since it is the only dynamically allocated memory of this application. Finally, the `InitDocument` method is called, which initializes an empty document.

```
void DeleteParagraph(Paragraph* paragraphPtr) {
  for (LineInfo* lineInfoPtr : paragraphPtr->LinePtrList()) {
    delete lineInfoPtr;
  }

  delete paragraphPtr;
}

void WordDocument::ClearDocument() {
  nextFont = SystemFont;

  for (Paragraph* paragraphPtr : paragraphList) {
    DeleteParagraph(paragraphPtr);
  }

  charList.Clear();
  paragraphList.Clear();
  InitDocument();
}
```

The `WriteDocumentToStream` method writes all the information about the document to the stream: the `application` mode (edit or mark), the index of the edit character, the indexes of the first and last marked characters, the number of pages in the document, and the next font. The idea is that the document will be opened in the exact same shape as it was written.

```
bool WordDocument::WriteDocumentToStream(String name,
                                         ostream& outStream) const {
  if (EndsWith(name, TEXT(".wrd")) &&
      WritePageSetupInfoToStream(outStream)) {
    outStream.write((char*) &wordMode, sizeof wordMode);
    outStream.write((char*) &editIndex, sizeof editIndex);
```

```
outStream.write((char*) &firstMarkIndex,
                    sizeof firstMarkIndex);
outStream.write((char*) &lastMarkIndex, sizeof lastMarkIndex);
outStream.write((char*) &totalPages, sizeof totalPages);
nextFont.WriteFontToStream(outStream);

{ int charInfoListSize = charList.Size();
  outStream.write((char*) &charInfoListSize,
                    sizeof charInfoListSize);
  for (CharInfo charInfo : charList) {
    charInfo.WriteCharInfoToStream(outStream);
  }
}

{ int paragraphListSize = paragraphList.Size();
  outStream.write((char*) &paragraphListSize,
                    sizeof paragraphListSize);

  for (const Paragraph* paragraphPtr : paragraphList) {
    paragraphPtr->WriteParagraphToStream(outStream);
  }
}
}
```

However, if the file suffix is .txt, we save the word in text format and discard all formatting.

```
else if (EndsWith(name, TEXT(".txt"))) {
  for (CharInfo charInfo : charList) {
    char c = (char) charInfo.Char();
    outStream.write(&c, sizeof c);
  }
}

return ((bool) outStream);
}
```

The ReadDocumentFromStream method reads the information written by the WriteDocumentToStream method. Note that the MakeVisible method is called at the end in order to make the current position visible.

```
bool WordDocument::ReadDocumentFromStream(String name,
                                        istream& inStream) {
  if (EndsWith(name, TEXT(".wrd")) &&
      ReadPageSetupInfoFromStream(inStream)){
    inStream.read((char*) &wordMode, sizeof wordMode);
    inStream.read((char*) &editIndex, sizeof editIndex);
    inStream.read((char*) &firstMarkIndex, sizeof firstMarkIndex);
```

```
inStream.read((char*) &lastMarkIndex, sizeof lastMarkIndex);
inStream.read((char*) &totalPages, sizeof totalPages);
nextFont.ReadFontFromStream(inStream);

{ charList.Clear();
  int charInfoListSize;
  inStream.read((char*) &charInfoListSize,
                sizeof charInfoListSize);

  for (int count = 0; count < charInfoListSize; ++count) {
    CharInfo charInfo;
    charInfo.ReadCharInfoFromStream(inStream);
    charList.PushBack(charInfo);
  }
}

{ paragraphList.Clear();
  int paragraphListSize;
  inStream.read((char*) &paragraphListSize,
                sizeof paragraphListSize);

  for (int count = 0; count < paragraphListSize; ++count) {
    Paragraph* paragraphPtr = new Paragraph();
    assert(paragraphPtr != nullptr);
    paragraphPtr->ReadParagraphFromStream(this, inStream);
    paragraphList.PushBack(paragraphPtr);
  }
}
}
```

However, if the file has the file suffix `.txt`, we just read the characters, and all characters are given the system font.

```
else if (EndsWith(name, TEXT(".txt"))) {
  wordMode = WordEdit;
  editIndex = 0;
  firstMarkIndex = 0;
  lastMarkIndex = 0;
  totalPages = 0;
  nextFont = SystemFont;

  Paragraph* paragraphPtr = new Paragraph(0, 0, Left, 0);
  int charIndex = 0, paragraphIndex = 0;
  char c;

  while (inStream >> c) {
    CharInfo charInfo(paragraphPtr, (TCHAR) c,
                      SystemFont, ZeroRect);
```

```
    charList.PushBack(charInfo);

    if (c == '\n') {
      paragraphPtr->Last() = charIndex;
      for (int index = paragraphPtr->First();
           index <= paragraphPtr->Last(); ++index) {
        charList[index].ParagraphPtr() = paragraphPtr;
      }

      GenerateParagraph(paragraphPtr);
      paragraphList.PushBack(paragraphPtr);
      Paragraph* paragraphPtr =
        new Paragraph(charIndex + 1, 0, Left, ++paragraphIndex);
    }

    ++charIndex;
  }

  paragraphPtr->Last() = charIndex;
  for (int index = paragraphPtr->First();
       index <= paragraphPtr->Last(); ++index) {
    charList[index].ParagraphPtr() = paragraphPtr;
  }

  GenerateParagraph(paragraphPtr);
  paragraphList.PushBack(paragraphPtr);
  CalculateDocument();
}

MakeVisible();
return ((bool) inStream);
}
```

Cut, copy, and paste

The **Copy** item in the **Edit** menu is enabled in `mark` mode:

```
bool WordDocument::CopyEnable() const {
  return (wordMode == WordMark);
}
```

As long as the `CopyEnable` method mentioned previously returns `true`, we are always ready to copy in every format. Therefore, we must let the `IsCopyAsciiReady`, `IsCopyUnicodeReady`, and `IsCopyGenericReady` methods return `true` (if they return `false` in the `StandardDocument` class).

```
bool WordDocument::IsCopyAsciiReady() const {
  return true;
}

bool WordDocument::IsCopyUnicodeReady() const {
  return true;
}

bool WordDocument::IsCopyGenericReady(int /* format */) const {
  return true;
}
```

The `CopyAscii` method simply calls the `CopyUnicode` method, since the text is stored in the generic text format and is transformed into ASCII and Unicode when saved to the global clipboard. The `CopyUnicode` method iterates through the marked paragraphs and, for each marked paragraph, extracts the marked text that is stored in the paragraph to the `textList` parameter. When it encounters a newline, it pushes the current text in the `textList` parameter.

```
void WordDocument::CopyAscii(vector<String>& textList) {
  CopyUnicode(textList);
}

void WordDocument::CopyUnicode(vector<String>& textList) {
  int minCharIndex = min(firstMarkIndex, lastMarkIndex),
      maxCharIndex = max(firstMarkIndex, lastMarkIndex);

  String text;
  for (int charIndex = minCharIndex; charIndex < maxCharIndex;
       ++charIndex) {
    CharInfo charInfo = charList[charIndex];
    text.push_back(charInfo.Char());

    if (charInfo.Char() == NewLine) {
      textList.push_back(text);
      text.clear();
    }
  }

  textList.push_back(text);
}
```

The `CopyGeneric` method is simpler than the `CopyUnicode` method. It first saves the number of characters to be copied, then iterates through the marked characters (not the paragraphs), and then calls the `WriteCharInfoToClipboard` method for each character. This works, since each pair of paragraphs is already separated by a newline in the charList list. We really do not care about the format, since there is just one format (WordFormat) for generic cut, copy, and paste operations in this application.

```
void WordDocument::CopyGeneric(int /* format */,
                               InfoList& infoList) const {
  int minCharIndex = min(firstMarkIndex, lastMarkIndex),
      maxCharIndex = max(firstMarkIndex, lastMarkIndex);
  int copySize = maxCharIndex - minCharIndex;
  infoList.AddValue<int>(copySize);

  for (int charIndex = minCharIndex; charIndex < maxCharIndex;
       ++charIndex) {
    CharInfo charInfo = charList[charIndex];
    charInfo.WriteCharInfoToClipboard(infoList);
  }
}
```

One difference between copying and pasting is that when the user selects **Cut** or **Copy**, the marked text is copied in all three formats (ASCII, Unicode, and generic) given in the preceding StandardDocument constructor. Their order does not really matter. When pasting, on the other hand, the StandardDocument constructor tries to paste the text in the formats order given in the constructor call. If it finds pasted information in one format in the global clipboard, it does not continue to check the other format. In this application, it means that if there is text copied in the generic format (WordFormat), then that text is pasted regardless of whether there is text in the ASCII of Unicode format (AsciiFormat or UnicodeFormat).

The PasteAscii method calls the PasteUnicode method (again, both ASCII and Unicode text are transformed into the generic text type), which iterates through the textList parameter and inserts a new paragraph for each text. Note that we do not override the PasteEnable method, since the StandardDocument constructor handles it by checking if there is a clipboard buffer with any of the formats defined in the StandardDocument constructor call.

The idea is that the first and last text in text list will be merged by the first and last part of the edit paragraph. The potential remaining text will be inserted as paragraphs in between. First we delete the marked text, if present, ensure edit mode, and clear the nextFont parameter (setting it to SystemFont).

```
void WordDocument::PasteUnicode(const vector<String>& textList) {
  if (wordMode == WordMark) {
    Delete(firstMarkIndex, lastMarkIndex);
    EnsureEditStatus();
  }
```

```
else {
  ClearNextFont();
}
```

We remove the edit paragraph from the paragraph list, which makes it easier to insert the pasted paragraphs later on.

```
Paragraph* paragraphPtr = charList[editIndex].ParagraphPtr();
paragraphList.Erase(paragraphPtr->Index());
```

We use the font of the edit character and the alignment of the edit paragraph for the pasted characters and paragraphs.

```
Alignment alignment = paragraphPtr->AlignmentField();
Font font = charList[editIndex].CharFont();
```

We save the number of the remaining characters of the edit paragraph. We also save the current edit index in order to calculate the total number of pasted characters at the end.

```
int restChars = paragraphPtr->Last() - editIndex,
    prevEditIndex = editIndex, textListSize = textList.size();
```

We insert the characters of each text in the edit paragraph.

```
for (int textIndex = 0; textIndex < textListSize; ++textIndex) {
  for (TCHAR tChar : textList[textIndex]) {
    charList.Insert(editIndex++,
                CharInfo(paragraphPtr, tChar, font));
  }
```

Since each text will finish a paragraph, except the last one, we create and insert a new paragraph.

```
  if (textIndex < (textListSize - 1)) {
    charList.Insert(editIndex++,
                CharInfo(paragraphPtr, NewLine));
    paragraphPtr->Last() = editIndex - 1;
    for (int index = paragraphPtr->First();
         index <= paragraphPtr->Last(); ++index) {
      charList[index].ParagraphPtr() = paragraphPtr;
    }
    GenerateParagraph(paragraphPtr);
    paragraphList.Insert(paragraphPtr->Index(), paragraphPtr);
    paragraphPtr = new Paragraph(editIndex, 0, alignment,
                                  paragraphPtr->Index() + 1);
  }
```

For the last text, we use the original edit paragraph and change its last character index.

```
else {
  paragraphPtr->Last() = editIndex + restChars;
  for (int index = paragraphPtr->First();
       index <= paragraphPtr->Last(); ++index) {
    charList[index].ParagraphPtr() = paragraphPtr;
  }
  GenerateParagraph(paragraphPtr);
  paragraphList.Insert(paragraphPtr->Index(), paragraphPtr);
}
}
```

We may also need to update the index of the succeeding paragraphs, since more than one paragraph may have been pasted. Since we know that at least one character has been pasted, we certainly need to at least modify the first and last index of the succeeding paragraphs.

```
int totalAddedChars = editIndex - prevEditIndex;
for (int parIndex = paragraphPtr->Index() + 1;
     parIndex < paragraphList.Size(); ++parIndex) {
  Paragraph* paragraphPtr = paragraphList[parIndex];
  paragraphPtr->Index() = parIndex;
  paragraphPtr->First() += totalAddedChars;
  paragraphPtr->Last() += totalAddedChars;
}

CalculateDocument();
UpdateCaret();
UpdateWindow();
}
```

The `PasteGeneric` method reads and inserts the generic paragraph information stored in the clipboard in a way similar to the preceding `PasteUnicode` method. The difference is that the paragraphs are separated to be newlines and that each pasted character comes with its own font.

```
void WordDocument::PasteGeneric(int /* format */,
                                InfoList& infoList) {
  if (wordMode == WordMark) {
    Delete(firstMarkIndex, lastMarkIndex);
    EnsureEditStatus();
  }
  else {
    ClearNextFont();
  }
```

We erase the edit paragraph in order to make the insertion easier, just as in the preceding `PasteUnicode` method. We use the alignment of the edit paragraph, but not the font of the edit character since each pasted character has its own font.

```
Paragraph* paragraphPtr = charList[editIndex].ParagraphPtr();
paragraphList.Erase(paragraphPtr->Index());
Alignment alignment = paragraphPtr->AlignmentField();
```

We read the paste size, which is the number of character to be pasted.

```
int pasteSize, restChars = paragraphPtr->Last() - editIndex;
infoList.GetValue<int>(pasteSize);
```

We read each character from the paste buffer and insert the characters into the character list. When we encounter a newline, we insert a new paragraph.

```
for (int pasteCount = 0; pasteCount < pasteSize; ++pasteCount) {
  CharInfo charInfo(paragraphPtr);
  charInfo.ReadCharInfoFromClipboard(infoList);
  charList.Insert(editIndex++, charInfo);

  if (charInfo.Char() == NewLine) {
    paragraphPtr->Last() = editIndex - 1;
    GenerateParagraph(paragraphPtr);
    paragraphList.Insert(paragraphPtr->Index(), paragraphPtr);
    paragraphPtr = new Paragraph(editIndex, 0, alignment,
                                 paragraphPtr->Index() + 1);
    assert(paragraphPtr != nullptr);
  }
}

paragraphPtr->Last() = editIndex + restChars;
for (int charIndex = editIndex;
     charIndex <= paragraphPtr->Last(); ++charIndex) {
  charList[charIndex].ParagraphPtr() = paragraphPtr;
}
```

We need to calculate the original paragraph before we insert it.

```
GenerateParagraph(paragraphPtr);
paragraphList.Insert(paragraphPtr->Index(), paragraphPtr);
```

Similar to the preceding `PasteUnicode` case, we may need to update the index of the succeeding paragraphs, since more than one paragraph may have been pasted. We also need to modify their first and last index, since at least one character has been pasted.

```
    for (int parIndex = paragraphPtr->Index() + 1;
      parIndex < paragraphList.Size(); ++parIndex) {
      Paragraph* paragraphPtr = paragraphList[parIndex];
      paragraphPtr->Index() = parIndex;
      paragraphPtr->First() += pasteSize;
      paragraphPtr->Last() += pasteSize;
    }

    CalculateDocument();
    UpdateCaret();
    UpdateWindow();
  }
```

Delete

In edit mode, it is possible to delete a character unless it is located at the very end of the document. In mark mode, the marked text can always always be deleted:

```
bool WordDocument::DeleteEnable() const {
  switch (wordMode) {
    case WordEdit:
      return (editIndex < (charList.Size() - 1));

    case WordMark:
      return true;
  }

  return false;
}
```

In edit mode, we delete the edit character, and in mark mode, we delete the marked text. In both cases, we call the Delete method to perform the actual deleting.

```
void WordDocument::OnDelete() {
  switch (wordMode) {
    case WordEdit:
      ClearNextFont();
      Delete(editIndex, editIndex + 1);
      break;

    case WordMark:
      Delete(firstMarkIndex, lastMarkIndex);
      editIndex = min(firstMarkIndex, lastMarkIndex);
      wordMode = WordEdit;
      break;
  }
```

```
        SetDirty(true);
        CalculateDocument();
        UpdateCaret();
        UpdateWindow();
    }
```

The `Delete` method is called by the `OnDelete`, `EnsureEditStatus`, `PasteUnicode`, and `PasteGeneric` methods. It removes the characters between the given indexes, which do not have to be in order. The removed paragraphs are deleted and the succeeding paragraphs are updated.

```
    void WordDocument::Delete(int firstIndex, int lastIndex) {
      int minCharIndex = min(firstIndex, lastIndex),
          maxCharIndex = max(firstIndex, lastIndex);

      Paragraph* minParagraphPtr =
        charList[minCharIndex].ParagraphPtr();
      Paragraph* maxParagraphPtr =
        charList[maxCharIndex].ParagraphPtr();
```

The deleted area covers at least two paragraphs, we set the characters of the maximal paragraph to point at the minimal paragraph, since they will be merged. We also set their rectangles to zero, to ensure that they will be redrawn.

```
      if (minParagraphPtr != maxParagraphPtr) {
        for (int charIndex = maxParagraphPtr->First();
             charIndex <= maxParagraphPtr->Last(); ++charIndex) {
          CharInfo& charInfo = charList[charIndex];
          charInfo.ParagraphPtr() = minParagraphPtr;
          charInfo.CharRect() = ZeroRect;
        }
      }
```

The characters are removed from the `charList` list and the last index of the minimal paragraph is updated. It is set to the last character of the maximal paragraph (that may be the same paragraph as the minimal paragraph) minus the number of the characters to be deleted. The minimal paragraph is then regenerated.

```
      int deleteChars = maxCharIndex - minCharIndex;
      minParagraphPtr->Last() = maxParagraphPtr->Last() - deleteChars;
      charList.Remove(minCharIndex, maxCharIndex - 1);
      GenerateParagraph(minParagraphPtr);
```

The paragraphs between the minimal and maximal paragraphs, if any, are deleted and the indexes of the succeeding paragraphs are set. We call `DeleteParagraph` for each paragraph to delete their dynamically allocated memory.

```
    int minParIndex = minParagraphPtr->Index(),
        maxParIndex = maxParagraphPtr->Index();

    if (minParIndex < maxParIndex) {
      for (int parIndex = minParIndex + 1;
           parIndex <= maxParIndex; ++parIndex) {
        DeleteParagraph(paragraphList[parIndex]);
      }
      paragraphList.Remove(minParIndex + 1, maxParIndex);
    }
```

Finally, we need to set the indexes of the succeeding paragraphs. Note that we have to update the first and last index regardless of whether any paragraphs have been removed, since we have removed at least one character.

```
    int deleteParagraphs = maxParIndex - minParIndex;
    for (int parIndex = minParagraphPtr->Index() + 1;
         parIndex < paragraphList.Size(); ++parIndex) {
      Paragraph* paragraphPtr = paragraphList[parIndex];
      paragraphPtr->Index() -= deleteParagraphs;
      paragraphPtr->First() -= deleteChars;
      paragraphPtr->Last() -= deleteChars;
    }
```

When the delete process is finished, the application is set to `edit` mode, and the edit index is set to the first marked character.

```
    wordMode = WordEdit;
    editIndex = minCharIndex;
  }
```

Page break

The **PageBreak** menu item is enabled in `edit` mode, and the `OnPageBreak` method is also quite simple. It just inverses the page break status of the edit paragraph:

```
bool WordDocument::PageBreakEnable() const {
  return (wordMode == WordEdit);
}

void WordDocument::OnPageBreak() {
  Paragraph* paragraphPtr = charList[editIndex].ParagraphPtr();
  paragraphPtr->PageBreak() = !paragraphPtr->PageBreak();
  CalculateDocument();
  UpdateCaret();
}
```

Font

The OnFont method is called when the user selects the **Font** menu item and it displays the font dialog. In edit mode, we first need to find the default font to use in the dialog. If the nextFont parameter is active (does not equal SystemFont), we use it. If it is not active, we check whether the edit character is the first character in the paragraph. If it is the first character, we use its font. If it is not the first character, we use the font of its preceding character. This is the same procedure as in the preceding UpdateCaret method:

```
void WordDocument::OnFont() {
  switch (wordMode) {
    case WordEdit: {
      Font font;

      if (nextFont != SystemFont) {
        font = nextFont;
      }
      else if (editIndex ==
              charList[editIndex].ParagraphPtr()->First()) {
        font = charList[editIndex].CharFont();
      }
      else {
        font = charList[editIndex - 1].CharFont();
      }
```

If the user closes the font dialog by choosing **Ok**, we set the nextFont parameter and recalculate the edit paragraph.

```
      if (StandardDialog::FontDialog(this, font)) {
        nextFont = font;
        Paragraph* paragraphPtr =
          charList[editIndex].ParagraphPtr();
        GenerateParagraph(paragraphPtr);
        SetDirty(true);
        CalculateDocument();
        UpdateCaret();
        UpdateWindow();
      }
    }
    break;
```

In `mark` mode, we choose the font of the marked character with the lowest index to be the default font in the font dialog.

```
case WordMark: {
    int minCharIndex = min(firstMarkIndex, lastMarkIndex),
        maxCharIndex = max(firstMarkIndex, lastMarkIndex);
    Font font = charList[minCharIndex].CharFont();
```

If the user chooses **Ok**, we set the font of every marked character and recalculate each of their paragraphs.

```
    if (StandardDialog::FontDialog(this, font)) {
      for (int charIndex = minCharIndex;
          charIndex < maxCharIndex; ++charIndex) {
        charList[charIndex].CharFont() = font;
      }
      int minParIndex =
          charList[minCharIndex].ParagraphPtr()->Index(),
        maxParIndex =
          charList[maxCharIndex].ParagraphPtr()->Index();

      for (int parIndex = minParIndex;
          parIndex <= maxParIndex; ++parIndex) {
        Paragraph* paragraphPtr = paragraphList[parIndex];
        GenerateParagraph(paragraphPtr);
      }

      SetDirty(true);
      CalculateDocument();
      UpdateCaret();
      UpdateWindow();
    }
  }
  break;
  }
}
```

Alignment

All the radio alignment listeners call the `IsAlignment` method, and all selection listeners call the `SetAlignment` method.

```
bool WordDocument::LeftRadio() const {
  return IsAlignment(Left);
}
```

```
void WordDocument::OnLeft() {
  SetAlignment(Left);
}

bool WordDocument::CenterRadio() const {
  return IsAlignment(Center);
}

void WordDocument::OnCenter() {
  SetAlignment(Center);
}

bool WordDocument::RightRadio() const {
  return IsAlignment(Right);
}

void WordDocument::OnRight() {
  SetAlignment(Right);
}

bool WordDocument::JustifiedRadio() const {
  return IsAlignment(Justified);
}

void WordDocument::OnJustified() {
  SetAlignment(Justified);
}
```

In edit mode, the IsAlignment method checks whether the edit paragraph has the given alignment. In mark mode, it checks if all partly or completely marked paragraph have the given alignment. This implies that if several paragraphs are marked with different alignments, no alignment menu item will be marked with a radio button.

```
bool WordDocument::IsAlignment(Alignment alignment) const {
  switch (wordMode) {
    case WordEdit: {
        Alignment editAlignment =
          charList[editIndex].ParagraphPtr()->AlignmentField();
        return (editAlignment == alignment);
      }
    case WordMark: {
        int minCharIndex = min(firstMarkIndex, lastMarkIndex),
            maxCharIndex = max(firstMarkIndex, lastMarkIndex);

        int minParIndex =
              charList[minCharIndex].ParagraphPtr()->Index(),
            maxParIndex =
              charList[maxCharIndex].ParagraphPtr()->Index();
```

```
            for (int parIndex = minParIndex; parIndex < maxParIndex;
                 ++parIndex) {
              Alignment markAlignment =
                paragraphList[parIndex]->AlignmentField();

              if (markAlignment != alignment) {
                return false;
              }
            }

            return true;
          }
        }

        assert(false);
        return false;
      }
```

The `SetAlignment` method sets the alignment of the edited or marked paragraphs. In `edit` mode, we just set the alignment of the edit paragraph. Remember that this method can only be called when the paragraph has another alignment. In `mark` mode, we traverse the marked paragraphs and set the alignment on those paragraphs that do not have the alignment already in question. Also remember that this method can only be called if at least one paragraph does not hold the alignment in question. The paragraphs that have changed alignment need to be recalculated. However, the new alignment does not affect the height of the paragraph, which implies that we do not need to call the `CalculateDocument` method for the remaining paragraphs.

```
      void WordDocument::SetAlignment(Alignment alignment) {
        switch (wordMode) {
          case WordEdit: {
              Paragraph* paragraphPtr =
                charList[editIndex].ParagraphPtr();
              paragraphPtr->AlignmentField() = alignment;
              GenerateParagraph(paragraphPtr);
              UpdateCaret();
            }
            break;

          case WordMark: {
              int minCharIndex = min(firstMarkIndex, lastMarkIndex),
                  maxCharIndex = max(firstMarkIndex, lastMarkIndex);

              int minParIndex =
                    charList[minCharIndex].ParagraphPtr()->Index(),
                  maxParIndex =
                    charList[maxCharIndex].ParagraphPtr()->Index();
```

```
          for (int parIndex = minParIndex; parIndex < maxParIndex;
              ++parIndex) {
            Paragraph* paragraphPtr = paragraphList[parIndex];
            paragraphPtr->AlignmentField() = alignment;
            GenerateParagraph(paragraphPtr);
          }
        }
        break;
    }

    UpdateWindow();
}
```

Summary

In this chapter, you started to develop a word processor capable of handling individual characters. The word processor supports the following:

- Individual font and style of each character
- Left, center, right, and justified alignment of each paragraph
- Paragraphs that are distributed over the pages
- Scrolling and zooming
- Touchscreen
- Cut, copy, and paste with ASCII or Unicode text, as well as application-specific generic information

In Chapter 7, *Keyboard Input and Character Calculation*, we will continue with the keyboard input and character calculation.

7
Keyboard Input and Character Calculation

In this chapter, we will continue our work on the word processor from Chapter 6, *Building a Word Processor*. More specifically, we will look into keyboard input and character calculation. The keyboard handling section deals with regular character input and a rather large set of special keys, such as *Home, End, Page Up* and *Page Down, Return, Backspace,* and arrows.

The calculation section deals with the calculation of each character with regards to its font and the alignment of its paragraph as well as the page settings. In the end, we will calculate the position and size of each individual character in the document.

Keyboard handling

To begin with, we look into the input of regular characters. The OnChar method is called every time a user presses a graphical character (with an ASCII value between 32 and 127, inclusive) or the *Return* key. If a part of the text is marked, that part is removed first. Then the character is added to the character list by the InsertChar method of the OverwriteChar class, depending on the keyboard mode.

```
void WordDocument::OnChar(TCHAR tChar) {
  if (isprint(tChar) || (tChar == NewLine)) {
    if (wordMode == WordMark) {
      OnDelete();
    }

    Paragraph* paragraphPtr = charList[editIndex].ParagraphPtr();
```

```
switch (GetKeyboardMode()) {
  case InsertKeyboard:
    OnInsertChar(tChar, paragraphPtr);
    break;

  case OverwriteKeyboard:
    OnOverwriteChar(tChar, paragraphPtr);
    break;
}

SetDirty(true);
GenerateParagraph(paragraphPtr);
CalculateDocument();

if (MakeVisible()) {
  Invalidate();
  UpdateWindow();
}

UpdateCaret();
  }
}
```

When inserting a character, we have three cases, which are similar to the UpdateCaret and OnFont methods from Chapter 6, *Building a Word Processor*. If the nextFont parameter is active (if it does not equal SystemFont), we use it for the new character. Then, the nextFont parameter is cleared by the ClearNextFont method.

```
void WordDocument::OnInsertChar(TCHAR tChar,
                                Paragraph* paragraphPtr) {
  if (nextFont != SystemFont) {
    charList.Insert(editIndex++,
                    CharInfo(paragraphPtr, tChar, nextFont));
    ClearNextFont();
  }
```

If the nextFont parameter is not active and the input is not at the beginning of the paragraph, we use the font of the preceding character for the new character.

```
  else if (charList[editIndex].ParagraphPtr()->First() <
           editIndex) {
    Font font = charList[editIndex - 1].CharFont();
    charList.Insert(editIndex++,
                    CharInfo(paragraphPtr, tChar, font));
  }
```

However, if the input is at the beginning of the paragraph, we use the font of the first character in the paragraph.

```
else {
  Font font = charList[editIndex].CharFont();
  charList.Insert(editIndex++,
                  CharInfo(paragraphPtr, tChar, font));
}
```

In order to make room for the inserted character, we increase the last index of its paragraph. We also increase the first and last index of the succeeding paragraphs.

```
++paragraphPtr->Last();

for (int parIndex = paragraphPtr->Index() + 1;
     parIndex <= paragraphList.Size() - 1; ++parIndex) {
  ++paragraphList[parIndex]->First();
  ++paragraphList[parIndex]->Last();
}
}
```

In the `overwrite` mode, we have two cases. If the input is at the very end of the document, we insert the character instead of overwriting it; otherwise, we overwrite the newline terminating the last paragraph. However, we are free to overwrite the terminating newline of every paragraph except the last one, in which case, the two paragraphs are merged into one.

Similar to the `InsertChar` method, we use the `nextFont` parameter if it is not equal to the `SystemFont` parameter. If it is equal to the `SystemFont` parameter, we use the font of the character we overwrite rather than the preceding character as we did in the `InsertChar` case.

```
void WordDocument::OnOverwriteChar(TCHAR tChar,
                                   Paragraph* paragraphPtr) {
  if (editIndex == (charList.Size() - 1)) {
    if (nextFont != SystemFont) {
      charList.Insert(editIndex++,
        CharInfo(paragraphPtr, tChar, nextFont));
      charList[editIndex] =
        CharInfo(paragraphPtr, NewLine, nextFont);
      ClearNextFont();
    }
    else {
      Font font = charList[editIndex].CharFont();
      charList.Insert(editIndex++,
                      CharInfo(paragraphPtr, tChar, font));
    }
```

```
        ++paragraphPtr->Last();
    }
    else {
      if (nextFont != SystemFont) {
        charList[editIndex++] =
          CharInfo(paragraphPtr, tChar, nextFont);
        ClearNextFont();
      }
      else {
        Font font = charList[editIndex].CharFont();
        charList[editIndex++] = CharInfo(paragraphPtr, tChar, font);
      }
    }
  }
}
```

The `ClearNextFont` method clears the `nextFont` parameter by setting its value to the `SystemFont` font. It also recalculates the edit paragraph and the document, since the removal of the `nextFont` parameter may cause the edit line (and thereby the edit paragraph) to be lowered. The fonts of the character on the line may all be lower than the `nextFont` parameter, which causes the line to be lower when the `nextFont` parameter is removed from the line.

```
void WordDocument::ClearNextFont() {
  if (nextFont != SystemFont) {
    nextFont = SystemFont;
    Paragraph* paragraphPtr = charList[editIndex].ParagraphPtr();
    GenerateParagraph(paragraphPtr);
    CalculateDocument();
    UpdateWindow();
  }
}
```

The `OnKeyDown` method is called every time the user presses a key. Depending on the key and whether the *Shift* key is pressed, the `OnKeyDown` method in turn calls the `OnShiftKey`, `OnRegularKey`, or `OnNeutralKey` method. The *Delete*, *Backspace*, and *Return* keys perform the same actions irrespective of whether the *Shift* key is pressed.

```
bool WordDocument::OnKeyDown(WORD key, bool shiftPressed,
                            bool /* controlPressed */) {
  switch (key) {
    case KeyLeft:
    case KeyRight:
    case KeyUp:
    case KeyDown:
    case KeyHome:
    case KeyEnd: {
```

```
        if (shiftPressed) {
          OnShiftKey(key);
        }
        else {
          OnRegularKey(key);
        }
      }
      return true;

    case KeyBackspace:
    case KeyReturn:
      OnNeutralKey(key);
      return true;
  }

  return false;
}
```

When the user presses a graphical key, the application will be set to the edit mode. The EnsureEditStatus method makes sure of it. The key stroke may move the caret to a position outside the visible part of the client area. Therefore, we call the MakeVisible method to move the scroll bars if necessary, so that the caret appears in the visible part of the client area. The idea is to make the caret and the edit character always visible in the window.

```
void WordDocument::OnRegularKey(WORD key) {
  EnsureEditStatus();

  switch (key) {
    case KeyLeft:
      OnLeftArrowKey();
      break;

    case KeyRight:
      OnRightArrowKey();
      break;

    case KeyUp:
      OnUpArrowKey();
      break;

    case KeyDown:
      OnDownArrowKey();
      break;
```

```
        case KeyHome:
          OnHomeKey();
          break;

        case KeyEnd:
          OnEndKey();
          break;
    }

    if (MakeVisible()) {
      Invalidate();
      UpdateWindow();
      UpdateCaret();
    }
}
```

We must make sure that the application is set to the `edit` mode when the user presses *Page Up*, *Page Down*, or one of the arrow keys, without pressing the *Shift* key. The `EnsureEditStatus` method takes care of that. The `editIndex` is set to `lastMarkIndex`.

```
void WordDocument::EnsureEditStatus() {
  if (wordMode == WordMark) {
    wordMode = WordEdit;
    editIndex = lastMarkIndex;
    InvalidateBlock(firstMarkIndex, lastMarkIndex);
    UpdateCaret();
    UpdateWindow();
  }
}
```

Arrow keys

The `OnLeftArrowKey` method is called when the user presses the left arrow key. Its purpose is to move the caret one step to the left, which is simple enough. We must make sure that the edit position is not already at the beginning of the document. If we move the position to the left, we also need to clear the `nextFont` parameter, since it will be active only when the user is about to input a new character.

```
void WordDocument::OnLeftArrowKey() {
  if (editIndex > 0) {
    ClearNextFont();
    --editIndex;
  }
}
```

The `OnRightArrowKey` method is called when the user presses the right arrow key. If the caret position is not at the end of the document, we move it one step to the right.

```
void WordDocument::OnRightArrowKey() {
  if (editIndex < (charList.Size() - 1)) {
    ClearNextFont();
    ++editIndex;
  }
}
```

When the user presses the up arrow key, we have to find the key above the edit line. We do that by simulating a mouse click slightly above (one logical unit) the line. Note that we have to look up the edit line. It is not enough to use the character rectangle, since the characters may differ in height and ascent (refer to the next section) and we cannot be sure that the character rectangle is the highest rectangle on the line. Therefore, we look up the height of the edit line. In the following screenshot, the text is surrounded by rectangles for the purpose of clarification. The code does not actually draw the rectangles. If we would use the rectangle of the digit four, we would not reach the preceding line because the rectangle of the digit **5** is higher. Instead, we have to use the line rectangle of the line **456**.

```
void WordDocument::OnUpArrowKey() {
  CharInfo charInfo = charList[editIndex];

  Paragraph* paragraphPtr = charInfo.ParagraphPtr();
  Point topLeft(0, paragraphPtr->Top());

  LineInfo* lineInfoPtr = charInfo.LineInfoPtr();
  Rect lineRect =
    topLeft + Rect(0, lineInfoPtr->Top(), PageInnerWidth(),
                   lineInfoPtr->Top() + lineInfoPtr->Height());
```

We need to check that the edit character is not located on the first line of the document. If the edit character is already located on the first line then nothing will happen to the output.

```
if (lineRect.Top() > 0) {
  ClearNextFont();
  Rect charRect = topLeft + charInfo.CharRect();
  editIndex =
    MousePointToIndex(Point(charRect.Left(), lineRect.Top()-1));
}
}
```

When the user presses the down arrow key, we simulate a mouse click by calling the MousePointToIndexDown method. In the call, we use the position slightly under the edit line (1 unit) in order to find the index of the character in the same horizontal position on the next line. One difference compared to the preceding UpArrowKey case is that we call the MousePointToIndexDown method instead of the MousePointToIndex method because it might be the last line of the paragraph, and there might be some space before the next paragraph. In that case, we would want the index of the character following the empty space, which the MousePointToIndexDown method returns, while the MousePointToIndex method returns the index of the character preceding the empty space.

```
void WordDocument::OnDownArrowKey() {
  CharInfo charInfo = charList[editIndex];
  Paragraph* paragraphPtr = charInfo.ParagraphPtr();
  Point topLeft(0, paragraphPtr->Top());
  LineInfo* lineInfoPtr = charInfo.LineInfoPtr();
  Rect lineRect =
    topLeft + Rect(0, lineInfoPtr->Top(), PageInnerWidth(),
                      lineInfoPtr->Top() + lineInfoPtr->Height());
```

Similar to the preceding OnUpArrowKey case, we need to ensure that the edit line is not the last line in the document. We do so by comparing it to the bottom of the last paragraph. If it is the last line then nothing will happen to the output.

```
Paragraph* lastParagraphPtr = paragraphList.Back();
int bottom = lastParagraphPtr->Top() +
              lastParagraphPtr->Height();

if (lineRect.Bottom() < bottom) {
  ClearNextFont();
  Rect charRect = topLeft + charInfo.CharRect();
  editIndex =
    MousePointToIndexDown(Point(charRect.Left(),
                            lineRect.Bottom() + 1));
}
}
```

The `MousePointToIndexDown` method returns the index of the character on which we click. If the mouse point is between two paragraphs, the index of the preceding character is returned.

```
int WordDocument::MousePointToIndexDown(Point mousePoint) const{
  for (int parIndex = 0; parIndex < paragraphList.Size();
      ++parIndex) {
    Paragraph* paragraphPtr = paragraphList[parIndex];

    if (mousePoint.Y() <=
        (paragraphPtr->Top() + paragraphPtr->Height())) {
      return MousePointToParagraphIndex
          (paragraphList[parIndex], mousePoint);
    }
  }
```

As this method always finds the correct paragraph, this point will never be reached, but we assert that in case of coding error it behaves otherwise.

```
  assert(false);
  return 0;
}
```

The `OnPageUp` and `OnPageDown` methods look up the height of the current vertical scroll bar in order to simulate a mouse click one page up or down.

```
void WordDocument::OnPageUpKey() {
  CharInfo charInfo = charList[editIndex];
  Rect editRect = charInfo.CharRect();

  Paragraph* paragraphPtr = charInfo.ParagraphPtr();
  Point topLeft(0, paragraphPtr->Top());

  int scrollPage = GetVerticalScrollPageHeight();
  Point editPoint((editRect.Left() + editRect.Right()) / 2,
      ((editRect.Top() + editRect.Bottom()) / 2) - scrollPage);

  editIndex = MousePointToIndex(topLeft + editPoint);
}

void WordDocument::OnPageDownKey() {
  CharInfo charInfo = charList[editIndex];
  Rect editRect = charInfo.CharRect();

  Paragraph* paragraphPtr = charInfo.ParagraphPtr();
  Point topLeft(0, paragraphPtr->Top());

  int scrollPage = GetVerticalScrollPageHeight();
```

```
Point editPoint((editRect.Left() + editRect.Right()) / 2,
       ((editRect.Top() + editRect.Bottom()) / 2) + scrollPage);

editIndex = MousePointToIndex(topLeft + editPoint);
}
```

Home and End

The OnHomeKey method is called when the user presses the *Home* key. It looks up the index of the first character on the edit line by following its paragraph and line pointers. It uses the index of the first character of the line.

```
void WordDocument::OnHomeKey() {
  CharInfo charInfo = charList[editIndex];
  int homeCharIndex = charInfo.ParagraphPtr()->First() +
                      charInfo.LineInfoPtr()->First();
```

If the edit character is not already at the beginning of the line, the nextFont parameter is cleared by the ClearNextFont method, the edit index is updated, and the caret is updated.

```
  if (homeCharIndex < editIndex) {
    ClearNextFont();
    editIndex = homeCharIndex;
    UpdateCaret();
  }
}
```

The OnEndKey method is called when the user presses the *End* key. It looks up the index of the last character on the edit line by following its paragraph and line pointers and using the index of the last character of the line.

```
void WordDocument::OnEndKey() {
  CharInfo charInfo = charList[editIndex];
  int endCharIndex = charInfo.ParagraphPtr()->First() +
                     charInfo.LineInfoPtr()->Last();
```

If the edit character is not already at the end of the line, the nextFont parameter is cleared by the ClearNextFont method, the edit index is updated, and the caret is updated.

```
  if (editIndex < endCharIndex) {
    ClearNextFont();
    editIndex = endCharIndex;
    UpdateCaret();
  }
}
```

Shift arrow keys

The `OnShiftKey` method is called when the user presses a key together with the *Shift* key:

```
void WordDocument::OnShiftKey(WORD key) {
  EnsureMarkStatus();
  switch (key) {
    case KeyLeft:
      OnShiftLeftArrowKey();
      break;

    case KeyRight:
      OnShiftRightArrowKey();
      break;

    case KeyUp:
      OnShiftUpArrowKey();
      break;

    case KeyDown:
      OnShiftDownArrowKey();
      break;

    case KeyPageUp:
      OnShiftPageUpKey();
      break;

    case KeyPageDown:
      OnShiftPageDownKey();
      break;

    case KeyHome:
      OnShiftHomeKey();
      break;

    case KeyEnd:
      OnShiftEndKey();
      break;
  }

  if (MakeVisible()) {
    Invalidate();
    UpdateWindow();
    UpdateCaret();
  }
}
```

If the user presses a key together with the *Shift* key, we must make sure that the application is set to the mark mode; the EnsureMarkMode method deals with that. It clears the nextFont parameter (by setting it to SystemFont), sets the application to the mark mode, and assigns both the first and last marked index to the edit index.

```
void WordDocument::EnsureMarkStatus() {
  if (wordMode == WordEdit) {
    ClearNextFont();
    wordMode = WordMark;
    firstMarkIndex = editIndex;
    lastMarkIndex = editIndex;
    UpdateCaret();
  }
}
```

The OnShiftLeftArrowKey method decreases the last marked index. Note that we only invalidate the indexes between the old and new value of the lastMarkIndex method in order to avoid dazzle:

```
void WordDocument::OnShiftLeftArrowKey() {
  if (lastMarkIndex > 0) {
    InvalidateBlock(lastMarkIndex, --lastMarkIndex);
  }
}
```

The OnShiftRightArrowKey method moves the position of the last marked character in a way similar to the OnShiftLeftArrowKey method.

```
void WordDocument::OnShiftRightArrowKey() {
  if (lastMarkIndex < charList.Size()) {
    InvalidateBlock(lastMarkIndex, lastMarkIndex++);
  }
}
```

The OnShiftUpArrowKey and OnShiftDownArrowKey methods are called when the user presses the up or down arrow key together with the *Shift* key. Its task is to move the last marked position one line upward. We simulate the mouse click in the same way as we did for the OnUpArrowKey and OnDownArrowKey method earlier.

```
void WordDocument::OnShiftUpArrowKey() {
  CharInfo charInfo = charList[lastMarkIndex];

  Paragraph* paragraphPtr = charInfo.ParagraphPtr();
  Point topLeft(0, paragraphPtr->Top());

  LineInfo* lineInfoPtr = charInfo.LineInfoPtr();
```

```
   Rect lineRect =
     topLeft + Rect(0, lineInfoPtr->Top(), PageInnerWidth(),
                        lineInfoPtr->Top() + lineInfoPtr->Height());

  if ((paragraphPtr->Top() + lineRect.Top()) > 0) {
    Rect charRect = topLeft + charInfo.CharRect();
    int newLastMarkIndex =
      MousePointToIndex(Point(charRect.Left(), lineRect.Top()-1));
    InvalidateBlock(lastMarkIndex, newLastMarkIndex);
    lastMarkIndex = newLastMarkIndex;
  }
}

void WordDocument::OnShiftDownArrowKey() {
  CharInfo charInfo = charList[lastMarkIndex];

  Paragraph* paragraphPtr = charInfo.ParagraphPtr();
  Point topLeft(0, paragraphPtr->Top());

  LineInfo* lineInfoPtr = charInfo.LineInfoPtr();
  Rect lineRect =
     topLeft + Rect(0, lineInfoPtr->Top(), PageInnerWidth(),
                        lineInfoPtr->Top() + lineInfoPtr->Height());

  Paragraph* lastParagraphPtr = paragraphList.Back();
  int bottom = lastParagraphPtr->Top() +
               lastParagraphPtr->Height();

  if (lineRect.Bottom() < bottom) {
    Rect charRect = topLeft + charInfo.CharRect();
    int newLastMarkIndex =
      MousePointToIndexDown(Point(charRect.Left(),
                                 lineRect.Bottom() + 1));
    InvalidateBlock(lastMarkIndex, newLastMarkIndex);
    lastMarkIndex = newLastMarkIndex;
  }
}
```

Shift Page Up and Page Down

The `OnShiftPageUpKey` and `OnShiftPageDown` methods move the edit character index one page-height by simulating a mouse click on *Page Up* or *Page Down*:

```
void WordDocument::OnShiftPageUpKey() {
  Rect lastRectMark = charList[lastMarkIndex].CharRect();
  int scrollPage = GetVerticalScrollPageHeight();
  Point lastPointMark
    ((lastRectMark.Left() + lastRectMark.Right()) / 2,
     (lastRectMark.Top()+lastRectMark.Bottom()) / 2 - scrollPage);

  int newLastMarkIndex = MousePointToIndex(lastPointMark);
  InvalidateBlock(lastMarkIndex, newLastMarkIndex);
  lastMarkIndex = newLastMarkIndex;
}

void WordDocument::OnShiftPageDownKey() {
  Rect lastRectMark = charList[lastMarkIndex].CharRect();

  int scrollPage = GetVerticalScrollPageHeight();
  Point lastPointMark
    ((lastRectMark.Left() + lastRectMark.Right()) / 2,
     (lastRectMark.Top()+lastRectMark.Bottom())/2 + scrollPage);

  int newLastMarkIndex = MousePointToIndexDown(lastPointMark);
  InvalidateBlock(lastMarkIndex, newLastMarkIndex);
  lastMarkIndex = newLastMarkIndex;
}
```

Shift Home and End

The `OnShiftHomeKey` and `OnShiftEndKey` methods are called when the user presses the *Home* or *End* key together with the *Shift* key. Their task is to mark the line from the current position to the beginning or end of the line:

```
void WordDocument::OnShiftHomeKey() {
  CharInfo charInfo = charList[editIndex];
  int homeCharIndex = charInfo.ParagraphPtr()->First() +
                      charInfo.LineInfoPtr()->First();

  if (homeCharIndex < lastMarkIndex) {
    InvalidateBlock(lastMarkIndex, homeCharIndex);
    lastMarkIndex = homeCharIndex;
  }
}
```

```
void WordDocument::OnShiftEndKey() {
  CharInfo charInfo = charList[editIndex];
  int endCharIndex = charInfo.ParagraphPtr()->First() +
                     charInfo.LineInfoPtr()->Last();

  if (lastMarkIndex < endCharIndex) {
    InvalidateBlock(lastMarkIndex, endCharIndex);
    lastMarkIndex = endCharIndex;
  }
}
```

Control Home and End

The OnControlHomeKey and OnControlEndKey methods set the edit character position to
the beginning or end of the document. Since these methods are listeners and not called by
the OnRegularKey method, we need to call the EnsureEditStatus, MakeVisible, and
UpdateCaret methods:

```
void WordDocument::OnControlHomeKey() {
  EnsureEditStatus();

  if (editIndex > 0) {
    editIndex = 0;
    if (MakeVisible()) {
      Invalidate();
      UpdateWindow();
    }

    UpdateCaret();
  }
}

void WordDocument::OnControlEndKey() {
  EnsureEditStatus();

  if (editIndex < (charList.Size() - 1)) {
    editIndex = charList.Size() - 1;

    if (MakeVisible()) {
      Invalidate();
      UpdateWindow();
    }

    UpdateCaret();
  }
}
```

Shift Control Home and End

The `OnShiftControlHomeKey` and `OnShiftControlEndKey` methods set the last mark index to the beginning or end of the document:

```
void WordDocument::OnShiftControlHomeKey() {
  EnsureMarkStatus();
  ClearNextFont();

  if (lastMarkIndex > 0) {
    InvalidateBlock(0, lastMarkIndex);
    lastMarkIndex = 0;

    if (MakeVisible()) {
      Invalidate();
      UpdateWindow();
    }

    UpdateCaret();
  }
}

void WordDocument::OnShiftControlEndKey() {
  EnsureMarkStatus();

  if (lastMarkIndex < (charList.Size() - 1)) {
    int lastIndex = charList.Size() - 1;
    InvalidateBlock(lastMarkIndex, lastIndex);
    lastMarkIndex = lastIndex;

    if (MakeVisible()) {
      Invalidate();
      UpdateWindow();
    }

    UpdateCaret();
  }
}
```

Neutral keys

The *Backspace* and *Return* keys are neutral keys in the sense that we do not care whether the user presses the *Shift* or *Ctrl* key. Note that the *Delete* key is not handled by the `OnNeutralKey` method because the **Delete** menu item has the *Delete* key as its accelerator:

```
void WordDocument::OnNeutralKey(WORD key) {
  switch (key) {
    case KeyBackspace:
      OnBackspaceKey();
      break;
    case KeyReturn:
      OnReturnKey();
      break;
  }

  if (MakeVisible()) {
    Invalidate();
    UpdateWindow();
    UpdateCaret();
  }
}
```

What the `OnBackSpaceKey` method does is quite simple–it just calls the `OnDelete` method. In the `edit` mode, we first move one step to the left unless the edit position is not already at the beginning of the document. If it is, nothing happens. In the `mark` mode, the *Delete* key and the *Backspace* key have the same effect–they both delete the marked text.

```
void WordDocument::OnBackspaceKey() {
  switch (wordMode) {
    case WordEdit:
      if (editIndex > 0) {
        OnLeftArrowKey();
        OnDelete();
      }
      break;

    case WordMark:
      OnDelete();
      break;
  }
}
```

The `OnReturnKey` method is called when the user presses the *Return* key. First, we call the `OnChar` method with a newline. The `OnChar` method is never called with newline on any other occasion, since newline is not a graphical character.

```
void WordDocument::OnReturnKey() {
  OnChar(NewLine);
```

After the newline has been added to the character list, we need to split the edit paragraph into two. The `editIndex` field has been updated by the `OnChar` method, and it is now the index of the character after the newline. The second paragraph starts at the edit index and ends at the end of the first paragraph. The first paragraph's last index is set to the edit index minus one. This means that the first paragraph holds the characters up to the newline, inclusive, while the second paragraph holds the characters one step beyond the newline.

```
Paragraph* firstParagraphPtr =
  charList[editIndex].ParagraphPtr();
Paragraph* secondParagraphPtr =
  new Paragraph(editIndex, firstParagraphPtr->Last(),
                firstParagraphPtr->AlignmentField(),
                firstParagraphPtr->Index() + 1);
assert(firstParagraphPtr != nullptr);
firstParagraphPtr->Last() = editIndex - 1;
```

We insert the second paragraph in the paragraph list; we also need to set the characters in the second paragraph to point to the second paragraph.

```
paragraphList.Insert(firstParagraphPtr->Index() + 1,
                     secondParagraphPtr);
for (int charIndex = secondParagraphPtr->First();
     charIndex <= secondParagraphPtr->Last(); ++charIndex) {
  charList[charIndex].ParagraphPtr() = secondParagraphPtr;
}
```

We need to recalculate both the first and second paragraph, since the first paragraph has lost characters and the second paragraph has been recently created.

```
GenerateParagraph(firstParagraphPtr);
GenerateParagraph(secondParagraphPtr);
```

Since we have added a paragraph, we need to increase the indexes of the succeeding paragraphs.

```
for (int parIndex = secondParagraphPtr->Index() + 1;
     parIndex < paragraphList.Size(); ++parIndex) {
  ++paragraphList[parIndex]->Index();
}

SetDirty(true);
CalculateDocument();
UpdateCaret();
UpdateWindow();
}
```

Visible characters

When the user uses the keyboard, the edit character or the last marked character will always be visible. We start by finding the area that is visible; in edit mode, it is the area of the edit character. In the mark mode, it is the area of the character before the last marked index, unless it is zero, in which case the index is set to zero.

```
bool WordDocument::MakeVisible() {
  Rect visibleArea;

  switch (wordMode) {
    case WordEdit: {
        Paragraph* editParagraphPtr =
          charList[editIndex].ParagraphPtr();
        Point topLeft(0, editParagraphPtr->Top());
        visibleArea = topLeft + charList[editIndex].CharRect();
      }
      break;

    case WordMark: {
        Paragraph* lastParagraphPtr =
          charList[max(0, lastMarkIndex - 1)].ParagraphPtr();
        Point topLeft(0, lastParagraphPtr->Top());
        visibleArea =
          topLeft + charList[max(0,lastMarkIndex - 1)].CharRect();
      }
      break;
  }
```

We test whether the visible area is in fact visible at the moment. If it is not visible, we adjust the scroll bars in order to make it visible.

```
  int horiScrollLeft = GetHorizontalScrollPosition(),
      horiScrollPage = GetHorizontalScrollPageWidth(),
      vertScrollTop = GetVerticalScrollPosition(),
      vertScrollPage = GetVerticalScrollPageHeight();
  int horiScrollRight = horiScrollLeft + horiScrollPage,
      vertScrollBottom = vertScrollTop + vertScrollPage;
```

If the left border of the visible area is not visible, we set the horizontal scroll position to its left border. In the same way, we set the vertical scroll position to the top border of the visible area if it is not visible.

```
  if (visibleArea.Left() < horiScrollLeft) {
    SetHorizontalScrollPosition(visibleArea.Left());
    return true;
  }
```

```
if (visibleArea.Top() < vertScrollTop) {
  SetVerticalScrollPosition(visibleArea.Top());
  return true;
}
```

It becomes a little bit more complicated when it comes to the right and bottom border of the visible area. We start by calculating the distance between the right border of the visible area and the right scroll position (the left scroll position plus the size of the horizontal scroll bar) and increase the horizontal scroll position by that distance. In the same way, we calculate the distance between the right border of the visible area and the bottom scroll position (the top scroll position plus the size of the vertical scroll bar) and increase the vertical scroll position by that distance.

```
if (visibleArea.Right() > horiScrollRight) {
  int horiDifference = visibleArea.Right() - horiScrollRight;
  SetHorizontalScrollPosition(horiScrollLeft + horiDifference);
  return true;
}

if (visibleArea.Bottom() > vertScrollBottom) {
  int vertDifference = visibleArea.Bottom() - vertScrollBottom;
  SetVerticalScrollPosition(vertScrollTop + vertDifference);
  return true;
}

return false;
}
```

Character calculation

The GenerateParagraph fucnction generates the character rectangles and the line lists of a paragraph every time characters are added or removed or when the font or alignment is changed. First, we generate lists of sizes and ascents for every character as well as the line list by calling the GenerateSizeAndAscentList and GenerateLineList methods. Then, we iterate through the line list and generate the character rectangles by calling the GenerateLineRectList method. Finally, we invalidate the characters that have been changed by comparing them to the original rectangle lists:

```
void WordDocument::GenerateParagraph(Paragraph* paragraphPtr) {
  if (!charList.Empty()) {
    DynamicList<Size> sizeList;
    DynamicList<int> ascentList;
    DynamicList<CharInfo> prevCharList;
```

```
    charList.Copy(prevCharList, paragraphPtr->First(),
                  paragraphPtr->Last());

    GenerateSizeAndAscentList(paragraphPtr, sizeList, ascentList);
    GenerateLineList(paragraphPtr, sizeList, ascentList);

    for (LineInfo* lineInfoPtr : paragraphPtr->LinePtrList()) {
      if (paragraphPtr->AlignmentField() == Justified) {
        GenerateJustifiedLineRectList(paragraphPtr, lineInfoPtr,
                                      sizeList, ascentList);
      }
      else {
        GenerateRegularLineRectList(paragraphPtr, lineInfoPtr,
                                    sizeList, ascentList);
      }
    }

    GenerateRepaintSet(paragraphPtr, prevCharList);
  }
}
```

Character size and ascent line

The ascent line separates the upper and lower part of a letter, which is shown in the following figure:

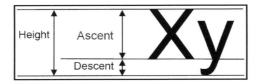

The `GenerateSizeAndAscentList` method fills the given lists with the size (width and height) and ascent of every character in the paragraph:

```
void WordDocument::GenerateSizeAndAscentList
        (Paragraph* paragraphPtr, DynamicList<Size>& sizeList,
          DynamicList<int>& ascentList) {
  int index = 0;

  for (int charIndex = paragraphPtr->First();
       charIndex <= paragraphPtr->Last(); ++charIndex) {
    CharInfo charInfo = charList[charIndex];
    TCHAR tChar = (charInfo.Char() == NewLine) ? Space
                                               : charInfo.Char();
```

```
      int width = GetCharacterWidth(charInfo.CharFont(), tChar),
          height = GetCharacterHeight(charInfo.CharFont()),
          ascent = GetCharacterAscent(charInfo.CharFont());

    sizeList.PushBack(Size(width, height));
    ascentList.PushBack(ascent);
  }
}
```

Line generation

The GenerateLineList method generates the line list. The main point is that we have to decide how many words fit on each line. We iterate through the characters and calculate the size of each word. When the next word does not fit on the line, we start a new line. We save the index of the first and last character on the line as well as its top position. We also save its maximum height and ascent, which is the height and ascent of the largest character on the line:

```
void WordDocument::GenerateLineList(Paragraph* paragraphPtr,
                                    DynamicList<Size>& sizeList,
                                    DynamicList<int>& ascentList) {
  int maxHeight = 0, maxAscent = 0, lineWidth = 0,
      spaceLineHeight = 0, spaceLineAscent = 0,
      startIndex = paragraphPtr->First(), spaceIndex = -1;
```

We delete the lines previously stored in the line list. The line list and the paragraph height are cleared. The lineTop variable is set to zero and is used when calculating the top position of each line.

```
  for (LineInfo* lineInfoPtr : paragraphPtr->LinePtrList()) {
    delete lineInfoPtr;
  }

  paragraphPtr->Height() = 0;
  paragraphPtr->LinePtrList().Clear();
  int lineTop = 0;

  for (int charIndex = paragraphPtr->First();
       charIndex <= paragraphPtr->Last(); ++charIndex) {
    CharInfo charInfo = charList[charIndex];

    if (charInfo.Char() != NewLine) {
      lineWidth +=
        sizeList[charIndex - paragraphPtr->First()].Width();
    }
```

If the `nextFont` parameter is active (does not equal `SystemFont`) and we have reached the edit index in edit mode, we calculate the height and ascent of the `nextFont` parameter. In this case, we are only interested in the height and ascent of the font, and we do not need to calculate the width of its average character.

```
if ((nextFont != SystemFont) && (charIndex == editIndex) &&
    (wordMode == WordEdit)) {
  maxHeight = max(maxHeight, GetCharacterHeight(nextFont));
  maxAscent = max(maxAscent, GetCharacterAscent(nextFont));
}
```

Note that we have to subtract the first index of the paragraph, since the indexes of each line are relative to the beginning of the paragraph. Remember that the character list is common to all paragraphs in the document.

```
else {
  maxHeight = max(maxHeight,
    sizeList[charIndex - paragraphPtr->First()].Height());
  maxAscent = max(maxAscent,
    ascentList[charIndex - paragraphPtr->First()]);
}

if (charInfo.Char() == Space) {
  spaceIndex = charIndex;

  spaceLineHeight = max(spaceLineHeight, maxHeight);
  spaceLineAscent = max(spaceLineAscent, maxAscent);

  maxHeight = 0;
  maxAscent = 0;
}
```

When we find a newline, we have reached the end of the paragraph.

```
if (charInfo.Char() == NewLine) {
  spaceLineHeight = max(spaceLineHeight, maxHeight);
  spaceLineAscent = max(spaceLineAscent, maxAscent);

  LineInfo* lineInfoPtr =
    new LineInfo(startIndex - paragraphPtr->First(),
                 charIndex - paragraphPtr->First(),
                 lineTop, spaceLineHeight, spaceLineAscent);
  assert(lineInfoPtr != nullptr);
```

```
        for (int index = lineInfoPtr->First();
            index <= lineInfoPtr->Last(); ++index) {
          charList[paragraphPtr->First() + index].LineInfoPtr() =
            lineInfoPtr;
        }

        paragraphPtr->Height() += spaceLineHeight;
        paragraphPtr->LinePtrList().PushBack(lineInfoPtr);
        break;
    }
```

When the width of the edit line exceeds the page width, we have, in fact, three different cases:

- The line is made up by at least one complete word (space is not equal to minus one)
- The line is made up by one word too long to fit on the page (space is equal to minus one and charIndex is greater than startIndex)
- The line is made up by one single character wider than the page (space is equal to minus one and charIndex equals startIndex

The third case is unlikely but possible.

```
if (lineWidth > PageInnerWidth()) {
  LineInfo* lineInfoPtr = new LineInfo();
  assert(lineInfoPtr != nullptr);
  lineInfoPtr->Top() = lineTop;
  lineTop += spaceLineHeight;
```

If the line is constituted by at least one complete word followed by a space, we discard the latest space and start the new line from the next character.

```
if (spaceIndex != -1) {
  lineInfoPtr->First() = startIndex - paragraphPtr->First();
  lineInfoPtr->Last() = spaceIndex - paragraphPtr->First();
  lineInfoPtr->Ascent() = spaceLineAscent;
  lineInfoPtr->Height() = spaceLineHeight;
  startIndex = spaceIndex + 1;
}
```

If the line is constituted by one single word (with at least two letters) such that its width does not fit on the page, we define the line to hold the word including the last fitting character, and we start the new line with the succeeding character.

```
else {
  if (charIndex > startIndex) {
    lineInfoPtr->First() =
      startIndex - paragraphPtr->First();
    lineInfoPtr->Last() =
      charIndex - paragraphPtr->First() - 1;
    startIndex = charIndex;
  }
```

Finally, in the unlikely event that one single character is wider than the page, we just let that character constitute the whole line and let the next index be the start index.

```
else {
  lineInfoPtr->First() =charIndex - paragraphPtr->First();
  lineInfoPtr->Last() = charIndex - paragraphPtr->First();
  startIndex = charIndex + 1;
}
```

The height and ascent of the line are the maximal height and ascent (the height and ascent of the character with the largest height and ascent).

```
  lineInfoPtr->Height() = maxHeight;
  lineInfoPtr->Ascent() = maxAscent;
}
```

We set all characters on the line to point at the line.

```
for (int index = lineInfoPtr->First();
    index <= lineInfoPtr->Last(); ++index) {
  charList[paragraphPtr->First() + index].LineInfoPtr() =
    lineInfoPtr;
}
```

The height of the paragraph is increased by the height of the line, and the line pointer is added to the line pointer list.

```
paragraphPtr->Height() += spaceLineHeight;
paragraphPtr->LinePtrList().PushBack(lineInfoPtr);
```

In order to prepare for the next iteration, the line width, the maximal height, and ascent are cleared.

```
lineWidth = 0;
maxAscent = 0;
maxHeight = 0;
```

The `charIndex` loop variable is set to the latest space index and the `spaceIndex` is set to
−1, indicating that we have not yet found a space on the new line.

```
        charIndex = startIndex;
        spaceIndex = -1;
      }
    }
  }
```

Regular and justified rectangle list generation

When we have decided the size and ascent line for each character and divided the
characters into lines, it is time to generate the character rectangles. For a regular (left, center,
or right-aligned) paragraph, we do that in three steps. The justified-aligned paragraph is
handled by the `GenerateJustifiedLineRectList` method as follows:

1. We sum the width of each line.
2. We find the leftmost position.
3. We generate the rectangles for the characters.

```
void WordDocument::GenerateRegularLineRectList
                    (Paragraph* paragraphPtr,LineInfo* lineInfoPtr,
                     DynamicList<Size>& sizeList,
                     DynamicList<int>& ascentList) {
```

We iterate through the characters of the line and sum its width. If the character after the last
character of the line is not a space or newline, we generate its rectangle too.

```
    for (int charIndex = lineInfoPtr->First();
         charIndex < lineInfoPtr->Last(); ++charIndex) {
      if (charList[paragraphPtr->First() + charIndex].Char() !=
          NewLine) {
        lineWidth +=
          sizeList[charIndex - lineInfoPtr->First()].Width();
      }
    }

    if ((charList[paragraphPtr->First()+lineInfoPtr->Last()].Char()
        != Space) &&
        (charList[paragraphPtr->First()+lineInfoPtr->Last()].Char()
        !=NewLine)) {
      lineWidth +=
        sizeList[lineInfoPtr->Last()-lineInfoPtr->First()].Width();
    }
```

Then, we find the leftmost position of the line to start the rectangle generation. In the case of left alignment, the starting position is always zero. In the case of center alignment, it is half the difference between the page and text width. In the case of right alignment, it is the whole difference between the page and text width.

```
int leftPos;

switch (paragraphPtr->AlignmentField()) {
  case Left:
    leftPos = 0;
    break;

  case Center:
    leftPos = (PageInnerWidth() - lineWidth) / 2;
    break;

  case Right:
    leftPos = PageInnerWidth() - lineWidth;
    break;
}
```

Next, we iterate through the line and generate each rectangle. If the character after the last character of the line is a space, we generate its rectangle too.

```
for (int charIndex = lineInfoPtr->First();
     charIndex <= lineInfoPtr->Last(); ++charIndex) {
  Size charSize = sizeList[charIndex];
  int ascent = ascentList[charIndex];
  int topPos = lineInfoPtr->Top() +
               lineInfoPtr->Ascent() - ascent;
  charList[paragraphPtr->First() + charIndex].CharRect() =
    Rect(leftPos, topPos, leftPos + charSize.Width(),
         topPos + charSize.Height());
  leftPos += charSize.Width();
  }
}
```

The `GenerateJustifiedLineRectList` method is slightly more complicated than the `GenerateRegularLineRectList` method. We follow the same three steps as mentioned previously. However, when calculating the width of the text, we omit the width of spaces from the text width. Instead, we count the number of spaces.

```
void WordDocument::GenerateJustifiedLineRectList
    (Paragraph* paragraphPtr, LineInfo* lineInfoPtr,
     DynamicList<Size>& sizeList, DynamicList<int>& ascentList) {
  int spaceCount = 0, lineWidth = 0;
```

```
for (int charIndex = lineInfoPtr->First();
     charIndex <= lineInfoPtr->Last(); ++charIndex) {
  CharInfo charInfo =
    charList[paragraphPtr->First() + charIndex];
```

We include every character on the line in `lineWidth`, except spaces and newlines.

```
  if (charInfo.Char() == Space) {
    ++spaceCount;
  }
  else if (charInfo.Char() != NewLine) {
    lineWidth += sizeList[charIndex].Width();
  }
}

if ((charList[paragraphPtr->First()+lineInfoPtr->Last()].Char()
    != Space) &&
    (charList[paragraphPtr->First()+lineInfoPtr->Last()].Char()
    !=NewLine)) {
  lineWidth += sizeList[lineInfoPtr->Last()].Width();
}
```

Similar to the previous left-alignment case, the leftmost position in justified alignment is always zero. If there is at least one space on the line, we calculate the width of the spaces by dividing the difference between the page and text width with the number of spaces. We need to check that the number of spaces is greater than zero. Otherwise, we would be dividing by zero. On the other hand, if the number of spaces is zero, we do not need the space width.

```
int leftPos = 0, spaceWidth;
if (spaceCount > 0) {
  spaceWidth = (PageInnerWidth() - lineWidth) / spaceCount;
}

for (int charIndex = lineInfoPtr->First();
     charIndex <= lineInfoPtr->Last(); ++charIndex) {
  Size charSize = sizeList[charIndex];
  int ascent = ascentList[charIndex], charWidth;
```

If the character is a space, we use the calculated space width instead of its actual width.

```
  if (charList[paragraphPtr->First() + charIndex].Char() ==
      Space) {
    charWidth = spaceWidth;
  }
  else {
    charWidth = charSize.Width();
  }
```

```
    int topPos =
      lineInfoPtr->Top() + lineInfoPtr->Ascent() - ascent;
    charList[paragraphPtr->First() + charIndex].CharRect() =
      Rect(leftPos, topPos, leftPos + charWidth,
          topPos + charSize.Height());
    leftPos += charWidth;
  }
}
```

Invalidate rectangle set generation

Finally, we need to invalidate the set of rectangles that have been changed. There are two cases to be considered. First, we have the rectangles themselves. We iterate through the character list, and for each character we compare its previous and current rectangle, and invalidate both of them if they differ (which causes both their areas to be repainted). Remember that invalidate means that we prepare the areas to be repainted next time the window is updated. Then we to look into the line list and add the areas to the left and right of the text on the line, if present.

```
    void WordDocument::GenerateRepaintSet(Paragraph* paragraphPtr,
                              DynamicList<CharInfo>& prevCharList) {
  Point topLeft(0, paragraphPtr->Top());

  for (int charIndex = paragraphPtr->First();
       charIndex <= paragraphPtr->Last(); ++ charIndex) {
    Rect prevRect =
      prevCharList[charIndex - paragraphPtr->First()].CharRect(),
        currRect = charList[charIndex].CharRect();

    if (prevRect != currRect) {
      Invalidate(topLeft + prevRect);
      Invalidate(topLeft + currRect);
    }
  }
  int pageWidth = PageInnerWidth();

  for (LineInfo* lineInfoPtr : paragraphPtr->LinePtrList()) {
    Rect firstRect = charList[paragraphPtr->First() +
                          lineInfoPtr->First()].CharRect();

    if (firstRect.Left() > 0) {
      Rect leftRect(0, lineInfoPtr->Top(), firstRect.Left(),
                lineInfoPtr->Top() + lineInfoPtr->Height());
      Invalidate(topLeft + leftRect);
    }
```

```
      Rect lastRect = charList[paragraphPtr->First() +
                          lineInfoPtr->Last()].CharRect();

    if (lastRect.Right() < pageWidth) {
      Rect rightRect(lastRect.Right(), lineInfoPtr->Top(),
            pageWidth, lineInfoPtr->Top()+lineInfoPtr->Height());
      Invalidate(topLeft + rightRect);
    }
  }
}
```

Summary

In this chapter, we finished the development of our word processor by looking into keyboard handling and character calculation. In Chapter 8, *Building a Spreadsheet Application*, we will start developing a spreadsheet program.

8
Building a Spreadsheet Application

In this chapter, we will start developing the last application of this book–a spreadsheet program capable of calculating numerical expressions as well as cutting and pasting cells with relative references. Similar to the word processor in the previous chapters, the spreadsheet program cuts and pastes ASCII and Unicode text as well as application-specific information. Moreover, it is possible to change the font and color of the cells and their horizontal and vertical alignment.

In this chapter, we will look at the following:

- Mouse and keyboard input
- Drawing a spreadsheet
- Saving and loading the spreadsheet
- Cutting, copying, and pasting cell blocks
- Fonts, colors, and alignments of cell blocks

The MainWindow class

The `MainWindow` definition in this chapter looks very much like the previous definitions.

MainWindow.cpp

```
#include "..\\SmallWindows\\SmallWindows.h"
#include "Token.h"
#include "Error.h"
#include "Scanner.h"
```

```
#include "TreeNode.h"
#include "Parser.h"
#include "Cell.h"
#include "CalcDocument.h"

void MainWindow(vector<String> /* argumentList */,
                WindowShow windowShow) {
  Application::ApplicationName() = TEXT("Calc");
  Application::MainWindowPtr() = new CalcDocument(windowShow);
}
```

The CalcDocument class

The CalcDocument class is the main class of the application. It catches mouse and keyboard events, handles scrolling and painting, and processes menu actions. However, the cell-level operations are handled by the Cell class, which we will cover in Chapter 9, *Formula Interpretation*.

The user can mark one or several cells, in which case, the private field calcMode is set to Mark. The user can also edit the text in one cell, in which case the calcMode field is set to Edit. Similar to the word processor in the previous chapters, we refer to the current value of the calcMode field in expressions such as **in mark mode** and **in edit mode**.

```
class CalcDocument : public StandardDocument {
  public:
    CalcDocument(WindowShow windowShow);
```

The OnMouseDown, OnMouseMove, and OnDoubleClick methods catch the mouse actions in the same way as in the previous applications. Note that we do not override the OnMouseUp method. Contrary to the word processor of Chapter 7, *Keyboard Input and Character Calaculation*, this application remains in the mark mode until the user actually inputs a character, even if they mark only one cell. The user can also mark several cells by dragging the mouse.

```
    void OnMouseDown(MouseButton mouseButtons, Point mousePoint,
                     bool shiftPressed, bool controlPressed);
    void OnMouseMove(MouseButton mouseButtons, Point mousePoint,
                     bool shiftPressed, bool controlPressed);
    void OnDoubleClick(MouseButton mouseButtons, Point mousePoint,
                       bool shiftPressed, bool controlPressed);
    void OnMouseUp(MouseButton mouseButtons, Point mousePoint,
                   bool shiftPressed, bool controlPressed);
```

The OnHorizontalScroll and OnVerticalScroll methods are called when the user changes the scroll bars. In the previous applications, we did not override these functions, but in this application, we want each scroll movement to result in a movement of an exact number of cells. Besides, in the StandardDocument constructor call, we use the LogicalWithoutScroll coordinate system in order to be able to handle the row and column headers of the spreadsheet, which are always located at the top and to the left of the client area regardless of the scroll bar settings. This implies that we have to handle scroll bar movements manually.

```
virtual void OnHorizontalScroll(WORD flags, WORD x);
virtual void OnVerticalScroll(WORD flags, WORD y);
```

The user can mark all cells by clicking on the **all** box in the top-left corner (ClickAll), all cells in a column by clicking on the column header (ClickCol), all cells in a row by clicking on the row header (ClickRow), or just one of the cells (ClickCell) by clicking on the cell.

```
enum ClickArea {ClickAll, ClickRow, ClickColumn, ClickCell};
```

The GetMouseLocation method analyzes a mouse click and returns one of the ClickArea values. If the user clicks on the right of the spreadsheet, the rightmost cell on the row is selected, and if they click below the spreadsheet, the cell at the bottom of the column is selected. The Reference class is defined in Chapter 12, *The Auxiliary Classes*.

```
ClickArea GetMouseLocation(Point mousePoint,
                           Reference& cellRef) const;
```

The MarkBlock method marks the blocks in the click area depending on the marks.

```
void MarkBlock(ClickArea clickArea, Reference newFirstMarkRef,
               Reference newLastMarkRef);
```

The OnDraw method draws the row and column header as well as the cells themselves. In the edit mode, the UpdateCaret method sets the caret in the cell being edited.

```
void OnDraw(Graphics& graphics, DrawMode drawMode) const;
void UpdateCaret();
```

When the user marks cells with the keyboard, the latest marked cell will always be visible. The IsCellVisible method returns true if it is visible, while the MakeCellVisible method makes sure it is visible by scrolling, if necessary.

The `MakeCellVisible` method without parameters calls the `MakeCellVisible` method with the parameter with the edited cell, or the last marked cell, depending on whether the application holds the `edit` or `mark` mode.

```
bool IsCellVisible(Reference cellRef) const;
void MakeCellVisible();
void MakeCellVisible(Reference cellRect);
```

When the user finishes input text in a cell, the `ToMarkMode` method is called, which tries to change the application mode from `edit` to `mark`. It returns `false` if the input fails (if a formula with syntax error has been input):

```
bool ToMarkMode();
```

The `Remark` method is called when the user has marked one or several cells. In order to avoid dazzle, it does not mark already marked cells:

```
void Remark(Reference newFirstRef, Reference newLastRef);
```

The `OnChar` method is called when the user inputs a character in `mark` mode; the application is changed to `edit` mode:

```
void OnChar(TCHAR tChar);
```

The `OnKeyDown` method calls one of the specific key handling methods, which changes the caret position in the `edit` mode and changes the cell markings in the `mark` mode:

```
bool OnKeyDown(WORD key, bool shiftPressed,
               bool controlPressed);
void OnLeftArrowKey(bool shiftPressed);
void OnRightArrowKey(bool shiftPressed);
void OnUpArrowKey(bool shiftPressed);
void OnDownArrowKey(bool shiftPressed);
void OnHomeKey(bool shiftPressed, bool controlPressed);
void OnEndKey(bool shiftPressed, bool controlPressed);
```

The `OnReturnKey` and `OnTabulatorKey` methods finish the input in the `edit` mode (unless a syntax error occurs) and moves the mark position one step down (*Return*), to the left (*Shift + Tab*) or to the right (*Tab*). However, in case of an error, an error message box is displayed and the `edit` mode remains. The only way for the user to finish the input of a formula with a syntax error is to press the *Esc* key, in which case the `OnEscapeKey` method is called and the cell's value is reset to the value which it held at the beginning of the input:

```
void OnReturnKey();
void OnTabulatorKey(bool shiftPressed);
void OnEscapeKey();
```

The `OnDeleteKey` and `OnBackspaceKey` methods remove the current character from the edit mode and clear the marked cells in the `mark` mode:

```
void OnDeleteKey();
void OnBackspaceKey();
```

Similar to the previous applications, the `ClearDocument` method is called when the user selects the **New** menu item, the `ReadDocumentFromStream` method is called when they select the **Open** menu item, and the `WriteDocumentToStream` method is called when they select the **Save** or **Save As** menu items:

```
void ClearDocument();
bool ReadDocumentFromStream(String name, istream& inStream);
bool WriteDocumentToStream(String name, ostream& outStream)
                      const;
```

A text that begins with an equal sign (=) followed by a numerical expression with cell references is regarded as a **formula**. Technically, an equal sign followed by something other than a numerical expression is also considered a formula. However, in that case, it is a formula with a syntax error. When the user inputs a formula, the cells referred to in the formula constitute the cell's **source set**. The **target set** of a cell is made up by the cells that have it at a source (the sets are more exactly defined at the end of this chapter). The `WriteSetMapToStream` and `ReadSetMapFromStream` methods write and read the source and target set maps:

```
static bool WriteSetMapToStream(const map<Reference,
            set<Reference>>& setMap, ostream& outStream);
static bool ReadSetMapFromStream(map<Reference,set<Reference>>
                      &setMap, istream& inStream);
```

In this application, we overwrite the methods `IsCopyAsciiReady`, `IsCopyUnicodeReady`, and `IsCopyGenericReady` from the `StandardDocument` class. They are called by the `OnCopy` method in the `StandardDocument` class:

```
bool CopyEnable() const;
bool IsCopyAsciiReady() const {return true;}
bool IsCopyUnicodeReady() const {return true;}
bool IsCopyGenericReady(int format) const {return true;}
```

It may seem strange that both the `CopyEnable` method and the three more specific enable methods are overridden. However, the `CopyEnable` method returns `true` if the application is ready for copying (which it is in the `mark` mode), while the other methods are called by the `OnCopy` method in the `StandardDocument` class to decide whether the application is ready to copy in the given format.

Their default implementation is to return `false`, but we need to override them, as it is always possible to copy the marked cells in `mark` mode:

```
void CopyAscii(vector<String>& textList) const;
void CopyUnicode(vector<String>& textList) const;
void CopyGeneric(int format, InfoList& infoList) const;
```

We could override the `PasteEnable` method from the `StandardDocument` class in the same way we override the `CopyEnable` method. However, in this application, we need some finer testing. Therefore, we override the `IsPasteAsciiReady`, `IsPasteUnicodeReady`, and `IsPasteGenericReady` methods instead. In the word processor of the previous chapters, we could always paste text, irrespective of the number of characters or paragraphs. In this application, however, we need to check whether the block to be pasted fits in the spreadsheet:

```
bool IsPasteAsciiReady(const vector<String>& textList) const;
bool IsPasteUnicodeReady(const vector<String>& textList)const;
bool IsPasteGenericReady(int format, InfoList& infoList)const;
```

Similar to the word processor, we override the `PasteAscii`, `PasteUnicode`, and `PasteGeneric` methods. Remember that these methods are called in the order in which the formats are given in the list in the `CalcDocument` constructor call. When the corresponding enable method `IsPasteAsciiReady`, `IsPasteUnicodeReady`, or `IsPasteGenericReady` returns `true`, the `PasteAscii`, `PasteUnicode`, or `PasteGeneric` method is called. Only the first paste method is called. If none of the enable methods returns `true`, none of the paste methods is called:

```
void PasteAscii(const vector<String>& textList);
void PasteUnicode(const vector<String>& textList);
void PasteGeneric(int format, InfoList& infoList);
```

The `DeleteEnable` method always returns `true` in the `mark` mode, since there is always at least one cell marked and ready to be deleted. It returns `true` in the `edit` mode if the caret is not located at the end of the text of the edited cell. The `OnDelete` method simply calls the `OnDeleteKey` method, because the **Delete** menu item has the same effect as that of a user pressing the *Delete* key:

```
bool DeleteEnable() const;
void OnDelete();
```

The `OnFont` and `OnBackgroundColor` methods are called when the user selects the **Font** or **Background Color** menu item. They display the standard **Font** or **Color** dialog:

```
DEFINE_VOID_LISTENER(CalcDocument, OnFont);
DEFINE_VOID_LISTENER(CalcDocument, OnBackgroundColor);
```

Horizontally, the text of a cell can be aligned to left, center, right, or justified. Vertically, it can be aligned to top, center, or bottom. All the radio methods call the `IsHorizontalAlignment` or `IsVerticalAlignment` methods, and all the selection methods call the `SetHorizontalAlignment` or `SetVerticalAlignment` methods:

```
DEFINE_BOOL_LISTENER(CalcDocument, HorizontalLeftRadio);
DEFINE_BOOL_LISTENER(CalcDocument, HorizontalCenterRadio);
DEFINE_BOOL_LISTENER(CalcDocument, HorizontalRightRadio);
DEFINE_BOOL_LISTENER(CalcDocument, HorizontalJustifiedRadio);

DEFINE_VOID_LISTENER(CalcDocument, OnHorizontalLeft);
DEFINE_VOID_LISTENER(CalcDocument, OnHorizontalCenter);
DEFINE_VOID_LISTENER(CalcDocument, OnHorizontalRight);
DEFINE_VOID_LISTENER(CalcDocument, OnHorizontalJustified);

bool IsHorizontalAlignment(Alignment alignment) const;
void SetHorizontalAlignment(Alignment alignment);

DEFINE_BOOL_LISTENER(CalcDocument, VerticalTopRadio);
DEFINE_BOOL_LISTENER(CalcDocument, VerticalCenterRadio);
DEFINE_BOOL_LISTENER(CalcDocument, VerticalBottomRadio);

DEFINE_VOID_LISTENER(CalcDocument, OnVerticalTop);
DEFINE_VOID_LISTENER(CalcDocument, OnVerticalCenter);
DEFINE_VOID_LISTENER(CalcDocument, OnVerticalBottom);

bool IsVerticalAlignment(Alignment alignment) const;
void SetVerticalAlignment(Alignment alignment);
```

The `InterpretEditCell` method interprets the cell after the user has finished the input and creates a **syntax tree** (described in Chapter 9, *Formula Interpretation*) in the case of a formula (or throws an exception in the case of syntax error). The `IsCircular` method returns `true` if the cell is part of a circular reference (the cell formula refers to itself, directly or indirectly). The `RemoveTargetSetMap` method removes the targets of the cell, and the `AddTargetSetMap` method adds targets to the cell. The `EvaluateCell` method evaluates the value of one cell, while the `EvaluateRecursive` method recursively evaluates the values of all its target cells. Finally, the `InvalidateCell` method invalidates the cell so that it can be redrawn later:

```
bool InterpretEditCell();
bool IsCircular(Reference cellRef, set<Reference>& targetSet);
void RemoveTargetSetMap(Reference cellRef);
void AddTargetSetMap(Reference cellRef,
                     set<Reference>& newSourceSet);
void InvalidateCell(Reference cellRef);
```

```
    void EvaluateRecursive(Reference cellRef,
                          set<Reference>& invalidateSet);
    void EvaluateCell(Reference cellRef);
```

As mentioned at the beginning of this section, the `calcMode` method is set to `Mark` or `Edit`, and we refer to its current value as **in mark mode** and **in edit mode**:

```
private:
    enum CalcMode {Edit, Mark} calcMode = Mark;
```

The `markOk` field is set by the `OnMouseDown` method to signal the `OnMouseMove` method that it is clear to mark cells:

```
    bool markOk;
```

The `firstMarkRef` and `lastMarkRef` fields refer to the first and last marked cell in the spreadsheet in the `mark` mode. Note that they refer to their chronological order rather than their physical order, which means that the first marked reference can be larger than the last marked reference. When necessary, in some methods, the minimum and maximum references are calculated:

```
    Reference firstMarkRef, lastMarkRef, editRef;
```

In the `edit` mode, `editRef` refers to the cell currently edited and `editIndex` to the index of the next input position in the cell text (and the caret position):

```
    int editIndex;
```

The `cellMatrix` field holds the spreadsheet of the application. `Rows` and `Cols` are constant values and `Cell` is the class holding the information of each cell. `Matrix` is defined in `Chapter 9`, *Formula Interpretation*.

```
    Matrix<Rows,Cols,Cell> cellMatrix;
```

When the user inputs a formula in a cell, each reference in the formula becomes a source. In the same way, each of the source cells is given a cell as a target. The source and target sets of the cells are stored in the `sourceSetMap` and `targetSetMap` methods:

```
    map<Reference,set<Reference>> sourceSetMap, targetSetMap;
```

The value of the `CalcFormat` method used when identifying cut, copy, and paste format is arbitrarily chosen to be 1003:

```
    static const unsigned int CalcFormat = 1003;
```

When the user finishes the input of a cell with the *Esc* key, the previous content of the cell (what was stored in the cell before the input began) gets stored in the `prevCell` variable and is copied back to the cell:

```
        Cell prevCell;
    };
```

CalcDocument.cpp

```
    #include "..\\SmallWindows\\SmallWindows.h"
    #include "Token.h"
    #include "Error.h"
    #include "Scanner.h"
    #include "TreeNode.h"
    #include "Parser.h"
    #include "Cell.h"
    #include "CalcDocument.h"
```

The constructor calls the `StandardDocument` constructor in the same way as in the word processor of the previous chapters. However, note that we choose the `LogicalWithoutScroll` coordinate system (in the word processor, we chose `LogicalWithScroll`). This implies that the coordinates of the client area are not updated when the user changes the scroll bar settings. Instead, we have to catch the scroll bar movements with the `OnHorizontalScroll` and `OnVerticalScroll` methods. This is because the row and column headers are always placed at the top and to the left of the client area, regardless of the current scroll bar settings. Besides, we also want the scrolling to result in exact row and column movements. We also give `false` as the seventh parameter, indicating that we omit the **Print** and **Print Preview** file items in the **File** menu in this application:

```
    CalcDocument::CalcDocument (WindowShow windowShow)
     :StandardDocument(LogicalWithoutScroll, USLetterPortrait,
                    TEXT("Calc Files, clc; Text Files, txt"),
                    nullptr, OverlappedWindow, windowShow,
                    {CalcFormat, UnicodeFormat, AsciiFormat},
                    {CalcFormat, UnicodeFormat, AsciiFormat}) {
```

In this application, we only add the **Format** menu besides the **File, Edit**, and **Help** standard menus to the standard menu bar. The **Format** menu holds the **Font** and **Background Color** items as well as the sub menus **Horizontal Alignment** and **Vertical Alignment**.

```
    Menu menuBar(this);
    menuBar.AddMenu(StandardFileMenu(false));
    menuBar.AddMenu(StandardEditMenu());
```

```
Menu formatMenu(this, TEXT("F&ormat"));
formatMenu.AddItem(TEXT("&Font ...\tCtrl+F"), OnFont);
formatMenu.AddItem(TEXT("&Background Color ...\tCtrl+B"),
                OnBackgroundColor);

Menu horizontalMenu(this, TEXT("&Horizontal Alignment"));
horizontalMenu.AddItem(TEXT("&Left"), OnHorizontalLeft,
                nullptr, nullptr, HorizontalLeftRadio);
horizontalMenu.AddItem(TEXT("&Center"), OnHorizontalCenter,
                nullptr, nullptr, HorizontalCenterRadio);
horizontalMenu.AddItem(TEXT("&Right"), OnHorizontalRight,
                nullptr, nullptr, HorizontalRightRadio);
horizontalMenu.AddItem(TEXT("&Justified"),OnHorizontalJustified,
                nullptr, nullptr, HorizontalJustifiedRadio);
Menu verticalMenu(this, TEXT("&Vertical Alignment"));
verticalMenu.AddItem(TEXT("&Top"), OnVerticalTop,
                nullptr, nullptr, VerticalTopRadio);
verticalMenu.AddItem(TEXT("&Center"), OnVerticalCenter,
                nullptr, nullptr, VerticalCenterRadio);

verticalMenu.AddItem(TEXT("&Bottom"), OnVerticalBottom,
                nullptr, nullptr, VerticalBottomRadio);

formatMenu.AddMenu(horizontalMenu);
formatMenu.AddMenu(verticalMenu);
menuBar.AddMenu(formatMenu);

menuBar.AddMenu(StandardHelpMenu());
SetMenuBar(menuBar);
```

The `GenerateCaretList` method is called for each cell in the spreadsheet, even though every cell is empty to start with. However, there is an extra caret rectangle generated for the position to the right of the text, which we need in case the user double-clicks on an empty cell. If they do, we use the caret list to find the index of the character clicked on (which naturally is zero for an empty cell):

```
for (int row = 0; row < Rows; ++row) {
  for (int col = 0; col < Cols; ++col) {
    cellMatrix[Reference(row, col)].GenerateCaretList(this);
  }
}
```

Mouse input

The OnMouseDown and OnMouseMove methods look up the part of the spreadsheet with the mouse position and mark the appropriate set of cells. If the user inputs a formula with a syntax error, it is not possible to change the mode from edit to mark, so an error message is displayed in a message box, and the edit mode remains as it is. In that case, the markOk method is set to false, indicating that the OnMouseMove and OnDoubleClick methods will take no actions:

```
void CalcDocument::OnMouseDown(MouseButton mouseButtons,
                Point mousePoint, bool shiftPressed /*=false*/,
                bool controlPressed /* = false */) {
  if ((calcMode == Mark) || ToMarkMode()) {
    markOk = true;
    Reference newFirstMarkRef;
    ClickArea clickArea =
      GetMouseLocation(mousePoint, newFirstMarkRef);
    MarkBlock(clickArea, newFirstMarkRef, newFirstMarkRef);
    UpdateCaret();
  }
  else {
    markOk = false;
  }
}
```

Note that the OnMouseMove method only takes action if the markOk method is set to true in the OnMouseDown method. Since the OnMouseDown method is always called before the OnMouseMove method, the markOk method is always properly set. One difference between the OnMouseDown and OnMouseMove methods is that the OnMouseDown method sets the first and last marked cell reference, while the OnMouseMove method only sets the last marked cell reference:

```
void CalcDocument::OnMouseMove(MouseButton mouseButtons,
                Point mousePoint, bool shiftPressed /*=false*/,
                bool controlPressed /* = false */) {
  if ((mouseButtons == LeftButton) && markOk) {
    Reference newLastMarkRef;
    ClickArea clickArea =
      GetMouseLocation(mousePoint, newLastMarkRef);
    MarkBlock(clickArea, firstMarkRef, newLastMarkRef);
  }
}
```

When the user double-clicks, the input position (and caret) is set to the character clicked on. We look up the clicked area in the same way as in the OnMouseDown and OnMouseMove methods. However, the double-click only takes effect if the user clicks on a cell, not the all-box or one of the row or column headers. We mark the clicked cell, set the application to the edit mode, and extract the edit index from the cell by calling the MouseToIndex method:

```
void CalcDocument::OnDoubleClick(MouseButton mouseButtons,
                   Point mousePoint, bool shiftPressed /*=false*/,
                   bool controlPressed /* = false */) {
  if ((mouseButtons == LeftButton) && markOk) {
    ClickArea clickArea = GetMouseLocation(mousePoint, editRef);

    if (clickArea == ClickCell) {
      calcMode = Edit;
      Cell& editCell = cellMatrix[editRef];
      prevCell = editCell;
      editCell.DisplayFormula();
      editIndex = editCell.MouseDown(mousePoint.X() % ColWidth);
      InvalidateCell(editRef);
      UpdateWindow();
      UpdateCaret();
    }
  }
}
```

Scrolling and marking

The OnHorizontalScroll and OnVerticalScroll methods are called when the user changes the scroll bar settings. We adjust the position to the nearest column or row and set the scroll position. These methods (together with GetMouseLocation) are the reason we chose the LogicalWithoutScroll coordinate system in the CalcDocument constructor call:

```
void CalcDocument::OnHorizontalScroll(WORD flags, WORD x) {
  int col = x / ColWidth;
  SetHorizontalScrollPosition(col * ColWidth);
}

void CalcDocument::OnVerticalScroll(WORD flags, WORD y) {
  int row = y / RowHeight;
  SetVerticalScrollPosition(row * RowHeight);
}
```

The `GetMouseLocation` method takes the position of a mouse click and returns one of the four areas of the client window: the all-box in the top-left corner (`ClickAll`), one of the column headers (`ClickCol`), one of the row headers (`ClickRow`), or one of the cells in the spreadsheet (`ClickCell`). In order for these methods to work properly, we have to choose the `LogicalWithoutScroll` coordinate system in the `CalcDocument` constructor call. We must be able to find the mouse position without any regard to the current scroll settings.

If the user clicks on the all-box (where both the horizontal and vertical positions are within the header dimension), we return the `ClickAll` method:

```
CalcDocument::ClickArea CalcDocument::GetMouseLocation
                       (Point mousePoint, Reference& cellRef) const {
  if ((mousePoint.X() <= HeaderWidth) &&
      (mousePoint.Y() <= HeaderHeight)) {
    return ClickAll;
  }
```

If the mouse click is not located within the all-box but within the header width, we return the `ClickRow` method and set the cell reference to the row clicked on. If the mouse click is below the bottom row, the bottom row is selected:

```
  else if (mousePoint.X() <= HeaderWidth) {
    mousePoint.Y() += GetVerticalScrollPosition() - HeaderHeight;
    cellRef = Reference(min(Rows-1, mousePoint.Y()/RowHeight), 0);
    return ClickRow;
  }
```

If the mouse click is not located within the all-box or in a row header but within the header height, we return the `ClickCol` method and set the cell reference to the column clicked on. If the mouse click is to the right of the rightmost column, the rightmost column is selected:

```
  else if (mousePoint.Y() <= HeaderHeight) {
    mousePoint.X() += GetHorizontalScrollPosition() - HeaderWidth;
    cellRef = Reference(0, min(Cols - 1,
                                mousePoint.X() / ColWidth));
    return ClickColumn;
  }
```

If the mouse click is not located within the all-box or at a row or column header, we return the `ClickCell` method and set the cell reference to the cell clicked on. If the mouse click is below the bottom row, the bottom row is selected, and if the mouse click is to the right of the rightmost column, the rightmost column selected:

```
    else {
      mousePoint.X() += GetHorizontalScrollPosition() - HeaderWidth;
      mousePoint.Y() += GetVerticalScrollPosition() - HeaderHeight;
      cellRef = Reference(min(Rows - 1, mousePoint.Y() / RowHeight),
                          min(Cols - 1, mousePoint.X() / ColWidth));
      return ClickCell;
    }
  }
}
```

Here is an outline of the different parts of the spreadsheet:

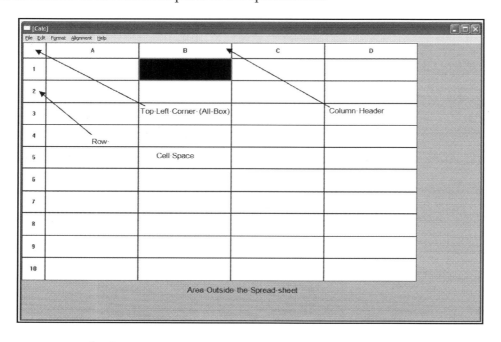

The `MarkBlock` method marks a part of the spreadsheet due to the `clickArea` parameter:

```
void CalcDocument::MarkBlock(ClickArea clickArea,
        Reference newFirstMarkRef, Reference newLastMarkRef) {
  switch (clickArea) {
```

If the user clicks on the all-box, all cells in the spreadsheet are marked:

```
    case ClickAll:
      Remark(ZeroReference, Reference(Rows - 1, Cols - 1));
      break;
```

If they click on a row, all cells in that row are marked:

```
case ClickRow:
  Remark(Reference(newFirstMarkRef.Row(), 0),
         Reference(newLastMarkRef.Row(), Cols - 1));
  break;
```

If they click on a column, all cells in that column are marked:

```
case ClickColumn:
  Remark(Reference(0, newFirstMarkRef.Col()),
         Reference(Rows - 1, newLastMarkRef.Col()));
  break;
```

If they click on a cell, only that cell gets marked:

```
case ClickCell:
  Remark(newFirstMarkRef, newLastMarkRef);
  break;
  }
}
```

Painting

The OnDraw method is called when the window client area needs to be repainted partly or completely. The client area can be divided into five parts as outlined earlier: the top-left corner, the row header, the column header, the cell space, and the area outside the spreadsheet:

```
void CalcDocument::OnDraw(Graphics& graphics,
                          DrawMode /* drawMode */) const {
  int horizontalScroll = GetHorizontalScrollPosition(),
      verticalScroll = GetVerticalScrollPosition();
```

We use the scroll bar settings to find the top and leftmost row and column. We cannot simply draw all cells (unless the scroll bar settings are zero) since it would overwrite the row or column headers:

```
  int startRow = horizontalScroll / RowHeight,
      startCol = verticalScroll / ColWidth;
```

The all-box is simply a rectangle:

```
  graphics.DrawRectangle(Rect(0, 0, HeaderWidth, HeaderHeight),
                         Black);
```

When drawing the column headers, we calculate the horizontal position of the cell's left border by multiplying the column index by the column width. We also need to subtract the current setting of the horizontal scroll bar and add the width of the header. The first column has index zero and will be named A, so we add the column index to the character A in order to find its name:

```
for (int col = startCol; col < Cols; ++col) {
  int x = (col * ColWidth) - horizontalScroll + HeaderWidth;
  Rect headerRect(x, 0, x + ColWidth, HeaderHeight);
  graphics.DrawRectangle(Rect(x, 0, x + ColWidth, HeaderHeight),
                         Black);
  TCHAR buffer[] = { (TCHAR) (TEXT('A') + col), TEXT('\0') };
  graphics.DrawText(headerRect, buffer,
                    SystemFont, Black, White);
}
```

In the same way, when drawing the row headers, we calculate the vertical position of the cell's top border by multiplying the row index by the row height. We also need to subtract the current setting of the vertical scroll bar and add the height of the header:

```
for (int row = startRow; row < Rows; ++row) {
  int y = (row * RowHeight) - verticalScroll + HeaderHeight;
  Rect headerRect(0, y, HeaderWidth, y + RowHeight);
  graphics.DrawRectangle(Rect(0, y, HeaderWidth, y + RowHeight),
                         Black);
  String buffer = to_String(row + 1);
  graphics.DrawText(headerRect, buffer,
                    SystemFont, Black, White);
}
```

Since the marked cells will be inverted and the `firstMarkRef` and `lastMarkRef` methods refer to the chronological order of the marking, we calculate the minimal and maximal markings:

```
int minMarkRow = min(firstMarkRef.Row(), lastMarkRef.Row()),
    minMarkCol = min(firstMarkRef.Col(), lastMarkRef.Col()),
    maxMarkRow = max(firstMarkRef.Row(), lastMarkRef.Row()),
    maxMarkCol = max(firstMarkRef.Col(), lastMarkRef.Col());
```

Finally, we draw the cells. For the cells marked or being edited, the third `DrawCell` parameter is `true` and the cell is inversed:

```
for (int row = startRow; row < Rows; ++row) {
  for (int col = startCol; col < Cols; ++col) {
    bool edit = (calcMode == Edit) &&
                (row == editRef.Row()) && (col == editRef.Col());
```

```
      bool mark = (calcMode == Mark) &&
                  (row >= minMarkRow) && (row <= maxMarkRow) &&
                  (col >= minMarkCol) && (col <= maxMarkCol);

      Reference cellRef(row, col);
      Cell cell = cellMatrix[cellRef];
      cell.DrawCell(graphics, cellRef, edit || mark);
    }
  }
}
```

Visibility

The IsCellVisible method returns true if the cell is visible in the window's client area. The index of the first and last visible row and column is calculated from the current scroll bar settings. The given cell reference is then compared to the references of the visible cells:

```
bool CalcDocument::IsCellVisible(Reference cellRef) const{
  int horizontalScrollPos = GetHorizontalScrollPosition(),
      horizontalScrollPage = GetHorizontalScrollPageWidth();
  int firstVisibleRow = horizontalScrollPos / RowHeight;
  int lastVisibleRow = firstVisibleRow +
                     (horizontalScrollPage / RowHeight);

  int verticalScrollPos = GetVerticalScrollPosition(),
      verticalScrollPage = GetVerticalScrollPageHeight();
  int firstVisibleCol = verticalScrollPos / ColWidth;
  int lastVisibleCol = firstVisibleCol +
                     (verticalScrollPage / ColWidth);

  int row = cellRef.Row(), col = cellRef.Col();
  return (row >= firstVisibleRow) && (row <= lastVisibleRow) &&
         (col >= firstVisibleCol) && (col <= lastVisibleCol);
}
```

The MakeCellVisible method makes the cell being edited visible in edit mode and the last marked cell visible in the mark mode:

```
void CalcDocument::MakeCellVisible() {
  switch (calcMode) {
    case Edit:
      MakeCellVisible(editRef);
      break;
```

```
        case Mark:
          MakeCellVisible(lastMarkRef);
          break;
      }
    }
```

The `MakeCellVisible` method makes the cell visible by comparing it to the current scroll bar settings. If necessary, it changes the scroll bar settings:

```
void CalcDocument::MakeCellVisible(Reference cellRef) {
  Point topLeft(cellRef.Col() * ColWidth,
                cellRef.Row() * RowHeight);
  Rect cellRect(topLeft, Size(ColWidth, RowHeight));
  Size clientSize = GetClientSize();
```

First, we check whether the width of the spreadsheet is larger than the width of the client area, in which case it may be necessary to change the setting of the horizontal scroll bar:

```
  if (clientSize.Width() < (HeaderWidth + Cols * ColWidth)) {
    int left = GetHorizontalScrollPosition(),
        xPage = GetHorizontalScrollPageWidth();
    int right = left + xPage - 1;
```

If the cell's left border is located to the left of the client area's left border or if the cell's right border is located to the right of the client area's right border, we change the scroll bar setting, as follows:

```
    if (cellRect.Left() < left) {
      SetHorizontalScrollPosition(cellRect.Left());
      Invalidate();
      UpdateWindow();
    }
    if (cellRect.Right() > right) {
      int distance = cellRect.Right() - right;
      distance += ColWidth - distance % ColWidth;
      SetHorizontalScrollPosition(left + distance);
      Invalidate();
      UpdateWindow();
    }
  }
```

If the height of the spreadsheet is more than the height of the client area, it may be necessary to change the setting of the horizontal scroll bar:

```
  if (clientSize.Height() < (HeaderHeight + Rows * RowHeight)) {
    int top = GetHorizontalScrollPosition(),
        yPage = GetHorizontalScrollPageWidth();
    int bottom = top + yPage - 1;
```

If the cell's top border is located above the client area's top border or if the cell's bottom border is located below the client area's bottom border, we change the scroll bar settings:

```
      if (cellRect.Top() < top) {
        SetVerticalScrollPosition(cellRect.Top());
        Invalidate();
        UpdateWindow();
      }

      if (cellRect.Bottom() > bottom) {
        int distance = cellRect.Bottom() - bottom;
        distance += RowHeight - distance % RowHeight;
        SetVerticalScrollPosition(top + distance);
        Invalidate();
        UpdateWindow();
      }
    }
  }
```

Marking and updating

The `UpdateCaret` method sets the caret in `edit` mode if the edited cell is visible. Otherwise, it clears the caret. We have to check whether the cell is visible. Otherwise, the caret may be shown in one of the header areas. In the keyboard `insert` mode, the caret is a vertical bar, and in the `overwrite` mode, it is a rectangle the size of the current character.

```
    void CalcDocument::UpdateCaret() {
      if ((calcMode == Edit) && IsCellVisible(editRef)) {
        Point topLeft(HeaderWidth + (editRef.Col() * ColWidth) +
                      CellMargin, HeaderHeight + (editRef.Row() *
                      RowHeight) + CellMargin);
        Cell& editCell = cellMatrix[editRef];
        Rect caretRect = editCell.CaretList()[editIndex];

        if (GetKeyboardMode() == InsertKeyboard) {
          caretRect.Right() = caretRect.Left() + 1;
        }

        SetCaret(topLeft + caretRect);
      }
      else {
        ClearCaret();
      }
    }
```

The `ToMarkMode` method is called when the user ends the input of the text in the cell by pressing the *Return* or *Tab* key or by clicking the mouse. Its first task is to check whether the input is valid by calling the `InterpretEditCell` method, which returns `false` if the text contains a formula with a syntax error. In that case, the `edit` mode remains unchanged and `false` is returned. However, if the cell interpretation goes well, the application is set to the `mark` mode and we get `true` in return:

```
bool CalcDocument::ToMarkMode() {
  if (calcMode == Edit) {
    if (InterpretEditCell()) {
      calcMode = Mark;
      firstMarkRef = editRef;
      lastMarkRef = editRef;
      return true;
    }

    return false;
  }

  return true;
}
```

The `Remark` method unmarks the marked cells and marks the new block given by the parameters without any unnecessary updating. That is, cells already marked shall not be invalidated. Note that the first and last marked cells refer to their chronological order rather than their locations on the spreadsheet. The last row or column may be less reflective than the first one. Therefore, we introduce the minimal and maximal variables to reflect their actual locations in the spreadsheet:

```
void CalcDocument::Remark(Reference newFirstRef,
                          Reference newLastRef) {
  Reference
    minOldMarked(min(firstMarkRef.Row(), lastMarkRef.Row()),
                 min(firstMarkRef.Col(), lastMarkRef.Col())),
    maxOldMarked(max(firstMarkRef.Row(), lastMarkRef.Row()),
                 max(firstMarkRef.Col(), lastMarkRef.Col())),
    minNewMarked(min(newFirstRef.Row(), newLastRef.Row()),
                 min(newFirstRef.Col(), newLastRef.Col())),
    maxNewMarked(max(newFirstRef.Row(), newLastRef.Row()),
                 max(newFirstRef.Col(), newLastRef.Col()));
```

In the previous marked block, all cells that are not located in the new marked block are invalidated in order for them to be redrawn as unmarked cells. No old cells within the new marked blocks become invalidated:

```
for (int row = minOldMarked.Row();
      row <= maxOldMarked.Row(); ++row) {
  for (int col = minOldMarked.Col();
        col <= maxOldMarked.Col(); ++col) {
    Reference cellRef(row, col);
    if (!cellRef.Inside(minNewMarked, maxNewMarked)) {
      InvalidateCell(cellRef);
    }
  }
}
```

In the new marked block, all cells that are not located in the old marked block are invalidated in order for them to be redrawn as unmarked cells. No already marked cells become invalidated:

```
for (int row = minNewMarked.Row();
      row <= maxNewMarked.Row(); ++row) {
  for (int col = minNewMarked.Col();
        col <= maxNewMarked.Col(); ++col) {
    Reference cellRef(row, col);
    if (!cellRef.Inside(minOldMarked, maxOldMarked)) {
      InvalidateCell(Reference(row, col));
    }
  }
}
```

The first and last marked reference is set and the invalidated cells are updated:

```
  firstMarkRef = newFirstRef;
  lastMarkRef = newLastRef;
  UpdateWindow();
}
```

Keyboard input

The OnCharDown method is called every time the user presses a graphical key on the keyboard. In the mark mode, the application is changed to the edit mode, where the edit reference is set to the first marked reference, the edit index is set to zero since the start of the input resets the cell, and the prevCell variable is set as backup in case the user finishes the input by pressing the *Esc* key:

```
void CalcDocument::OnChar(TCHAR tChar) {
  if (calcMode == Mark) {
    calcMode = Edit;
    editRef = firstMarkRef;
    Remark(editRef, editRef);
```

```
      editIndex = 0;
      Cell& editCell = cellMatrix[editRef];
      prevCell = *editCell;
      editCell.Reset();
   }
```

The cell to be edited is made visible, the character is added to the text, and the caret rectangle is regenerated. Finally, the caret and window are updated, since the cell has been altered and the edit index has been updated:

```
      MakeCellVisible(editRef);
      Cell& cell = cellMatrix[editRef];
      cell.CharDown(editIndex++, tChar, GetKeyboardMode());
      cell.GenerateCaretList(this);
      InvalidateCell(editRef);
      UpdateCaret();
      UpdateWindow();
   }
```

The OnKeyDown method is called every time the user presses a key. The appropriate method is called in the case of the arrow keys, *Page Up, Page Down, Home, End, Return, Tab, Insert, Delete,* or *Backspace*:

```
bool CalcDocument::OnKeyDown(WORD key, bool shiftPressed,
                             bool controlPressed) {
  switch (key) {
    case KeyLeft:
      OnLeftArrowKey(shiftPressed);
      break;

    case KeyRight:
      OnRightArrowKey(shiftPressed);
      break;

    case KeyUp:
      OnUpArrowKey(shiftPressed);
      break;

    case KeyDown:
      OnDownArrowKey(shiftPressed);
      break;

    case KeyHome:
      OnHomeKey(shiftPressed, controlPressed);
      break;
```

```
        case KeyEnd:
          OnEndKey(shiftPressed, controlPressed);
          break;

        case KeyReturn:
          OnReturnKey();
          break;

        case KeyTabulator:
          OnTabulatorKey(shiftPressed);
          break;

        case KeyEscape:
          OnEscapeKey();
          break;

        case KeyDelete:
          OnDeleteKey();
          break;

        case KeyBackspace:
          OnBackspaceKey();
          break;
      }
    UpdateCaret();
    UpdateWindow();
    return true;
  }
```

The `OnLeftArrowKey` method is called when the user presses the left arrow key. We have three different cases to consider depending on the `edit` or `mark` mode and on whether the user presses the *Shift* key. In the `edit` mode, we make the edit cell visible, move the edit index one step to the left if it is not already at the leftmost position, and update the caret:

```
void CalcDocument::OnLeftArrowKey(bool shiftPressed) {
  switch (calcMode) {
    case Edit: {
        MakeCellVisible(editRef);
        if (editIndex > 0) {
          --editIndex;
        }
      }
      break;
```

In the `mark` mode, we have to take into consideration whether the *Shift* key is pressed. If it is not, we place the marked block (both the first and last marked cells) one step to the left of the last marked cell unless it is already at the leftmost column:

```
case Mark:
  if (lastMarkRef.Col() > 0) {
    if (!shiftPressed) {
      Reference newLastMarkRef(lastMarkRef.Row(),
                               lastMarkRef.Col() - 1);
      MakeCellVisible(newLastMarkRef);
      Remark(newLastMarkRef, newLastMarkRef);
    }
```

If the *Shift* key is pressed, we move the last marked cell one step to the left unless it is already at the leftmost position. The first marked cell is not affected:

```
    else {
      Reference newLastRefMark(lastMarkRef.Row(),
                               lastMarkRef.Col() - 1);
      MakeCellVisible(newLastRefMark);
      Remark(firstMarkRef, newLastRefMark);
    }
  }
  break;
  }
}
```

The `OnRightArrowKey` method is called when the user presses the right arrow key. It works similarly to the `OnLeftArrowKey` method. In the `edit` mode, we make the edit cell visible, move the edit index one step to the right if it is not already at the rightmost position, and update the caret:

```
void CalcDocument::OnRightArrowKey(bool shiftPressed) {
  switch (calcMode) {
    case Edit: {
        MakeCellVisible(editRef);

        if (editIndex <
            ((int) cellMatrix[editRef].GetText().length())) {
          ++editIndex;
        }
      }
      break;
```

In the `mark` mode, we have to take into consideration whether the *Shift* key is pressed. If it is not pressed, we place the marked block one step to the right of the first marked cell, unless it already is at the rightmost column:

```
    case Mark:
      if (lastMarkRef.Col() < (Cols - 1)) {
        if (!shiftPressed) {
          Reference newLastMarkRef(lastMarkRef.Row(),
                                   lastMarkRef.Col() + 1);
          MakeCellVisible(newLastMarkRef);
          Remark(newLastMarkRef, newLastMarkRef);
        }
```

If the *Shift* key is pressed, we move the last marked cell one step to the right unless it is already at the rightmost position. The first marked cell is not affected:

```
        else {
          Reference newLastRefMark(lastMarkRef.Row(),
                                   lastMarkRef.Col() + 1);
          MakeCellVisible(newLastRefMark);
          Remark(firstMarkRef, newLastRefMark);
        }
      }
      break;
  }
}
```

The `OnUpArrowKey` method is called when the user presses the up arrow key. In the `edit` mode, no action is taken:

```
void CalcDocument::OnUpArrowKey(bool shiftPressed) {
  switch (calcMode) {
    case Edit:
      break;
```

If the *Shift* key is not pressed in the `mark` mode, we place the marked cell one step up relative to the first marked cell if it is not already in the top row. In that case, we place the marked block in the first marked cell:

```
    case Mark:
      if (lastMarkRef.Row() > 0) {
        if (!shiftPressed) {
          Reference newLastMarkRef(lastMarkRef.Row() - 1,
                                   lastMarkRef.Col());
          MakeCellVisible(newLastMarkRef);
          Remark(newLastMarkRef, newLastMarkRef);
        }
```

If the *Shift* key is pressed, we move the last marked cell one step up unless it is already in the top row. The first marked cell is not affected:

```
      else {
        Reference newLastRefMark(lastMarkRef.Row() - 1,
                                 lastMarkRef.Col());
        MakeCellVisible(newLastRefMark);
        Remark(firstMarkRef, newLastRefMark);
      }
    }
    break;
  }
}
```

The `OnDownArrowKey` method is called when the user presses the down arrow key. It works in a way similar to the `OnUpArrowKey` method. In the `edit` mode, no action is taken:

```
void CalcDocument::OnDownArrowKey(bool shiftPressed) {
  switch (calcMode) {
    case Edit:
      break;
```

If the *Shift* key is not pressed in the `mark` mode, we place the marked block one step relatively under the first marked cell, unless it already is in the bottom row:

```
    case Mark:
      if (lastMarkRef.Row() < (Rows - 1)) {
        if (!shiftPressed) {
          Reference newMarkRef(lastMarkRef.Row() + 1,
                               lastMarkRef.Col());
          MakeCellVisible(newMarkRef);
          Remark(newMarkRef, newMarkRef);
        }
```

If the *Shift* key is pressed, we move the last marked cell one step down unless it is already in the bottom row. The first marked cell is not affected:

```
      else {
        Reference newLastRefMark(lastMarkRef.Row() + 1,
                                 lastMarkRef.Col());
        MakeCellVisible(newLastRefMark);
        Remark(firstMarkRef, newLastRefMark);
      }
    }
    break;
  }
}
```

The `OnHomeKey` method is called when the user presses the *Home* key. In the `edit` mode, we make the edit cell visible, move the edit index to the leftmost index, and update the caret:

```
void CalcDocument::OnHomeKey(bool shiftPressed,
                             bool controlPressed) {
  switch (calcMode) {
    case Edit: {
        MakeCellVisible(editRef);
        editIndex = 0;
        UpdateCaret();
      }
      break;
```

If neither the *Shift* or *Ctrl* keys is pressed in the `mark` mode, we move the marked block to the leftmost column of the first marked row. If the *Shift* key is pressed, we move the last marked cell to the leftmost column of the last marked row. The first marked cell is not affected:

```
    case Mark:
      if (!shiftPressed && !controlPressed) {
        Remark(Reference(firstMarkRef.Row(), 0),
               Reference(firstMarkRef.Row(), 0));
        MakeCellVisible(firstMarkRef);
      }
      else if (shiftPressed && !controlPressed) {
        Remark(firstMarkRef, Reference(firstMarkRef.Row(), 0));
        MakeCellVisible(lastMarkRef);
      }
```

If the *Ctrl* key is pressed, but not the *Shift* key, we move the marked block to the top-left cell. If the *Ctrl* key is not pressed, we move the last marked cell to the leftmost position in the row:

```
      else if (!shiftPressed && controlPressed) {
        Remark(ZeroReference, ZeroReference);
        MakeCellVisible(lastMarkRef);
      }
      else if (shiftPressed && controlPressed) {
        Remark(firstMarkRef, ZeroReference);
        MakeCellVisible(lastMarkRef);
      }
      break;
    }
}
```

The `OnEndKey` method is called when the user presses the *End* key, and it works in a way similar to the `OnHomeKey` method. In the `edit` mode, we make the edit cell visible, move the edit index to the rightmost index, and update the caret:

```
void CalcDocument::OnEndKey(bool shiftPressed, bool controlPressed) {
  switch (calcMode) {
    case Edit: {
        MakeCellVisible(editRef);
        editIndex = cellMatrix[editRef].GetText().length();
        UpdateCaret();
      }
      break;
```

If neither the *Shift* nor the *Ctrl* key is pressed in the `mark` mode, we move the marked block to the rightmost column of the first marked row. If the *Shift* key is pressed, we move the last marked cell to the rightmost column of the last marked row. The first marked cell is not affected:

```
    case Mark:
      if (!shiftPressed && !controlPressed) {
        Remark(Reference(firstMarkRef.Row(), Cols - 1),
               Reference(firstMarkRef.Row(), Cols - 1));
        MakeCellVisible(firstMarkRef);
      }
      else if (shiftPressed && !controlPressed) {
        Remark(firstMarkRef,
               Reference(firstMarkRef.Row(), Cols - 1));
        MakeCellVisible(lastMarkRef);
      }
```

If the *Ctrl* key is pressed, but not the *Shift* key, we move the marked block to the bottom-right cell. If the *Ctrl* key is not pressed, we move the last marked cell to the rightmost position in the row:

```
      else if (!shiftPressed && controlPressed) {
        Remark(Reference(Rows - 1, Cols - 1),
               Reference(Rows - 1, Cols - 1));
        MakeCellVisible(lastMarkRef);
      }
      else if (shiftPressed && controlPressed) {
        Remark(firstMarkRef, Reference(Rows - 1, Cols - 1));
        MakeCellVisible(lastMarkRef);
      }
      break;
  }
}
```

The *Return* key finishes the editing session unless the user has input a formula with a syntax error, in which case an error message box is displayed. The user can also finish by pressing the *Tab* key or by clicking the mouse; in either case, the `Remark` method takes care of finishing the editing process. When the editing is finished, we try to mark the cell:

```
void CalcDocument::OnReturnKey() {
  if ((calcMode == Mark) || ToMarkMode()) {
    Reference newMarkedRef(min(firstMarkRef.Row() + 1, Rows - 1),
                           firstMarkRef.Col());
    Remark(newMarkedRef, newMarkedRef);
    MakeCellVisible(newMarkedRef);
  }
}
```

The *Tab* key does almost the same thing as the *Return* key. The only difference is that the next marked cell is, if possible, the cell to right or the cell to the left (if the user pressed the *Shift* key):

```
void CalcDocument::OnTabulatorKey(bool shiftPressed) {
  if ((calcMode == Mark) || ToMarkMode()) {
    if (shiftPressed && (lastMarkRef.Col() > 0)) {
      Reference firstMarkRef(lastMarkRef.Row(),
                             firstMarkRef.Col() - 1);
      Remark(firstMarkRef, firstMarkRef);
      MakeCellVisible(firstMarkRef);
    }
    if (!shiftPressed && (lastMarkRef.Col() < (Cols - 1))) {
      Reference firstMarkRef(firstMarkRef.Row(),
                             firstMarkRef.Col() + 1);
      Remark(firstMarkRef, firstMarkRef);
      MakeCellVisible(firstMarkRef);
    }
  }
}
```

The `OnEscapeKey` method is called when the user presses the *Esc* key and resets the cell to the value of the `prevCell` variable:

```
void CalcDocument::OnEscapeKey() {
  if (calcMode == Edit) {
    Cell& editCell = cellMatrix[editRef];
    editCell = prevCell;
    InvalidateCell(editRef);
    calcMode = Mark;
    firstMarkRef = lastMarkRef = editRef;
  }
}
```

The `OnDeleteKey` method is called when the user presses the *Delete* key or selects the **Delete** menu item to delete a character in the `edit` mode or the contents of the marked block in the `mark` mode. In the `edit` mode, we delete the character of the edit index unless it is at the end of the text. In the `mark` mode, we just reset the marked cell. When the cells are reset, we need to re-evaluate their target cells recursively:

```
void CalcDocument::OnDeleteKey() {
  switch (calcMode) {
    case Edit: {
        Cell& editCell = cellMatrix[editRef];
        String& cellText = editCell.GetText();

        if (editIndex < ((int) cellText.length())) {
          String leftPart = cellText.substr(0, editIndex),
                  rightPart = cellText.substr(editIndex + 1);
          editCell.SetText(leftPart + rightPart);
          editCell.GenerateCaretList(this);
          InvalidateCell(editRef);
          UpdateWindow();
          SetDirty(true);
        }
      }
      break;

    case Mark: {
        int minMarkRow = min(firstMarkRef.Row(), lastMarkRef.Row()),
            minMarkCol = min(firstMarkRef.Col(), lastMarkRef.Col()),
            maxMarkRow = max(firstMarkRef.Row(), lastMarkRef.Row()),
            maxMarkCol = max(firstMarkRef.Col(), lastMarkRef.Col());

        set<Reference> invalidateSet;
        for (int row = minMarkRow; <= minMarkRow; ++row) {
          for (int col = minMarkCol; col <= minMarkCol; ++col) {
            Reference cellRef = Reference(row, col);
            cellMatrix[cellRef].Reset();
            EvaluateRecursive(editRef, invalidateSet);
          }
        }
        for (Reference cellRef : invalidateSet) {
          InvalidateCell(cellRef);
        }
        UpdateWindow();
        SetDirty(true);
      }
      break;
  }
}
```

The OnBackspaceKey method is called when the user presses the *Backspace* key to delete a character in a cell in the edit mode or the contents of the marked block in the mark mode. In the edit mode, we decrement the edit index and remove the character by calling the OnDeleteKey method at the new index, unless the edit position is already at the beginning of text. In the mark mode, we just call the OnDeleteKey method:

```
void CalcDocument::OnBackspaceKey() {
  switch (calcMode) {
    case Edit:
      if (editIndex > 0) {
        --editIndex;
        OnDeleteKey();
      }
      break;

    case Mark:
      OnDeleteKey();
      break;
  }
}
```

File management

Similar to the previous applications, the ClearDocument method is called by the StandardDocument class when the user selects the **New** menu item, the WriteDocumentToStream method is called when the user selects **Save** or **Save As**, and the ReadDocumentFromStream method is called when the user selects **Open** menu item.

In the ClearDocument method, every cell is cleared along with their source and target sets. When a cell is reset, its text is cleared. When it is cleared, its font and color are also cleared. Finally, the application is set to the mark mode, where the top-left cell is marked:

```
void CalcDocument::ClearDocument() {
  for (int row = 0; row < Rows; ++row) {
    for (int col = 0; col < Cols; ++col) {
      cellMatrix[Reference(row, col)].Clear();
    }
  }

  sourceSetMap.clear();
  targetSetMap.clear();
```

```
  calcMode = Mark;
  firstMarkRef.Clear();
  lastMarkRef.Clear();
}
```

The `WriteCellToStream` method is a callback function that, given a cell and an output stream, writes the cell to the stream. In the same way, the `ReadCellFromStream` method reads a cell from an input stream:

```
void WriteCellToStream(Cell cell, ostream& outStream) {
  cell.WriteCellToStream(outStream);
}

void ReadCellFromStream(Cell& cell, istream& inStream) {
  cell.ReadCellFromStream(inStream);
}
```

The `WriteDocumentToStream` and `ReadDocumentFromStream` methods write and read the spreadsheet. More specifically, they read and write the `application` mode, the edit index and reference, the mark references, the source and target sets, and the cells in the cell matrix:

```
bool CalcDocument::WriteDocumentToStream(String name,
                                           ostream& outStream)const{
  if (EndsWith(name, TEXT(".clc"))) {
    outStream.write((char*) &calcMode, sizeof calcMode);
    outStream.write((char*) &editIndex, sizeof editIndex);
    editRef.WriteReferenceToStream(outStream);
    firstMarkRef.WriteReferenceToStream(outStream);
    lastMarkRef.WriteReferenceToStream(outStream);
    prevCell.WriteCellToStream(outStream);
    WriteSetMapToStream(sourceSetMap, outStream);
    WriteSetMapToStream(targetSetMap, outStream);

    for (int row = 0; row < Rows; ++row) {
      for (int col = 0; col < Cols; ++col) {
        cellMatrix[row][col].WriteCellToStream(outStream);
      }
    }
  }
  else if (EndsWith(name, TEXT(".txt"))) {
    for (int row = 0; row < Rows; ++row) {
      if (row > 0) {
        outStream << "\n";
      }
```

```
      for (int col = 0; col < Cols; ++col) {
        if (col > 0) {
          outStream << "\t";
        }

        const Cell& cell = cellMatrix[row][col];
        String text = cell.IsFormula()
                      ? (TEXT("=") + cell.TreeToString())
                      : cell.GetText();

        for (TCHAR c : text) {
          outStream << ((char) c);
        }
      }
    }
  }

  return ((bool) outStream);
}
```

Note that we call the `MakeCellVisible` method at the end of the
`ReadDocumentFromStream` method. The idea is that the user should be able to pick up the
spreadsheet where they left it:

```
bool CalcDocument::ReadDocumentFromStream(String name,
                                          istream& inStream) {
  if (EndsWith(name, TEXT(".clc")) &&
      ReadPrintSetupInfoFromStream(inStream)){
    inStream.read((char*)&calcMode, sizeof calcMode);
    inStream.read((char*) &editIndex, sizeof editIndex);
    editRef.ReadReferenceFromStream(inStream);
    firstMarkRef.ReadReferenceFromStream(inStream);
    lastMarkRef.ReadReferenceFromStream(inStream);
    prevCell.ReadCellFromStream(inStream);
    ReadSetMapFromStream(sourceSetMap, inStream);
    ReadSetMapFromStream(targetSetMap, inStream);
    MakeCellVisible();

    for (int row = 0; row < Rows; ++row) {
      for (int col = 0; col < Cols; ++col) {
        cellMatrix[Reference(row, col)].
            ReadCellFromStream(inStream);
      }
    }
  }
```

```
    else if (EndsWith(name, TEXT(".txt"))) {
      String text;
      int row = 0, col = 0;

      while (inStream) {
        char c;
        inStream.read(&c, sizeof c);

        if (inStream) {
          switch (c) {
            case ';':
              cellMatrix[Reference(row, col++)].SetText(text);
              text.clear();
              break;

            case '\n':
              cellMatrix[Reference(row++, col)].SetText(text);
              text.clear();
              col = 0;
              break;

            default:
              text.push_back((TCHAR) c);
              break;
          }
        }
      }
    }

    return ((bool) inStream);
  }
```

The `WriteSetMapToStream` and `ReadSetMapFromStream` methods write and read the source and target sets. They are static, since they are called for both `sourceSetMap` and `targetSetMap`. For each cell in the spreadsheet, the size of the set as well as the references of the sets are written and read:

```
bool CalcDocument::WriteSetMapToStream(const
                   map<Reference,set<Reference>>& setMap,
                   ostream& outStream) {
  int mapSize = setMap.size();
  outStream.write((char*) &mapSize, sizeof mapSize);

  for (pair<Reference,set<Reference>> entry : setMap) {
    Reference cellRef = entry.first;
    cellRef.WriteReferenceToStream(outStream);
```

```
      set<Reference> set = entry.second;
      int setSize = set.size();
      outStream.write((char*) &setSize, sizeof setSize);

      for (Reference ref : set) {
        ref.WriteReferenceToStream(outStream);
      }
    }

    return ((bool) outStream);
  }

bool CalcDocument::ReadSetMapFromStream
                  (map<Reference,set<Reference>>& setMap,
                   istream& inStream) {
    int mapSize;
    inStream.read((char*) &mapSize, sizeof mapSize);

    for (int mapIndex = 0; mapIndex < mapSize; ++mapIndex) {
      Reference cellRef;
      cellRef.ReadReferenceFromStream(inStream);

      int setSize;
      inStream.read((char*) &setSize, sizeof setSize);

      set<Reference> set;
      for (int setIndex = 0; setIndex < setSize; ++setIndex) {
        Reference ref;
        ref.ReadReferenceFromStream(inStream);
        set.insert(ref);
      }

      setMap[cellRef] = set;
    }

    return ((bool) inStream);
  }
```

Cut, copy, and paste

The **Copy** menu item is enabled in the `mark` mode. Note that we do not override the `PasteEnable` method, since the `StandardDocument` class enables the **Paste** menu item if there is a clipboard buffer with one of the application formats–the `AsciiFormat`, `UnicodeFormat`, or `CalcFormat` format:

```
bool CalcDocument::CopyEnable() const {
  return (calcMode == Mark);
}
```

The `CopyAscii` method simply calls `CopyUnicode`, which in turn fills the `textList` list with the copied text. Each text in the `textList` list holds one row, and the columns are divided by semicolons (';'):

```
void CalcDocument::CopyAscii(vector<String>& textList) const {
  CopyUnicode(textList);
}
```

```
void CalcDocument::CopyUnicode(vector<String>& textList) const {
  int minMarkRow = min(firstMarkRef.Row(), lastMarkRef.Row()),
      maxMarkRow = max(firstMarkRef.Row(), lastMarkRef.Row()),
      minMarkCol = min(firstMarkRef.Col(), lastMarkRef.Col()),
      maxMarkCol = max(firstMarkRef.Col(), lastMarkRef.Col());

  for (int row = minMarkRow; row <= maxMarkRow; ++row) {
    String text;

    for (int col = minMarkCol; col <= maxMarkCol; ++col) {
      Reference markRef = Reference(row, col);
      const Cell& markCell = cellMatrix[markRef];
      text.append(((col > 0) ? TEXT(";") : TEXT("")) +
                  markCell.TreeToString());
    }

    textList.push_back(text);
  }
}
```

The `CopyGeneric` method stores the top-left position and size of the marked block and calls the `WriteCellToClipboard` method for each marked cell:

```
void CalcDocument::CopyGeneric(int /* format */,
                              InfoList& infoList) const {
  int minRow = min(firstMarkRef.Row(), lastMarkRef.Row()),
      minCol = min(firstMarkRef.Col(), lastMarkRef.Col()),
      copyRows = abs(firstMarkRef.Row() - lastMarkRef.Row()) + 1,
      copyCols = abs(firstMarkRef.Col() - lastMarkRef.Col()) + 1;

  infoList.AddValue<int>(copyRows);
  infoList.AddValue<int>(copyCols);
  infoList.AddValue<int>(minRow);
  infoList.AddValue<int>(minCol);
```

```
      for (int row = 0; row < copyRows; ++row) {
        for (int col = 0; col < copyCols; ++col) {
          Reference sourceRef(minRow + row, minCol + col);
          const Cell& cell = cellMatrix[sourceRef];
          cell.WriteCellToClipboard(infoList);
        }
      }
    }
```

The `IsPasteAsciiReady` method simply calls the `IsPasteUnicodeReady` method, which returns `true` if there is only one cell currently marked and the block to be pasted fits in the spreadsheet, or if the currently marked block has the same size as the block to be pasted. Note that in the first case, if only one cell is marked, the block to be pasted does not have to have an equal number of columns for each row, as long as they fit in the spreadsheet:

```
bool CalcDocument::IsPasteAsciiReady
                  (const vector<String>& textList) const {
  return IsPasteUnicodeReady(textList);
}
bool CalcDocument::IsPasteUnicodeReady
                  (const vector<String>& textList) const {
  int markedRows = abs(firstMarkRef.Row() - lastMarkRef.Row()) +1,
      markedCols = abs(firstMarkRef.Col() - lastMarkRef.Col()) +1,
      minMarkedRow = min(firstMarkRef.Row(), lastMarkRef.Row()),
      minMarkedCol = min(firstMarkRef.Col(), lastMarkRef.Col());
  if ((markedRows == 1) && (markedCols == 1)) {
    int copyRows = textList.size();
    int maxCopyCols = 0;
    for (String text : textList) {
      maxCopyCols = max(maxCopyCols,
                        ((int) Split(text, ';').size()));
    }
    return ((minMarkedRow + copyRows) < Rows) &&
           ((minMarkedCol + maxCopyCols) < Cols);
  }
  else {
    if (textList.size() != markedRows) {
      return false;
    }
    for (String text : textList) {
      if (((int) Split(text, ';').size()) != markedCols) {
        return false;
      }
    }
    return true;
  }
}
```

Similar to the `IsPasteUnicodeReady` method, the `IsPasteGenericReady` method returns `true` if there is only cell marked at the moment and the block to be pasted fits in the spreadsheet or if the currently marked block and the block to be pasted have the same size. However, unlike the Unicode case we saw earlier, the rows of the generic block to be pasted all have the same size:

```
bool CalcDocument::IsPasteGenericReady(int /* format */,
                                   InfoList& infoList) const {
  int markedRows = abs(firstMarkRef.Row() - lastMarkRef.Row()) +1,
      markedCols = abs(firstMarkRef.Col() - lastMarkRef.Col()) +1,
      minMarkedRow = min(firstMarkRef.Row(), lastMarkRef.Row()),
      minMarkedCol = min(firstMarkRef.Col(), lastMarkRef.Col()),
      copyRows, copyCols;

  infoList.PeekValue<int>(copyRows, 0);
  infoList.PeekValue<int>(copyCols, sizeof(int));

  return (((markedRows == copyRows)&&(markedCols == copyCols)) ||
          ((markedRows == 1) && (markedCols == 1))) &&
         ((minMarkedRow + copyRows) <= Rows) &&
         ((minMarkedCol + copyCols) <= Cols);
}
```

The `PasteAscii` method simply calls the `PasteUnicode` method that first takes a backup of the cell matrix as well as the source and target set maps, since the cells to be pasted may contain a formula with syntax errors, in which case the pasting process will be aborted. Then, it iterates through the text to be pasted and splits each row in to columns. The text of each column is copied to the pasted cell:

```
void CalcDocument::PasteAscii(const vector<String>& textList) {
  PasteUnicode(textList);
}

void CalcDocument::PasteUnicode(const vector<String>& textList) {
  Matrix<Rows,Cols,Cell> backupMatrix =
    Matrix<Rows,Cols,Cell>(cellMatrix);
  map<Reference,set<Reference>> backupSourceSetMap = sourceSetMap,
                              backupTargetSetMap = targetSetMap;

  try {
    set<Reference> invalidateSet;
    int row = min(firstMarkRef.Row(), lastMarkRef.Row()),
        minCol = min(firstMarkRef.Col(), lastMarkRef.Col());
    Reference diffRef(row, minCol);
```

```
for (String rowText : textList) {
  int col = minCol;
  vector<String> columnList = Split(rowText, ';');
```

The text of the column is interpreted, and if it holds a formula with a syntax error, an exception is thrown, stopping the iteration and restoring the backup matrix together with the source and target set maps. This is actually the reason why the `EvaluateRecursive` method fills the set of references to be invalidated instead of just invalidating them. If the pasting process fails due to a formula with a syntax error, we would not want any cells to become invalidated and updated:

```
for (String colText : columnList) {
  Reference targetRef(row, col++);
  RemoveTargetSetMap(targetRef);
  Cell& targetCell = cellMatrix[targetRef];
  targetCell.Reset();
  targetCell.SetText(colText)
  set<Reference> sourceSet;
  targetCell.InterpretCell(sourceSet);
  targetCell.GenerateCaretList(this);
```

When the text has been interpreted, we need to update the references, in case it holds a formula, by comparing the location of the marked block with the original location (from where it was copied) of the pasted block in order for the reference to be relative:

```
if (!diffRef.IsEmpty()) {
  sourceSet.clear();
  targetCell.UpdateTree(diffRef, sourceSet);
}
```

Finally, we set the source and target sets of the cell, evaluate its value, and generate its caret rectangle list. The evaluation may result in an error (missing value, reference out of range, circular reference, or division by zero), in which case an error message is stored in the cell text:

```
      AddTargetSetMap(targetRef, sourceSet);
      sourceSetMap[targetRef] = sourceSet;
      EvaluateRecursive(targetRef, invalidateSet);
      targetCell.GenerateCaretList(this);
    }
    ++row;
  }
```

The pasted cells are not invalidated until we have iterated through them and none of them has been found to hold a formula with a syntax error. Note that there may be more than just the pasted cells to be invalidated, the other cells outside the pasted block that are targets of the pasted cells, and thereby evaluated, need to be invalidated:

```
    for (Reference cellRef : invalidateSet) {
      InvalidateCell(cellRef);
    }
  }
```

If one of the pasted cells holds a formula with a syntax error, we simply restore the backup and display a message box:

```
  catch (Error error) {
    cellMatrix = backupMatrix;
    sourceSetMap = backupSourceSetMap;
    targetSetMap = backupTargetSetMap;
    MessageBox(error.ErrorText(), TEXT("Syntax Error"), Ok, Stop);
  }
}
```

The `PasteGeneric` method is simpler than the `PasteUnicode` method: since there is no need for cell interpretation (as the cell has been copied from the spreadsheet and thereby holds valid formulas), there in no need for backup and no exception is thrown:

```
void CalcDocument::PasteGeneric(int /* format */,
                                InfoList& infoList) {
  int minMarkedRow = min(firstMarkRef.Row(), lastMarkRef.Row()),
      minMarkedCol = min(firstMarkRef.Col(), lastMarkRef.Col()),
      copyRows, copyCols, minCopyRow, minCopyCol;

  infoList.GetValue<int>(copyRows);
  infoList.GetValue<int>(copyCols);
  infoList.GetValue<int>(minCopyRow);
  infoList.GetValue<int>(minCopyCol);

  Reference diffRef(minMarkedRow - minCopyRow,
                    minMarkedCol - minCopyCol);
  int maxCopyRow = minCopyRow + copyRows - 1,
      maxCopyCol = minCopyCol + copyCols - 1;
```

Each pasted cell is read from the buffer and then the source cell is assigned to it. The target set is removed and then added by the pasted cell:

```
  for (int row = minCopyRow; row <= maxCopyRow; ++row) {
    for (int col = minCopyCol; col <= maxCopyCol; ++col) {
      Cell pastedCell;
```

```
    pastedCell.ReadCellFromClipboard(infoList);

    Reference pastedRef(row, col);
    Reference targetRef = pastedRef + diffRef;

    RemoveTargetSetMap(targetRef);
    Cell& targetCell = cellMatrix[targetRef];
    targetCell = pastedCell;

    set<Reference> sourceSet;
    if (diffRef.IsEmpty()) {
      targetCell.GenerateSourceSet(sourceSet);
    }
    else {
      targetCell.UpdateTree(diffRef, sourceSet);
    }

    AddTargetSetMap(targetRef, sourceSet);
    sourceSetMap[targetRef] = sourceSet;

    set<Reference> invalidateSet;
    EvaluateRecursive(targetRef, invalidateSet);

    for (Reference cellRef : invalidateSet) {
      InvalidateCell(cellRef);
    }
    }
  }

  UpdateWindow();
  SetDirty(true);
}
```

The **Delete** menu item is enabled in the `edit` mode unless the edit index is at the end of the cell's text. The item is always enabled in the `mark` mode, since there is always at least one marked cell marked to be deleted:

```
bool CalcDocument::DeleteEnable() const {
  if (calcMode == Edit) {
    const Cell& editCell = cellMatrix[editRef];
    return (editIndex < ((int)editCell.GetText().length()));
  }
  else {
    return true;
  }
}
```

The `OnDelete` method (the menu item) just calls `OnDeleteKey` (the key pressed), since they perform the same action:

```
void CalcDocument::OnDelete() {
  OnDeleteKey();
}
```

Font and color

The `OnFont` and `OnBackgroundColor` methods work in the same manner–they are called when the user selects the **Font** or **Background Color** items in the **Format** menu. They apply the change on the edited or marked cells, and the window and (in the edit case) the caret is updated. If at least one cell has been modified, the dirty flag is set:

```
void CalcDocument::OnFont() {
  switch (calcMode) {
    case Edit: {
        Cell& editCell = cellMatrix[editRef];
        Font font = editCell.CellFont();
        Font previousFont = font;
```

In the `edit` mode, the font of the edited cell is changed if the `FontDialog` method returns `true` (the user has pressed the **Ok** button) and has chosen a different font. Note that the `FontDialog` method also sets the color of the font:

```
        if (StandardDialog::FontDialog(this, font) &&
            (font != previousFont)) {
          editCell.CellFont() = font;
          editCell.GenerateCaretList(this);
          InvalidateCell(editRef);
          SetDirty(true);
          UpdateCaret();
          UpdateWindow();
        }
    }
    break;
```

In the `mark` mode, the font of each marked cell is set to the new font if the `FontDialog` method returns `true`. If the font of at least one cell is set (which we do not know from the start), the dirty flag is set:

```
    case Mark: {
        Font font = cellMatrix[lastMarkRef].CellFont();
```

```
    if (StandardDialog::FontDialog(this, font)) {
      int minMarkRow = min(firstMarkRef.Row(),
                           lastMarkRef.Row()),
          maxMarkRow = max(firstMarkRef.Row(),
                           lastMarkRef.Row()),
          minMarkCol = min(firstMarkRef.Col(),
                           lastMarkRef.Col()),
          maxMarkCol = max(firstMarkRef.Col(),
                           lastMarkRef.Col());

      for (int row = minMarkRow; row <= maxMarkRow; ++row) {
        for (int col = minMarkCol; col <= maxMarkCol; ++col) {
          Reference markRef = Reference(row, col);
          Cell& markCell = cellMatrix[markRef];

          if (markCell.CellFont() != font) {
            markCell.CellFont() = font;
            markCell.GenerateCaretList(this);
            InvalidateCell(markRef);
            SetDirty(true);
          }
        }
      }

      UpdateWindow();
    }
  }
  break;
}
}
```

The `OnBackgroundColor` method is similar to the `OnFont` method. The only difference is that the `OnBackgroundColor` method calls the `ColorDialog` method instead of the `FontDialog` method, and that `BackgroundColor` is called for each cell instead of `Font`:

```
void CalcDocument::OnBackgroundColor() {
  switch (calcMode) {
    case Edit: {
        Cell& editCell = cellMatrix[editRef];
        Color color = editCell.BackgroundColor();
        Color previousColor = color;

        if (StandardDialog::ColorDialog(this, color) &&
            (color != previousColor)){
          editCell.BackgroundColor() = color;
          InvalidateCell(editRef);
          SetDirty(true);
        }
```

```
        }
        break;

    case Mark: {
        Color color = cellMatrix[lastMarkRef].BackgroundColor();

        if (StandardDialog::ColorDialog(this, color)) {
            int minMarkRow = min(firstMarkRef.Row(),
                                 lastMarkRef.Row()),
                maxMarkRow = max(firstMarkRef.Row(),
                                 lastMarkRef.Row()),
                minMarkCol = min(firstMarkRef.Col(),
                                 lastMarkRef.Col()),
                maxMarkCol = max(firstMarkRef.Col(),
                                 lastMarkRef.Col());

            for (int row = minMarkRow; row <= maxMarkRow; ++row) {
                for (int col = minMarkCol; col <= maxMarkCol; ++col) {
                    Reference markRef = Reference(row, col);
                    Cell& markCell = cellMatrix[markRef];

                    if (markCell.BackgroundColor() != color) {
                        markCell.BackgroundColor() = color;
                        InvalidateCell(markRef);
                        SetDirty(true);
                    }
                }
            }
        }
        break;
    }

    UpdateWindow();
}
```

Alignment

The horizontal and vertical alignments follow the same pattern. The radio methods call the
IsHorizontalAlignment or IsVerticalAlignment method, which return true if the
edited cells or all the marked cells hold the alignment in question. The selection methods
call the SetHorizontalAlignment or SetVerticalAlignment method, which set the
alignment of the edited cell or every marked cell. If at least one cell has been modified, the
dirty flag is set. Finally, the window and (in the edit case) caret are updated.

The `HorizontalLeftRadio`, `HorizontalCenterRadio`, `HorizontalRightRadio`, and `HorizontalJustifiedRadio` methods call the `IsHorizontalAlignment` method, as you'll see next:

```
bool CalcDocument::HorizontalLeftRadio() const {
  return (IsHorizontalAlignment(Left));
}

bool CalcDocument::HorizontalCenterRadio() const {
  return (IsHorizontalAlignment(Center));
}

bool CalcDocument::HorizontalRightRadio() const {
  return (IsHorizontalAlignment(Right));
}

bool CalcDocument::HorizontalJustifiedRadio() const {
  return (IsHorizontalAlignment(Justified));
}
```

The `IsHorizontalAlignment` method returns `true` if the alignment of the edited cell or at least one of the marked cells holds the alignment in question:

```
bool CalcDocument::IsHorizontalAlignment(Alignment alignment)
                                                  const {
  switch (calcMode) {
    case Edit:
      return cellMatrix[editRef].HorizontalAlignment() ==
             alignment;

    case Mark: {
        int minMarkRow = min(firstMarkRef.Row(),
                             lastMarkRef.Row()),
            maxMarkRow = max(firstMarkRef.Row(),
                             lastMarkRef.Row()),
            minMarkCol = min(firstMarkRef.Col(),
                             lastMarkRef.Col()),
            maxMarkCol = max(firstMarkRef.Col(),
                             lastMarkRef.Col());

        for (int row = minMarkRow; row <= maxMarkRow; ++row) {
          for (int col = minMarkCol; col <= maxMarkCol; ++col) {
            Reference markRef = Reference(row, col);
            if (cellMatrix[markRef].VerticalAlignment() !=
                alignment) {
              return true;
            }
          }
        }
```

```
    }
      return false;
    }
  }

  return true;
}
```

The OnHorizontalLeft, OnHorizontalCenter, OnHorizontalRight, and OnHorizontalJustified methods call the SetHorizontalAlignment method, as follows:

```
void CalcDocument::OnHorizontalLeft() {
  SetHorizontalAlignment(Left);
}

void CalcDocument::OnHorizontalCenter() {
  SetHorizontalAlignment(Center);
}

void CalcDocument::OnHorizontalRight() {
  SetHorizontalAlignment(Right);
}

void CalcDocument::OnHorizontalJustified() {
  SetHorizontalAlignment(Justified);
}
```

The SetHorizontalAlignment method sets the alignment of the edited cell or all marked cells:

```
void CalcDocument::SetHorizontalAlignment(Alignment alignment) {
  switch (calcMode) {
    case Edit: {
        Cell& editCell = cellMatrix[editRef];
        editCell.HorizontalAlignment() = alignment;
        editCell.GenerateCaretList(this);
        InvalidateCell(editRef);
        UpdateCaret();
      }
      break;
    case Mark: {
        int minMarkRow = min(firstMarkRef.Row(),
                             lastMarkRef.Row()),
          maxMarkRow = max(firstMarkRef.Row(),
                           lastMarkRef.Row()),
          minMarkCol = min(firstMarkRef.Col(),
                           lastMarkRef.Col()),
                             lastMarkRef.Col()),
```

```
        maxMarkCol = max(firstMarkRef.Col(),
                         lastMarkRef.Col());

    for (int row = minMarkRow; row <= maxMarkRow; ++row) {
      for (int col = minMarkCol; col <= maxMarkCol; ++col) {
        Reference markRef = Reference(row, col);
        Cell& markCell = cellMatrix[markRef];
```

For each cell whose alignment is changed, its caret rectangle list is regenerated and the cell becomes invalidated:

```
        if (markCell.HorizontalAlignment() != alignment) {
          markCell.HorizontalAlignment() = alignment;
          markCell.GenerateCaretList(this);
          InvalidateCell(markRef);
        }
      }
    }
  }
  break;
}
```

The dirty flag is set, since at least one cell has been modified. Otherwise, the alignment menu item would not be enabled:

```
UpdateWindow();
SetDirty(true);
}
```

The vertical alignment methods are similar to the horizontal alignment methods, as we can see here:

```
bool CalcDocument::VerticalTopRadio() const {
  return (IsVerticalAlignment(Top));
}

bool CalcDocument::VerticalCenterRadio() const {
  return (IsVerticalAlignment(Center));
}

bool CalcDocument::VerticalBottomRadio() const {
  return (IsVerticalAlignment(Bottom));
}

bool CalcDocument::IsVerticalAlignment(Alignment alignment) const {
  switch (calcMode) {
    case Edit:
      return cellMatrix[editRef].VerticalAlignment() == alignment;
```

```
      case Mark: {
          int minMarkRow = min(firstMarkRef.Row(),
                               lastMarkRef.Row()),
              maxMarkRow = max(firstMarkRef.Row(),
                               lastMarkRef.Row()),
              minMarkCol = min(firstMarkRef.Col(),
                               lastMarkRef.Col()),
              maxMarkCol = max(firstMarkRef.Col(),
                               lastMarkRef.Col());

          for (int row = minMarkRow; row <= maxMarkRow; ++row) {
            for (int col = minMarkCol; col <= maxMarkCol; ++col) {
              Reference markRef = Reference(row, col);
              if (cellMatrix[markRef].VerticalAlignment() !=
                  alignment){
                return true;
              }
            }
          }
          return false;
        }
    }

    return true;
}

void CalcDocument::OnVerticalTop() {
  SetVerticalAlignment(Top);
}

void CalcDocument::OnVerticalCenter() {
  SetVerticalAlignment(Center);
}

void CalcDocument::OnVerticalBottom() {
  SetVerticalAlignment(Bottom);
}

void CalcDocument::SetVerticalAlignment(Alignment alignment) {
  switch (calcMode) {
    case Edit: {
        Cell& editCell = cellMatrix[editRef];
        editCell.VerticalAlignment() = alignment;
        editCell.GenerateCaretList(this);
        InvalidateCell(editRef);
        UpdateCaret();
      }
      break;
```

```
case Mark: {
    int minMarkRow = min(firstMarkRef.Row(),
                         lastMarkRef.Row()),
        maxMarkRow = max(firstMarkRef.Row(),
                         lastMarkRef.Row()),
        minMarkCol = min(firstMarkRef.Col(),
                         lastMarkRef.Col()),
        maxMarkCol = max(firstMarkRef.Col(),
                         lastMarkRef.Col());

    for (int row = minMarkRow; row <= maxMarkRow; ++row) {
      for (int col = minMarkCol; col <= maxMarkCol; ++col) {
        Reference markRef = Reference(row, col);
        Cell& markCell = cellMatrix[markRef];

        if (markCell.VerticalAlignment() != alignment) {
          markCell.VerticalAlignment() = alignment;
          markCell.GenerateCaretList(this);
          InvalidateCell(markRef);
        }
      }
    }
  }
  break;
}

UpdateWindow();
SetDirty(true);
}
```

Source and target sets

Each cell in the spreadsheet holds a numerical value, a formula, or a (possibly empty) plain text. As mentioned at the beginning of the chapter, a formula is a text beginning with the equal sign (=) followed by a numerical expression with cell references. If the cell holds a value, it may affect the values in other cells (if it does not hold a value, it might cause evaluation errors in target cells). If the cell contains a formula, its value may depend on the values in other cells. This implies that each cell needs a set of cells that it depends on, that is, its source set, and a set of cells that depend on it, that is, its target set.

Only a formula has a non-empty source set, which is the set of all references of the formula. The target set, on the other hand, is more complicated–a cell does not decide its own target set; it is decided indirectly by the formulas that have it as its source cell.

In mathematical terms, the cells with its source and target sets constitute a **directed graph**. Technically, they constitute two different directed graphs, one each for the source and target sets. However, the graphs are just inverses of each other, so in all practical ways, they can be regarded as the same graph.

For instance, in the screenshot that follows the source set of a3 holds a1 and c1 because its formula includes a1 and c1. In the same way, the source set of c3 holds c1 because its formula includes c1. The source set of a1 and c1 are empty, because they do not hold formulas.

As c1 is included in both the formulas of a3 and c3, the value of c1 affects the values of a3 and c3. This implies that the target set of c1 holds a3 and c3. In the same way, as a1 is included in the formula of a3, the target set of a1 holds a3. As the values of a3 and c3 do not affect the values of any other cells, their target sets are empty.

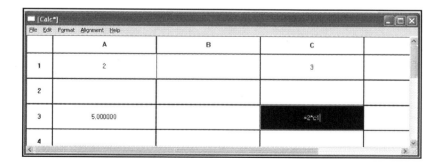

The following is a screenshot of the same spreadsheet with the c3 cell being edited instead of the a3 cell:

The first of the following diagrams shows the acyclic graph of the source sets of the preceding spreadsheet, the second diagram shows the acyclic graph of the target sets. As mentioned previously (and shown by the graphs), the source and targets sets are the inverse of each other. Technically, we can manage with only one of the sets. However, as the sets are needed on different occasions, the code is clearer with both of them.

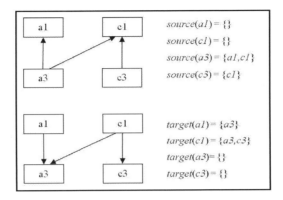

When the value of a cell is changed, its target set is traversed and the values of those cells are updated. Then the target sets of these cells are traversed, and so on. The search terminates when there are no more cells to evaluate or when we detect a circular reference. The circular reference is detected by a deep-search algorithm, which is described in the next section.

Graph searching

When the user changes the value of a cell, we need to find the cells that need to be re-evaluated. Again, note the difference between source and target sets. While only formula cells can have non-empty source sets, all kinds of cells (also empty cells) can have non-empty target sets. Another difference between the two sets is that the target sets are defined indirectly by formulas in other cells. If a formula of another cell holds a reference to a particular cell, the reference to the formula cell is added to the target set of the particular cell. In the same way, when a formula is altered or cleared, the reference to that cell is removed from the target sets of all its source cells. When a cell is updated, all its targets are evaluated recursively–the targets cells are re-evaluated, then their target cells are re-evaluated, and so on. The evaluation always terminates when there are no more targets left, or when a circular reference is encountered. We always run out of targets or encounter a circular reference, since there is a finite number of cells in the spreadsheet.

The `InterpretEditCell` method is called when the user finishes the input of a cell. It interprets the cell by calling the `InterpretCell` method, which fills the `sourceSet` method but throws an exception in the case of a formula with a syntax error:

```
bool CalcDocument::InterpretEditCell() {
  try {
    Cell& editCell = cellMatrix[editRef];
    set<Reference> sourceSet;
    editCell.InterpretCell(sourceSet);
```

However, if the parsing goes well, the previous source set is removed and the new source set is added:

```
    RemoveTargetSetMap(editRef);
    AddTargetSetMap(editRef, sourceSet);
    sourceSetMap[editRef] = sourceSet;
```

Then the cell is recursively evaluated and all its direct or indirect target cells are updated:

```
    set<Reference> invalidateSet;
    EvaluateRecursive(editRef, invalidateSet);
    editCell.GenerateCaretList(this);
```

Finally, all evaluated cells are invalidated, the dirty flag is set, and `true` is returned:

```
    for (Reference cellRef : invalidateSet) {
      InvalidateCell(cellRef);
    }

    SetDirty(true);
    return true;
  }
```

If a syntax error is detected and an exception is thrown, an error message is displayed and `false` is returned. In that case, the application remains in `edit` mode if the user has finished the input. If the `InterpretEditCell` method has been called due to pasting, the pasting process is aborted:

```
  catch (Error error) {
    MessageBox(error.ErrorText(), TEXT("Syntax Error"), Ok, Stop);
    return false;
  }
}
```

The `InvalidateCell` method invalidates the area occupied by the cell with the given reference:

```
void CalcDocument::InvalidateCell(Reference cellRef) {
  Point topLeft(HeaderWidth + (cellRef.Col() * ColWidth),
                HeaderHeight + (cellRef.Row() * RowHeight));
  Size cellSize(ColWidth, RowHeight);
  Rect cellRect(topLeft, cellSize);
  Invalidate(cellRect);
}
```

The sources and targets sets can be searched and evaluated in two ways: **depth-first** and **breadth-first**. As the names implies, depth-first tries to search as deep as possible. When it reaches a dead end, it backtracks and tries another way, if there is one. Breadth-first, on the other hand, evaluates all cells at the same distance from the start cell. Not until every cell at a distance has been evaluated, are the cells at the next distance examined.

When the user adds or alters a formula, it is essential that we detect potential circular references in the graph. The `IsCircular` method decides whether the cell is part of a circular reference, that is, a direct reference to its own cell or a chain of references leading to its own cell. We perform a depth-first search, which is easier than the breadth-first search, since we can take advantage of recursive calls. The breadth-first method is, on the other hand, necessary in order to evaluate the targets of a modified cell in the `EvaluateRecursive` method, as shown here:

```
bool CalcDocument::IsCircular(Reference cellRef,
                             set<Reference>& targetSet){
  for (Reference targetRef : targetSet) {
    if ((cellRef == targetRef) ||
        IsCircular(cellRef, targetSetMap[targetRef])) {
      return true;
    }
  }

  return false;
}
```

When the value of a cell is modified, it is essential that the formulas having references to the cell are notified and that their values are re-evaluated. The `EvaluateRecursive` method performs a breadth-first search by following the target sets forward.

Unlike the check for circular references, which we saw earlier, we cannot perform a depth-first search, since it would introduce the risk of the cells being evaluated in the wrong order:

```
void CalcDocument::EvaluateCell(Reference cellRef) {
  Cell& cell = cellMatrix[cellRef];

  if (IsCircular(cellRef, targetSetMap[cellRef])) {
    cell.SetText(Error(CircularReference).ErrorText());
  }
  else {
    set<Reference> sourceSet = sourceSetMap[cellRef];
    map<Reference, double> valueMap;

    for (Reference sourceRef : sourceSet) {
      Cell& sourceCell = cellMatrix[sourceRef];

      if (sourceCell.HasValue()) {
        valueMap[sourceRef] = sourceCell.GetValue();
      }
    }

    cell.Evaluate(valueMap);
  }

  cell.GenerateCaretList(this);
}
```

When a cell is being evaluated, it needs the values of the cells in its source set; the `valueMap` parameter holds the values of the source cells that holds some value. Every source cell not holding a value is omitted from the map:

```
void CalcDocument::EvaluateRecursive(Reference cellRef,
                     set<Reference>& invalidateSet) {
```

If this cell is not a part of a circular reference, we add the values of the referred cells with values to the `valueMap` parameter. Refereed cells without values are simply omitted from the `valueMap` parameter:

```
set<Reference> targetSet, evaluatedSet;
targetSet.insert(cellRef);

while (!targetSet.empty()) {
  Reference targetRef = *targetSet.begin();
  targetSet.erase(targetRef);
```

```
    if (evaluatedSet.count(targetRef) == 0) {
      EvaluateCell(targetRef);
      evaluatedSet.insert(targetRef);
      invalidateSet.insert(targetRef);
      set<Reference> nextTargetSet = targetSetMap[targetRef];
      targetSet.insert(nextTargetSet.begin(),
                       nextTargetSet.end());
    }
  }
}
```

Regardless of whether the cell was properly evaluated or was found to be part of a circular reference, we need to regenerate its caret rectangle list. It is either given a proper value or an error message, and in both cases, the text is changed:

```
    cell.GenerateCaretList(this);
  }
```

The RemoveTargetSetMap method traverses the source set of the cell in the cell matrix and, for each source cell, removes the cell as a target. In the same way, the AddTargetSetMap method traverses the source set of the cell in the cell matrix and, for each source cell, adds the cell as a target:

```
void CalcDocument::RemoveTargetSetMap(Reference cellRef) {
  for (Reference sourceRef : sourceSetMap[cellRef]) {
    int row = sourceRef.Row(), col = sourceRef.Col();
    if ((row >= 0) && (row < Rows) && (col >= 0) && (col < Cols)){
      targetSetMap[sourceRef].erase(cellRef);
    }
  }
}
```

```
void CalcDocument::AddTargetSetMap(Reference cellRef,
                                   set<Reference>& sourceSet) {
  for (Reference sourceRef : sourceSet) {
    int row = sourceRef.Row(), col = sourceRef.Col();
    if ((row >= 0) && (row < Rows) && (col >= 0) && (col < Cols)){
      targetSetMap[sourceRef].insert(cellRef);
    }
  }

  sourceSetMap[cellRef] = sourceSet;
}
```

Error handling

The evaluation errors are as follows:

- **Missing value**: This error occurs when the cell referred in a formula does not hold a value
- **Reference out of range**: This error occurs when a reference is outside the scope of the spreadsheet
- **Circular reference**: This error occurs when a cell is referring to itself, directly or indirectly
- **Division by zero**: This error occurs when the denominator in a division expression is zero

There is also the syntax error that occurs when the user inputs a syntactically incorrect formula.

Error.h

```
enum ErrorId {SyntaxError, CircularReference, ReferenceOutOfRange,
              DivisionByZero, MissingValue};

class Error : public exception {
  public:
    Error(ErrorId errorId);
    String ErrorText() const;

  private:
    ErrorId errorId;
};
```

Error.cpp

```
#include "..\\SmallWindows\\SmallWindows.h"
#include "Error.h"

Error::Error(ErrorId errorId)
 :errorId(errorId) {
  // Empty.
}

String Error::ErrorText() const{
  switch (errorId) {
    case SyntaxError:
      return TEXT("Syntax Error.");
```

```
      case CircularReference:
        return TEXT("#Circular reference#");

      case DivisionByZero:
        return TEXT("#Division by Zero#");

      case MissingValue:
        return TEXT("#Missing Value#");

      case ReferenceOutOfRange:
        return TEXT("#Reference out of Range.#");
    }

    return TEXT("");
}
```

Summary

In this chapter, we looked into how a spreadsheet program is implemented: the mouse and keyboard input; cut, copy, and paste; file management; and font, color, and alignment. Chapter 9, *Formula Interpretation*, will introduce cell handling and formula interpretation, including parsing, scanning, and caret rectangle list generation.

9

Formula Interpretation

The spreadsheet program is capable of handling text, numerical values, and formulas composed by the four arithmetic operators. In order to do so, we need to interpret the formulas. We also need to find the sources of a formula (the cells referred to in the formula) and the targets of a cell (the cells affected by a change).

In this chapter, we will take a look at the following topics:

- Interpretation (scanning and parsing) of numerical expressions
- Parse and syntax trees
- Evaluation of formulas
- References and matrices
- Drawing of cells
- Loading and saving of cells

In the following spreadsheet, the C3 cell is being edited:

Formula interpretation

The core of a spreadsheet program is its ability to interpret formulas. When the user inputs a formula in a cell, it is interpreted and its value is evaluated. The process of formula interpretation is divided into three separate steps. First, given the input string, the **Scanner** generates a **Token List**, then the **Parser** generates a **Syntax Tree**, and the **Evaluator** determines the value.

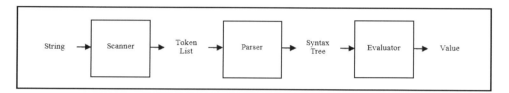

A token is the least significant part of the formula. For instance, *a1* is interpreted as a reference and *1.2* is interpreted as a value. Assuming that the cells have values according to the following sheet, the formula interpretation process will be as follows. Remember that a formula is text beginning with an equal sign (=).

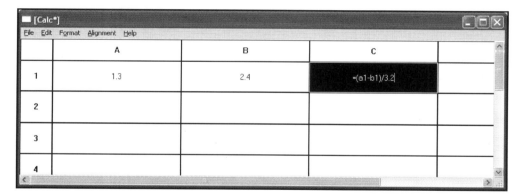

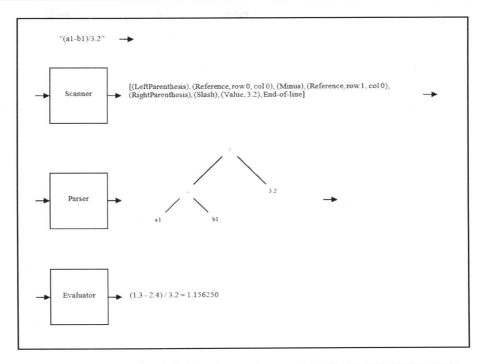

The tokens

The scanner takes a string as input and finds its least significant parts-its tokens. Spaces between the tokens are ignored, and the scanner makes out no difference between capital and small letters. The `Value` token needs an extra piece of information to keep track of the actual value, which is called an **attribute**. In the same way, `Reference` needs an attribute to keep track of reference. In this application, there are nine different tokens:

Token.h

```
enum TokenId {Plus, Minus, Star, Slash, LeftParenthesis,
              RightParenthesis, RefToken, Number, EndOfLine};
```

Token	Description
`Plus`, `Minus`, `Star`, and `Slash`	These are the four arithmetic operators: "+", "–", "*", and "/"
`LeftParenthesis` and `RightParenthesis`	These are the left and right parentheses: " (" and ") "
Value	This is a numerical value, for instance, `124`, `3.14`, or `-0.23`. It does not matter whether the value is integral or decimal. Nor does it matter if the decimal point (if present) is preceded or succeeded by digits. However, the value must contain at least one digit. This needs a value of type double as an attribute.
Reference	This is a reference, for instance, `b8`, `c6`. This needs `Reference` object as an attribute.
EndOfLine	This is at the end of the line, there are no more (non-space) characters in the string.

As stated previously, the string *1.2 * (b2 + c3)* generates the tokens in the table on the next page. The end-of-line token is added at the end of the list.

Text	Token	Attribute
1.2	Value	1.2
*	Star	
(	LeftParenthesis	
b2	Reference	row 1, col 1
+	Plus	
c3	Reference	row 2, col 2
)	RightParanthesis	
	EndOfLine	

The tokens are defined in the `Token` class. A token is made up of a token identifier, a double value in case of the value token, and a `Reference` object in case of the reference token.

Token.h

```
class Token {
  public:
    Token(TokenId tokenId);
    Token(double value);
    Token(Reference reference);

    TokenId Id() const {return tokenId;}
    double Value() const {return value;}
    Reference ReferenceField() const {return reference;}

  private:
    TokenId tokenId;
    double value;
    Reference reference;
};
```

Token.cpp

```
#include "..\\SmallWindows\\SmallWindows.h"
#include "Token.h"

Token::Token(TokenId tokenId)
 :tokenId(tokenId) {
  // Empty.
}
```

```
Token::Token(double value)
 :tokenId(Number),
  value(value) {
  // Empty.
}

Token::Token(Reference reference)
 :tokenId(RefToken),
  reference(reference) {
  // Empty.
}
```

The tree node

As mentioned earlier, the parser generates a syntax tree. More specifically, it generates an object of the Tree class (described in Chapter 12, *Auxiliary Classes*), which is a template class with a node type: TreeNode. There are 10 identities for a node and, similar to Token, a value node has a double value as its attribute and a reference node has a reference object as attribute.

TreeNode.h

```
enum TreeId {EmptyTree, UnaryAdd, UnarySubtract, BinaryAdd, BinarySubtract,
             Multiply, Divide, Parenthesis, RefId, ValueId};
```

The default constructor is used when reading the value from a file or the clipboard buffer.

```
class TreeNode {
  public:
    TreeNode();
    TreeNode(TreeId id);
    TreeNode(Reference reference);
    TreeNode(double value);
```

A cell of a spreadsheet can be saved to a file as well as cut, copied, and pasted, thus we included the following methods:

```
        bool WriteTreeNodeToStream(ostream& outStream) const;
        bool ReadTreeNodeFromStream(istream& inStream);
        void WriteTreeNodeToClipboard(InfoList& infoList) const;
        void ReadTreeNodeFromClipboard(InfoList& infoList);
```

The identity and value of the node can only be inspected, not modified. However, the reference can be modified, since it is updated when the user copies a cell and then pastes it to another location:

```
    TreeId Id() const {return id;}
    double Value() const {return value;}
    Reference ReferenceField() const {return reference;}
    Reference& ReferenceField() {return reference;}


  private:
    TreeId id;
    Reference reference;
    double value;
};
```

TreeNode.cpp

```cpp
#include "..\\SmallWindows\\SmallWindows.h"
#include "TreeNode.h"

TreeNode::TreeNode()
 :id(EmptyTree),
  value(0) {
  // Empty.
}

TreeNode::TreeNode(TreeId id)
 :id(id),
  value(0) {
    // Empty.
}

TreeNode::TreeNode(Reference reference)
: id(RefId),
  value(0),
  reference(reference) {
  // Empty.
}

TreeNode::TreeNode(double value)
 :id(ValueId),
  value(value) {
  // Empty.
}
```

The node identity, the value, and the reference are written and read, as follows:

```
bool TreeNode::WriteTreeNodeToStream(ostream& outStream) const {
  outStream.write((char*) &id, sizeof id);
  outStream.write((char*) &value, sizeof value);
  reference.WriteReferenceToStream(outStream);
  return ((bool) outStream);
}

bool TreeNode::ReadTreeNodeFromStream(istream& inStream) {
  inStream.read((char*) &id, sizeof id);
  inStream.read((char*) &value, sizeof value);
  reference.ReadReferenceFromStream(inStream);
  return ((bool) inStream);
}

void TreeNode::WriteTreeNodeToClipboard(InfoList& infoList) const {
  infoList.AddValue<TreeId>(id);
  infoList.AddValue<double>(value);
  reference.WriteReferenceToClipboard(infoList);
}

void TreeNode::ReadTreeNodeFromClipboard(InfoList& infoList) {
  infoList.GetValue<TreeId>(id);
  infoList.GetValue<double>(value);
  reference.ReadReferenceFromClipboard(infoList);
}
```

The Scanner – Generating the list of tokens

The task of the `Scanner` class is to group characters into tokens. For instance, *12.34* is interpreted as the value *12.34*. The constructor takes a string as parameter while `Scan` generates a list of tokens by repeatedly calling `NextToken` until the string is empty.

Scanner.h

```
class Scanner {
  public:
    Scanner(String buffer);
    list<Token> Scan();
```

The `NextToken` method returns `EndOfLine` when it encounters the end of the string. The `ScanValue` and `ScanReference` methods return `true` if they encounter a value or a reference:

```
Token NextToken();
bool ScanValue(double& value);
bool ScanReference(Reference& reference);
```

The next token is continually read from the buffer until it is empty:

```
private:
   String buffer;
};
```

Scanner.cpp

```
#include "..\\SmallWindows\\SmallWindows.h"
#include "Token.h"
#include "Error.h"
#include "Scanner.h"
```

TEXT('\0') is added to the string for simplicity; instead of checking whether the remaining text is empty, we look for the null character:

```
Scanner::Scanner(String buffer)
 :buffer(buffer + TEXT('\0')) {
   // Empty.
}
```

The Scan method adds the token from the buffer to tokenList until it encounters EndOfLine. Finally, the list is returned:

```
list<Token> Scanner::Scan() {
   list<Token> tokenList;

   while (true) {
     Token token = NextToken();
     tokenList.push_back(token);

     if (token.Id() == EndOfLine) {
       break;
     }
   }

   return tokenList;
}
```

The NextToken method does the actual work of the scanner by finding the next token in the buffer. First, we skip the blanks. It is rather simple to extract the token when it comes to the arithmetic symbols and the parentheses. We just check the next character of the buffer. It becomes slightly more difficult when it comes to numerical values or references. We have two auxiliary methods for that purpose: `ScanValue` and `ScanReference`. Take a look at the following code:

```
Token Scanner::NextToken() {
  while (buffer[0] == TEXT(' ')) {
    buffer.erase(0, 1);
  }

  switch (buffer[0]) {
  case TEXT('\0'):
    return Token(EndOfLine);

  case TEXT('+'):
    buffer.erase(0, 1);
    return Token(Plus);

  case TEXT('-'):
    buffer.erase(0, 1);
    return Token(Minus);

  case TEXT('*'):
    buffer.erase(0, 1);
    return Token(Star);

  case TEXT('/'):
    buffer.erase(0, 1);
    return Token(Slash);

  case TEXT('('):
    buffer.erase(0, 1);
    return Token(LeftParenthesis);

  case TEXT(')'):
    buffer.erase(0, 1);
    return Token(RightParenthesis);
```

If none of the trivial cases apply, the token may be a value or a reference. The `ScanValue` and `ScanReference` methods find out if that is the case. If not, the scanner has encountered an unknown character and a syntax error exception is thrown:

```
  default: {
    double value;
    Reference reference;
    if (ScanValue(value)) {
      return Token(value);
    }
```

```
      else if (ScanReference(reference)) {
        return Token(reference);
      }
      else {
        throw Error(SyntaxError);
      }
    }
  }
  break;
  }
}
```

`ScanValue` uses the `_stscanf_s` standard function, which is the safe generic version of `sscanf`. The returned value is stored in `fieldCount`, which is set to 1 if the double value was successfully read. We also need the number of the character read, which is stored in `charCount`, in order to erase the correct number of characters from the buffer:

```
bool Scanner::ScanValue(double& value) {
  int charCount;
  int fieldCount = _stscanf_s(buffer.c_str(), TEXT("%lf%n"),
                              &value, &charCount);

  if (fieldCount > 0) {
    buffer.erase(0, charCount);
    return true;
  }

  return false;
}
```

`ScanReference` checks whether the first two characters are a letter and a digit. If so, it extracts the column and the row of the reference:

```
bool Scanner::ScanReference(Reference& reference) {
  if (isalpha(buffer[0]) && (isdigit(buffer[1]))) {
```

We extract the column by subtracting the lowercase letter from *a*, which gives that the first column has the index zero, and erases the letter from the buffer.

```
    reference.Col() = tolower(buffer[0]) - TEXT('a');
    buffer.erase(0, 1);
```

Similar to `ScanValue`, we extract the row by calling `_stscanf_s`, which reads the row integer value and the number of characters, which we use to erase the characters read from the buffer:

```
    int row;
    int charCount;
    _stscanf_s(buffer.c_str(), TEXT("%d%n"), &row, &charCount);
    reference.Row() = row - 1;
    buffer.erase(0, charCount);
    return true;
  }

  return false;
}
```

The parser – Generating the syntax tree

The user inputs a formula beginning with an equal sign (=). The parser's task is to translate the scanner's token list into a syntax tree. The syntax of a valid formula can be defined by a **grammar**. Let's start with a grammar that handles expressions that make use of the arithmetic operators:

> 1. *Formula → Expression EndOfLine*
> 2. *Expression → Expression + Expression*
> 3. *Expression → Expression – Expression*
> 4. *Expression → Expression * Expression*
> 5. *Expression → Expression / Expression*
> 6. *Expression → (Expression)*
> 7. *Expression → Value*
> 8. *Expression → Reference*

A grammar is a set of rules. In the preceding grammar, there are eight rules. **Formula** and **Expression** are called **non-terminals**; **EndOfLine**, **Value**, and the characters +, –, *, /, (, and) are called **terminals**. Terminals and non-terminals are called symbols. One of the rules is the grammar's **start rule**, in our case the first rule. The symbol to the left of the start rules is called the grammar's **start symbol**, in our case **Formula**.

The arrow can be read as "**is**", and the preceding grammar can be read as:

A formula is an expression followed by end-of-line. An expression is the sum of two expressions, the difference of two expressions, the product of two expressions, the quotient of two expressions, an expression enclosed by parentheses, a reference, or a numerical value.

This is a good start, but there are a few problems. Let's test if the string *1 + 2 * 3* is accepted by the grammar. We can test that by doing a **derivation**, where we start with the start symbol Formula and apply the rules until there are only terminals. The digits in the following derivation refer to the grammar rules:

$$Formula \overset{1}{\Rightarrow} Expression \ EndOfFile \overset{2}{\Rightarrow} Expression + Expression \ EndOfFile \overset{4}{\Rightarrow}$$

$$Expression + Expression * Expression \ EndOfFile \overset{7}{\Rightarrow} Value(1) + Expression * Expression$$

$$EndOfFile \overset{7}{\Rightarrow} Value(1) + Value(2) * Expression \ EneOfLine \overset{7}{\Rightarrow} Value(1) + Value(2) * Value(3)$$

$$EndOfFile$$

The derivation can be illustrated by the development of a **parse tree**.

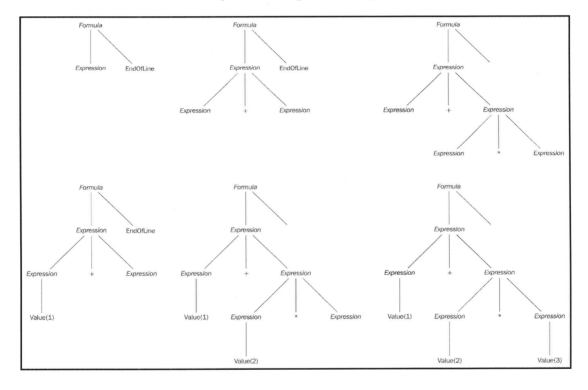

Let's try another derivation of the same string, with the rules applied in a different order.

$Formula \overset{1}{\Rightarrow} Expression\ EndOfLine \overset{4}{\Rightarrow} Expression * Expression\ EndOfLine \overset{2}{\Rightarrow}$

$Expression + Expression * Expression\ EndOfLine \overset{7}{\Rightarrow} Value(1) + Expression * Expression$

$EndOfLine \overset{7}{\Rightarrow} Value(1) + Value(2) * Expression\ EndOfLine \overset{7}{\Rightarrow} Value(1) + Value(2) * Value(3)$

$EndOfLine$

This derivation generates a different parse tree, which is as follows:

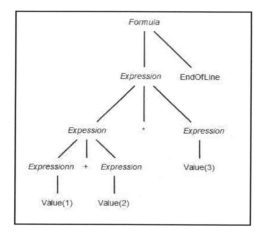

The grammar is said to be ambiguous as it can generate two different parse trees for the same input string, which we would like to avoid. The second tree is obviously a violation of the laws of mathematics, stating that multiplication has higher precedence than addition, but the grammar does not know that. One way to avoid ambiguity is to introduce a new set of rules for each level of precedence:

1. *Formula → Expression EndOfLine*
2. *Expression → Expression + Term*
3. *Expression → Expression – Term*
4. *Expression → Term*
5. *Term → Term * Factor*
6. *Term → Term / Factor*
7. *Term → Factor*
8. *Factor → Value*
9. *Factor → Reference*
10. *Factor → (Expression)*

The new grammar is not ambiguous. If we try our string with this grammar, we can only generate one parse tree, regardless of the order that we choose to apply the rules. There are formal methods to prove that the grammar is not ambiguous; however, that is outside the scope of this book. Check out the references at the end of this chapter for references.

$$Formula \overset{1}{\Rightarrow} Expression\ EndOfLine \overset{2}{\Rightarrow} Expression + Term\ EndOfLine \overset{4}{\Rightarrow}$$

$$Term + Term\ EndOfLine \overset{7}{\Rightarrow} Factor + Term\ EndOfLine \overset{8}{\Rightarrow} Value(1) + Term\ EndOfLine \overset{5}{\Rightarrow}$$

$$Value(1) + Term * Factor\ EndOfLine \overset{7}{\Rightarrow} Value(1) + Factor * Factor\ EndOfLine \overset{8}{\Rightarrow}$$

$$Value(1) + Value(2) * Factor\ EndOfLine \overset{7}{\Rightarrow} Value(1) + Value(2) * Value(3)\ EndOfLine$$

This derivation gives the following tree. As it is not possible to derive two different trees from the same input string, the grammar is **unambiguous**.

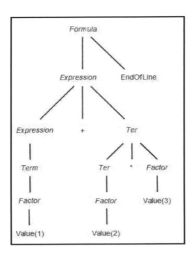

We are now ready to write a parser. Essentially, there are two types of parsers: **top-down parser** and **bottom-up parser**. As the terms imply, a top-down parser starts by the grammar's start symbol together with the input string, and it tries to apply rules until we are left with only terminals. A bottom-up parser starts with the input string and tries to apply rules backward, reducing the rules until we reach the start symbol.

It is a complicated matter to construct a bottom-up parser. It is usually not done manually; instead, there are **parser generators** constructing a **parser table** for the given grammar and skeleton code for the implementation of the parser. However, the theory of bottom-up parsing is outside the scope of this book.

It is easier to construct a top-down parser than a bottom-up parser. One way to construct a simple, but inefficient, top-down parser would be to apply all possible rules in random order. If we reach a dead end, we simply backtrack and try another rule. A more efficient, but rather simple, parser is a look-ahead parser. Given a suitable grammar, we only need to look at the next token in order to uniquely determine the rule to apply. If we reach a dead end, we do not have to backtrack; we simply draw the conclusion that the input string is incorrect according to the grammar-it is said to be **syntactically incorrect**, that is, it has a **syntax error**.

The first attempt to implement a look-ahead parser could be to write a function for each rule in the grammar. Unfortunately, we cannot do that quite yet because that would result in a function `Expression` like this:

```
Tree<TreeNode>* Parser::Expression() {
  Token token = tokenList.front();

  switch (token.Id()) {
    case Plus:
      Tree<TreeNode>* plusTree = Expression();
      // ...
      break;
  }
}
```

Do you see the problem? The method calls itself without changing the input stream, which would result in an infinite number of recursive calls. This is called **left recursion**. We can solve the problem, however, with the help of a simple translation.

> $Expression \rightarrow Expression + Term$
> $Expression \rightarrow Expression - Term$
> $Expression \rightarrow Term$

The preceding rules can be translated to the equivalent set of rules (where epsilon ε denotes empty string):

> $Expression \rightarrow Term\ NextExpression$
> $NextExpression \rightarrow +Term\ NextExpression$
> $NextExpression \rightarrow -Term\ NextExpression$
> $NextExpression \rightarrow \varepsilon$

If we apply this transformation to the **Expression** and **Term** rules in the preceding grammar, we receive the following grammar:

1. *Formula → Expression EOL*
2. *Expression → Term NextExpression*
3. *NextExpression → +Term NextExpression*
4. *NextExpression → −Term NextExpression*
5. *NextExpression → ε*
6. *Term → Factor NextTerm*
7. *NextTerm → *Factor NextTerm*
8. *NextTerm → / Factor NextTerm*
9. *NextTerm → ε*
10. *Factor → Value*
11. *Factor → Reference*
12. *Factor → (Expression)*

Let's try this new grammar with our string *1 + 2 * 3*.

$$Formula \overset{1}{\Rightarrow} Expression\ EndOfLine \overset{2}{\Rightarrow} Term\ NextExpression\ EndOfLine \overset{3}{\Rightarrow}$$

$$Term + Term\ NextExpression\ EndOfLine \overset{6}{\Rightarrow}$$

$$Factor\ NextTerm + Term\ NextExpression\ EndOfLine \overset{9}{\Rightarrow}$$

$$Factor + Term\ NextExpression\ EndOfLine \overset{10}{\Rightarrow}$$

$$Value(1) + Term\ NextExpression\ EndOfLine \overset{6}{\Rightarrow}$$

$$Value(1) + Factor\ NextTerm\ NextExpression\ EndOfLine \overset{10}{\Rightarrow}$$

$$Value(1) + Value(2)\ NextTerm\ NextExpression\ EndOfLine \overset{7}{\Rightarrow}$$

$$Value(1) + Value(2) * Factor\ NextTerm\ NextExpression\ EndOfLine \overset{10}{\Rightarrow}$$

$$Value(1) + Value(2) * Value(3)\ NextTerm\ NextExpression\ EndOfLine \overset{9}{\Rightarrow}$$

$$Value(1) + Value(2) * Value(3)\ NextExpression\ EndOfLine \overset{5}{\Rightarrow}$$

$$Value(1) + Value(2) * Value(3)\ EndOfLine$$

The derivation generates the following parse tree:

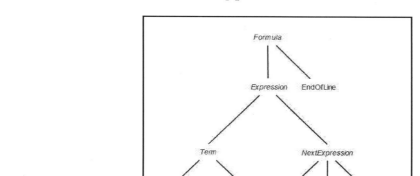

The requirement for a grammar to be suitable for a look-ahead parser is that every set of rules with the same left-hand side symbol must begin with different terminals at its right-hand side. If it does not have an empty rule, it may have at the most one rule with a non-terminal as the first symbol on the right-hand side. The preceding grammar we covered meets these requirements.

Now we are ready to write the parser. However, the parser should also generate some kind of output, representing the string. One such representation is the **syntax tree**, which can be viewed as an abstract parse tree-we keep only the essential information. For instance, the previous parse tree has a matching syntax, which is as follows:

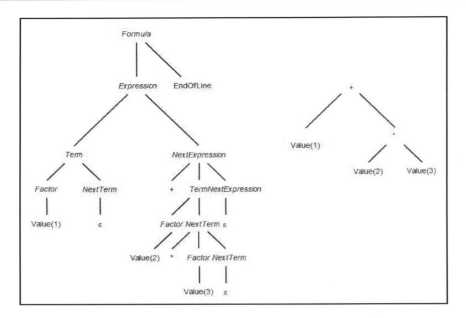

The following is the `Parser` class. The idea is that we write a method for every set of rules with the same left-hand symbol. Each such method generates a part of the resulting syntax tree. The constructor takes the text to parse and lets the scanner generate a list of tokens. Then, `Parse` starts the parsing process, and returns the generated syntax tree. If an error occurs during the parsing process, a syntax error exception is thrown. When the token list has been parsed, we should make sure that there are no extra tokens left in the list except `EndOfLine`. Also, if the input buffer is completely empty (the user inputs only a single equal sign), there is still the `EndOfLine` token in the list.

The result of the parsing is a syntax tree representing the formula. For instance, the formula *a1 * c3 / 3.6 + 2.4 * (b2 − 2.4)* generates the following syntax tree, and we take advantage of the `Tree` class of `Chapter 12`, *Auxiliary Classes.*

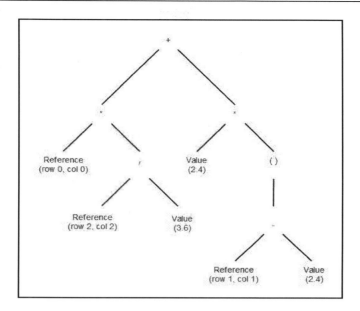

As mentioned in the `TreeNode` section earlier, there are nine types of syntax tree: the four arithmetic operators, unary addition and subtraction, expressions in parentheses, references, and numerical values. We do not actually need the parentheses to store the formula correctly, as the priority of the expression is stored in the syntax tree itself. However, we need it to regenerate the original string from the syntax tree when written in a cell.

Parser.h

```
class Parser {
  public:
    Parser(String buffer);
    Tree<TreeNode>* Parse();
    void Match(int tokenId);
    Tree<TreeNode>* Expression();
    Tree<TreeNode>* NextExpression(Tree<TreeNode>* leftTermPtr);
    Tree<TreeNode>* Term();
    Tree<TreeNode>* NextTerm(Tree<TreeNode>* leftFactorPtr);
    Tree<TreeNode>* Factor();

  private:
    list<Token> tokenList;
};
```

The `Parse` method is called in order to interpret the text that the user has input. It receives the token list from the scanner, which holds at least the `EndOfLine` token and parses the token list and receives a pointer to the syntax tree. When the token list has been parsed, it checks whether the next token is `EndOfLine` to make sure that there are no extra characters (except spaces) left in the buffer:

Parser.cpp

```
#include "..\\SmallWindows\\SmallWindows.h"
#include "Token.h"
#include "Error.h"
#include "Scanner.h"
#include "TreeNode.h"
#include "Parser.h"

Parser::Parser(String buffer) {
  Scanner scanner(buffer);
  tokenList = scanner.Scan();
}

Tree<TreeNode>* Parser::Parse() {
  Tree<TreeNode>* resultTreePtr = Expression();
  Match(EndOfLine);
  return resultTreePtr;
}
```

The `Match` method is used to match the next token in the list with the expected token. If they do not match or if the token list is empty, a syntax error exception is thrown. Otherwise, the next token is removed from the list:

```
void Parser::Match(int tokenId) {
  if (tokenList.empty() || (tokenList.front().Id() != tokenId)) {
    throw Error(SyntaxError);
  }

  tokenList.pop_front();
}
```

The rest of the methods implement the grammar we discussed earlier. There is one method for each for the symbols `Expression`, `NextExpression`, `Term`, `NextTerm`, and `Factor`:

```
Tree<TreeNode>* Parser::Expression() {
  Tree<TreeNode>* termTreePtr = Term();
  return NextExpression(termTreePtr);
}
```

The `NextExpression` method takes care of addition and subtraction. If the next token is

Plus or Minus, we match it and parse its right operand. Then, we create and return a new syntax tree with the operator in question. If the next token is neither Plus nor Minus, we just assume that another rule applies and return the given left syntax tree:

```
Tree<TreeNode>* Parser::NextExpression(Tree<TreeNode>*
                                       leftTermTreePtr) {
  Token token = tokenList.front();
  switch (token.Id()) {
    case Plus: {
      Match(Plus);
      Tree<TreeNode>* rightTermTreePtr = Term();
      Tree<TreeNode>* sumTreePtr =
        new Tree<TreeNode>(TreeNode(BinaryAdd),
                           {leftTermTreePtr, rightTermTreePtr});
      assert(sumTreePtr != nullptr);
      return NextExpression(sumTreePtr);
    }

    case Minus: {
      Match(Minus);
      Tree<TreeNode>* rightTermTreePtr = Term();
        Tree<TreeNode>* diffTreePtr =
            new Tree<TreeNode>(TreeNode(BinarySubtract),
                               {leftTermTreePtr, rightTermTreePtr});
      assert(diffTreePtr != nullptr);
      return NextExpression(diffTreePtr);
    }

    default:
      return leftTermTreePtr;
  }
}

Tree<TreeNode>* Parser::Term() {
  Tree<TreeNode>* pFactorTree = Factor();
  return NextTerm(pFactorTree);
}
```

The NextTerm method works with multiplication and division in a way similar to NextExpression. Remember that we need a set of methods for each precedence level of the grammar.

```
Tree<TreeNode>* Parser::NextTerm(Tree<TreeNode>*leftFactorTreePtr) {
  Token token = tokenList.front();
```

```
    switch (token.Id()) {
      case Star: {
        Match(Star);
        Tree<TreeNode>* rightFactorTreePtr = Factor();
        Tree<TreeNode>* productTreePtr =
          new Tree<TreeNode>(TreeNode(Multiply),
        Tree<TreeNode>* productTreePtr =
          new Tree<TreeNode>(TreeNode(Multiply),
                         {leftFactorTreePtr, rightFactorTreePtr});
        assert(productTreePtr != nullptr);
        return NextExpression(productTreePtr);
      }

      case Slash: {
        Match(Slash);
        Tree<TreeNode>* rightFactorTreePtr = Factor();
        Tree<TreeNode>* quotientTreePtr =
          new Tree<TreeNode>(TreeNode(Divide),
                         {leftFactorTreePtr, rightFactorTreePtr});
        assert(quotientTreePtr != nullptr);
        return NextExpression(quotientTreePtr);
      }
      default:
        return leftFactorTreePtr;
    }
  }
```

The `Factor` method parses values, references, and expressions enclosed by parentheses. If the next token is a unary operator (plus or minus), we parse its expression and create a syntax tree holding the expression:

```
Tree<TreeNode>* Parser::Factor() {
  Token token = tokenList.front();

  switch (token.Id()) {
    case Plus: {
      Match(Plus);
      Tree<TreeNode>* nextExprTreePtr = Expression();
      Tree<TreeNode>* plusTreePtr =
        new Tree<TreeNode>(TreeNode(UnaryAdd),
                       {nextExprTreePtr});
      assert(plusTreePtr!= nullptr);
      return plusTreePtr;
    }

    case Minus: {
      Match(Minus);
      Tree<TreeNode>* nextExprTreePtr = Expression();
```

```
      Tree<TreeNode>* minusTreePtr =
        new Tree<TreeNode>(TreeNode(UnaryAdd),
                            {nextExprTreePtr});
      assert(minusTreePtr!= nullptr);
      return minusTreePtr;
    }
```

If the next token is a left parenthesis, we match it, parse the following expression, and match the closing right parenthesis:

```
    case LeftParenthesis: {
      Match(LeftParenthesis);
      Tree<TreeNode>* innerExprTreePtr = Expression();
      Match(RightParenthesis);
      Tree<TreeNode>* resultTreePtr =
        new Tree<TreeNode>(TreeNode(Parenthesis),
                            {innerExprTreePtr});
      assert(resultTreePtr != nullptr);
      return resultTreePtr;
    }
```

If the next token is a reference, we receive the reference attribute with its row and column and match the reference token. We create a new syntax tree holding a reference. Note that the parser does not check whether the reference is valid (refers to a cell inside the spreadsheet); that is the task of the evaluation of the formula's value:

```
    case RefToken: {
      Match(RefToken);
      Tree<TreeNode>* resultTreePtr =
        new Tree<TreeNode>(TreeNode(token.ReferenceField()));
      assert(resultTreePtr != nullptr);
      return resultTreePtr;
    }

    case Number: {
      Match(Number);
      Tree<TreeNode>* resultTreePtr =
        new Tree<TreeNode>(TreeNode(token.Value()));
      assert(resultTreePtr != nullptr);
      return resultTreePtr;
    }
```

If none of the preceding tokens applies, the user has input an invalid expression and a syntax error exception is thrown:

```
    default:
       throw Error(SyntaxError);
    }
  }
```

Matrix and reference

The `Matrix` class is used when storing the cells of spreadsheet, and the `Reference` class is used when accessing cells in the spreadsheet.

The reference class

The `Reference` class holds the row and column of a cell in the `Matrix` class, as shown in the next section:

Reference.h

```
namespace SmallWindows {
  class Reference;
  extern const Reference ZeroReference;

  class Reference {
    public:
```

The default constructor initializes the row and column to zero. A reference can be initialized by and assigned to another reference:

```
      Reference();
      Reference(int row, int col);
      Reference(const Reference& ref);
      Reference& operator=(const Reference& ref);
```

The compare operators first compare the rows. If they are equal, the columns are then compared:

```
      friend bool operator==(const Reference& ref1,
                             const Reference& ref2);
      friend bool operator!=(const Reference& ref1,
                             const Reference& ref2);
      friend bool operator<(const Reference& ref1,
                            const Reference& ref2);
      friend bool operator<=(const Reference& ref1,
                             const Reference& ref2);
```

```
friend bool operator>(const Reference& ref1,
                          const Reference& ref2);
friend bool operator>=(const Reference& ref1,
                          const Reference& ref2);
```

The addition operators add and subtract the rows and columns separately:

```
Reference& operator+=(const Reference& ref);
Reference& operator-=(const Reference& ref);
friend Reference operator+(const Reference& ref1,
                          const Reference& ref2);
friend Reference operator-(const Reference& ref1,
                          const Reference& ref2);
```

The `Clear` method sets both the row and column to zero, and `IsEmpty` returns `true` if the row and column is zero:

```
void Clear() {row = 0; col = 0;}
bool IsEmpty() const {return ((row == 0) && (col == 0));}
```

The `ToString` method returns a string representing the reference:

```
String ToString() const;
```

A reference is inside a block of references defined by a smallest and a largest reference if it is greater than or equal to the smallest one and less than or equal to the largest one:

```
bool Inside(Reference minRef, Reference maxRef);
```

The reference can be written to and read from a file stream, the clipboard, and the registry:

```
bool WriteReferenceToStream(ostream& outStream) const;
bool ReadReferenceFromStream(istream& inStream);
void WriteReferenceToClipboard(InfoList& infoList) const;
void ReadReferenceFromClipboard(InfoList& infoList);
void WriteReferenceToRegistry(String key) const;
void ReadReferenceFromRegistry(String key,
                Reference defaultRef = ZeroReference);
```

The row and column are inspected by the constant methods and modified by the non-constant methods:

```
int Row() const {return row;}
int Col() const {return col;}
int& Row() {return row;}
int& Col() {return col;}
```

```
    private:
        int row, col;
    };
};
```

Reference.cpp

```cpp
#include "..\\SmallWindows\\SmallWindows.h"
namespace SmallWindows {
  const Reference ZeroReference(0, 0);
  Reference::Reference()
   :row(0),
    col(0) {
    // Empty.
  }

  Reference::Reference(int row, int col)
   :row(row),
    col(col) {
    // Empty.
  }

  Reference::Reference(const Reference& ref)
   :row(ref.row),
    col(ref.col) {
    // Empty.
  }

  Reference& Reference::operator=(const Reference& ref) {
    if (this != &ref) {
      row = ref.row;
      col = ref.col;
    }
    return *this;
  }

  bool operator==(const Reference& ref1, const Reference& ref2) {
    return (ref1.row == ref2.row) && (ref1.col == ref2.col);
  }

  bool operator!=(const Reference& ref1, const Reference& ref2) {
    return !(ref1 == ref2);
  }

  bool operator<(const Reference& ref1, const Reference& ref2) {
    return (ref1.row < ref2.row) ||
           ((ref1.row == ref2.row) && (ref1.col < ref2.col));
  }
```

```
bool operator<=(const Reference& ref1, const Reference& ref2) {
  return (ref1 < ref2) || (ref1 == ref2);
}

bool operator>(const Reference& ref1, const Reference& ref2) {
  return !(ref1 <= ref2);
}

bool operator>=(const Reference& ref1, const Reference& ref2) {
  return !(ref1 < ref2);
}

Reference& Reference::operator+=(const Reference& ref) {
  row += ref.row;
  col += ref.col;
  return *this;
}

Reference& Reference::operator-=(const Reference& ref) {
  row -= ref.row;
  col -= ref.col;
  return *this;
}

Reference operator+(const Reference& ref1,
                    const Reference& ref2) {
  return Reference(ref1.row + ref2.row, ref1.col + ref2.col);
}

Reference operator-(const Reference& ref1,
                    const Reference& ref2) {
  return Reference(ref1.row - ref2.row, ref1.col - ref2.col);
}
```

The `ToString` method returns to reference as a string. We increase the number of rows by one, implying that row zero corresponds to *1*. The column is converted to characters, implying that column zero corresponds to *a*. If the number of rows or columns is less than zero, *?* is returned:

```
String Reference::ToString() const {
  String result;

  if (row >= 0) {
    result.push_back((TCHAR) (col + TEXT('a')));
  }
  else {
    result.push_back(TEXT('?'));
  }
```

```
    if (col >= 0) {
      result.append(to_String(row + 1));
    }
    else {
      result.push_back(TEXT('?'));
    }

    return result;
}

bool Reference::Inside(Reference minRef, Reference maxRef) {
    return ((minRef.row <= row) && (row <= maxRef.row) &&
            (minRef.col <= col) && (col <= maxRef.col));
}

bool Reference::WriteReferenceToStream(ostream& outStream) const {
    outStream.write((char*) &row, sizeof row);
    outStream.write((char*) &col, sizeof col);
    return ((bool) outStream);
}

bool Reference::ReadReferenceFromStream(istream& inStream) {
    inStream.read((char*) &row, sizeof row);
    inStream.read((char*) &col, sizeof col);
    return ((bool) inStream);
}

void Reference::WriteReferenceToClipboard(InfoList& infoList) const {
    infoList.AddValue<int>(row);
    infoList.AddValue<int>(col);
}

void Reference::ReadReferenceFromClipboard(InfoList& infoList) {
    infoList.GetValue<int>(row);
    infoList.GetValue<int>(col);
}
```

When communicating with the registry, we use the `WriteBuffer` and `ReadBuffer` static methods. In order for that to work, we place the row and column values in the `ReferenceStruct` structure:

```
struct ReferenceStruct {int row, col;};

void Reference::WriteReferenceToRegistry(String key) const {
    ReferenceStruct writeStruct = {row, col};
    Registry::WriteBuffer(key, &writeStruct, sizeof writeStruct);
}
```

```
void Reference::ReadReferenceFromRegistry(String key,
                    Reference defaultRef /* = ZeroReference */){
  ReferenceStruct readStruct;
  ReferenceStruct defaultStruct =
    {defaultRef.row, defaultRef.col};
  Registry::ReadBuffer(key, &readStruct, sizeof readStruct,
                    &defaultStruct);
  row = readStruct.row;
  col = readStruct.col;
  }
}
```

The Matrix class

The Matrix class holds a set of cells organized in rows and columns.

Matrix.h

```
namespace SmallWindows {
  template <int Rows, int Cols, class Type>

  class Matrix {
    public:
```

The matrix can be initialized by or assigned to another matrix; in both cases, they call Init to do the actual initialization:

```
  public:
    Matrix();
    Matrix(const Matrix& matrix);
    Matrix& operator=(const Matrix& matrix);

  private:
    void Init(const Matrix<Rows,Cols,Type>& matrix);
```

The index operator takes a row or a Reference object. In the case of a row, an array of columns is returned (technically, the address of its first value is returned), which can be further indexed by the regular index operator to obtain the value in the buffer. In the case of a reference, the value is accessed directly by indexing the row and column of the buffer. Note that in this class, the vertical row coordinate holds the first index and the horizontal column coordinate the second index:

```
  public:
    const Type* operator[](int row) const
                    {return ((const Type*) buffer[row]);}
```

```
    Type& operator[](const Reference& ref)
                    {return buffer[ref.Row()][ref.Col()];}
    Type operator[](const Reference& ref) const
                    {return buffer[ref.Row()][ref.Col()];}

  private:
    Type buffer[Rows][Cols];
};
```

Since Matrix is a template class, we place the definition of its methods in the header file. The default constructor lets the default cell constructor initialize the cells:

```
template <int Rows, int Cols, class Type>
Matrix<Rows,Cols,Type>::Matrix() {
  // Empty.
}
```

The copy constructor and the assignment operator copies the cells by calling Init:

```
template <int Rows, int Cols, class Type>
Matrix<Rows,Cols,Type>::Matrix(const Matrix<Rows,Cols,Type>&
                                    matrix) {
  Init(matrix);
}

template<int Rows, int Cols, class Type>
Matrix<Rows,Cols,Type>& Matrix<Rows,Cols,Type>::operator=
                    (const Matrix<Rows,Cols,Type>& matrix) {
  if (this != &matrix) {
    Init(matrix);
  }

  return *this;
}

template <int Rows, int Cols, class Type>
void Matrix<Rows,Cols,Type>::Init
                    (const Matrix<Rows,Cols,Type>& matrix) {
  for (int row = 0; row < Rows; ++row) {
    for (int col = 0; col < Cols; ++col) {
      buffer[row][col] = matrix.buffer[row][col];
    }
  }
}
```

The cell

The cell can hold three modes: (possible empty) text, a numerical value, or a formula. Its mode is stored in the `cellMode` field. It can hold the value `TextMode`, `ValueMode`, or `FormulaMode`. Similar to `CalcDocument` in this chapter and `WordDocument` in the previous chapters, we refer to the current value of `cellMode` in expressions such as **in text mode, in value mode**, and **in formula mode**.

`HeaderWidth`, `HeaderHeight`, `ColWidth`, and `RowHeight` are the size of the headers and cells of the spreadsheet. In order for the cell text to not overwrite the cell's borders, `CellMargin` is used. The spreadsheet is made up of ten rows and four columns.

Cell.h

```
extern const int HeaderWidth, HeaderHeight,
                 ColWidth, RowHeight, CellMargin;

#define Rows 10
#define Cols 4
```

A cell can be aligned at the left, center, right or justified in the horizontal direction, and it can be aligned at the top, center, or bottom in the vertical direction:

```
enum Alignment {Left, Center, Right, Justified, Top, Bottom};

class Cell {
  public:
    Cell();
    ~Cell();

    Cell(const Cell& cell);
    Cell& operator=(const Cell& cell);
```

The `Clear` method is called when the user selects the new menu item and clears the font and background color of the cell before calling `Reset`, which clears the text and sets the cell to the text mode. `Reset` is also called when the user deletes the cell, in that case, the text is cleared, but not the font or color:

```
void Clear();
void Reset();
```

The `CharDown` method is called when the user inputs a character that is inserted before the current character or overwrites it depending on the value of the `keyboardMode` parameter. When the user double-clicks on the text in a cell, `MouseToIndex` calculates the index of the character clicked on:

```
void CharDown(int editIndex, TCHAR tChar,
              KeyboardMode keyboardMode);
int MouseToIndex(int x) const;
```

The `Text` and `CaretList` methods return the text and caret rectangle list of the cell.

```
vector<Rect> CaretList() const {return caretList;}

String GetText() const {return text;}
void SetText(String& t) {text = t;}

bool IsFormula() const {return (cellMode == FormulaMode);}
```

The font and background color of the cell can both be modified and inspected, so can the horizontal and vertical alignment:

```
Font CellFont() const {return font;}
Font& CellFont() {return font;}
Color BackgroundColor() const {return backgroundColor;}
Color& BackgroundColor() {return backgroundColor;}

Alignment HorizontalAlignment() const
                    {return horizontalAlignignment;}
Alignment& HorizontalAlignment()
                    {return horizontalAlignignment;}
Alignment VerticalAlignment() const
                    {return verticalAlignignment;}
Alignment& VerticalAlignment() {return verticalAlignignment;}
```

The `DrawCell` method draws the border of the cell in black, fills the cell with the background color, and draws the text. All colors are inverted if the inverse parameter is true, which it is if the cell is either being edited or is marked:

```
void DrawCell(Graphics& graphics, Reference cellRef,
              bool inverse) const;
void GenerateCaretList(Window* windowPtr);
```

The `DisplayFormula` method is called when the user starts editing the cell. A cell with a formula can be displayed with its value or its formula. When the user edits the cell, the formula is displayed. When they mark it, its value is displayed. The `DisplayFormula` method replaces the value by the formula (or an error message in case of an incorrect formula):

```
void DisplayFormula ();
```

The `InterpretCell` method interprets the text of the cell, which is interpreted as text, a numerical value, or a formula. If the formula contains a syntax error, an exception is thrown:

```
void InterpretCell(set<Reference>& sourceSet);
```

In the `formula` mode, `GenerateSourceSet` analyzes the formula and returns the (possibly empty) set of all its references. In the `text` or `value` mode, an empty set is returned:

```
void GenerateSourceSet(set<Reference>& sourceSet) const;
void GenerateSourceSet(Tree<TreeNode>* syntaxNodePtr,
                       set<Reference>& sourceSet) const;
```

In the `formula` mode, `TreeToString` returns the formula converted from the syntax tree to the string that is displayed in the cell when being edited:

```
String TreeToString() const;
String TreeToString(Tree<TreeNode>* syntaxNodePtr) const;
```

When the user cuts, copies, and pastes cells, their references are updated. `UpdateTree` updates all references in the formula mode:

```
void UpdateTree(Reference diffRef, set<Reference>& sourceSet);
void UpdateTree(Tree<TreeNode>* syntaxNodePtr,
               Reference diffRef, set<Reference>& sourceSet);
```

The `HasValue` method returns `true` if the cell holds a value: `true` in the `value` mode, `false` in the `text` mode, and `true` in the `formula` mode if it has been evaluated to a value, `false` if an evaluation error (missing value, reference out of scope, circular reference, or division by zero) occurred:

```
bool HasValue() const;
double GetValue() const {return value;}
```

The `Evaluate` method evaluates the syntax tree of the formula; `valueMap` holds the values of the cells in the source set:

```
void Evaluate(map<Reference,double>& valueMap);
double Evaluate(Tree<TreeNode>* syntaxNodePtr,
                map<Reference,double>& valueMap);
```

The cell can be saved to a file or cut, copied, and pasted:

```
bool WriteCellToStream(ostream& outStream) const;
bool ReadCellFromStream(istream& inStream);

void WriteCellToClipboard(InfoList& infoList) const;
void ReadCellFromClipboard(InfoList& infoList);
```

As mentioned at the beginning of this section, the cell can hold (possibly empty) text, a numerical value, or a formula, indicated by the value `cellMode`:

```
private:
    enum CellMode {TextMode, ValueMode, FormulaMode} cellMode;
```

All characters in the cell hold the same font and background color. The cell can be aligned at the left, center, right, or justified horizontally, and it can be aligned at the top, center, or bottom vertically:

```
Font font;
Color backgroundColor;
Alignment horizontalAlignignment, verticalAlignignment;
```

The `text` field holds the text displayed in the cell. In the `edit` mode, it is the text currently input by the user. In the `mark` mode, it is the text input by the user (in text mode), a numerical value input by the user converted to text, the calculated value of a formula, or an error message (missing value, reference out of scope, circular reference, or division by zero):

```
String text;
```

The caret list holds the caret rectangle of each character in `text`. It also holds the rectangle for the index after the last character, which means that the size of the caret list is always one more than the text:

```
vector<Rect> caretList;
```

When the value of a formula is being calculated, it may result in a value or any of the errors we discussed earlier. If the cell holds a value, `hasValue` is `true` and `value` holds the actual value:

```
bool hasValue;
double value;
```

When the user inputs a formula starting with =, it is interpreted as a syntax tree by the `Scanner` and `Parser` classes, and it is stored in `syntaxTreePtr`:

```
Tree<TreeNode>* syntaxTreePtr;
};
```

Cell.cpp

```cpp
#include "..\\SmallWindows\\SmallWindows.h"
#include "Token.h"
#include "Error.h"
#include "Scanner.h"
#include "TreeNode.h"
#include "Parser.h"
#include "Cell.h"

const int CellMargin = 100,
          ColWidth = 4000, RowHeight = 1000,
          HeaderWidth = 1000, HeaderHeight = 700;
```

The width of a cell is the width of the column minus the margins, and its height is the row height minus the margins:

```cpp
const int CellWidth = ColWidth - (2 * CellMargin),
          CellHeight = RowHeight - (2 * CellMargin);
```

When a cell is created, it is empty, it holds the text mode, it is center aligned in both horizontal and vertical directions, and it holds the system font with black text on white background:

```cpp
Cell::Cell()
 :cellMode(TextMode),
  font(SystemFont),
  backgroundColor(White),
  horizontalAlignignment(Center),
  verticalAlignignment(Center),
  hasValue(false),
  value(0),
  syntaxTreePtr(nullptr) {
  // Empty.
}
```

The copy constructor and assignment operator check whether `syntaxTreePtr` is `null`, if it is not null it is copied dynamically, its constructor continues copying its children recursively. It is not enough to simply copy the pointer, since one of the formulas of either the original or copy cell may be changed, but not the other one:

```
Cell::Cell(const Cell& cell)
 :cellMode(cell.cellMode),
  font(cell.font),
  backgroundColor(cell.backgroundColor),
  horizontalAlignignment(cell.horizontalAlignignment),
  verticalAlignignment(cell.verticalAlignignment),
  text(cell.text),
  caretList(cell.caretList),
  hasValue(cell.hasValue),
  value(cell.value) {
  if (cell.syntaxTreePtr != nullptr) {
    syntaxTreePtr = new Tree<TreeNode>(*cell.syntaxTreePtr);
    assert(syntaxTreePtr != nullptr);
  }
  else {
    syntaxTreePtr = nullptr;
  }
}
```

One difference between the copy constructor and the assignment operator is that we delete the syntax tree pointer in the assignment operator since it may point at dynamically allocated memory, which is not the case in the copy constructor. If it points at `null`, the `delete` operator does nothing:

```
Cell& Cell::operator=(const Cell& cell) {
  if (this != &cell) {
    cellMode = cell.cellMode;
    font = cell.font;
    backgroundColor = cell.backgroundColor;
    horizontalAlignignment = cell.horizontalAlignignment;
    verticalAlignignment = cell.verticalAlignignment;
    text = cell.text;
    caretList = cell.caretList;
    hasValue = cell.hasValue;
    value = cell.value;
    delete syntaxTreePtr;

    if (cell.syntaxTreePtr != nullptr) {
      syntaxTreePtr = new Tree<TreeNode>(*cell.syntaxTreePtr);
      assert(syntaxTreePtr != nullptr);
    }
```

```
  else {
    syntaxTreePtr = nullptr;
  }
}

return *this;
}
```

The syntax tree is the only dynamically allocated memory of the cell. Again, in case of a null pointer, `delete` does nothing:

```
Cell::~Cell() {
  delete syntaxTreePtr;
}
```

The difference between `Clear` and `Reset` is:

- `Clear` is called when the user selects the **New** menu item and the spreadsheet shall be totally cleared and also the cell's font, color and alignment shall be reset.
- `Reset` is called when the user deletes a cell and its mode and text shall be reset.

```
void Cell::Clear() {
  font = SystemFont;
  backgroundColor = White;
  horizontalAlignignment = Center;
  verticalAlignignment = Center;
  Reset();
}

void Cell::Reset() {
  cellMode = TextMode;
  text.clear();
  delete syntaxTreePtr;
  syntaxTreePtr = nullptr;
}
```

Character input

The `CharDown` method is called by `WindowProc` (which in turn is called by the Windows system) every time the user presses a graphical character. If the input index is at the end of the text (one step to the right of the text), we just add the character at the end. If it is not at the end of the text, we have to take into consideration the keyboard mode, which is either insert or overwrite.

In case of an insert, we insert the character, and in case of overwrite, we overwrite the character previously located at the edit index. Unlike the word processor in the previous chapters, we do not have to deal with the font, since all characters in the cell have the same font:

```
void Cell::CharDown(int editIndex, TCHAR tChar,
                    KeyboardMode keyboardMode) {
  if (editIndex == text.length()) {
    text.append(1, tChar);
  }
  else {
    switch (keyboardMode) {
      case InsertKeyboard:
        text.insert(editIndex, 1, tChar);
        break;

      case OverwriteKeyboard:
        text[editIndex] = tChar;
        break;
    }
  }
}
```

The `MouseToIndex` method is called when the user double-clicks on the cell. First, we need to subtract the cell margin from the mouse position, then we iterate the caret list and return the position of the character hit by the mouse. If the user hits to the left of the first character (aligned at the center or right), zero index is returned, and if they hit to the right of the last character (aligned to the left or center), the size of the text is returned, which corresponds to the index to the right of the last character:

```
int Cell::MouseToIndex(int x) const {
  x -= CellMargin;

  if (x < caretList[0].Left()) {
    return 0;
  }

  int size = text.length();
  for (int index = 0; index < size; ++index) {
    if (x < caretList[index].Right()) {
      return index;
    }
  }

  return size;
}
```

Drawing

The `Draw` method is called when the contents of the cell are to be drawn. The drawing of the text is rather straightforward-for each character in the character list, we just draw the character in its caret rectangle. This particular cell may be marked or in the process of being edited, in which case the inverse is true. In that case, the text, background, and border colors are inverted. In order to not overwrite the border of the cell, we also take the cell margin into consideration:

```
void Cell::DrawCell(Graphics& graphics, Reference cellRef,
                    bool inverse) const {
  Point topLeft(HeaderWidth + cellRef.Col() * ColWidth,
                HeaderHeight + cellRef.Row() * RowHeight);
  Size cellSize(ColWidth, RowHeight);
  Rect cellRect(topLeft, cellSize);

  Color textColor = font.FontColor(),
        backColor = backgroundColor, borderColor = Black;

  if (inverse) {
    textColor = textColor.Inverse();
    backColor = backColor.Inverse();
    borderColor = borderColor.Inverse();
  }

  graphics.FillRectangle(cellRect, borderColor, backColor);
  Size marginSize(CellMargin, CellMargin);
  int size = text.length();

  for (int index = 0; index < size; ++index) {
    TCHAR tChar = text[index];
    Rect caretRect = caretList[index];

    Rect charRect = (topLeft + marginSize) + caretRect;
    TCHAR text[] = {tChar, TEXT('\0')};
    graphics.DrawText(charRect, text, font, textColor, backColor);
  }
}
```

Caret rectangle list generation

When the user adds or removes a character of the text of a cell or changes its font or alignment, the caret rectangles need to be recalculated. GenerateCaretList can be considered a simplified version of GenerateParagraph in the word processor of the previous chapters. Its task is to calculate the character rectangles, which are used when setting the caret, drawing the text, and calculating the index of a mouse click.

First, we need to calculate the width of each character as well as the width of the text in order to set its horizontal start position. In case of justified alignment, we calculate the text width without spaces and count the spaces:

```
void Cell::GenerateCaretList(Window* windowPtr) {
  vector<int> widthList;
  int textWidth = 0, spaceCount = 0, noSpaceWidth = 0;

  for (const TCHAR tChar : text) {
    int charWidth = windowPtr->GetCharacterWidth(font, tChar);
    widthList.push_back(charWidth);
    textWidth += charWidth;

    if (horizontalAlignignment == Justified) {
      if (tChar == TEXT(' ')) {
        ++spaceCount;
      }
      else {
        noSpaceWidth += charWidth;
      }
    }
  }
}
```

When we have calculated the text width, we set the horizontal start position. In case of left or justified alignment, the start position is set to the cell margin. In the case of justified alignment, we also set the width of each space in the text. In the case of right alignment, we add the difference between the width of the cell and the text to the cell margin in order to place the rightmost part of the text at the right border in the cell. In the case of center alignment, we add half the difference in order for the text to be placed in the middle of the cell:

```
int startPos = 0, spaceWidth, cellWidth = ColWidth - (2 * CellMargin);

switch (horizontalAlignignment) {
  case Left:
    startPos = CellMargin;
    break;
```

```
    case Justified: {
        startPos = CellMargin;
        if (spaceCount > 0) {
            spaceWidth = max(0, (cellWidth-noSpaceWidth)/spaceCount);
        }
    }
    break;

    case Right:
        startPos = CellMargin + max(0, cellWidth - textWidth);
        break;

    case Center:
        startPos = CellMargin + max(0, (cellWidth - textWidth) / 2);
        break;
}
```

The vertical top position is set in a similar manner. In the case of top alignment, the top position is set to the cell margin. In the case of bottom alignment, we add the difference between the height of the cell and the text to the cell margin in order to place the bottom part of the text at the bottom border in the cell. In the case of center alignment, we add half the difference in order to place the text in the middle of the cell:

```
int topPos = 0,
    textHeight = windowPtr->GetCharacterHeight(font),
    cellHeight = RowHeight - (2 * CellMargin);

switch (verticalAlignignment) {
    case Top:
        topPos = CellMargin;
        break;

    case Bottom:
        topPos = CellMargin + max(0, cellHeight - textHeight);
        break;

    case Center:
        topPos = CellMargin + max(0, (cellHeight - textHeight) / 2);
        break;
}
```

When the horizontal start position and the top vertical position has been set, we iterate through the characters and add the rectangles to `caretList` for each of them. Note that we use the value of `spaceWidth` for spaces in the case of justified alignment:

```
caretList.clear();
int size = text.size();
for (int index = 0; index < size; ++index) {
  int charWidth = widthList[index];

  if ((horizontalAlignignment == Justified) &&
      (text[index] == TEXT(' '))) {
    charWidth = spaceWidth;
  }

  Point topLeft(startPos, topPos);
  Size charSize(charWidth, textHeight);
  caretList.push_back(Rect(topLeft, charSize));
  startPos += charWidth;
}
```

When each rectangle is added, we add the rectangle for the character to the right of the text. We set its width to the width of an average character of the cell's font:

```
  Point topLeft(startPos, topPos);
  int averageWidth = windowPtr->GetCharacterAverageWidth(font);
  Size charSize(averageWidth, textHeight);
  caretList.push_back(Rect(topLeft, charSize));
}
```

Formula interpretation

When the user single-clicks or double-clicks on a cell, its text remains unchanged in the text or value mode, but it gets changed in the formula mode. In the formula mode, the calculated value of the formula is displayed in the mark mode, while in the edit mode, the formula itself is displayed. `DisplayFormula` calls `TreeToString` in the formula mode, which generates the text of the formula:

```
void Cell::DisplayFormula() {
  switch (cellMode) {
    case TextMode:
    case ValueMode:
      break;

    case FormulaMode:
      text = TEXT("=") + TreeToString(syntaxTreePtr);
      break;
  }
}
```

The `InterpretCell` method is called when the user terminates the text input by pressing the *Enter* or *Tab* key or clicking the mouse. If the user has input a formula (starting with =), it is parsed. `Parse` returns a syntax tree holding the formula or throws an exception in the case of a syntax error. Note that `InterpretCell` only report the syntax error. All other errors (missing value, references out of range, circular reference, or division by zero) are handled by the following `Evaluate`:

```
void Cell::InterpretCell(set<Reference>& sourceSet) {
  String trimText = Trim(text);

  if (IsNumeric(trimText)) {
    cellMode = ValueMode;
    value = stod(trimText);
  }
  else if (!trimText.empty() && (trimText[0] == TEXT('='))) {
    cellMode = FormulaMode;
    Parser parser(trimText.substr(1));
    syntaxTreePtr = parser.Parse();
    GenerateSourceSet(syntaxTreePtr, sourceSet);
  }
  else {
    cellMode = TextMode;
  }
}
```

The `GenerateSourceSet` method traverses the syntax tree and extracts a (possible empty) set of all its references in the formula mode. In the case of text or value mode, the set is empty, since only formulas hold references:

```
void Cell::GenerateSourceSet(set<Reference>& sourceSet) const{
  if (cellMode == FormulaMode) {
    GenerateSourceSet(syntaxTreePtr, sourceSet);
  }
}
```

In case of unary addition or subtraction or an expression enclosed by parentheses, the source set of its child node is returned:

```
void Cell::GenerateSourceSet(Tree<TreeNode>* syntaxNodePtr,
                             set<Reference>& sourceSet) const{
  DynamicList<Tree<TreeNode>*> childList =
    syntaxNodePtr->ChildList();
  switch (syntaxNodePtr->NodeValue().Id()) {
    case UnaryAdd:
    case UnarySubtract:
    case Parenthesis:
      return GenerateSourceSet(childList[0]);
```

In the case of a binary expression, the union of the source sets of the two children is returned:

```
case BinaryAdd:
case BinarySubtract:
case Multiply:
case Divide: {
    set<Reference> leftSet = GenerateSourceSet(childList[0]),
                   rightSet = GenerateSourceSet(childList[1]);
    leftSet.insert(rightSet.begin(), rightSet.end());
    return leftSet;
}
```

In the case of a reference, a set holding only the reference is returned if it is located in the spreadsheet. No references outside the spreadsheet are included in the set:

```
case RefId: {
    set<Reference> singleSet;
    Reference sourceRef =
       syntaxNodePtr->NodeValue().ReferenceField();

    if ((sourceRef.Row() >= 0) && (sourceRef.Row() < Rows) &&
        (sourceRef.Col() >= 0) && (sourceRef.Col() < Cols)) {
      singleSet.insert(sourceRef);
    }

    return singleSet;
}
```

Finally, in the case of a value, an empty set is returned:

```
        case ValueId:
          return set<Reference>();
    }

    assert(false);
    return set<Reference>();
}
```

The `TreeToString` method traverses the syntax tree and converts it to a string. Note that it is quite possible to have a formula with a reference out of scope. However, the `Reference` class returns ? in that case:

```
String Cell::TreeToString() const {
  if (cellMode == FormulaMode) {
    return TEXT("=") + TreeToString(syntaxTreePtr);
  }
```

```
    else {
      return text;
    }
  }
```

In the case of unary addition or subtraction, + or – is added to the text of the child node:

```
String Cell::TreeToString(Tree<TreeNode>* syntaxNodePtr) const {
  DynamicList<Tree<TreeNode>*> childList =
    syntaxNodePtr->ChildList();

  switch (syntaxNodePtr->NodeValue().Id()) {
    case UnaryAdd:
      return TEXT("+") + TreeToString(childList[0]);

    case UnarySubtract:
      return TEXT("-") + TreeToString(childList[0]);
      break;
```

In the case of a binary expressions +, –, *, or / is inserted between the text of the child nodes:

```
    case BinaryAdd:
      return TreeToString(childList[0]) + TEXT("+") +
            TreeToString(childList[1]);

    case BinarySubtract:
      return TreeToString(childList[0]) + TEXT("-") +
            TreeToString(childList[1]);

    case Multiply:
      return TreeToString(childList[0]) + TEXT("*") +
            TreeToString(childList[1]);

    case Divide:
      return TreeToString(childList[0]) + TEXT("/") +
            TreeToString(childList[1]);
```

In the case of an expression enclosed by parentheses, the text of the child node enclosed by parentheses is returned:

```
    case Parenthesis:
      return TEXT("(") + TreeToString(childList[0]) + TEXT(")");
```

In the case of a reference, its text is returned. Again, if the reference is out of range, ? is returned:

```
case RefId:
  return syntaxNodePtr->
        NodeValue().ReferenceField().ToString();
```

In the case of a value, its converted text is returned:

```
case ValueId:
  return to_String(syntaxNodePtr->NodeValue().Value());
}

assert(false);
return TEXT("");
}
```

When the user copies and pastes a block of cells, the references of each formula are relative and will be updated. `UpdateTree` looks for and updates references in the syntax tree. In all other cases, it iterates through the child list and calls `UpdateTree` recursively for each child (one child each in a unary expression and a parentheses expression, two children in a binary expression, and no children in values or references):

```
void Cell::UpdateTree(Reference diffRef, set<Reference>&sourceSet) {
  if (cellMode == FormulaMode) {
    UpdateTree(syntaxTreePtr, diffRef, sourceSet);
  }
}

void Cell::UpdateTree(Tree<TreeNode>* syntaxNodePtr,
                Reference diffRef, set<Reference>& sourceSet) {
  if (syntaxNodePtr->NodeValue().Id() == RefId) {
    syntaxNodePtr->NodeValue().ReferenceField() += diffRef;
    sourceSet.insert(syntaxNodePtr->NodeValue().ReferenceField());
  }
  else {
    for (Tree<TreeNode>* childNodePtr :
        syntaxNodePtr->ChildList()) {
      UpdateTree(childNodePtr, diffRef, sourceSet);
    }
  }
}
```

When the value of a formula is evaluated, it may return a valid value, in which case `hasValue` is set to `true`. However, if an error occurs during the evaluation (missing value, references out of range, circular reference, or division by zero), `hasValue` is set to `false`. `hasValue` is called when a value of a formula of another cell is being evaluated. If it returns `false`, the evaluation will result in the missing value error:

```
bool Cell::HasValue() const{
  switch (cellMode) {
    case TextMode:
      return false;
    case ValueMode:
      return true;

    case FormulaMode:
      return hasValue;
  }

  assert(false);
  return false;
}
```

In the formula mode, the formula is being evaluated to a value. If an error occurs (missing value, reference out of range, circular reference, or division by zero), an exception is thrown by `Evaluate`, and the cell text is set to the error message text. Note that it is possible to input references out of scope, which `InterpretCell` accepts. However, `Evaluate` throws an exception with an error message that is displayed in the cell.

Moreover, it is quite possible to cut, copy, and paste a cell so that its references get located out of the scope and then cut, copied, and pasted again so that the references become valid. However, if the user edits a formula with references out of the scope, `?` is returned by the `ToString` method in the `Reference` class, since it is difficult to express references with negative columns:

```
void Cell::Evaluate(map<Reference,double>& valueMap) {
  if (cellMode == FormulaMode) {
    try {
      value = Evaluate(syntaxTreePtr, valueMap);
      text = to_String(value);
      hasValue = true;
    }
    catch (Error error) {
      text = error.ErrorText();
      hasValue = false;
    }
  }
}
```

The `Evaluate` method finds the current value of the cell by looking up the values of the cells referred to by the formula:

```
double Cell::Evaluate(Tree<TreeNode>* syntaxNodePtr,
                      map<Reference,double>& valueMap) {
  DynamicList<Tree<TreeNode>*> childList =
    syntaxNodePtr->ChildList();
```

In the case of a unary or binary expression, the value is calculated (unary addition is only present for the sake of completeness and does not change the value):

```
switch (syntaxNodePtr->NodeValue().Id()) {
  case UnaryAdd:
    return Evaluate(childList[0], valueMap);

  case UnarySubtract:
    return -Evaluate(childList[0], valueMap);

  case BinaryAdd:
    return Evaluate(childList[0], valueMap) +
           Evaluate(childList[1], valueMap);

  case BinarySubtract:
    return Evaluate(childList[0], valueMap) -
           Evaluate(childList[1], valueMap);

  case Multiply:
    return Evaluate(childList[0], valueMap) *
           Evaluate(childList[1], valueMap);
```

In case of division by zero, an exception is thrown.

```
  case Divide: {
      double remainder = Evaluate(childList[1], valueMap);

      if (remainder != 0) {
        return Evaluate(childList[0], valueMap) / remainder;
      }
      else {
        throw Error(DivisionByZero);
      }
    }
    break;
```

In the case of an expression within parentheses, we simply return its evaluated value:

```
  case Parenthesis:
    return Evaluate(childList[0], valueMap);
```

In the case of a reference, we look up the source cell in `valueMap`. In the case of a source cell with a missing value (not present in `valueMap`) or a reference out of scope (referring to a cell outside the spreadsheet), exceptions are thrown:

```
case RefId: {
    Reference sourceRef =
        syntaxNodePtr->NodeValue().ReferenceField();

    if ((sourceRef.Row() >= 0) && (sourceRef.Row() < Rows) &&
        (sourceRef.Col() >= 0) && (sourceRef.Col() < Cols)) {
      if (valueMap.find(sourceRef) != valueMap.end()) {
        return valueMap[sourceRef];
      }
      else {
        throw Error(MissingValue);
      }
    }
    else {
      throw Error(ReferenceOutOfRange);
    }
  }
  break;
```

In the case of a value, we simply return the value:

```
    case ValueId:
        return syntaxNodePtr->NodeValue().Value();
  }

  assert(false);
  return 0;
}
```

File management

The `WriteDocumentToStream` method is called by `CalcDocument` every time the user selects the **Save** or **Save As** menu items from the file menu. In the formula mode, we call `WriteTreeToStream` on the syntax tree:

```
bool Cell::WriteCellToStream(ostream& outStream) const {
  outStream.write((char*) &cellMode, sizeof cellMode);
  outStream.write((char*) &horizontalAlignignment,
                  sizeof horizontalAlignignment);
  outStream.write((char*) &verticalAlignignment,
                  sizeof verticalAlignignment);
  outStream.write((char*) &hasValue, sizeof hasValue);
  outStream.write((char*) &value, sizeof value);

  backgroundColor.WriteColorToStream(outStream);
  font.WriteFontToStream(outStream);

  int charListSize = text.size();
  outStream.write((char*) &charListSize, sizeof charListSize);

  for (const TCHAR tChar : text) {
    outStream.write((char*) &tChar, sizeof tChar);
  }

  for (const Rect caretRect : caretList) {
    caretRect.WriteRectToStream(outStream);
  }

  if (cellMode == FormulaMode) {
    syntaxTreePtr->WriteTreeToStream(outStream);
  }

  return ((bool) outStream);
}
```

In `ReadCellFromStream`, we dynamically create and read the syntax tree in the formula mode:

```
bool Cell::ReadCellFromStream(istream& inStream) {
  inStream.read((char*) &cellMode, sizeof cellMode);
  inStream.read((char*) &horizontalAlignignment,
                sizeof horizontalAlignignment);
  inStream.read((char*) &verticalAlignignment,
                sizeof verticalAlignignment);
  inStream.read((char*) &hasValue, sizeof hasValue);
  inStream.read((char*) &value, sizeof value);
```

```
  backgroundColor.ReadColorFromStream(inStream);
  font.ReadFontFromStream(inStream);

  int charListSize;
  inStream.read((char*) &charListSize, sizeof charListSize);

  for (int count = 0; count < charListSize; ++count) {
    TCHAR tChar;
    inStream.read((char*) &tChar, sizeof tChar);
    text.append(1, tChar);
  }

  for (int count = 0; count < (charListSize + 1); ++count) {
    Rect caretRect;
    caretRect.ReadRectFromStream(inStream);
    caretList.push_back(caretRect);
  }

  if (cellMode == FormulaMode) {
    syntaxTreePtr = new Tree<TreeNode>();
    assert(syntaxTreePtr != nullptr);
    syntaxTreePtr->ReadTreeFromStream(inStream);
  }
  else {
    syntaxTreePtr = nullptr;
  }

  return ((bool) inStream);
}
```

The `WriteCellToClipboard` and `ReadCellFromClipboard` methods are called by `CalcDocument` when the user cuts, copies, and pastes the cell. It works in the same way as `WriteDocumentToStream` and `ReadCellFromStream` we saw earlier:

```
void Cell::WriteCellToClipboard(InfoList& infoList) const {
  infoList.AddValue<CellMode>(cellMode);
  infoList.AddValue<Alignment>(horizontalAlignignment);
  infoList.AddValue<Alignment>(verticalAlignignment);
  infoList.AddValue<double>(value);
  infoList.AddValue<bool>(hasValue);

  font.WriteFontToClipboard(infoList);
  backgroundColor.WriteColorToClipboard(infoList);
  infoList.AddValue<int>(text.size());

  for (const TCHAR tChar : text) {
    infoList.AddValue<TCHAR>(tChar);
  }
```

```
      if (cellMode == FormulaMode) {
        syntaxTreePtr->WriteTreeToClipboard(infoList);
      }
    }

    void Cell::ReadCellFromClipboard(InfoList& infoList) {
      infoList.GetValue<CellMode>(cellMode);
      infoList.GetValue<Alignment>(horizontalAlignignment);
      infoList.GetValue<Alignment>(verticalAlignignment);
      infoList.GetValue<double>(value);
      infoList.GetValue<bool>(hasValue);

      font.ReadFontFromClipboard(infoList);
      backgroundColor.ReadColorFromClipboard(infoList);

      int listSize;
      infoList.GetValue<int>(listSize);

      for (int count = 0; count < listSize; ++count) {
        TCHAR tChar;
        infoList.GetValue<TCHAR>(tChar);
        text.push_back(tChar);
      }

      for (int count = 0; count < (listSize + 1); ++count) {
        Rect caretRect;
        caretRect.ReadRectFromClipboard(infoList);
        caretList.push_back(caretRect);
      }

      if (cellMode == FormulaMode) {
        syntaxTreePtr = new Tree<TreeNode>();
        assert(syntaxTreePtr != nullptr);
        syntaxTreePtr->ReadTreeFromClipboard(infoList);
      }
      else {
        syntaxTreePtr = nullptr;
      }
    }
```

Further reading

If the scanner and parser of this chapter have got you interested in compilers, I recommend that you refer to *Compilers: Principles, Techniques, and Tools* by A. V. Aho et al. (second edition. Addison Wesley, 2007). It is the second edition of the classic *Dragon Book*. The authors explain the theory and practice of compilers from scanning and parsing to advanced optimization.

If the concept of graphs has caught your interest, I recommend *Introduction to Graph Theory* by D. B. West (Prentice Hall, 2000), which reasons about graphs from a mathematical point of view.

Summary

In this chapter, we covered the spreadsheet program implementation. This chapter concludes the first part of this book: how to develop an application with Small Windows. Chapter 10, *The Framework*, introduces the second part: the implementation of Small Windows.

10
The Framework

The remaining chapters of this book explain the details of the Small Windows implementation. This chapter covers the following topics:

- An overview of the classes of Small Windows
- An example of the Hello World application, which we covered at the beginning of this book, written in the Win32 API7
- The `MainWindow` and `WinMain` functions
- The implementation of the main classes of Small Windows: `Application`, `Window`, and `Graphics`

An overview of Small Windows

Here is a short description of the classes of Small Windows:

Chapter	Class	Description
10	Application	This is the main class of Small Windows. It manages the message loop and registration of Windows classes.
10	Window	This the root Window class. It creates individual windows and provides basic window functionality, such as mouse, touch, and keyboard input, drawing, zooming, timer, focus, size, and coordinate systems.
10	Graphics	This is the class for drawing lines, rectangles, ellipses, and text in the client area of the window.

11	`Document` **extends** `Window`	This extends the window with document functionality, such as scrolling, caret handling, and drop files.
11	`Menu`	This handles menu bars, menus, menu items, and the menu separator.
11	`Accelerator`	This extracts accelerator information from the menu item texts.
11	`StandardDocument` **extends** `Document`	This provides a document-based framework with the common **File**, **Edit**, and **Help** menu items.

12	`Size`
	`Point`
	`Rect`
		These are auxiliary classes that handle a two-dimensional point (x and y), size (width and height), or the four corners of a rectangle.

12	`Font`	This wraps the `LOGFONT` structure, which holds information about the font's name, size, and whether it is bold or italic.
12	`Cursor`	This sets the cursor and provides a set of standard cursors.
12	`DynamicList` **template**	This is a list of dynamic size and a set of callback methods.
12	`Tree` **template**	This is a tree structure where each node has a (possibly empty) list of child nodes.
12	`InfoList`	This is a list of generic information, which can be transformed to and from a memory buffer.
13	`Registry`	This provides an interface against the Windows registry.
13	`Clipboard`	This provides an interface against the Windows clipboard.
13	`StandardDialog`	This displays the standard dialogs for saving and opening files, choosing a font or color, and printing.
13	`PreviewDocument` **extends** `Document`	This sets up a document whose logical size is fixed regardless of its physical size.
14	`Dialog` **extends** `Window`	This provides a modal dialog. The controls below are added to the dialog.

14	Control **abstract**	This is the base class for dialog controls.
14	ButtonControl **extends** Control	This is the base class for button controls.
14	GroupBox, PushButton, CheckBox, RadioButton **extends** ButtonControl	These are classes for group boxes, push buttons, checkboxes, and radio buttons.
14	ListControl **extends** Control	This is the base class for list controls.
14	ListBox, MultipleListBox **extends** ListControl	These are classes for single and multiple list boxes.
14	ComboBox **extends** Control	This is the class for a combo (drop-down) box.
14	Label **extends** Control	This is the class for a simple label, often used as a prompt for TextField.
14	TextField **template extends** Control	This is a class for an editable field, where a converter may convert between a string and any type.
14	Converter **template**	This is a converter class that can be specified by any type.
14	PageSetupDialog **extends** Dialog	This is a dialog for page setup settings, such as margins, headers, and footer text.
14	PageSetupInfo	This has page setup information, which we saw previously.

"Hello" window for the Win32 API

First of all, let's take a look at the Hello application from the first chapter of this book. The following code snippet is the same application written directly with the Win32 API, without Small Windows. Note that the code is written in C rather than C++ as the Win32 API is a C function library rather than a C++ class library. As you can see, the code is a lot more complicated compared to the application in the first chapter.

Do not worry if it looks complicated. Its purpose is actually to demonstrate the complexity of the Win32 API; we'll discuss the details in this and the following chapters.

MainWindow.c

```
#include <Windows.h>
#include <Assert.h>
#include <String.h>
#include <TChar.h>

LRESULT CALLBACK WindowProc(HWND windowHandle, UINT message,
                            WPARAM wordParam, LPARAM longParam);
```

The `WinMain` method is called when the application starts to execute. It corresponds to `main` in Standard C.

```
int WINAPI WinMain(HINSTANCE instanceHandle,
                   HINSTANCE prevInstanceHandle,
                   char* commandLine, int commandShow) {
```

First, we need to register the `Windows` class for our window. Note that `Windows` classes are not C++ classes:

```
WNDCLASS windowClass;
memset(&windowClass, 0, sizeof windowClass);
windowClass.hInstance = instanceHandle;
```

The style of the `Windows` class will be redrawn when the window size is changed in the horizontal and vertical direction:

```
windowClass.style = CS_HREDRAW | CS_VREDRAW | CS_DBLCLKS;
```

The icon of the window is the standard application icon, the cursor is the standard arrow cursor, and the background of the client area is white.

```
windowClass.hIcon = LoadIcon(NULL, IDI_APPLICATION);
windowClass.hCursor = LoadCursor(NULL, IDC_ARROW);
windowClass.hbrBackground =
  (HBRUSH) GetStockObject(WHITE_BRUSH);
```

The `WindowProc` function is a callback function called every time the window receives a message:

```
windowClass.lpfnWndProc = WindowProc;
```

The name of the `Windows` class is `window`, which is used in the `CreateWindowEx` call here:

```
windowClass.lpszClassName = TEXT("window");
RegisterClass(&windowClass);
```

The `CreateWindowEx` method creates a window with the default position and size. Note that we can create many windows with the same `Windows` class:

```
HWND windowHandle =
  CreateWindowEx(0, TEXT("window"), NULL, WS_OVERLAPPEDWINDOW,
                 CW_USEDEFAULT, CW_USEDEFAULT, CW_USEDEFAULT,
                 CW_USEDEFAULT, NULL, CreateMenu(),
                 instanceHandle, NULL);
assert(windowHandle != NULL);
ShowWindow(windowHandle, commandShow);
RegisterTouchWindow(windowHandle, 0);
SetWindowText(windowHandle, TEXT("Hello Window"));
```

The `GetMessage` method waits for the next message, which is translated and dispatched to the window with an input focus. The `GetMessage` method returns `true` for all messages except the quit message, which is eventually sent when the user closes the window:

```
MSG message;
while (GetMessage(&message, NULL, 0, 0)) {
  TranslateMessage(&message);
  DispatchMessage(&message);
}
return ((int) message.wParam);
}

LRESULT CALLBACK WindowProc(HWND windowHandle, UINT message,
                            WPARAM wordParam, LPARAM longParam){

  switch (message) {
    case WM_PAINT: {
```

When painting the client area, we need to create a paint structure and a device context, which is created by `BeginPaint`:

```
PAINTSTRUCT paintStruct;
HDC deviceContextHandle =
  BeginPaint(windowHandle, &paintStruct);
SetMapMode(deviceContextHandle, MM_ISOTROPIC);
```

Since we want to use logical units (hundreds of a millimeters), we need to set the device context by calling `SetWindowExtEx` and `SetViewportExtEx`:

```
int horizontalSize =
    100 * GetDeviceCaps(deviceContextHandle, HORZSIZE),
  verticalSize =
    100 * GetDeviceCaps(deviceContextHandle,VERTSIZE);
```

```
SetWindowExtEx(deviceContextHandle, horizontalSize,
             verticalSize, NULL);
int horizontalResolution =
     (int) GetDeviceCaps(deviceContextHandle,HORZRES),
   verticalResolution =
     (int) GetDeviceCaps(deviceContextHandle,VERTRES);
SetViewportExtEx(deviceContextHandle,horizontalResolution,
               verticalResolution, NULL);
```

Since we also want to take scroll movements into consideration, we also call
`SetWindowOrgEx`:

```
int horizontalScroll =
  GetScrollPos(windowHandle, SB_HORZ),
    verticalScroll = GetScrollPos(windowHandle, SB_VERT);
SetWindowOrgEx(deviceContextHandle, horizontalScroll,
             verticalScroll, NULL);
```

Also, as we want to take scroll movements into consideration, we call `SetWindowOrgEx` to
set to logical origin of the client area:

```
RECT clientRect;
GetClientRect(windowHandle, &clientRect);
POINT bottomRight = {clientRect.right, clientRect.bottom};
DPtoLP(deviceContextHandle, &bottomRight, 1);
clientRect.right = bottomRight.x;
clientRect.top = bottomRight.y;
```

We need to set a LOGFONT structure to create the 12-point boldface `Times New Roman` font:

```
LOGFONT logFont;
memset(&logFont, 0, sizeof logFont);
_tcscpy_s(logFont.lfFaceName, LF_FACESIZE,
         TEXT("Times New Roman"));
int fontSize = 12;
```

Since we work with logical units that are hundreds of millimeters, one typographical point
is 1 inch divided by 72 and 1 inch is 25.4 millimeters. We multiply the font size by 2,540 and
divide it by 72:

```
logFont.lfHeight = (int) ((2540.0 * fontSize) / 72);
logFont.lfWeight = FW_BOLD;
logFont.lfItalic = FALSE;
```

When we use the font to write text in the client area, we need to create the font indirectly
and add it as a graphical object. We also need to save the previous object in order to restore
it later:

```
HFONT fontHandle = CreateFontIndirect(&logFont);
HFONT oldFontHandle =
  (HFONT) SelectObject(deviceContextHandle, fontHandle);
```

The text color is black and its background color is white. RGB is a macro that transforms the red, green, and blue parts of the color into a COLORREF value:

```
COLORREF black = RGB(0, 0, 0), white = RGB(255, 255, 255);
SetTextColor(deviceContextHandle, black);
SetBkColor(deviceContextHandle, white);
```

Finally, DrawText draws the text in the middle of the client area:

```
TCHAR* textPtr = TEXT("Hello, Small Windows!");
DrawText(deviceContextHandle, textPtr, _tcslen(textPtr),
         &clientRect, DT_SINGLELINE|DT_CENTER|DT_VCENTER);
```

Since fonts are system resources, we need to restore the previous font object and delete the new font object. We also need to restore the paint structure:

```
SelectObject(deviceContextHandle, oldFontHandle);
DeleteObject(fontHandle);
EndPaint(windowHandle, &paintStruct);
}
```

Since we have handled the WM_PAINT message, we return zero.

```
    break;
}
```

For all messages other than WM_PAINT, we call DefWindowProc to handle the message:

```
return DefWindowProc(windowHandle, message,
                     wordParam, longParam);
}
```

The MainWindow function

In regular C and C++, the execution of the application starts with the main function. In Small Windows, however, main has been replaced by MainWindow. MainWindow is implemented by the user of Small Windows for each project. Its task is to define the application name and create the main window object.

MainWindow.h

```
void MainWindow(vector<String> argumentList,
                SmallWindows::WindowShow windowShow);
```

The WinMain function

In the Win32 API, `WinMain` is the function equivalent to `main`. Each application must include the definition of the `WinMain` function. In order for Small Windows to work, `WinMain` is implemented as a part of Small Windows, while `MainWindow` has to be implemented by the user of Small Windows for each project. To sum it up, here are the three kinds of main functions:

Regular C/C++	Win32 API	Small Windows
main	WinMain	MainWindow

The `WinMain` function is called by the Windows system and takes the following parameters:

- `instanceHandle`: This holds the handle of the application
- `prevInstanceHandle`: This is present due to backward compatibility but is always `null`
- `commandLine`: This is a null-terminated character (`char`, not `TCHAR`) array holding the arguments for the application, separated by spaces
- `commandShow`: This holds the preferred appearance of the main window

WinMain.cpp

```
#include "SmallWindows.h"

int WINAPI WinMain(HINSTANCE instanceHandle,
                   HINSTANCE /* prevInstanceHandle */,
                   char* commandLine, int commandShow) {
```

The `WinMain` function performs the following tasks:

- It divides the space-separated words of the command line into a `String` list by calling `GenerateArgumentList`. Refer to `Chapter 12`, *Auxiliary Classes*, for the definitions of `CharPtrToGenericString` and `Split`.
- It instantiates an `Application` object.
- It calls the `MainWindow` function, which creates the main window of the application and sets its name.

- It calls the `RunMessageLoop` method of `Application`, which continues to handle Windows messages until the quit message is sent.

```
Application::RegisterWindowClasses(instanceHandle);
vector<String> argumentList =
  Split(CharPtrToGenericString(commandLine));
MainWindow(argumentList, (WindowShow) commandShow);
return Application::RunMessageLoop();
}
```

The Application class

The `Application` class handles the message loop of the application. The message loop waits for the next message from the Windows system and sends it to the right window. The `Application` class also defines the `Windows` classes (which are not C++ classes) for the `Window`, `Document`, `StandardDocument`, and `Dialog` C++ classes. The fields of the classes are static since `Application` is not intended to be instantiated.

From this point in Small Windows, every part of the Small Windows implementation is included in the `SmallWindows` namespace. A namespace is a C++ feature that encapsulates classes and functions. The declaration of `MainWindow`, we saw earlier, is not included in the `Smallwindows` namespace since the C++ language rules stipulate that it cannot be included in a namespace. The `WinMain` definition is also not included in the namespace, since it needs to be placed outside the namespace to be called by the Windows system.

Application.h

```
namespace SmallWindows {
  class Application {
    public:
```

The `RegisterWindowClasses` method defines the Windows classes for the `Window`, `Document`, `StandardDocument`, and `Dialog` C++ classes. The `RunMessageLoop` method runs the message loop of the Windows message system. It waits for the next message and sends it to the right window. When a special quit message is received it breaks the message loop, which leads to the termination of the `Application` class:

```
static void RegisterWindowClasses(HINSTANCE instanceHandle);
static int RunMessageLoop();
```

In Windows, each application holds a **handle** to the application instance. Handles are common in the Win32 API, and are used to access objects of the Windows system. They are similar to pointers but provide identification without revealing any location information.

The instance handle (of the `HINSTANCE` type) is used when creating windows in the constructor of the following `Window` class and when displaying standard dialogs in the Standard Dialogs section in `Chapter 14`, *Dialogs, Controls, and Page Setup*:

```
static HINSTANCE& InstanceHandle() {return instanceHandle;}
```

The application name is set by each application and is referred to by the standard **File**, **Help**, and **About** menus, the **Open** and **Save** dialogs, and the registry:

```
static String& ApplicationName() {return applicationName;}
```

The pointer to the main window of the application is referenced when the user closes a window. If it is the main window, the application exits. Moreover, when the user selects the **Exit** menu item, the main window is closed before the application exits:

```
static Window*& MainWindowPtr() {return mainWindowPtr;}

   private:
      static HINSTANCE instanceHandle;
      static String applicationName;
      static Window* mainWindowPtr;
   };
};
```

Application.cpp

```
#include "SmallWindows.h"

namespace SmallWindows {
   HINSTANCE Application::instanceHandle;
   String Application::applicationName;
   Window* Application::mainWindowPtr;
```

The Win32 API Windows classes

The `Windows` classes are registered in `Application`. A Windows class needs to be registered only once. After it has been registered, more than one window can be created for each `Windows` class. Again, note that windows classes are not C++ classes. Each `Windows` class is stored by its name: `lpszClassName`. The `lpfnWndProc` field defines the freestanding function that receives the window messages from the message loop. Each window allows double-clicks as well as horizontal and vertical redraw styles, which means that the `WM_PAINT` message is sent to the window and the `OnPaint` method is called each time the user changes the size of the window. Moreover, each window has the standard application icon in its top-right corner and the standard arrow cursor. The client area is white, except for the dialog, where the client area is light gray:

```
void Application::RegisterWindowClasses(HINSTANCE
                                        instanceHandle) {
  Application::instanceHandle = instanceHandle;
  assert(instanceHandle != nullptr);

  WNDCLASS windowClass;
  memset(&windowClass, 0, sizeof windowClass);
  windowClass.hInstance = instanceHandle;
  windowClass.style = CS_HREDRAW | CS_VREDRAW | CS_DBLCLKS;
  windowClass.hIcon = LoadIcon(nullptr, IDI_APPLICATION);
  windowClass.hCursor = LoadCursor(nullptr, IDC_ARROW);
  windowClass.hbrBackground =
    (HBRUSH) GetStockObject(WHITE_BRUSH);

  windowClass.lpfnWndProc = WindowProc;
  windowClass.lpszClassName = TEXT("window");
  ::RegisterClass(&windowClass);

  windowClass.lpfnWndProc = DocumentProc;
  windowClass.lpszClassName = TEXT("document");
  ::RegisterClass(&windowClass);

  windowClass.lpfnWndProc = DocumentProc;
  windowClass.lpszClassName = TEXT("standarddocument");
  ::RegisterClass(&windowClass);
}
```

The message loop

The `RunMessageLoop` method holds the classic Windows message loop. There are two cases: if the main window pointer points at an object of the `Window` class, we just need to handle the message queue with the Win32 API functions `GetMessage`, `TranslateMessage`, and `DispatchMessage` without caring about accelerators. However, if it points at an object of `Document` or any of its subclasses, the message loop becomes more complicated because we need to take accelerators into consideration:

```
int Application::RunMessageLoop() {
  assert(!applicationName.empty());
  assert(mainWindowPtr != nullptr);

  MSG message;
```

```
  if (dynamic_cast<Document*>(mainWindowPtr) == nullptr) {
    while (::GetMessage(&message, nullptr, 0, 0)) {
      ::TranslateMessage(&message);
      ::DispatchMessage(&message);
    }
  }
```

If the main window pointer points at an object of Document or any of its subclasses, we set up a buffer for the accelerator table defined in Document, which we use in the message loop. The Win32 API TranslateAccelerator function looks up the accelerator and decides whether a key stroke message should be treated as the menu item associated with the accelerator:

```
  else {
    Document* documentPtr = (Document*) mainWindowPtr;
    int size = documentPtr->AcceleratorSet().size(), index = 0;
```

The TranslateAccelerator method wants an array of ACCEL structures, so we convert the accelerator set to an array:

```
    ACCEL* acceleratorTablePtr = new ACCEL[size];
    assert(acceleratorTablePtr != nullptr);

    for (ACCEL accelerator : documentPtr->AcceleratorSet()) {
      acceleratorTablePtr[index++] = accelerator;
    }

    HACCEL acceleratorTable =
            ::CreateAcceleratorTable(acceleratorTablePtr, size);

    while (::GetMessage(&message, nullptr, 0, 0)) {
      if (!::TranslateAccelerator(mainWindowPtr->WindowHandle(),
                                  acceleratorTable, &message)) {
        ::TranslateMessage(&message);
        ::DispatchMessage(&message);
      }
    }
```

When the accelerator array is used, it is deleted:

```
    delete [] acceleratorTablePtr;
  }
```

When the message loop is finished, we return the last massage:

```
    return ((int) message.wParam);
  }
```

The Window class

The `Window` class is the root class of the document classes; it handles basic window functionality such as the timer, input focus, coordinate transformation, window size and position, text metrics, and the message box as well as mouse, keyboard, and touch screen input. Moreover, `Window` defines enumerations for window styles and appearances, buttons, icons, and coordinate systems.

Window.h

```
namespace SmallWindows {
  extern map<HWND,Window*> WindowMap;
```

There is large set of window styles. The window may be equipped with a border, a thick frame, scroll bars, or minimize and maximize boxes:

```
enum WindowStyle {NoStyle = 0, Border = WS_BORDER,
                  ThickFrame = WS_THICKFRAME,
                  Caption = WS_CAPTION, Child = WS_CHILD,
                  ClipChildren = WS_CLIPCHILDREN,
                  ClipSibling = WS_CLIPSIBLINGS,
                  Disabled = WS_DISABLED,
                  DialogFrame = WS_DLGFRAME, Group = WS_GROUP,
                  HScroll = WS_HSCROLL, Minimize = WS_MINIMIZE,
                  Maximize = WS_MAXIMIZE,
                  MaximizeBox = WS_MAXIMIZEBOX,
                  MinimizeBox = WS_MINIMIZEBOX,
                  Overlapped = WS_OVERLAPPED,
                  OverlappedWindow = WS_OVERLAPPEDWINDOW,
                  Popup = WS_POPUP,PopupWindow = WS_POPUPWINDOW,
                  SystemMenu = WS_SYSMENU,
                  Tabulatorstop = WS_TABSTOP,
                  Thickframe = WS_THICKFRAME,
                  Tiled = WS_TILED, Visible = WS_VISIBLE,
                  VScroll = WS_VSCROLL};
```

The window can be displayed in minimized, maximized, or normal mode:

```
enum WindowShow {Restore = SW_RESTORE, Default = SW_SHOWDEFAULT,
                 Maximized = SW_SHOWMAXIMIZED,
                 Minimized = SW_SHOWMINIMIZED,
                 MinNoActive = SW_SHOWMINNOACTIVE,
                 NoActive = SW_SHOWNA,
                 NoActivate = SW_SHOWNOACTIVATE,
                 Normal = SW_SHOWNORMAL,
                 Show = SW_SHOW, Hide = SW_HIDE};
```

A mouse may hold the left, middle, and right button. The mouse wheel can be rolled upwards or downwards:

```
enum MouseButton {NoButton = 0x00, LeftButton = 0x01,
                  MiddleButton = 0x02, RightButton = 0x04};
enum WheelDirection {WheelUp, WheelDown};
```

There are four kinds of coordinate system as follows:

- `LogicalWithScroll`: In this, each unit is one hundredth of a millimeter, regardless of the physical screen resolution, with the current scroll bar settings taken into consideration
- `LogicalWithoutScroll`: This is the same as `LogicalWithScroll`, except that the scroll bars settings are ignored
- `PreviewCoordinate`: In this, the window client area always holds a specific logical size, which means that the size of the logical units is changed when the size of the window is changed

```
enum CoordinateSystem {LogicalWithScroll, LogicalWithoutScroll,
                       PreviewCoordinate};
```

The message box comes equipped with a set of button combinations, icons, and answers. Note that the answer corresponding to the **OK** button is named `OkAnswer` in the `Answer` enumeration in order to avoid name clashes with the `OK` button in the `ButtonGroup` enumeration:

```
enum ButtonGroup {Ok = MB_OK, OkCancel = MB_OKCANCEL,
                  YesNo = MB_YESNO,
                  YesNoCancel = MB_YESNOCANCEL,
                  RetryCancel = MB_RETRYCANCEL,
                  CancelTryContinue = MB_CANCELTRYCONTINUE,
                  AbortRetryIgnore = MB_ABORTRETRYIGNORE};

enum Icon {NoIcon = 0, Information = MB_ICONINFORMATION,
           Stop = MB_ICONSTOP, Warning = MB_ICONWARNING,
           Question = MB_ICONQUESTION};

enum Answer {OkAnswer = IDOK, Cancel = IDCANCEL, Yes = IDYES,
             No = IDNO, Retry = IDRETRY, Continue = IDCONTINUE,
             Abort = IDABORT, Ignore = IDIGNORE} const;
```

The default definitions of `OnPaint` and `OnPrint` both call `OnDraw`. In order to distinguish the two cases, the `OnDraw` parameter has the value `Paint` or `Print`:

```
enum DrawMode {Paint, Print};
```

The first `Window` constructor is public and intended to be used when a window is created directly. The `pageSize` field refers to the size of the window client area. The constructor also takes a pointer to the window's parent window (which is `null` if there is no parent window), the window's basic style and extended style, and its initial appearance, position, and size. If the position or size is zero, the window is located or dimensioned in accordance with the system's default settings.

Note the difference between the document and windows sizes in `PreviewCoordinate`: the document size is the size of the client area in units defined by the window's coordinate system, while the size and position of the window are given in the coordinate system of the parent window or in device units if there is no parent window. Moreover, the document size refers to the size of the client area while the window size refers to the size of the whole window:

```
class Application;

class Window {
  public:
    Window(CoordinateSystem system, Size pageSize = ZeroSize,
           Window* parentPtr = nullptr,
           WindowStyle style = OverlappedWindow,
           WindowStyle extendedStyle = NoStyle,
           WindowShow windowShow = Normal,
           Point topLeft = ZeroPoint, Size windowSize=ZeroSize);
```

The second constructor is protected and intended to be called by subclasses' constructors. The difference when compared to the first constructor is that is takes the name of the `window` class as its first parameter. As defined by the `Application` class, the class name can be `Window`, `Document`, `StandardDocument`, or `Dialog`:

```
  protected:
    Window(Window* parentPtr = nullptr);
    Window(String className, CoordinateSystem system,
           Size pageSize = ZeroSize,
           Window* parentPtr = nullptr,
           WindowStyle style = OverlappedWindow,
           WindowStyle extendedStyle = NoStyle,
           WindowShow windowShow = Normal,
           Point windowTopLeft = ZeroPoint,
           Size windowSize = ZeroSize);
```

A **device context** is used when painting the client area, when transforming between logical and device units, and when calculating the size of text. It is a connection to the client area of a window or to a printer. However, since it comes with a set of functions for drawing text of graphical objects, it can also be considered as a toolbox for drawing. However, before it is used, it needs to be prepared and adjusted in accordance with the current coordinate system:

```
void PrepareDeviceContext(HDC deviceContextHandle) const;
```

The destructor destroys the window and exits the application if the window is the application's main window:

```
public:
    virtual ~Window();
```

The window can be visible or invisible; it can also be enabled in such a way that it catches mouse, touch, and keyboard inputs:

```
void ShowWindow(bool visible);
void EnableWindow(bool enable);
```

The `OnSize` and `OnMove` methods are called when the user changes the size of the window or moves it. The size and position are given in logical coordinates. The `OnHelp` method is called when the user presses the *F1* key of the *Help* button in a message box. The methods are intended to be overridden by subclasses, and their default behavior is to do nothing:

```
virtual void OnSize(Size windowSize) {/* Empty. */}
virtual void OnMove(Point topLeft) {/* Empty. */}
virtual void OnHelp() {/* Empty. */}
```

The `WindowHandle` method returns the Win32 API window handle, which is used by standard dialog functions. The `ParentWindowPtr` method returns the pointer to the parent window, which is `null`, meaning that there is no parent window. The `SetHeader` method sets the title of the window, which is visible in the upper border:

```
HWND WindowHandle() const {return windowHandle;}
HWND& WindowHandle() {return windowHandle;}
Window* ParentWindowPtr() const {return parentPtr;}
Window*& ParentWindowPtr() {return parentPtr;}
void SetHeader(String headerText);
```

The client area of the window is zoomed in accordance with the zoom factor; 1.0 corresponds to the normal size:

```
double GetZoom() const {return zoom;}
void SetZoom(double z) {zoom = z;}
```

Several timers can be set or dropped as long as the values of the `timerId` parameter differ. The `OnTimer` method is called in accordance with the intervals in milliseconds; its default behavior is to do nothing.

```
void SetTimer(int timerId, unsigned int interval);
void DropTimer(int timerId);
virtual void OnTimer(int timerId) {/* Empty. */}
```

The SetFocus method sets the input focus to this window. The input focus directs the keyboard input and clipboard to the window. However, the mouse pointer may be aiming at another window. The window previously holding the input focus loses the focus; only one window can hold the focus at a given time. The HasFocus method returns true if the window has input focus.

```
void SetFocus() const;
bool HasFocus() const;
```

The OnGainFocus and OnLoseFocus methods are called when the window gains or loses input focus. They are intended to be overridden by subclasses, and their default behavior is to do nothing.

```
virtual void OnGainFocus() {/* Empty. */}
virtual void OnLoseFocus() {/* Empty. */}
```

In Windows, a mouse is regarded as holding three buttons, even if it does not do so physically. The mouse buttons can be pressed or released and the mouse can be moved. The OnMouseDown, OnMouseUp, and OnMouseMove methods are called when the user presses or releases one of the mouse buttons or moves the mouse with at least one button pressed. The user may press the *Shift* or *Ctrl* key at the same time, in which case shiftPressed or controlPressed is true:

```
virtual void OnMouseDown(MouseButton mouseButtons,
                         Point mousePoint,
                         bool shiftPressed,
                         bool controlPressed) {/* Empty. */}
virtual void OnMouseUp(MouseButton mouseButtons,
                       Point mousePoint,
                       bool shiftPressed,
                       bool controlPressed) {/* Empty. */}
virtual void OnMouseMove(MouseButton mouseButtons,
                         Point mousePoint,
                         bool shiftPressed,
                         bool controlPressed) {/* Empty. */}
```

The user can also double-click a mouse button, in which case OnDoubleClick is called. What constitutes a double-click is decided by the Windows system and can be set in the Control Panel. When the user single-clicks a button, OnMouseDown is called, followed by OnMouseMove in the case of potential mouse movements, and finally OnMouseUp. However, in the case of a double-click, OnMouseDown is not called, its call is replaced by

OnDoubleClick:

```
virtual void OnDoubleClick(MouseButton mouseButtons,
                  Point mousePoint, bool shiftPressed,
                  bool controlPressed) {/* Empty. */}
```

The OnMouseWheel method is called when the user rolls the mouse wheel one step upwards or downwards:

```
virtual void OnMouseWheel(WheelDirection direction,
                  bool shiftPressed,
                  bool controlPressed){/* Empty. */}
```

The OnTouchDown, OnTouchMove, and OnTouchUp methods are called when the user touches the screen. Unlike mouse clicks, the user can touch the screen at several locations at the same time. Therefore, the parameter is a list of points rather than a single point. The methods are intended to be overridden by subclasses. Their default behavior is to simulate a mouse click for each touch point with no button and with neither the *Shift* nor the *Ctrl* key pressed:

```
virtual void OnTouchDown(vector<Point> pointList);
virtual void OnTouchMove(vector<Point> pointList);
virtual void OnTouchUp(vector<Point> pointList);
```

The OnKeyDown and OnKeyUp methods are called when the user presses and releases a key. If the key is a graphical character (with ASCII number between 32 and 127, inclusive), OnChar is called in between. The OnKeyDown and OnKeyUp methods return bool; the idea is that the methods return true if the key was used. If not, they return false and the caller method is free to use the key to, for instance, control scroll movements:

```
virtual bool OnKeyDown(WORD key, bool shiftPressed,
                  bool controlPressed) {return false;}
virtual void OnChar(TCHAR tChar) {/* Empty. */}
virtual bool OnKeyUp(WORD key, bool shiftPressed,
                  bool controlPressed) {return false;}
```

The OnPaint method is called when the client area of the window needs to be redrawn, partly or completely, and OnPrint is called when the user selects the **Print** menu item. In both cases, the default definition calls OnDraw, which performs the actual drawing; drawMode is Paint when called by OnPaint and Print when called by OnPrint. The idea is that we let OnPaint and OnPrint perform actions specific to painting and printing and call OnDraw for the common drawing. The Graphics class is described in the next section:

```
virtual void OnPaint(Graphics& graphics) const
                  {OnDraw(graphics, Paint);}
```

```
virtual void OnPrint(Graphics& graphics, int page,
                 int copy, int totalPages) const
                 {OnDraw(graphics, Print);}
virtual void OnDraw(Graphics& graphics,
                 DrawMode drawMode) const {/* Empty. */}
```

The `Invalidate` method invalidates the client area, partly or completely; that is, it prepares the area to be redrawn by `OnPaint` or `OnDraw`. If `clear` is `true`, the area is first cleared (painted by the window client color). The `UpdateWindow` method forces a repainting of the invalidated parts of the client area:

```
void Invalidate(bool clear = true) const;
void Invalidate(Rect areaRect, bool clear = true) const;
void UpdateWindow();
```

The `OnClose` method is called when the user tries to close the window; its default behavior is to call `TryClose`. If `TryClose` returns `true` (which it does in its default definition), the window is closed. If that happens, `OnDestroy` is called, whose default behavior is to do nothing:

```
virtual bool TryClose() {return true;}
virtual void OnClose();
virtual void OnDestroy() {/* Empty. */}
```

The following method transforms a `Point`, `Rectangle`, or `Size` object between device units and logical units. They are protected since they are intended to be called by subclasses only:

```
protected:
Point DeviceToLogical(Point point) const;
Rect DeviceToLogical(Rect rect) const;
Size DeviceToLogical(Size size) const;
Point LogicalToDevice(Point point) const;
Rect LogicalToDevice(Rect rect) const;
Size LogicalToDevice(Size size) const;
```

The following method gets or sets the size and position of the window and the client area in device units:

```
public:
Point GetWindowDevicePosition() const;
void SetWindowDevicePosition(Point topLeft);
Size GetWindowDeviceSize() const;
void SetWindowDeviceSize(Size windowSize);
Size GetClientDeviceSize() const;
Rect GetWindowDeviceRect() const;
void SetWindowDeviceRect(Rect windowRect);
```

The following method gets or sets the logical size and position of the window and the client area, in logical units, in accordance with the coordinate system of the window:

```
Point GetWindowPosition() const;
void SetWindowPosition(Point topLeft);
Size GetWindowSize() const;
void SetWindowSize(Size windowSize);
Size GetClientSize() const;
Rect GetWindowRect() const;
void SetWindowRect(Rect windowRect) ;
```

The `CreateTextMetric` method initializes and returns a Win32 API `TEXTMETRIC` structure, which is then used by the text metric methods in order to calculate the logical size of text. It is private since it in intended to be called only by the `Window` methods:

```
private:
    TEXTMETRIC CreateTextMetric(Font font);
```

The following method calculates and returns the width, height, ascent, or average width of a character or text with the given font, in logical units:

```
public:
    int GetCharacterAverageWidth(Font font) const;
    int GetCharacterHeight(Font font) const;
    int GetCharacterAscent(Font font) const;
    int GetCharacterWidth(Font font, TCHAR tChar) const;
```

The `MessageBox` method displays a message box with a message, caption, a set of buttons, an icon, and on optional **Help** button:

```
Answer MessageBox(String message,
            String caption = TEXT("Error"),
            ButtonGroup buttonGroup = Ok,
            Icon icon = NoIcon, bool help = false) const;
```

The `pageSize` field holds the window client's logical size in the `PreviewCoordinate` coordinate system, which is used when transforming coordinates between logical and device coordinates. In the `LogicalWithScroll` and `LogicalWithoutScroll` coordinate systems, `pageSize` holds the logical size of the document, which does not necessarily equal the logical size of the client area, and is not changed when the window is resized. It is protected since it is also used by the `Document` and `StandardDocument` subclasses in the next chapter:

```
protected:
    const Size pageSize;
```

In the previous section, there was a handle to the application instance. `windowHandle` is a handle of type `HWND` to a Win32 API window; `parentPtr` is a pointer to the parent window, which is `null` if there is no parent window:

```
HWND windowHandle;
Window* parentPtr;
```

The coordinate system chosen for the window is stored in `system`. The `zoom` field holds the zooming factor of the window, where 1.0 is the default:

```
private:
  CoordinateSystem system;
  double zoom = 1.0;
```

The `WindowProc` method is called each time the window receives a message. It is a friend of `Window`, since it needs access to its private members:

```
friend LRESULT CALLBACK WindowProc(HWND windowHandle,
                                   UINT message, WPARAM wordParam,
                                   LPARAM longParam);
};
```

Finally, `WindowMap` maps the `HWND` handles to the `Window` pointers, which are used in `WindowProc` as follows:

```
extern map<HWND,Window*> WindowMap;
};
```

Window.cpp

```
#include "SmallWindows.h"

namespace SmallWindows {
  map<HWND,Window*> WindowMap;
```

Initialization

The first constructor simply calls the second constructor with the class name `window`:

```
Window::Window(CoordinateSystem system, Size pageSize
               /* = ZeroSize */, Window* parentPtr /*=nullptr*/,
               WindowStyle style /* = OverlappedWindow */,
               WindowStyle extendedStyle /* = NoStyle */,
               WindowShow windowShow /* = Normal */,
               Point windowTopLeft /* = ZeroPoint */,
               Size windowSize /* = ZeroSize */)
```

```
    :Window(TEXT("window"), system, pageSize, parentPtr, style,
            extendedStyle, windowShow, windowTopLeft, windowSize) {
    // Empty.
}
```

The second constructor initializes the `parentPtr`, `system`, and `pageSize` fields:

```
Window::Window(String className, CoordinateSystem system,
               Size pageSize /* = ZeroSize */,
               Window* parentPtr /* = nullptr */,
               WindowStyle style /* = OverlappedWindow */,
               WindowStyle extendedStyle /* = NoStyle */,
               WindowShow windowShow /* = Normal */,
               Point windowTopLeft /* = ZeroPoint */,
               Size windowSize /* = ZeroSize */)
    :parentPtr(parentPtr),
     system(system),
     pageSize(pageSize) {
```

If the window is a child window (the parent pointer is not `null`), its coordinates are converted to the coordinate system of its parent window:

```
if (parentPtr != nullptr) {
    windowTopLeft = parentPtr->LogicalToDevice(windowTopLeft);
    windowSize = parentPtr->LogicalToDevice(windowSize);
}
```

The Win32 API window creation process is divided into two steps. First, a Windows class needs to be registered, which was done in the `Application` constructor earlier. Then, the `Windows` class name is used in the call to the Win32 API `CreateWindowEx` function, which returns a handle to the window. If the size or position is zero, default values are used:

```
int left, top, width, height;

if (windowTopLeft != ZeroPoint) {
    left = windowTopLeft.X();
    top = windowTopLeft.Y();
}
else {
    left = CW_USEDEFAULT;
    top = CW_USEDEFAULT;
}

if (windowSize != ZeroSize) {
    width = windowSize.Width();
    height = windowSize.Height();
}
```

```
else {
  width = CW_USEDEFAULT;
  height = CW_USEDEFAULT;
}

HWND parentHandle = (parentPtr != nullptr) ?
                parentPtr->windowHandle : nullptr;

windowHandle =
  CreateWindowEx(extendedStyle, className.c_str(),
              nullptr, style, left, top, width, height,
              parentHandle,::CreateMenu(),
              Application::InstanceHandle(), this);

assert(windowHandle != nullptr);
```

In order for `WindowProc` to be able to receive messages and identify the recipient window, the handle is stored in `WindowMap`:

```
WindowMap[windowHandle] = this;
```

The Win32 API functions `ShowWindow` and `RegisterTouchWindow` are called to make the window visible in accordance with the `windowShow` parameter and to make the window receptive to touch movements:

```
    ::ShowWindow(windowHandle, windowShow);
    ::RegisterTouchWindow(windowHandle, 0);
}
```

The destructor calls `OnDestroy` and erases the window from `windowMap`. If the window has a parent window, it receives an input focus:

```
Window::~Window() {
  OnDestroy();
  WindowMap.erase(windowHandle);

  if (parentPtr != nullptr) {
    parentPtr->SetFocus();
  }
```

If the window is the application's main window, the Win32 API `PostQuitMessage` function is called. It posts a quit message, which is eventually caught by `RunMessageLoop` in the `Application` class that terminates the execution. Finally, the window is destroyed:

```
    if (this == Application::MainWindowPtr()) {
      ::PostQuitMessage(0);
    }
```

```
    WindowMap.erase(windowHandle);
    ::DestroyWindow(windowHandle);
}
```

Header and visibility

The `ShowWindow` and `EnableWindow` methods call the Win32 API functions `ShowWindow` and `EnableWindow` with the window handle as their first parameter:

```
void Window::ShowWindow(bool visible) {
    ::ShowWindow(windowHandle, visible ? SW_SHOW : SW_HIDE);
}
```

Note that the second parameter of `EnableWindow` is a value of the Win32 API type `BOOL`, which is not necessarily the same type as the C++ type `bool`. Therefore, since `enable` holds the type `bool` we need to convert it to `BOOL`:

```
void Window::EnableWindow(bool enable) {
    ::EnableWindow(windowHandle, enable ? TRUE : FALSE);
}
```

The `SetHeader` method sets the title of the window by calling the Win32 API function `SetWindowText`. As `headerText` is a `String` object and `SetWindowText` wants a C string (a zero-terminated char pointer) as parameter, we need to call the `c_str` function:

```
void Window::SetHeader(String headerText) {
    ::SetWindowText(windowHandle, headerText.c_str());
}
```

The `SetTimer` and `DropTimer` methods turn the timer with the given identity on and off by calling the Win32 API functions `SetTimer` and `KillTimer`. The interval in the `SetTimer` call is given in milliseconds:

```
void Window::SetTimer(int timerId, unsigned int interval) {
    ::SetTimer(windowHandle, timerId, interval, nullptr);
}

void Window::DropTimer(int timerId) {
    ::KillTimer(windowHandle, timerId);
}
```

The `SetFocus` method sets the focus by calling the corresponding Win32 API function `SetFocus`. The `HasFocus` method returns `true` if the window has the input focus by calling the `GetFocus` Win32 API function, which returns the handle to the window, holding the input focus that is compared to the window's handle:

```
void Window::SetFocus() const {
  ::SetFocus(windowHandle);
}

bool Window::HasFocus() const {
  return (::GetFocus() == windowHandle);
}
```

The touch screen

The default behavior of OnTouchDown, OnTouchMove, and OnTouchUp is to call the corresponding mouse input method for each touch point, with no button and neither the *Shift* nor the *Ctrl* key pressed:

```
void Window::OnTouchDown(vector<Point> pointList) {
  for (Point touchPoint : pointList) {
    OnMouseDown(NoButton, touchPoint, false, false);
  }
}

void Window::OnTouchMove(vector<Point> pointList) {
  for (Point touchPoint : pointList) {
    OnMouseMove(NoButton, touchPoint, false, false);
  }
}

void Window::OnTouchUp(vector<Point> pointList) {
  for (Point touchPoint : pointList) {
    OnMouseUp(NoButton, touchPoint, false, false);
  }
}
```

With a modern screen, the user can touch the screen in ways similar to mouse clicks. However, the user can touch the screen at several locations at once, and its positions are stored in a point list. The OnTouch method is an auxiliary method calling OnTouchDown, OnTouchMove, and OnTouchUp when the user touches the screen. It creates a list of points in logical coordinates:

```
void OnTouch(Window* windowPtr, WPARAM wordParam,
             LPARAM longParam, Point windowTopLeft) {
  UINT inputs = LOWORD(wordParam);
  HTOUCHINPUT touchInputHandle = (HTOUCHINPUT) longParam;
```

```
TOUCHINPUT* inputArray = new TOUCHINPUT[inputs];
assert(inputArray != nullptr);

if (::GetTouchInputInfo(touchInputHandle, inputs,
                        inputArray, sizeof(TOUCHINPUT))){
  vector<Point> pointList;

  for (UINT index = 0; index < inputs; ++index) {
    Point touchPoint
      ((inputArray[index].x / 100) - windowTopLeft.X(),
       (inputArray[index].y / 100) - windowTopLeft.Y());
    pointList.push_back(touchPoint);
  }
```

If the touch identity does not equal the first value in the input array, we have a touch down event; if it does, we have a touch move event:

```
  static DWORD touchId = -1;
  if (touchId != inputArray[0].dwID) {
    touchId = inputArray[0].dwID;
    windowPtr->OnTouchDown(pointList);
  }
  else {
    windowPtr->OnTouchMove(pointList);
  }

  ::CloseTouchInputHandle(touchInputHandle);
}

delete [] inputArray;
}
```

Invalidation and window updates

When the window's client area needs to be (partly or completely) repainted, one of the `Invalidate` methods is called. The `Invalidate` methods call the Win32 API function `InvalicateRect`, which posts a message that results in a call to `OnPaint` when `UpdateWindow` is called. The `clear` parameter indicates whether the invalidated area should be cleared (repainted with the window client area's color) before it is redrawn, which normally is the case. Similar to the `EnableWindow` method we saw earlier, we need to convert `clear` from type `bool` to `BOOL`:

```
void Window::Invalidate(bool clear /* = true */) const {
  ::InvalidateRect(windowHandle, nullptr, clear ? TRUE : FALSE);
}
```

The `Invalidate` method transforms the area from logical to device coordinates before the call to the Win32 API function `InvalidateRect` and stores the size in a `RECT` structure:

```
void Window::Invalidate(Rect areaRect, bool clear /* = true */)
                        const {
  RECT rect = (RECT) LogicalToDevice(areaRect);
  ::InvalidateRect(windowHandle, &rect, clear ? TRUE : FALSE);
}
```

The `UpdateWindow` method calls the Win32 API function `UpdateWindow`, which eventually results in a call to `OnPaint`:

```
void Window::UpdateWindow() {
  ::UpdateWindow(windowHandle);
}
```

Preparing the device context

When painting the windows's client area, we need a device context, which we need to prepare in accordance with the coordinate system in order to paint with logical coordinates. The Win32 API function `SetMapMode` sets the mapping mode of the logical coordinate system. `MISOTROPIC` forces that the *x* and *y* axis to have the same unit length (resulting in non-elliptic circles) that is suitable for the `LogicalWithScroll` and `LogicalWithoutScroll` systems, while `MANISOTROPIC` allows different unit lengths that are suitable for the `PreviewCoordinate` system. We establish a mapping between the logical and device systems by calling the Win32 API functions `SetWindowExtEx`, which takes the logical size of the client area, and `SetViewportExtEx`, which takes its physical (device) size.

In the case of the `PreviewCoordinate` system, we simply match the logical size (`pageSize`) of the client area to its device size (`clientDeviceRect`), given by the Win32 API function `GetClientRect`, resulting in the client area always having the same logical size, regardless of its physical size:

```
void Window::PrepareDeviceContext(HDC deviceContextHandle)const{
  switch (system) {
    case PreviewCoordinate: {
      RECT clientDeviceRect;
      ::GetClientRect(windowHandle, &clientDeviceRect);

      ::SetMapMode(deviceContextHandle, MM_ANISOTROPIC);
      ::SetWindowExtEx(deviceContextHandle, pageSize.Width(),
                   pageSize.Height(), nullptr);
```

```
::SetViewportExtEx(deviceContextHandle,
                   clientDeviceRect.right,
                   clientDeviceRect.bottom, nullptr);
    }
    break;
```

In the case of the logical coordinate system, we need to find the ratio between logical coordinates (hundreds of millimeters) and device coordinates (pixels). In other words, we need to establish the logical size of a pixel. We can find the number of pixels on the screen by calling the Win32 API function GetDeviceCaps with HORZSIZE and VERTSIZE, and the size of the screen in millimeters with HORZRES and VERTRES. We multiply the logical size by 100, since we have hundreds of millimeters as our logical unit. We also need to take into account the zooming factor of the window, which we do by multiplying the physical size by zoom.

Note that it's only in the PreviewCoordinate system that the client area always has the same logical size. In the other systems, the logical size changes when the size of the window is changed. The logical units are always the same in LogicalWithScroll and LogicalWithoutScroll: hundreds of millimeters:

```
case LogicalWithScroll:
case LogicalWithoutScroll:
  ::SetMapMode(deviceContextHandle, MM_ISOTROPIC);

  { int horizontalSize =
        100 * GetDeviceCaps(deviceContextHandle,HORZSIZE),
      verticalSize =
        100 * GetDeviceCaps(deviceContextHandle,VERTSIZE);
    ::SetWindowExtEx(deviceContextHandle, horizontalSize,
                     verticalSize, nullptr);
  }

  { int horizontalResolution = (int)
        (zoom*GetDeviceCaps(deviceContextHandle, HORZRES)),
      verticalResolution = (int)
        (zoom*GetDeviceCaps(deviceContextHandle, VERTRES));
    ::SetViewportExtEx(deviceContextHandle,
        horizontalResolution, verticalResolution, nullptr);
  }
```

In the case of the LogicalWithScroll logical coordinate system, we also need to adjust the origin of the window in accordance with the current scroll settings by calling the Win32 API function SetWindowOrg:

```
    if (system == LogicalWithScroll) {
      int horizontalScroll =
            ::GetScrollPos(windowHandle, SB_HORZ),
          verticalScroll =
            ::GetScrollPos(windowHandle, SB_VERT);
      ::SetWindowOrgEx(deviceContextHandle, horizontalScroll,
                       verticalScroll, nullptr);
    }
    break;
  }
}
```

Unit transformation

The `DeviceToLogical` method transforms the device coordinates of a point, rectangle, or size to logical coordinates by preparing the device context and then calling the Win32 API function `DPtoLP` (Device Point to Logical Point). Note that we establish the device context by calling the Win32 API function `GetDC` and we need to return it by calling `ReleaseDC`. Also, note that we need to convert the `Point` object to a `POINT` structure and back again, since `DPtoLP` takes a pointer to a `POINT`:

```
Point Window::DeviceToLogical(Point point) const {
  HDC deviceContextHandle = ::GetDC(windowHandle);
  PrepareDeviceContext(deviceContextHandle);
  POINT pointStruct = (POINT) point;
  ::DPtoLP(deviceContextHandle, &pointStruct, 1);
  ::ReleaseDC(windowHandle, deviceContextHandle);
  return Point(pointStruct);
}
```

When transforming a rectangle, we use the point method to transform its top-left and bottom-right corners. When transforming a size, we create a rectangle, call the rectangle method, and convert the rectangle to a size:

```
Rect Window::DeviceToLogical(Rect rect) const {
  return Rect(DeviceToLogical(rect.TopLeft()),
              DeviceToLogical(rect.BottomRight()));
}

Size Window::DeviceToLogical(Size size) const {
  return ((Size) DeviceToLogical(Rect(ZeroPoint, size)));
}
```

The `LogicalToDevice` method transforms the point, rectangle, or size from logical to device coordinates calling the Win32 API function `LPtoDP` (Logical Point to Device Point) in the same manner as the earlier methods. The only difference is that they call `LPtoDP` instead of `DPtoLP`:

```
Point Window::LogicalToDevice(Point point) const {
  HDC deviceContextHandle = ::GetDC(windowHandle);
  PrepareDeviceContext(deviceContextHandle);
  POINT pointStruct = (POINT) point;
  ::LPtoDP(deviceContextHandle, &pointStruct, 1);
  ::ReleaseDC(windowHandle, deviceContextHandle);
  return Point(pointStruct);
}

Rect Window::LogicalToDevice(Rect rect) const {
  return Rect(LogicalToDevice(rect.TopLeft()),
              LogicalToDevice(rect.BottomRight()));
}

Size Window::LogicalToDevice(Size size) const {
  return ((Size) LogicalToDevice(Rect(ZeroPoint, size)));
}
```

Window size and position

The `GetWindowDevicePosition`, `SetWindowDevicePosition`, `GetWindowDeviceSize`, `SetWindowDeviceSize`, and `GetClientDeviceSize` methods call the corresponding Win32 API functions `GetWindowRect`, `GetClientRect`, and `SetWindowPos`:

```
Point Window::GetWindowDevicePosition() const {
  return GetWindowDeviceRect().TopLeft();
}

void Window::SetWindowDevicePosition(Point topLeft) {
  ::SetWindowPos(windowHandle, nullptr, topLeft.X(),
              topLeft.Y(), 0, 0, SWP_NOSIZE);
}

Size Window::GetWindowDeviceSize() const {
  return GetWindowDeviceRect().GetSize();
}

void Window::SetWindowDeviceSize(Size windowSize) {
  ::SetWindowPos(windowHandle, nullptr, 0, 0,
              windowSize.Width(), windowSize.Height(), SWP_NOMOVE);
}
```

```
Size Window::GetClientDeviceSize() const {
  RECT rectStruct;
  ::GetClientRect(windowHandle, &rectStruct);
  return Size(rectStruct.right, rectStruct.bottom);
}

Rect Window::GetWindowDeviceRect() const {
  RECT windowRect;
  ::GetWindowRect(windowHandle, &windowRect);
  POINT topLeft = {windowRect.left, windowRect.top},
        bottomRight = {windowRect.right, windowRect.bottom};

  if (parentPtr != nullptr) {
    ::ScreenToClient(parentPtr->windowHandle, &topLeft);
    ::ScreenToClient(parentPtr->windowHandle, &bottomRight);
  }

  return Rect(Point(topLeft), Point(bottomRight));
}

void Window::SetWindowDeviceRect(Rect windowRect) {
  SetWindowDevicePosition(windowRect.TopLeft());
  SetWindowDeviceSize(windowRect.GetSize());
}
```

The `GetWindowPosition`, `SetWindowPosition`, `GetWindowSize`, `SetWindowSize`, and `GetClientSize` methods call the corresponding device methods together with `LogicalToDevice` or `DeviceToLogical`:

```
Point Window::GetWindowPosition() const {
  return DeviceToLogical(GetWindowDevicePosition());
}

void Window::SetWindowPosition(Point topLeft) {
  SetWindowDevicePosition(LogicalToDevice(topLeft));
}

Size Window::GetWindowSize() const {
  return DeviceToLogical(GetWindowDeviceSize());
}

void Window::SetWindowSize(Size windowSize) {
  SetWindowDeviceSize(LogicalToDevice(windowSize));
}

Size Window::GetClientSize() const {
  return DeviceToLogical(GetClientDeviceSize());
}
```

```
Rect Window::GetWindowRect() const {
  return DeviceToLogical(GetWindowDeviceRect());
}

void Window::SetWindowRect(Rect windowRect) {
  SetWindowDeviceRect(LogicalToDevice(windowRect));
}
```

Text metrics

Given a font, `CreateTextMetric` creates a metric structure holding the height, ascent line, and average width of a character of the font. The `CreateFontIndirect` and `SelectObject` methods prepare the font for `GetTextExtentPoint`:

```
TEXTMETRIC Window::CreateTextMetric(Font font) const {
  font.PointsToLogical();

  HDC deviceContextHandle = ::GetDC(windowHandle);
  PrepareDeviceContext(deviceContextHandle);

  HFONT fontHandle = ::CreateFontIndirect(&font.LogFont());
  HFONT oldFontHandle =
    (HFONT) ::SelectObject(deviceContextHandle, fontHandle);

  TEXTMETRIC textMetric;
  ::GetTextMetrics(deviceContextHandle, &textMetric);
```

Note that `CreateFontIndirect` must be matched by `DeleteObject` and the first call to `SelectObject` must be matched by a second call to `SelectObject` to reinstall the original object:

```
  ::SelectObject(deviceContextHandle, oldFontHandle);
  ::DeleteObject(fontHandle);
```

Also, note that the device context received from `GetDC` must be released with `ReleaseDC`:

```
  ::ReleaseDC(windowHandle, deviceContextHandle);
  return textMetric;
}
```

The `GetCharacterHeight`, `GetCharacterAscent`, and `GetCharacterAverageWidth` methods call `CreateTextMetric` and return the relevant information:

```
int Window::GetCharacterHeight(Font font) const {
  return CreateTextMetric(font).tmHeight;
}
```

```
int Window::GetCharacterAscent(Font font) const {
  return CreateTextMetric(font).tmAscent;
}

int Window::GetCharacterAverageWidth(Font font) const {
  return CreateTextMetric(font).tmAveCharWidth;
}
```

The `GetCharacterWidth` method calls `GetTextExtentPoint` to establish the width of a character of the given font. Since the font height is given in typographical points (1 point = 1/72 of an inch = 1/72 * 25.4 mm $\approx$ 0.35 mm) and needs to be given in millimeters, we call `PointsToLogical`. Similar to what we did earlier in `CreateTextMetric`, `CreateFontIndirect` and `SelectObject` prepare the font for `GetTextExtentPoint`:

```
int Window::GetCharacterWidth(Font font, TCHAR tChar) const {
  font.PointsToLogical();

  HDC deviceContextHandle = ::GetDC(windowHandle);
  PrepareDeviceContext(deviceContextHandle);

  HFONT fontHandle = ::CreateFontIndirect(&font.LogFont());
  HFONT oldFontHandle =
    (HFONT) ::SelectObject(deviceContextHandle, fontHandle);

  SIZE szChar;
  ::GetTextExtentPoint(deviceContextHandle, &tChar, 1, &szChar);

  ::SelectObject(deviceContextHandle, oldFontHandle);
  ::DeleteObject(fontHandle);
  ::ReleaseDC(windowHandle, deviceContextHandle);

  return szChar.cx;
}
```

Closing the window

When the user tries to close the window, the `Window` object (`this`) is deleted if `TryClose` returns `true`:

```
void Window::OnClose() {
  if (TryClose()) {
    delete this;
  }
}
```

The MessageBox method

The `MessageBox` method displays a message box holding a caption, a message, a combination of buttons (**OK, OK-Cancel, Retry-Cancel, Yes-No, Yes-No-Cancel, Cancel-Try-Continue**, or **Abort-Retry-Ignore**), an optional icon (**Information, Stop, Warning,** or **Question**), and an optional **Help** button. It returns the answer **OK Answer** (since OK is already taken by the `ButtonGroup` enumeration), **Cancel, Yes, No, Retry, Continue, Abort,** or **Ignore**:

```
Answer Window::MessageBox(String message,
                          String caption /*=TEXT("Error")*/,
                          ButtonGroup buttonGroup /* = Ok */,
                          Icon icon /* = NoIcon */,
                          bool help /* = false */) const {
  return (Answer) ::MessageBox(windowHandle, message.c_str(),
                        caption.c_str(), buttonGroup |
                        icon | (help ? MB_HELP : 0));
}
```

When a window is created by calling `CreateWindowEx` in the `Window` class constructor, the name of a `Windows` class that has earlier been given by the `Application` class constructor is enclosed. When the class is registered, a freestanding function is also given. For the `Window` class, the function is `WindowProc`, which is thereby called every time the window receives a message.

The `wordParam` and `longParam` parameters (`WPARAM` and `LPARAM` are both 4 bytes) hold message-specific information, which may be divided into low and high words (2 bytes) with the `LOWORD` and `HIWORD` macros:

```
LRESULT CALLBACK WindowProc(HWND windowHandle, UINT message,
                            WPARAM wordParam, LPARAM longParam){
```

First we need to find the `Window` object associated with the window handle by looking up the handle in the static field `WindowMap`:

```
if (WindowMap.count(windowHandle) == 1) {
  Window* windowPtr = WindowMap[windowHandle];
```

When receiving the `WSETFOCUS`, `WKILLFOCUS`, and `WTIMER` messages, the corresponding methods in `Window` are simply called. When the messages have been handled, they do not need to be further processed; therefore, zero is returned:

```
switch (message) {
  case WM_SETFOCUS:
    windowPtr->OnGainFocus();
    return 0;

  case WM_KILLFOCUS:
    windowPtr->OnLoseFocus();
    return 0;
```

The identity of the timer (the `timerId` parameter in `SetTimer` and `DropTimer`) is stored in `wordParam`:

```
  case WM_TIMER:
    windowPtr->OnTimer((int) wordParam);
    return 0;
```

When receiving the `WMOVE` and `WSIZE` messages, the `Point` value stored in `longParam` is given in device units that need to be transformed into logical units by calling `DeviceToLogical` in the calls to `OnMove` and `OnSize` in `Window`:

```
  case WM_MOVE: {
      Point windowTopLeft =
        {LOWORD(longParam), HIWORD(longParam)};
      windowPtr->OnMove
              (windowPtr->DeviceToLogical(windowTopLeft));
  }
  return 0;

  case WM_SIZE: {
      Size clientSize =
        {LOWORD(longParam), HIWORD(longParam)};
      windowPtr->
        OnSize(windowPtr->DeviceToLogical(clientSize));
  }
  return 0;
```

If the user presses the *F1* key or the **Help** button in a message box, the `WM_HELP` message is sent. We call `OnHelp` in `Window`:

```
  case WM_HELP:
    windowPtr->OnHelp();
    break;
```

When handling mouse or keyboard input messages, it is useful to decide whether the user simultaneously presses the *Shift* or *Ctrl* key. This can be established by calling the Win32 API function, `GetKeyState`, which returns an integer value less than zero if the key is pressed when called with `VK_SHIFT` or `VK_CONTROL`:

```
case WM_KEYDOWN: {
    WORD key = wordParam;
    bool shiftPressed = (::GetKeyState(VK_SHIFT) < 0);
    bool controlPressed = (::GetKeyState(VK_CONTROL) < 0);
```

If `OnKeyDown` returns `true`, the key message has been processed and we return zero. If it returns `false`, the Win32 API function `DefWindowProc`, as shown here, will be called, which further processes the message:

```
    if (windowPtr->OnKeyDown(wordParam, shiftPressed,
                             controlPressed)) {
      return 0;
    }
}
break;
```

If the pressed key is a graphical character (ASCII numbers between 32 and 127, inclusive), `OnChar` is called:

```
case WM_CHAR: {
    int asciiCode = (int) wordParam;

    if ((asciiCode >= 32) && (asciiCode <= 127)) {
      windowPtr->OnChar((TCHAR) asciiCode);
      return 0;
    }
}
break;

case WM_KEYUP: {
    bool shiftPressed = (::GetKeyState(VK_SHIFT) < 0);
    bool controlPressed = (::GetKeyState(VK_CONTROL) < 0);

    if (windowPtr->OnKeyUp(wordParam, shiftPressed,
                           controlPressed)) {
      return 0;
    }
}
break;
```

All mouse input points stored in `longParam` are given in device coordinates, which need to be transformed into logical coordinates by `DeviceToLogical`. The mouse-down message is normally followed by the corresponding mouse-up message. Unfortunately, that is not the case if the user presses the mouse button in one window and releases it in another window, in which case the mouse-up message is sent to the other window. However, the problem can be solved by the Win32 API function, `SetCapture`, which makes sure that every mouse message is sent to the window until `ReleaseCapture` is called:

```
case WM_LBUTTONDOWN: {
    bool shiftPressed = (::GetKeyState(VK_SHIFT) < 0);
    bool controlPressed = (::GetKeyState(VK_CONTROL) < 0);
    ::SetCapture(windowPtr->windowHandle);
    Point mousePoint =
      Point({LOWORD(longParam), HIWORD(longParam)});
    windowPtr->OnMouseDown(LeftButton,
                windowPtr->DeviceToLogical(mousePoint),
                shiftPressed, controlPressed);
}
  return 0;

case WM_MBUTTONDOWN: {
    bool shiftPressed = (::GetKeyState(VK_SHIFT) < 0);
    bool controlPressed = (::GetKeyState(VK_CONTROL) < 0);
    ::SetCapture(windowPtr->windowHandle);
    Point mousePoint =
      Point({LOWORD(longParam), HIWORD(longParam)});
    windowPtr->OnMouseDown(MiddleButton,
                windowPtr->DeviceToLogical(mousePoint),
                shiftPressed, controlPressed);
}
  return 0;

case WM_RBUTTONDOWN: {
    bool shiftPressed = (::GetKeyState(VK_SHIFT) < 0);
    bool controlPressed = (::GetKeyState(VK_CONTROL) < 0);
    ::SetCapture(windowPtr->windowHandle);
    Point mousePoint =
      Point({LOWORD(longParam), HIWORD(longParam)});
    windowPtr->OnMouseDown(RightButton,
                windowPtr->DeviceToLogical(mousePoint),
                shiftPressed, controlPressed);
}
  return 0;
```

When the user moves the mouse, they may at the same time press a combination of buttons, stored in `buttonMask`:

```
case WM_MOUSEMOVE: {
    MouseButton buttonMask = (MouseButton)
      (((wordParam & MK_LBUTTON) ? LeftButton : 0) |
       ((wordParam & MK_MBUTTON) ? MiddleButton : 0) |
       ((wordParam & MK_RBUTTON) ? RightButton : 0));
```

```
            if (buttonMask != NoButton) {
                bool shiftPressed = (::GetKeyState(VK_SHIFT) < 0);
                bool controlPressed = (::GetKeyState(VK_CONTROL)<0);
                Point mousePoint =
                    Point({LOWORD(longParam), HIWORD(longParam)});
                windowPtr->OnMouseMove(buttonMask,
                            windowPtr->DeviceToLogical(mousePoint),
                            shiftPressed, controlPressed);
            }
        }
        return 0;
```

Note that `ReleaseCapture` is called at the end of the mouse-up methods in order to release the mouse message from the window and make it possible for mouse messages to be sent to other windows:

```
        case WM_LBUTTONUP: {
            bool shiftPressed = (::GetKeyState(VK_SHIFT) < 0);
            bool controlPressed = (::GetKeyState(VK_CONTROL) < 0);
            Point mousePoint =
                Point({LOWORD(longParam), HIWORD(longParam)});
            windowPtr->OnMouseUp(LeftButton,
                        windowPtr->DeviceToLogical(mousePoint),
                        shiftPressed, controlPressed);
            ::ReleaseCapture();
        }
        return 0;

        case WM_MBUTTONUP: {
            bool shiftPressed = (::GetKeyState(VK_SHIFT) < 0);
            bool controlPressed = (::GetKeyState(VK_CONTROL) < 0);
            Point mousePoint =
                Point({LOWORD(longParam), HIWORD(longParam)});
            windowPtr->OnMouseUp(MiddleButton,
                        windowPtr->DeviceToLogical(mousePoint),
                        shiftPressed, controlPressed);
            ::ReleaseCapture();
        }
        return 0;

        case WM_RBUTTONUP: {
            bool shiftPressed = (::GetKeyState(VK_SHIFT) < 0);
            bool controlPressed = (::GetKeyState(VK_CONTROL) < 0);
            Point mousePoint =
                Point({LOWORD(longParam), HIWORD(longParam)});
            windowPtr->OnMouseUp(RightButton,
                        windowPtr->DeviceToLogical(mousePoint),
                        shiftPressed, controlPressed);
```

```
    ::ReleaseCapture();
  }
  return 0;

case WM_LBUTTONDBLCLK: {
    bool shiftPressed = (::GetKeyState(VK_SHIFT) < 0);
    bool controlPressed = (::GetKeyState(VK_CONTROL) < 0);
    Point mousePoint =
      Point({LOWORD(longParam), HIWORD(longParam)});
    windowPtr->OnDoubleClick(LeftButton,
                windowPtr->DeviceToLogical(mousePoint),
                shiftPressed, controlPressed);
  }
  return 0;

case WM_MBUTTONDBLCLK: {
    bool shiftPressed = (::GetKeyState(VK_SHIFT) < 0);
    bool controlPressed = (::GetKeyState(VK_CONTROL) < 0);
    Point mousePoint =
      Point({LOWORD(longParam), HIWORD(longParam)});
    windowPtr->OnDoubleClick(MiddleButton,
                windowPtr->DeviceToLogical(mousePoint),
                shiftPressed, controlPressed);
  }
  return 0;

case WM_RBUTTONDBLCLK: {
    bool shiftPressed = (::GetKeyState(VK_SHIFT) < 0);
    bool controlPressed = (::GetKeyState(VK_CONTROL) < 0);
    Point mousePoint =
      Point({LOWORD(longParam), HIWORD(longParam)});
    windowPtr->OnDoubleClick(RightButton,
                windowPtr->DeviceToLogical(mousePoint),
                shiftPressed, controlPressed);
  }
  return 0;
```

When a touch message is sent, `OnTouch` is called, which needs the position of the window in device units:

```
case WM_TOUCH:
  OnTouch(windowPtr, wordParam, longParam,
          windowPtr->GetWindowDevicePosition());
  return 0;
```

When creating a device context in response to a paint message, we use the Win32 API functions `BeginPaint` and `EndPaint` instead of `GetDC` and `ReleaseDC` to handle the device context. However, the device context still needs to be prepared for the window's coordinate system, which is accomplished by `PrepareDeviceContext`:

```
case WM_PAINT: {
    PAINTSTRUCT paintStruct;
    HDC deviceContextHandle =
        ::BeginPaint(windowHandle,&paintStruct);
    windowPtr->PrepareDeviceContext(deviceContextHandle);
    Graphics graphics(windowPtr, deviceContextHandle);
    windowPtr->OnPaint(graphics);
    ::EndPaint(windowHandle, &paintStruct);
}
return 0;
```

When the user tries to close the window by clicking on the close box in the top-right corner, `OnClose` is called. It calls `TryClose` and closes the window if `TryClose` returns true:

```
        case WM_CLOSE:
            windowPtr->OnClose();
            return 0;
    }
}
```

If we reach this point, the Win32 API function `DefWindowProc` is called, which performs the default message handling:

```
    return DefWindowProc(windowHandle, message, wordParam, longParam);
    }
};
```

The Graphics class

The `Graphics` class is a wrapper class for a device context. It also provides functionality for drawing lines, rectangles, and ellipses; writing text; saving and restoring graphic states; setting the origin of the device context; and clipping the painting area. The constructor is private since `Graphics` objects are intended to be created internally by Small Windows only.

Graphics.h

```
namespace SmallWindows {
```

When drawing a line, it can be solid, dashed, dotted, dashed and dotted, as well as dashed and double-dotted:

```
class Window;
enum PenStyle {Solid = PS_SOLID, Dash = PS_DASH, Dot = PS_DOT,
               DashDot = PS_DASHDOT, DashDotDot =PS_DASHDOTDOT};
class Graphics {
  private:
    Graphics(Window* windowPtr, HDC deviceContextHandle);
```

The `Save` method saves the current state of the `Graphics` object and `Restore` restores it:

```
public:
  int Save();
  void Restore(int saveId);
```

The `SetOrigin` method sets the origin of the coordinate system and `IntersectClip` restricts the area to be painted:

```
void SetOrigin(Point centerPoint);
void IntersectClip(Rect clipRect);
```

The following methods draw lines, rectangles, and ellipses, and write text:

```
void DrawLine(Point startPoint, Point endPoint,
              Color penColor, PenStyle penStyle = Solid);
void DrawRectangle(Rect rect, Color penColor,
                   PenStyle = Solid);
void FillRectangle(Rect rect, Color penColor,
                   Color brushColor, PenStyle penStyle=Solid);
void DrawEllipse(Rect rect, Color penColor,
                 PenStyle = Solid);
void FillEllipse(Rect rect, Color penColor,
                 Color brushColor, PenStyle penStyle=Solid);
void DrawText(Rect areaRect, String text, Font font,
              Color textColor, Color backColor,
              bool pointsToMeters = true);
```

The `GetDeviceContextHandle` method returns the device context wrapped by the `Graphics` object:

```
HDC GetDeviceContextHandle() const
                        {return deviceContextHandle;}
```

The `windowPtr` field holds a pointer to the window about which client area is to be drawn, and `deviceContextHandle` holds the handle to the device context, of type `HDC`:

```
private:
  Window* windowPtr;
  HDC deviceContextHandle;
```

The `WindowProc` and `DialogProc` functions are friends of the `Graphics` class, since they need access to its private members. This is the same for the `PrintDialog` methods of the `StandardDialog` class:

```
friend LRESULT CALLBACK
   WindowProc(HWND windowHandle, UINT message,
             WPARAM wordParam, LPARAM longParam);
friend Graphics* StandardDialog::PrintDialog
                       (Window*parentPtr,int totalPages,
                        int& firstPage, int& lastPage,
                        int& copies, bool& sorted);
   };
};
```

Graphics.cpp

```
#include "SmallWindows.h"
```

The constructor initializes the window pointer and device context:

```
namespace SmallWindows {
  Graphics::Graphics(Window* windowPtr, HDC deviceContextHandle)
   :windowPtr(windowPtr),
    deviceContextHandle(deviceContextHandle) {
    // Empty.
  }
```

Sometimes, it is desirable to save the current state of the `Graphics` object with `Save`, which returns an identity number that can be used to restore the `Graphics` object with `Restore`:

```
int Graphics::Save() {
  return ::SaveDC(deviceContextHandle);
}

void Graphics::Restore(int saveId) {
  ::RestoreDC(deviceContextHandle, saveId);
}
```

The default origin (x = 0 and y = 0) of the coordinate system is the top-left corner of the window client area. This can be changed with `SetOrigin`, which takes the new origin in logical units. The win32 API function `SetWindowOrgEx` sets the new origin:

```
void Graphics::SetOrigin(Point centerPoint) {
  ::SetWindowOrgEx(deviceContextHandle, centerPoint.X(),
             centerPoint.Y(), nullptr);
}
```

The part of the client area to be painted can be restricted with `IntersectClip`, resulting in the area outside the given rectangle not being affected. The Win32 API function `IntersectClip` sets the restricted area:

```
void Graphics::IntersectClip(Rect clipRect) {
  ::IntersectClipRect(deviceContextHandle, clipRect.Left(),
          clipRect.Top(),clipRect.Right(),clipRect.Bottom());
}
```

It is possible to draw lines, rectangles, and ellipses using a pen, which is obtained by the Win32 API functions `CreatePen` and `SelectObject`. Note that we save the previous object in order to restore it later:

```
void Graphics::DrawLine(Point startPoint, Point endPoint,
                Color color, PenStyle penStyle/* = Solid */){
  HPEN penHandle = ::CreatePen(penStyle, 0, color.ColorRef());
  HPEN oldPenHandle =
    (HPEN) ::SelectObject(deviceContextHandle,penHandle);
```

By the way, the technique of moving the pen to the start point and then drawing the line to the end point with `MoveToEx` and `LineTo` is called **Turtle graphics**, referring to a turtle moving over the client area with the pen up or down:

```
::MoveToEx(deviceContextHandle, startPoint.X(),
        startPoint.Y(), nullptr);
::LineTo(deviceContextHandle, endPoint.X(), endPoint.Y());
```

Similar to `CreateTextMetrics` and `GetCharacterWidth` in `Window`, we need to select the previous object and restore the pen:

```
::SelectObject(deviceContextHandle, oldPenHandle);
::DeleteObject(penHandle);
}
```

When drawing a rectangle, we need a solid pen and a hollow brush, which we create with the Win32 API function `CreateBrushIndirect` with a LOGBRUSH structure parameter:

```
void Graphics::DrawRectangle(Rect rect, Color penColor,
                    PenStyle penStyle /* = Solid */) {

  HPEN penHandle =
    ::CreatePen(penStyle, 0, penColor.ColorRef());

  LOGBRUSH lbBrush;
  lbBrush.lbStyle = BS_HOLLOW;
  HBRUSH brushHandle = ::CreateBrushIndirect(&lbBrush);
```

```
    HPEN oldPenHandle =
      (HPEN) ::SelectObject(deviceContextHandle,penHandle);
    HBRUSH oldBrushHandle =
      (HBRUSH)  ::SelectObject(deviceContextHandle, brushHandle);

    ::Rectangle(deviceContextHandle, rect.Left(), rect.Top(),
              rect.Right(), rect.Bottom());

    ::SelectObject(deviceContextHandle, oldBrushHandle);
    ::DeleteObject(brushHandle);

    ::SelectObject(deviceContextHandle, oldPenHandle);
    ::DeleteObject(penHandle);
  }
```

When filling a rectangle, we also need a solid brush, which we create with the Win32 API function CreateSolidBrush:

```
  void Graphics::FillRectangle(Rect rect, Color penColor,
            Color brushColor, PenStyle penStyle /* = Solid */){

    HPEN penHandle =
      ::CreatePen(penStyle, 0, penColor.ColorRef());
    HBRUSH brushHandle =
      ::CreateSolidBrush(brushColor.ColorRef());

    HPEN oldPenHandle =
      (HPEN)::SelectObject(deviceContextHandle,penHandle);
    HBRUSH oldBrushHandle =
      (HBRUSH) ::SelectObject(deviceContextHandle, brushHandle);

    ::Rectangle(deviceContextHandle, rect.Left(), rect.Top(),
              rect.Right(), rect.Bottom());

    ::SelectObject(deviceContextHandle, oldBrushHandle);
    ::DeleteObject(brushHandle);

    ::SelectObject(deviceContextHandle, oldPenHandle);
    ::DeleteObject(penHandle);
  }
```

The DrawEllipse and FillEllipse methods are similar to DrawRectangle and FillRectangle. The only difference is that they call the Win32 API function Ellipse instead of Rectangle:

```
  void Graphics::DrawEllipse(Rect rect, Color penColor,
                          PenStyle penStyle /* = Solid */) {
```

```
    HPEN penHandle =
       ::CreatePen(penStyle, 0, penColor.ColorRef());

    LOGBRUSH lbBrush;
    lbBrush.lbStyle = BS_HOLLOW;
    HBRUSH brushHandle = ::CreateBrushIndirect(&lbBrush);

    HPEN oldPenHandle =
       (HPEN)::SelectObject(deviceContextHandle,penHandle);
    HBRUSH oldBrushHandle =
       (HBRUSH) ::SelectObject(deviceContextHandle, brushHandle);

    ::Ellipse(deviceContextHandle, rect.Left(), rect.Top(),
              rect.Right(), rect.Bottom());

    ::SelectObject(deviceContextHandle, oldBrushHandle);
    ::DeleteObject(brushHandle);

    ::SelectObject(deviceContextHandle, oldPenHandle);
    ::DeleteObject(penHandle);
}

void Graphics::FillEllipse(Rect rect, Color penColor,
              Color brushColor, PenStyle penStyle /* = Solid */){
    HPEN penHandle =
       ::CreatePen(penStyle, 0, penColor.ColorRef());
    HBRUSH brushHandle =
       ::CreateSolidBrush(brushColor.ColorRef());

    HPEN oldPenHandle =
       (HPEN) ::SelectObject(deviceContextHandle,penHandle);
    HBRUSH oldBrushHandle =
       (HBRUSH) ::SelectObject(deviceContextHandle, brushHandle);

    ::Ellipse(deviceContextHandle, rect.Left(), rect.Top(),
              rect.Right(), rect.Bottom());

    ::SelectObject(deviceContextHandle, oldBrushHandle);
    ::DeleteObject(brushHandle);

    ::SelectObject(deviceContextHandle, oldPenHandle);
    ::DeleteObject(penHandle);
}
```

When drawing text, we first need to check whether the font is given in typographical points and needs to be transformed into logical units (if `pointToMeters` is true), which is the case in the `LogicalWithScroll` and `LogicalWithoutScroll` coordinates systems. However, in the `PreviewCoordinate` system, the size of the text is already given in logical units and should not be transformed. Moreover, before we write the text, we need to create and select a font object and set the text and background colors. The Win32 `DrawText` function centers the text within the given rectangle:

```
void Graphics::DrawText(Rect areaRect, String text, Font font,
                        Color textColor, Color backColor,
                        bool pointsToMeters /* = true */) {
  if (pointsToMeters) {
    font.PointsToLogical();
  }

  HFONT fontHandle = ::CreateFontIndirect(&font.LogFont());
  HFONT oldFontHandle =
    (HFONT) ::SelectObject(deviceContextHandle, fontHandle);

  ::SetTextColor(deviceContextHandle, textColor.ColorRef());
  ::SetBkColor(deviceContextHandle, backColor.ColorRef());

  RECT rectStruct = (RECT) areaRect;
  ::DrawText(deviceContextHandle, text.c_str(), text.length(),
             &rectStruct, DT_SINGLELINE |DT_CENTER |DT_VCENTER);

  ::SelectObject(deviceContextHandle, oldFontHandle);
  ::DeleteObject(fontHandle);
  }
};
```

Summary

In this chapter, we looked into the core of Small Windows: the `MainWindow` function and the `Application`, `Window`, and `Graphics` classes. In `Chapter 11`, *The Document*, we look into the document classes of Small Windows: `Document`, `Menu`, `Accelerator`, and `StandardDocument`.

11
The Document

In the previous chapter we looked into the implementation of the `Application` and `Window` classes, which are useful for general Windows applications. In this chapter, we will look into the implementation of the `Document`, `StandardDocument`, `Menu`, and `Accelerator` classes, which are useful for document-based Windows applications.

The Document class

In this book, a **document** is a window intended for common document-based applications, such as the drawing program, spreadsheet program, and word processor of this book. The `Document` class implements the document described previously and is a direct subclass of the `Window` class. It supports caret and dirty flag, keyboard status, menus, accelerators, the mouse wheel, scroll bars, and drop files.

Document.h

```
namespace SmallWindows {
   extern const Size USLetterPortrait, LineSize;
```

The keyboard holds either the `insert` or `overwrite` mode.

```
   enum KeyboardMode {InsertKeyboard, OverwriteKeyboard};
```

Similar to `Window`, `Document` has a public constructor intended for instantiation and a protected constructor intended for subclasses. A document of the `Document` class can accept drop files, and the line size is used by the scroll bar methods:

```
   class Document : public Window {
     public:
       Document(CoordinateSystem system, Size pageSize,
                Window* parentPtr = nullptr,
```

```
                WindowStyle style=OverlappedWindow,
                WindowShow windowShow = Normal,
                bool acceptDropFiles = true,
                Size lineSize = LineSize);

        protected:
          Document(String className, CoordinateSystem system,
                Size pageSize, Window* parentPtr = nullptr,
                WindowStyle style = OverlappedWindow,
                WindowShow windowShow = Normal,
                bool acceptDropFiles = true,
                Size lineSize = LineSize);
```

A dirty flag is set if the window has been modified and needs to be saved before closing (the document has been *dirty*). The content of the document can be zoomed in accordance with a zoom factor; the default is 1.0. The name of the document is displayed in the document header by `GenerateHeader`, together with the zoom factor expressed as a percentage, and an asterisk (*) if the dirty flag is `true`. However, the zoom factor is not displayed if it is 100%:

```
        public:
          ~Document();

          String GetName() const;
          void SetName(String name);
          void SetZoom(double zoom);
          bool IsDirty() const;
          void SetDirty(bool dirty);
        private:
          void GenerateHeader();
```

The `OnSize` method is overridden to modify the size of the scroll bar in accordance with the client size. Note that the parameter to `OnSize` is the logical size of the client area, not the size of the window:

```
        public:
          virtual void OnSize(Size clientSize);
```

The `OnMouseWheel` method is overridden to scroll the vertical scroll bar one line for each wheel click:

```
          virtual void OnMouseWheel(WheelDirection direction,
                      bool shiftPressed, bool controlPressed);
```

The `Document` class supports the caret, and the `OnGainFocus` and `OnLoseFocus` methods are overridden to show or hide the caret. The `SetCaret` and `ClearCaret` methods create and destroy the caret:

```
void OnGainFocus();
void OnLoseFocus();
void SetCaret(Rect caretLogicalRect);
void ClearCaret();
```

The `UpdateCaret` method is called when the caret needs to be modified, it is intended to be overridden and its default behavior is to do nothing:

```
virtual void UpdateCaret() {/* Empty. */}
```

The `SetMenuBar` method sets the menu bar of the window. The `OnCommand` method is called every time the user selects a menu item or presses an accelerator key, and `CommandInit` is called before the menus become visible in order to set a check mark or a radio button at the menu item or to enable or disable it:

```
void SetMenuBar(Menu& menuBar);
void OnCommand(WORD commandId);
void OnCommandInit();
```

If the `acceptDropFiles` parameter in the constructor is `true`, the document accepts drop files. If the user moves one or several files and drops them in the document window, `OnDropFile` is called with the list of path names as parameters. It is intended to be overridden by subclasses, and its default behavior is to do nothing:

```
virtual void OnDropFile(vector<String> pathList)
                        {/* Empty. */}
```

The `GetKeyboardMode` and `SetKeyboardMode` methods set and get the `keyboard` mode. The `OnKeyboardMode` method is called when the `keyboard` mode is changed; it is intended to be overridden and its default behavior is to do nothing:

```
KeyboardMode GetKeyboardMode() const {return keyboardMode;}
void SetKeyboardMode(KeyboardMode mode)
                    {keyboardMode = mode;}
virtual void OnKeyboardMode(KeyboardMode mode)
                    {/* Empty. */}
```

The `OnHorizontalScroll` and `OnVerticalScroll` methods handle the scroll messages. The scroll bar is set in accordance with the message settings:

```
virtual void OnHorizontalScroll(WORD flags,WORD thumbPos=0);
virtual void OnVerticalScroll(WORD flags, WORD thumbPos =0);
```

The `KeyToScroll` method takes a key and performs an appropriate scroll bar action depending on the key and whether the *Shift* or *Ctrl* key is pressed. For instance, the *Page Up* key moves the vertical scroll bar one page upward:

```
virtual bool KeyToScroll(WORD key, bool shiftPressed,
                         bool controlPressed);
```

The following methods set or get the logical position, line size, page size, and total size of the horizontal and vertical scroll bar:

```
void SetHorizontalScrollPosition(int scrollPos);
int GetHorizontalScrollPosition() const;
void SetVerticalScrollPosition(int scrollPos);
int GetVerticalScrollPosition() const;

void SetHorizontalScrollLineWidth(int lineWidth);
int GetHorizontalScrollLineHeight() const;
void SetVerticalScrollLineHeight(int lineHeight);
int GetVerticalScrollLineHeight() const;

void SetHorizontalScrollPageWidth(int pageWidth);
int GetHorizontalScrollPageWidth() const;
void SetVerticalScrollPageHeight(int pageHeight);
int GetVerticalScrollPageHeight() const;

void SetHorizontalScrollTotalWidth(int scrollWidth);
int GetHorizontalScrollTotalWidth() const;
void SetVerticalScrollTotalHeight(int scrollHeight);
int GetVerticalScrollTotalHeight() const;
```

The command map stores the menu items of the document; for each menu item, the selection, enable, check, and radio listeners are stored:

```
public:
   map<WORD,Command>& CommandMap() {return commandMap;}
```

The accelerator set holds the accelerators of the document irrespective of whether it is a regular key or virtual key (for instance, *F2*, *Home*, or *Delete*) and whether the *Ctrl*, *Shift*, or *Alt* key is pressed. The set is used by the message loop in `Application`:

```
list<ACCEL>& AcceleratorSet() {return acceleratorSet;}

private:
   map<WORD, Command> commandMap;
   list<ACCEL> acceleratorSet;
```

The `name` field is the name of the document displayed at the top of the window; `caretPresent` is true when the caret is visible:

```
String name;
bool caretPresent = false;
```

When the user presses one of the arrow keys, `OnKeyDown` is called. However, if `OnKeyDown` returns `false`, the scroll bar is changed; in that case, we need `lineSize` to define the size of a line to be scrolled:

```
Size lineSize;
```

The `dirtyFlag` field is `true` when the user has changed the document without saving, resulting in the **Save** menu item being enabled and the user being asked whether to save the document when closing the window or exiting the application:

```
bool dirtyFlag = false;
```

The `menuBarHandle` method is the Win32 API function that handles the menu bar of the document window:

```
HMENU menuBarHandle;
```

The keyboard can hold the `insert` or `overwrite` mode, which is stored in `keyboardMode`:

```
    KeyboardMode keyboardMode = InsertKeyboard;
};
```

The `DocumentProc` method is called when the document window receives a message, similar to `WindowProc` in the `Window` class:

```
LRESULT CALLBACK DocumentProc(HWND windowHandle, UINT message,
                    WPARAM wordParam, LPARAM longParam);
```

The `ExtractPathList` method extracts the paths of the dropped files when the window receives the `WM_DROPFILES` message:

```
    vector<String> ExtractPathList(WORD wordParam);
};
```

Initialization

The first `Document` constructor takes the coordinate system, the page size, parent window, style, appearance, whether the document accepts drop files, and the line size as its parameters. The size of a US Letter page in portrait mode (standing up) is 215.9 * 279.4 millimeters. A line (used by `KeyToScroll` when scrolling lines) is 5 millimeters in both the horizontal and vertical directions. Since a logical unit is one hundredth of a millimeter, we multiply each measure by one hundred.

Document.cpp

```
#include "SmallWindows.h"

namespace SmallWindows {
  const Size USLetterPortrait(21590, 27940), LineSize(500, 500);
```

The first constructor calls the second constructor with the `Windows` class named `Document` as the first parameter:

```
Document::Document(CoordinateSystem system, Size pageSize,
                   Window* parentPtr /* = nullptr */,
                   WindowStyle style /* = OverlappedWindow */,
                   WindowShow windowShow /* = Normal */,
                   bool acceptDropFiles /* = true */,
                   Size lineSize /* = LineSize */)
 :Document::Document(TEXT("document"), system, pageSize,
                     parentPtr, style, windowShow,
                     acceptDropFiles, lineSize) {
  // Empty.
}
```

The second constructor takes the same parameters as the first construct with the exception that it inserts the `Windows` class name as its first parameter:

```
Document::Document(String className, CoordinateSystem system,
                   Size pageSize, Window* parentPtr/*=nullptr*/,
                   WindowStyle style /* = OverlappedWindow */,
                   WindowShow windowShow /* = Normal */,
                   bool acceptDropFiles /* = true */,
                   Size lineSize /* = LineSize */)
 :Window(className, system, pageSize, parentPtr,
         style, NoStyle, windowShow),
```

The range and page size of the scroll bars are stored in the window's scroll bar settings. However, the size of the line needs to be stored in `lineSize`:

```
lineSize(lineSize) {
```

The header appears on the top bar of the document window:

```
GenerateHeader();
```

The default position of the scroll bars is :

```
SetHorizontalScrollPosition(0);
SetVerticalScrollPosition(0);
```

The size of the scroll bars is the logical width and height of the page:

```
SetHorizontalScrollTotalWidth(pageSize.Width());
SetVerticalScrollTotalHeight(pageSize.Height());
```

The page sizes of the scroll bars represent the visible part of the document, which is the logical size of the client area:

```
Size clientSize = GetClientSize();
SetHorizontalScrollPageWidth(clientSize.Width());
SetVerticalScrollPageHeight(clientSize.Height());
```

The Win32 API function `DragAcceptFiles` makes the window accept drop files. Note that we need to convert the C++ `bool` type of `acceptDropFiles` to the value `TRUE` or `FALSE` of the Win32 API `BOOL` type:

```
  ::DragAcceptFiles(windowHandle,
                    acceptDropFiles ? TRUE : FALSE);
}
```

The destructor destroys the caret if present:

```
Document::~Document() {
  if (caretPresent) {
    ::DestroyCaret();
  }
}
```

The Document header

The `GetName` method simply returns the name. However, `SetName` sets the name and regenerates the header of the document window. The same goes for `SetZoom` and `SetDirty`: they set the zoom factor and dirty flag and then regenerate the header:

```
String Document::GetName() const {
  return name;
}

void Document::SetName(String name) {
  this->name = name;
  GenerateHeader();
}
```

```
void Document::SetZoom(double zoom) {
  Window::SetZoom(zoom);
  GenerateHeader();
}

bool Document::IsDirty() const {
  return dirtyFlag;
}

void Document::SetDirty(bool dirty) {
  dirtyFlag = dirty;
  GenerateHeader();
}
```

The title of the document includes its name, whether the dirty flag is set (indicated by an asterisk), and the zoom status (as a percentage), unless it is 100%.

```
void Document::GenerateHeader() {
  String headerName = name.empty() ? TEXT("[No Name]") : name,
         dirtyText = dirtyFlag ? TEXT("*") : TEXT("");
  int zoomPerCent = (int) (100 * GetZoom());

  if (zoomPerCent!= 100) {
    String zoomText =
      TEXT(" ") + to_String(zoomPerCent) + TEXT("%");
    SetHeader(headerName + dirtyText + zoomText);
  }
  else {
    SetHeader(headerName + dirtyText);
  }
}
```

`OnSize` modifies the page sizes of the horizontal and vertical scroll bars in accordance with the new client size:

```
void Document::OnSize(Size clientSize) {
  SetHorizontalScrollPageWidth(clientSize.Width());
  SetVerticalScrollPageHeight(clientSize.Height());
}
```

The caret

As mentioned in `Chapter 1`, *Introduction*, a caret is the marker indicating where to input the next character. It is a thin vertical bar in the `insert` mode and a block in the `overwrite` mode. The `OnGainFocus` and `OnLoseFocus` methods show and hide the caret, if present:

```
void Document::OnGainFocus() {
  if (caretPresent) {
    ::ShowCaret(windowHandle);
  }
}

void Document::OnLoseFocus() {
  if (caretPresent) {
    ::HideCaret(windowHandle);
  }
}
```

The `SetCaret` method displays a caret with the given dimensions. If there already is a caret present, it is destroyed:

```
void Document::SetCaret(Rect caretLogicalRect) {
  if (caretPresent) {
    ::DestroyCaret();
  }
```

The size of the caret must be given in device units; there is a risk that the `LogicalToDevice` call rounds the width to zero (in the case of a vertical bar), in which case the width is set to 1:

```
Rect deviceCaretRect = LogicalToDevice(caretLogicalRect);
if (deviceCaretRect.Width() == 0) {
  deviceCaretRect.Right() = deviceCaretRect.Left() + 1;
}
```

The new caret is created by the Win32 API functions `CreateCaret`, `SetCaretPos`, and `ShowCaret`:

```
  ::CreateCaret(windowHandle, nullptr, deviceCaretRect.Width(),
                deviceCaretRect.Height());
  ::SetCaretPos(deviceCaretRect.Left(), deviceCaretRect.Top());
  ::ShowCaret(windowHandle);

  caretPresent = true;
}
```

The `ClearCaret` method destroys the caret, if present:

```
void Document::ClearCaret() {
  if (caretPresent) {
    ::DestroyCaret();
  }
  caretPresent = false;
}
```

The mouse wheel

When the user moves the mouse wheel, the vertical scroll bar is moved one line up or down (if they do not press the *Ctrl* key):

```
void Document::OnMouseWheel(WheelDirection wheelDirection,
                     bool shiftPressed, bool controlPressed){
  if (controlPressed) {
    switch (wheelDirection) {
      case WheelUp:
        OnVerticalScroll(SB_LINEUP);
        break;

      case WheelDown:
        OnVerticalScroll(SB_LINEDOWN);
        break;
    }
  }
```

If the user presses the *Ctrl* key, then the client area is zoomed. The permitted range is 10% to 1,000%:

```
  else {
    switch (wheelDirection) {
      case WheelUp:
        SetZoom(min(10.0, 1.11 * GetZoom()));
        break;

      case WheelDown:
        SetZoom(max(0.1, 0.9 * GetZoom()));
        break;
    }
  }
```

As the vertical scroll bar position has been modified, we need to repaint the whole client area:

```
  Invalidate();
  UpdateWindow();
  UpdateCaret();
}
```

The menu bar

The menu bar of the document is set by calling the Win32 API function `SetMenu`, which handles the document window and the menu bar; `menuBarHandle` is used when enabling or marking menu items in `OnCommandInit`, as shown here:

```
void Document::SetMenuBar(Menu& menuBar) {
  menuBarHandle = menuBar.menuHandle;
  ::SetMenu(windowHandle, menuBarHandle);
}
```

The `OnCommand` method is called when the user selects a menu item or an accelerator. It looks up and calls the selection listener associated with the given command identity number:

```
void Document::OnCommand(WORD commandId) {
  Command command = commandMap[commandId];
  command.Selection()(this);
}
```

The `OnCommandInit` method is called before a menu becomes visible. It iterates through every menu item and, for each of them, decides whether it should be annotated with a check mark or radio button, or enabled or disabled:

```
void Document::OnCommandInit() {
  for (pair<WORD,Command> pair : commandMap) {
    WORD commandId = pair.first;
    Command command = pair.second;
```

If the enable listener is not null, we call it and set the enable flag to `MF_ENABLED` or `MF_GRAYED` (disabled):

```
    if (command.Enable() != nullptr) {
      UINT enableFlag = command.Enable()(this) ?
                        MF_ENABLED : MF_GRAYED;
      ::EnableMenuItem(menuBarHandle, commandId,
                       MF_BYCOMMAND | enableFlag);
    }
```

If the check or radio listeners are not null, we call them and set `checkflag` or `radioFlag`:

```
    { bool checkFlag = false;
      if (command.Check() != nullptr) {
        BoolListener checkListener = command.Check();
        checkFlag = checkListener(this);
      }
      bool radioFlag = false;
      if (command.Radio() != nullptr) {
        BoolListener radioListener = command.Radio();
        radioFlag = radioListener(this);
      }
```

If either `checkFlag` or `radioFlag` is `true`, we check the menu item. Whether the menu item thereby becomes annotated with a check mark or a radio button is decided when the menu item is added to the menu, which is described in the `Menu` class in the next section. It is also stated in `Menu` that at least one of the check mark and radio listeners must be null, since it is not possible to annotate a menu item with both a check mark and a radio button:

```
        UINT checkFlags = (checkFlag | radioFlag) ?
                         MF_CHECKED : MF_UNCHECKED;
        ::CheckMenuItem(menuBarHandle, commandId,
                      MF_BYCOMMAND | checkFlags);
      }
    }
  }
```

The scroll bar

The `OnHorizontalScroll` and `OnVerticalScroll` methods are called every time the user scrolls by clicking the scroll bar arrows, the scroll bar itself, or by dragging the scroll thumb.

The `scrollPos` field holds the current scroll bar setting. The `scrollLine` variable is the size of the line, `scrollPage` is the size of the page (representing the logical size of the visible part of the document and equal to the logical size of the client area), and `scrollSize` is the total size of the scroll bar (representing the logical size of the document):

```
    void Document::OnHorizontalScroll(WORD flags,
                                   WORD thumbPos /*= 0 */) {
    int scrollPos = GetHorizontalScrollPosition(),
        scrollLine = GetHorizontalScrollLineHeight(),
        scrollPage = GetHorizontalScrollPageWidth(),
        scrollSize = GetHorizontalScrollTotalWidth();

    switch (flags) {
      case SB_LEFT:
        SetHorizontalScrollPosition(0);
        break;
```

In the case of leftward movement, we need to verify that the new scroll position doesn't go below zero:

```
      case SB_LINELEFT:
        SetHorizontalScrollPosition(max(0, scrollPos -
                                      scrollLine));
        break;
```

```
      case SB_PAGELEFT:
        SetHorizontalScrollPosition(max(0, scrollPos -
                                     scrollPage));
        break;
```

In the case of rightward movement, we need to verify that the scroll position does not exceed the scroll bar size:

```
      case SB_LINERIGHT:
        SetHorizontalScrollPosition(min(scrollPos + scrollLine,
                                     scrollSize - scrollLine));
        break;

      case SB_PAGERIGHT:
        SetHorizontalScrollPosition(min(scrollPos + scrollLine,
                                     scrollSize - scrollPage));
        break;

      case SB_RIGHT:
        SetHorizontalScrollPosition(scrollSize - scrollPage);
        break;
```

If the user drags the scroll bar thumb, we just set the new scroll position. The difference between the messages is that SB_THUMBTRACK is sent continually as the user drags the thumb, while SB_THUMBPOSITION is sent when the user releases the mouse button:

```
      case SB_THUMBTRACK:
      case SB_THUMBPOSITION:
        SetHorizontalScrollPosition(thumbPos);
        break;
    }
  }
```

Vertical scroll bar movements work in the same way as horizontal scroll bar movements:

```
  void Document::OnVerticalScroll(WORD flags,
                                  WORD thumbPos /* = 0 */) {
    int scrollPos = GetVerticalScrollPosition(),
        scrollLine = GetVerticalScrollLineHeight(),
        scrollPage = GetVerticalScrollPageHeight(),
        scrollSize = GetVerticalScrollTotalHeight();

    switch (flags) {
      case SB_TOP:
        SetVerticalScrollPosition(0);
        break;
```

```
            case SB_LINEUP:
                SetVerticalScrollPosition(max(0, scrollPos - scrollLine));
                break;

            case SB_PAGEUP:
                SetVerticalScrollPosition(max(0, scrollPos - scrollPage));
                break;

            case SB_LINEDOWN:
                SetVerticalScrollPosition(min(scrollPos + scrollLine,
                                              scrollSize - scrollLine));
                break;

            case SB_PAGEDOWN:
                SetVerticalScrollPosition(min(scrollPos + scrollLine,
                                              scrollSize - scrollPage));
                break;

            case SB_BOTTOM:
                SetVerticalScrollPosition(scrollSize - scrollPage);
                break;

            case SB_THUMBTRACK:
            case SB_THUMBPOSITION:
                SetVerticalScrollPosition(thumbPos);
                break;
        }
    }
```

The `KeyToScroll` function is called when the user presses a key. It examines the key, performs an appropriate scroll action, and returns `true` if the key was used, indicating as much:

```
bool Document::KeyToScroll(WORD key, bool shiftPressed,
                           bool controlPressed) {
    switch (key) {
        case KeyUp:
            OnVerticalScroll(SB_LINEUP);
            return true;

        case KeyDown:
            OnVerticalScroll(SB_LINEDOWN);
            return true;

        case KeyPageUp:
            OnVerticalScroll(SB_PAGEUP);
            return true;
```

```
      case KeyPageDown:
        OnVerticalScroll(SB_PAGEDOWN);
        return true;

      case KeyLeft:
        OnHorizontalScroll(SB_LINELEFT);
        return true;

      case KeyRight:
        OnHorizontalScroll(SB_LINERIGHT);
        return true;

      case KeyHome:
        OnHorizontalScroll(SB_LEFT);
        if (controlPressed) {
          OnVerticalScroll(SB_TOP);
        }
        return true;

      case KeyEnd:
        OnHorizontalScroll(SB_RIGHT);
        if (controlPressed) {
          OnVerticalScroll(SB_BOTTOM);
        }
        return true;
    }

    return false;
  }
```

If the scroll position has been changed, we set the new scroll position by calling the Win32 API function `SetScrollPos` and update the window and the caret:

```
void Document::SetHorizontalScrollPosition(int scrollPos) {
  if (scrollPos != GetHorizontalScrollPosition()) {
    ::SetScrollPos(windowHandle, SB_HORZ, scrollPos, TRUE);
    Invalidate();
    UpdateWindow();
    UpdateCaret();
  }
}
```

The Win32 API function `GetScrollPos` returns the current scroll bar position:

```
int Document::GetHorizontalScrollPosition() const {
  return ::GetScrollPos(windowHandle, SB_HORZ);
}
```

The methods for the vertical scroll position work in the same way as the methods for the horizontal scroll bar:

```
void Document::SetVerticalScrollPosition(int scrollPos) {
  if (scrollPos != GetVerticalScrollPosition()) {
    ::SetScrollPos(windowHandle, SB_VERT, scrollPos, TRUE);
    Invalidate();
    UpdateWindow();
    UpdateCaret();
  }
}

int Document::GetVerticalScrollPosition() const {
  return ::GetScrollPos(windowHandle, SB_VERT);
}
```

The `SetHorizontalScrollLineWidth`, `GetHorizontalScrollLineHeight`, `SetVerticalScrollLineHeight`, and `GetVerticalScrollLineHeight` methods have no Win32 API counterparts. Instead, we store the size of a scrolled line in the `lineSize` field:

```
void Document::SetHorizontalScrollLineWidth(int lineWidth) {
  lineSize.Width() = lineWidth;
}

int Document::GetHorizontalScrollLineHeight() const {
  return lineSize.Width();
}

void Document::SetVerticalScrollLineHeight(int lineHeight) {
  lineSize.Height() = lineHeight;
}

int Document::GetVerticalScrollLineHeight() const {
  return lineSize.Height();
}
```

The `SetHorizontalScrollPageWidth`, `GetHorizontalScrollPageWidth`, `SetVerticalScrollPageHeight`, and `GetVerticalScrollPageHeight` methods have no direct Win32 API counterparts. However, the `GetScrollInfo` and `SetScrollInfo` functions handle the general scroll information, and we can set and extract the page information:

```
void Document::SetHorizontalScrollPageWidth(int pageWidth) {
  SCROLLINFO scrollInfo = {sizeof(SCROLLINFO), SIF_PAGE};
  scrollInfo.nPage = pageWidth;
```

```
  ::SetScrollInfo(windowHandle, SB_HORZ, &scrollInfo, TRUE);
}

int Document::GetHorizontalScrollPageWidth() const {
  SCROLLINFO scrollInfo = {sizeof(SCROLLINFO), SIF_PAGE};
  ::GetScrollInfo(windowHandle, SB_HORZ, &scrollInfo);
  return scrollInfo.nPage;
}

void Document::SetVerticalScrollPageHeight(int pageHeight) {
  SCROLLINFO scrollInfo = {sizeof(SCROLLINFO), SIF_PAGE};
  scrollInfo.nPage = pageHeight;
  ::SetScrollInfo(windowHandle, SB_VERT, &scrollInfo, TRUE);
}

int Document::GetVerticalScrollPageHeight() const {
  SCROLLINFO scrollInfo = {sizeof(SCROLLINFO), SIF_PAGE};
  ::GetScrollInfo(windowHandle, SB_VERT, &scrollInfo);
  return scrollInfo.nPage;
}
```

The SetHorizontalScrollTotalWidth, GetHorizontalScrollTotalWidth, SetVerticalScrollTotalHeight, and GetVerticalScrollTotalHeight methods call the Win32 API functions SetScrollRange and GetScrollRange, which set and get the minimum and maximum scroll values. However, we ignore the minimum value since it is always 0:

```
void Document::SetHorizontalScrollTotalWidth(int scrollWidth) {
  ::SetScrollRange(windowHandle, SB_HORZ, 0, scrollWidth, TRUE);
}

int Document::GetHorizontalScrollTotalWidth() const {
  int minRange, maxRange;
  ::GetScrollRange(windowHandle, SB_HORZ, &minRange, &maxRange);
  return maxRange;
}

void Document::SetVerticalScrollTotalHeight(int scrollHeight) {
  ::SetScrollRange(windowHandle, SB_VERT, 0, scrollHeight, TRUE);
}

int Document::GetVerticalScrollTotalHeight() const {
  int minRange, maxRange;
  ::GetScrollRange(windowHandle, SB_VERT, &minRange, &maxRange);
  return maxRange;
}
```

The DocumentProc method

The `DocumentProc` method is called every time the document (of the `Document` class) receives a message. If it uses the message, 0 is returned; otherwise, `WindowProc` (described in the previous chapter) is called to further process the message:

```
LRESULT CALLBACK DocumentProc(HWND windowHandle, UINT message,
                          WPARAM wordParam, LPARAM longParam){
```

We look up the window in `WindowMap` in the `Window` class and take action only if the window is a `Document` object:

```
if ((windowHandle != nullptr) &&
    (WindowMap.count(windowHandle) == 1)) {
  Document* documentPtr =
    dynamic_cast<Document*>(WindowMap[windowHandle]);

  if (documentPtr != nullptr) {
    switch (message) {
```

The direction of the mouse wheel is downward if the word parameter's ninth bit is set:

```
case WM_MOUSEWHEEL: {
    bool down = (HIWORD(wordParam) & 0x0100) != 0;
    WheelDirection wheelDirection =
      down ? WheelDown : WheelUp;
    bool shiftPressed = (::GetKeyState(VK_SHIFT) < 0);
    bool controlPressed = (::GetKeyState(VK_CONTROL)<0);
    documentPtr->OnMouseWheel(wheelDirection,
                  shiftPressed, controlPressed);
}
return 0;
```

The key-down messages both check the *Insert* key and call `OnKeyDown` and `KeyToScroll`, returning 0 if one of them uses the key:

```
case WM_KEYDOWN: {
    WORD key = wordParam;
```

If the user presses the *Insert* key, the keyboard mode is swapped between the insert and overwrite mode. `SetKeyboardMode` sets the keyboard mode and calls `OnKeyboardMode`, which is intended to be overridden by subclasses to alert the application of the change:

```
if (key == KeyInsert) {
  switch (documentPtr->GetKeyboardMode()) {
```

```
    case InsertKeyboard:
      documentPtr->
        SetKeyboardMode(OverwriteKeyboard);
      documentPtr->
        OnKeyboardMode(OverwriteKeyboard);
      break;

    case OverwriteKeyboard:
      documentPtr->SetKeyboardMode(InsertKeyboard);
      documentPtr->OnKeyboardMode(InsertKeyboard);
      break;
  }

  return 0;
}
```

If the user does not press the *Insert* key, we check whether OnKeyDown uses the key (and thereby returns true). If it does not, we instead check whether KeyToScroll uses the key. If either OnKeyDown or KeyToScroll returns true, 0 is returned:

```
    else {
      bool shiftPressed = (::GetKeyState(VK_SHIFT) < 0);
      bool controlPressed=(::GetKeyState(VK_CONTROL)<0);

      if (documentPtr->OnKeyDown(wordParam,shiftPressed,
                                 controlPressed) ||
          documentPtr->KeyToScroll(key, shiftPressed,
                                   controlPressed)) {
        return 0;
      }
    }
  }
  break;
```

The WM_COMMAND case is sent when the user selects a menu item, and WM_INITMENUPOPUP is sent before a menu becomes visible. Messages are handled by calling OnCommand, which executes the selection listener connected to the menu item, and OnCommandInit, which enables or annotates menu items with check marks or radio buttons before they become visible:

```
case WM_COMMAND:
  documentPtr->OnCommand(LOWORD(wordParam));
  return 0;

case WM_INITMENUPOPUP:
  documentPtr->OnCommandInit();
  return 0;
```

When the user drops a set of files into the window, we need to extract their paths before calling `OnDropFile`. The `ExtractPath` method extracts the path of the files from the drop and returns a list of paths, which is sent to `OnDropFile`:

```
case WM_DROPFILES: {
    vector<String> pathList =
      ExtractPathList(wordParam);
    documentPtr->OnDropFile(pathList);
  }
  return 0;
```

The `WM_HSCROLL` and `WM_VSCROLL` messages are handled by calling their matching methods:

```
case WM_HSCROLL: {
    WORD flags = LOWORD(wordParam),
        thumbPos = HIWORD(wordParam);
    documentPtr->OnHorizontalScroll(flags, thumbPos);
  }
  return 0;

case WM_VSCROLL: {
    WORD flags = LOWORD(wordParam),
        thumbPos = HIWORD(wordParam);
    documentPtr->OnVerticalScroll(flags, thumbPos);
  }
  return 0;
  }
 }
}
```

Finally, if the message is not caught by `DocumentProc`, `WindowProc` (from the previous chapter) is called to further process the message:

```
    return WindowProc(windowHandle, message,
                    wordParam, longParam);
}
```

The `ExtractPathList` method extracts the paths of the dropped files by calling the Win32 API function `DragQueryFile` and returns the list of paths:

```
vector<String> ExtractPathList(WORD wordParam) {
  vector<String> pathList;
  HDROP dropHandle = (HDROP) wordParam;
```

The `DragQueryFile` method returns the number of files when the second parameter is `0xFFFFFFFF`:

```
      int size =
        ::DragQueryFile(dropHandle, 0xFFFFFFFF, nullptr, 0);
      for (int index = 0; index < size; ++index) {
```

The `DragQueryFile` method returns the size of the path string when the second parameter is a zero-based index and the third parameter is null:

```
        int bufferSize =
          ::DragQueryFile(dropHandle, index, nullptr, 0) + 1;
        TCHAR* path = new TCHAR[bufferSize];
        assert(path!= nullptr);
```

The `DragQueryFile` method copies the path itself when the third parameter is a pointer to a text buffer rather than null:

```
        assert(::DragQueryFile(dropHandle, index,
                               path, bufferSize) != 0);
        pathList.push_back(String(path));
        delete [] path;
      }

      return pathList;
    }
};
```

The Menu class

The `Menu` class handles a menu, made up of a list of menu items, separator bars, or submenus. When a menu item is added, its command information is stored in the document's command map to be used when receiving the `WM_COMMAND` and `WM_INITCOMMAND` messages. If the menu item text includes an accelerator, it is added to the document's accelerator set. The `Command` class is an auxiliary class holding pointers to the menu items: selection, enable, check, and radio listeners.

Command.h

```
namespace SmallWindows {
  typedef void (*VoidListener)(void* sourcePtr);
  typedef bool (*BoolListener)(void* sourcePtr);

  class Command {
    public:
      Command();
      Command(VoidListener selection, BoolListener enable,
              BoolListener check, BoolListener radio);
```

```
        VoidListener Selection() const {return selection;}
        BoolListener Enable() const {return enable;}
        BoolListener Check() const {return check;}
        BoolListener Radio() const {return radio;}

    private:
      VoidListener selection;
      BoolListener enable, check, radio;
  };
};
```

Command.cpp

```
#include "SmallWindows.h"

namespace SmallWindows {
  Command::Command()
   :selection(nullptr),
    enable(nullptr),
    check(nullptr),
    radio(nullptr) {
    // Empty.
  }

  Command::Command(VoidListener selection, BoolListener enable,
                   BoolListener check, BoolListener radio)
   :selection(selection),
    enable(enable),
    check(check),
    radio(radio) {
    // Empty.
  }
};
```

Menu and accelerator listeners are not regular methods. They are declared (they do not need to be defined) by the DECLARE_BOOL_LISTENER and DECLARE_VOID_LISTENER macros. This is because we cannot call a non-static method in an unknown class directly. Therefore, we let the macros declare a non-static method without parameters and define a static method with a void pointer as a parameter that calls the non-static method. The macros do not define the non-static method. That task is left for the user of Small Windows.

When the user adds a menu item with a listener, a Command object is created. It is actually the static method with the void pointer parameter that is added to the Command object. Moreover, when the user selects a menu item, it is the static method that is called. The static method in turn calls the non-static method, which is defined by the user.

The macros take the names of the current class and the listener as parameters. Note that the bool listener is constant, while the void listener is not constant. This is because bool listeners are intended to look up the values of one or several of the fields of the class, while void listeners also modify the fields.

Menu.h

```
#define DEFINE_BOOL_LISTENER(SubClass, Listener)   \
  virtual bool Listener() const;                   \
  static bool SubClass::Listener(void* voidPtr) {  \
    return ((SubClass*) voidPtr)->Listener();      \
  }

#define DEFINE_VOID_LISTENER(SubClass, Listener)   \
  virtual void Listener();                         \
  static void SubClass::Listener(void* voidPtr) {  \
    ((SubClass*) voidPtr)->Listener();             \
  }

namespace SmallWindows {
  class Document;

  class Menu {
    public:
      Menu(Document* documentPtr, String text = TEXT(""));
      Menu(const Menu& menu);

      void AddMenu(Menu& menu);
      void AddSeparator();
      void AddItem(String text, VoidListener selection,
                   BoolListener enable = nullptr,
                   BoolListener check = nullptr,
                   BoolListener radio = nullptr);
```

The document pointer is needed when accessing the command map and accelerator set of the document. Every menu except the menu bar has text that is displayed in the document window; menuHandle is the Win32 API menu handle wrapped by this class:

```
    private:
      Document* documentPtr;
      String text;
      HMENU menuHandle;

      friend class Document;
      friend class StandardDocument;
  };
};
```

Menu.cpp

```
#include "SmallWindows.h"
```

The constructor initializes the pointer document and the text. It also creates the menu by calling the Win32 API function `CreateMenu`. Since the menu bar does not need text, the `text` parameter is empty by default:

```
namespace SmallWindows {
  Menu::Menu(Document* documentPtr, String text /* = TEXT("") */)
   :documentPtr(documentPtr),
    text(text),
    menuHandle(::CreateMenu()) {
    // Empty.
  }
```

The copy constructor copies the fields of the menu. Note that we copy the `menuHandle` field rather than creating a new menu handle.

```
  Menu::Menu(const Menu& menu)
   :documentPtr(menu.documentPtr),
    text(menu.text),
    menuHandle(menu.menuHandle) {
    // Empty.
  }
```

The `AddMenu` method adds a menu (not a menu item) as a submenu to the menu, while `AddSeparator` adds a separator (a horizontal bar) to the menu:

```
  void Menu::AddMenu(Menu& menu) {
    ::AppendMenu(menuHandle, MF_STRING | MF_POPUP,
                 (UINT) menu.menuHandle, menu.text.c_str());
  }

  void Menu::AddSeparator() {
    ::AppendMenu(menuHandle, MF_SEPARATOR, 0, nullptr);
  }
```

The `AddItem` method adds a menu item (not a menu) to the menu, with the selection, enable, check, and radio listeners:

```
  void Menu::AddItem(String text, VoidListener selection,
                     BoolListener enable /* = nullptr */,
                     BoolListener check /* = nullptr */,
                     BoolListener radio /* = nullptr */) {
```

The selection listener is not allowed to be null, and at least one of the check marks and radio listeners must be null, since it is not possible to annotate a menu item with both a check mark and a radio button:

```
assert((selection != nullptr) &&
       ((check == nullptr) || (radio == nullptr)));
```

Each menu item is given a unique identity number, which we obtain from the current size of the command map:

```
map<WORD,Command>& commandMap = documentPtr->CommandMap();
int itemId = commandMap.size();
```

We add a `Command` object to the command map and add the menu item with the Win32 API function `AppendMenu`, which takes the menu handle, identity number, and text:

```
commandMap[itemId] = Command(listener, enable, check, radio);
::AppendMenu(menuHandle, MF_STRING,
             (UINT) itemId, text.c_str());
```

If the radio listener is not null, we need to call the Win32 API function `SetMenuItemInfo` in order for the radio button to appear with the menu item:

```
if (radio != nullptr) {
  MENUITEMINFO menuItemInfo;
  menuItemInfo.cbSize = sizeof menuItemInfo;
  menuItemInfo.fMask = MIIM_FTYPE;
  menuItemInfo.fType = MFT_RADIOCHECK;
  ::SetMenuItemInfo(menuHandle, (UINT) itemId,
                    FALSE, &menuItemInfo);
}
```

Finally, we call `TextToAccelerator` in `Accelerator` (described in the next section) to add an accelerator, if present, to the accelerator set of the document, which is used by the message loop of `Application`:

```
    Accelerator::TextToAccelerator(text, itemId,
                                   documentPtr->AcceleratorSet());
  }
};
```

The Accelerator class

It is possible to add an accelerator to a menu item. The accelerator text is preceded by a tabulator character (`\t`) and the text is made up of the optional prefixes `Ctrl+`, `Shift+`, or `Alt+` followed by a character (for instance, `&Open\tCtrl+O`) or the name of a virtual key (for instance, `&Save\tAlt+F2`).

Accelerator.h

```
namespace SmallWindows {
```

The Win32 API holds a set of virtual keys with names beginning with `VK_`. In Small Windows, they have been given other names, hopefully easier to understand. The virtual keys available are: **F1 – F12, Insert, Delete, Backspace, Tab, Home, End, Page Up, Page Down, Left, Right, Up, Down, Space, Escape,** and **Return**:

```
enum Keys {KeyF1 = VK_F1, KeyF2 = VK_F2, KeyF3 = VK_F3,
           KeyF4 = VK_F4, KeyF5 = VK_F5, KeyF6 = VK_F6,
           KeyF7 = VK_F7, KeyF8 = VK_F8, KeyF9 = VK_F9,
           KeyF10 = VK_F10, KeyF11 = VK_F11, KeyF12 = VK_F12,
           KeyInsert = VK_INSERT, KeyDelete = VK_DELETE,
           KeyBackspace = VK_BACK, KeyTabulator = VK_TAB,
           KeyHome = VK_HOME, KeyEnd = VK_END,
           KeyPageUp = VK_PRIOR, KeyPageDown = VK_NEXT,
           KeyLeft = VK_LEFT, KeyRight = VK_RIGHT,
           KeyUp = VK_UP, KeyDown = VK_DOWN,
           KeySpace = VK_SPACE, KeyEscape = VK_ESCAPE,
           KeyReturn = VK_RETURN};
```

The `Accelerator` class only holds the `TextToAccelerator` method, which takes text, extracts the accelerator, and adds it to the accelerator set, if present:

```
class Accelerator {
  public:
    static void TextToAccelerator(String& text, int idemId,
                                  list<ACCEL>& acceleratorSet);
  };
};
```

Accelerator.cpp

```
#include "SmallWindows.h"
```

`TextToVirtualKey` is an auxiliary function that takes text and returns the corresponding virtual key. The `keyTable` array holds the map between the texts and the available virtual keys:

```
namespace SmallWindows {
  WORD TextToVirtualKey(String& text) {
    static const struct {
      TCHAR* textPtr;
      WORD key;
    } keyTable[] = {
      {TEXT("F1"), KeyF1}, {TEXT("F2"), KeyF2},
      {TEXT("F3"), KeyF3}, {TEXT("F4"), KeyF4},
      {TEXT("F5"), KeyF5}, {TEXT("F6"), KeyF6},
      {TEXT("F7"), KeyF7}, {TEXT("F8"), KeyF8},
      {TEXT("F9"), KeyF9}, {TEXT("F10"), KeyF10},
      {TEXT("F11"), KeyF11}, {TEXT("F12"), KeyF12},
      {TEXT("Insert"), KeyInsert}, {TEXT("Delete"), KeyDelete},
      {TEXT("Back"), KeyBackspace}, {TEXT("Tab"), KeyTabulator},
      {TEXT("Home"), KeyHome}, {TEXT("End"), KeyEnd},
      {TEXT("Page Up"), KeyPageUp},
      {TEXT("Page Down"), KeyPageDown},
      {TEXT("Left"), KeyLeft}, {TEXT("Right"), KeyRight},
      {TEXT("Up"), KeyUp}, {TEXT("Down"), KeyDown},
      {TEXT("Space"), KeySpace}, {TEXT("Escape"), KeyEscape},
      {TEXT("Return"), KeyReturn}, {nullptr, 0}};
```

We loop through the table until we find the virtual key:

```
for (int index = 0; keyTable[index].textPtr != nullptr;
     ++index) {
  if (text == keyTable[index].textPtr) {
    return keyTable[index].key;
  }
}
```

If we do not find a key matching the text, an assert occurs:

```
    assert(false);
    return 0;
}
```

In `TextToAccelerator`, we store the **Control, Shift, Alt**, and virtual key status together with the key in a Win32 API ACCEL structure:

```
void Accelerator::TextToAccelerator(String& text, int itemId,
                              list<ACCEL>&acceleratorSet){
```

First, we check whether the text contains a *Tab* key (\t). If it does, we initialize the ACCEL structure with `itemId` and extract the accelerator part of the text:

```
int tabulatorIndex = text.find(TEXT("\t"));
if (tabulatorIndex != -1) {
  ACCEL accelerator;
  accelerator.fVirt = 0;
  accelerator.cmd = itemId;
  String acceleratorText = text.substr(tabulatorIndex + 1);
```

If the accelerator text contains the prefix Ctrl+, Alt+, or Shift+, we mask FCONTROL, FALT, or FSHIFT to the fVirt field and remove the prefix:

```
{ String controlText = TEXT("Ctrl+");
  int controlIndex = acceleratorText.find(controlText);

  if (controlIndex != -1) {
    accelerator.fVirt |= FCONTROL;
    acceleratorText.erase(controlIndex,
                          controlText.length());
  }
}

{ String altText = TEXT("Alt+");
  int altIndex = acceleratorText.find(altText);

  if (altIndex != -1) {
    accelerator.fVirt |= FALT;
    acceleratorText.erase(altIndex, altText.length());
  }
}

{ String shiftText = TEXT("Shift+");
  int shiftIndex = acceleratorText.find(shiftText);

  if (shiftIndex != -1) {
    accelerator.fVirt |= FSHIFT;
    acceleratorText.erase(shiftIndex, shiftText.length());
  }
}
```

After we remove the Ctrl+, Shift+, and Alt+ prefixes, we look into the remaining part of the accelerator text. If there is one single character (the length is one), we save it in the key field. However, we do not save the ASCII number. Instead, we save the letter number, which starts with 1 for a or A:

```
if (acceleratorText.length() == 1) {
  accelerator.key =
    (WORD) ((tolower(acceleratorText[0]) - ''a'') + 1);
}
```

If the remaining part of the accelerator text is made up of more than one character, we assume that it is a virtual key and call `TextToVirtualKey` to find it and mask the `FVIRTKEY` constant to the `fVirt` field:

```
else {
  accelerator.fVirt |= FVIRTKEY;
  accelerator.key = TextToVirtualKey(acceleratorText);
}
```

If `fVirt` is still zero, the accelerator does not contain `Ctrl+`, `Shift+`, `Alt+`, or a virtual key, which is not allowed:

```
assert(accelerator.fVirt != 0);
```

Finally, we add the accelerator to the accelerator set:

```
acceleratorSet.push_back(accelerator);
}
```

Note that no accelerator is added to the accelerator set if the text does not contain a tabulator:

```
  }
};
```

The StandardDocument class

The `StandardDocument` class is a direct subclass of `Document`; it handles the **File**, **Edit**, and **Help** menus and implements file handling, cut, copy, and paste, drop files, and printing. There is no specific message function for this class; all messages are sent to `DocumentProc` in the `Document` section covered previously. The document name and the dirty flag are automatically updated by the framework. `StandardDocument` does also handle the Page Setup dialog, which is more closely described in `Chapter 12`, *The Auxiliary Classes*.

StandardDocument.h

```
namespace SmallWindows {
  class StandardDocument : public Document {
    public:
```

Most constructor parameters are sent to the `Document` constructor. What is specific for `StandardDocument` is the file description text and the copy and paste format lists. The file description is used by the standard save and open dialogs. The copy and paste lists are used when copying and pasting information between the application and the global Clipboard:

```
StandardDocument(CoordinateSystem system, Size pageSize,
                 String fileDescriptionsText,
                 Window* parentPtr=nullptr,
                 WindowStyle style = OverlappedWindow,
                 WindowShow windowShow = Normal,
                 initializer_list<unsigned int>
                   copyFormatList = {},
                 initializer_list<unsigned int>
                   pasteFormatList = {},
                 bool acceptDropFiles = true,
                 Size lineSize = LineSize);

private:
    void InitializeFileFilter(String fileDescription);
```

The `StandardFileMenu`, `StandardEditMenu`, and `StandardHelpMenu` methods create and return the standard menus. If `print` in `StandardFileMenu` is `true`, the **Page Setup**, **Print**, and **Print Preview** menu items are included:

```
protected:
    Menu StandardFileMenu(bool print);
    Menu StandardEditMenu();
    Menu StandardHelpMenu();
```

The **Save** menu item is disabled when the document does not need to be saved (the dirty flag is `false`). The `SaveEnable` method is called before the **Save** menu item becomes visible and enables it if the dirty flag is `true`.

```
private:
    DEFINE_VOID_LISTENER(StandardDocument, OnNew);
    DEFINE_VOID_LISTENER(StandardDocument, OnOpen);
    DEFINE_BOOL_LISTENER(StandardDocument, SaveEnable);
    DEFINE_VOID_LISTENER(StandardDocument, OnSave);
    DEFINE_VOID_LISTENER(StandardDocument, OnSaveAs);
```

The `OnSave` method calls `SaveFileWithName` or `SaveFileWidhoutName` depending on whether the document has been given a name. However, `OnSaveAs` always calls `SaveFileWithoutName`, regardless of whether the document has a name.

```
private:
    void SaveFileWithName(String name);
    void SaveFileWithoutName();
```

The `ClearDocument`, `WriteDocumentToStream`, and `ReadDocumentFromStream` methods are called when the user selects the **New**, **Save**, **Save As**, or **Open** menu items and are intended to be overridden by subclasses to clear, write, and read the document:

```
protected:
  void ClearPageSetupInfo();
  bool ReadPageSetupInfoFromStream(istream &inStream);
  bool WritePageSetupInfoToStream(ostream &outStream) const;

  virtual void ClearDocument() {/* Empty. */}
  virtual bool WriteDocumentToStream(String name,
                  ostream& outStream) const {return true;}
  virtual bool ReadDocumentFromStream(String name,
                  istream& inStream) {return true;}
```

The OnCut, OnCopy, OnPaste, and OnDelete methods are called when the user selects the corresponding menu item in the **Edit** menu. The default behavior for OnCut is to call OnCopy followed by OnDelete:

```
DEFINE_VOID_LISTENER(StandardDocument, OnCut);
DEFINE_VOID_LISTENER(StandardDocument, OnCopy);
DEFINE_VOID_LISTENER(StandardDocument, OnPaste);
DEFINE_VOID_LISTENER(StandardDocument, OnDelete);
```

The CutEnable, CopyEnable, PasteEnable, and DeleteEnable methods are listeners deciding whether the menu items are enabled. The default behavior for CutEnable and DeleteEnable is to call CopyEnable:

```
DEFINE_BOOL_LISTENER(StandardDocument, CutEnable);
DEFINE_BOOL_LISTENER(StandardDocument, CopyEnable);
DEFINE_BOOL_LISTENER(StandardDocument, PasteEnable);
DEFINE_BOOL_LISTENER(StandardDocument, DeleteEnable);
```

The IsCopyAsciiReady, IsCopyUnicodeReady, and IsCopyGenericReady methods are called by CopyEnable. They are intended to be overridden and return true if the application is ready to be copied in the ASCII, Unicode, or generic formats. Their default behavior is to return false:

```
virtual bool IsCopyAsciiReady() const {return false;}
virtual bool IsCopyUnicodeReady() const {return false;}
virtual bool IsCopyGenericReady(int format)
                              const {return false;}
```

The CopyAscii, CopyUnicode, and CopyGeneric methods are called by OnCopy when the user selects the **Copy** menu item. They are intended to be overridden by subclasses and are called in accordance with the copy format list in the constructor and the copy-ready methods:

```
virtual void CopyAscii(vector<String>& textList) const
                    {/* Empty. */}
virtual void CopyUnicode(vector<String>& textList) const
                      {/* Empty. */}
virtual void CopyGeneric(int format, InfoList& infoList)
                    const {/* Empty. */}
```

The `IsPasteAsciiReady`, `IsPasteUnicodeReady`, and `IsPasteGenericReady` methods
are called by `PasteEnable`, which returns `true` if at least one of the methods returns `true`.
They are intended to be overridden and return `true` if the application is ready to be pasted
in the ASCII, Unicode, or generic formats. Their default behavior is to return `true`:

```
virtual bool IsPasteAsciiReady
        (const vector<String>&textList) const {return true;}
virtual bool IsPasteUnicodeReady
        (const vector<String>&textList) const {return true;}
virtual bool IsPasteGenericReady(int format,
            InfoList& infoList) const {return true;}
```

The `PasteAscii`, `PasteUnicode`, and `PasteGeneric` methods are called by `OnPaste`
when the user selects the **Paste** menu item. They are intended to be overridden by
subclasses and are called in accordance with the paste format list in the constructor and the
paste-ready methods. One difference between copying and pasting is that copying is
performed in all available formats while pasting is performed in the first available format
only:

```
virtual void PasteAscii(const vector<String>& textList)
                    {/* Empty. */}
virtual void PasteUnicode(const vector<String>& textList)
                      {/* Empty. */}
virtual void PasteGeneric(int format, InfoList& infoList)
                    {/* Empty. */}
```

The `OnDropFile` methods is called when the user drops a set of files in the window's client
area. If there is exactly one file with the suffix given in the constructor in the path list, that
file is read in the same way as if the user had selected it in the standard open dialog.
However, if there are no files or more than one file with the suffix in the list, an error
message is displayed:

```
void OnDropFile(vector<String> pathList);
```

The `PageOuterSize` methods returns the logical size of the page in portrait or landscape
mode depending on the page setup settings, without regard to the margins, while
`PageInnerSize`, `PageInnerWidth`, and `PageInnerHeight` return the size of the page
after subtracting the margins:

```
private:
  Size PageOuterSize() const;
  Size PageInnerSize() const;

protected:
  int PageInnerWidth() const{return PageInnerSize().Width();}
  int PageInnerHeight()const{return PageInnerSize().Height();}
```

The OnPageSetup, OnPrintPreview, and OnPrintItem methods are called when the user selects the **Page Setup, Print,** and **Print Preview** menu items. They display **Page Setup Dialog, Print Preview Window,** and **Print Dialog:**

```
public:
  DEFINE_VOID_LISTENER(StandardDocument, OnPageSetup);
  DEFINE_VOID_LISTENER(StandardDocument, OnPrintPreview);
  DEFINE_VOID_LISTENER(StandardDocument, OnPrintItem);
```

The PrintPage method is called by OnPrintItem and prints one page of the document:

```
bool PrintPage(Graphics* graphicsPtr, int page,
               int copy, int totalPages);
```

The OnPageSetup method is called to notify the application when the user has selected the **Page Setup** menu item and has changed the page setup information. It is intended to be overridden by subclasses and its default behavior is to do nothing:

```
virtual void OnPageSetup(PageSetupInfo info) {/* Empty. */}
```

The GetTotalPages method returns the number of pages to print; the default is 1. It is intended to be overridden by subclasses:

```
virtual int GetTotalPages() const {return 1;}
```

The OnPrint method is called once by OnPrintItem for each page and copy. Its default behavior is to write the header and footer in accordance with the setting in the **Page Setup Dialog,** and then call OnDraw for the application-specific contents of the document:

```
virtual void OnPrint(Graphics& graphics, int page,
                     int copy, int totalPages) const;
```

The OnExit method is called when the user selects the **Exit** menu item and quits the application if TryClose returns true. If the dirty flag is true, TryClose displays a message box, asking the user for permission to close the window:

```
DEFINE_VOID_LISTENER(StandardDocument, OnExit);
virtual bool TryClose();
```

The OnAbout method displays a simple message box with the application name:

```
DEFINE_VOID_LISTENER(StandardDocument, OnAbout);
```

The fileFilter fields are used by the **Open** and **Save** standard dialogs and fileSuffixList is used to check the file suffix of dropped files:

```
private:
  TCHAR fileFilter[MAX_PATH];
  vector<String> fileSuffixList;
```

The pageSetupInfo field is used when the user selects the **Page Setup** menu item. It stores information about the header and footer text and font, page orientation (portrait or landscape), margins, and whether the pages are surrounded by a frame. Refer to the next chapter for a closer description.

```
PageSetupInfo pageSetupInfo;
```

The copyFormatList and pasteFormatList fields hold the formats available for cutting, copying, and pasting:

```
    list<unsigned int> copyFormatList, pasteFormatList;
  };
};
```

Initialization

The first StandardDocument constructor takes a large set of parameters. The coordinate system, page size, parent window, style, appearance, whether the document accepts drop files, and the line size parameters are the same as in the Document case covered previously.

What remains is the file description text, whether the print menu is present, and the format list for copying and pasting. The description text holds a semicolon-separated list of file descriptions and file suffixes for the allowed files, for instance, **Calc Files**, *clc*; **Text Files**, *txt*. The copy and paste format list holds the allowed formats for copying and pasting information.

StandardDocument.cpp

```
#include "SmallWindows.h"
```

Most constructor parameters are sent to the Document constructor. However, the copy and paste format lists are stored in copyFormatList and pasteFormatList. The file filter and file suffix lists are initialized by InitializeFileFilter:

```
namespace SmallWindows {
  StandardDocument::StandardDocument(CoordinateSystem system,
                      Size pageSize,
                      String fileDescriptionsText,
                      Window* parentPtr /* = nullptr */,
                      WindowStyle style/* = OverlappedWindow */,
                      WindowShow windowShow /* = Normal */,
                      initializer_list<unsigned int>
                        copyFormatList /* = {} */,
                      initializer_list<unsigned int>
                        pasteFormatList /* = {}*/,
                      bool acceptDropFiles /* = true */,
                      Size lineSize /* = LineSize */)
   :Document(TEXT("standarddocument"), system, pageSize,
          parentPtr, style, windowShow,
          acceptDropFiles, lineSize),
    copyFormatList(copyFormatList),
    pasteFormatList(pasteFormatList) {
    InitializeFileFilter(fileDescriptionsText);
```

In `Window`, we used the page size for transforming between logical and physical units. In `Document`, we used it for setting the scroll page size. However, in `StandardDocument`, there are actually two kinds of page sizes: the outer and inner page size. The outer page size is the page size without taking the margins of the document into consideration. The inner page size is obtained by subtracting the margins from the outer page size. In `StandardDocument`, we use the inner page size to set the size of the scroll bar:

```
    SetHorizontalScrollTotalWidth(PageInnerWidth());
    SetVerticalScrollTotalHeight(PageInnerHeight());
}
```

Standard menus

The code for this is shown as follows:

```
  void StandardDocument::InitializeFileFilter(String fileListText)
  { OStringStream filterStream;
    vector<String> fileList = Split(fileListText, TEXT(';'));
    assert(fileList.size() > 0);

    for (String fileText : fileList) {
      vector<String> partList = Split(fileText, TEXT(','));
      assert(partList.size() == 2);
      String description = Trim(partList[0]),
             suffix = Trim(partList[1]);
      fileSuffixList.push_back(suffix);
```

```
        filterStream << description << TEXT(" (*.") << suffix
                     << TEXT(")\n") << TEXT("*.") << suffix
                     << TEXT("\n");
    }

    filterStream << TEXT("\n");

    int index = 0;
    for (TCHAR c : filterStream.str()) {
      fileFilter[index++] = (c == TEXT(''\n'')) ? TEXT(''\0'') : c;
    }
}
```

The standard **File** menu holds the **New, Open, Save, Save As,** and **Exit** menu items as well as (if `print` is `true`) the **Page Setup, Print Preview,** and **Print** menu items:

```
Menu StandardDocument::StandardFileMenu(bool print) {
  Menu fileMenu(this, TEXT("&File"));
  fileMenu.AddItem(TEXT("&New\tCtrl+N"), OnNew);
  fileMenu.AddItem(TEXT("&Open\tCtrl+O"), OnOpen);
  fileMenu.AddItem(TEXT("&Save\tCtrl+S"), OnSave, SaveEnable);
  fileMenu.AddItem(TEXT("Save &As\tCtrl+Shift+S"), OnSaveAs);

  if (print) {
    fileMenu.AddSeparator();
    fileMenu.AddItem(TEXT("Page Set&up"), OnPageSetup);
    fileMenu.AddItem(TEXT("Print Pre&view"), OnPrintPreview);
    fileMenu.AddItem(TEXT("&Print\tCtrl+P"), OnPrintItem);
  }

  fileMenu.AddSeparator();
  fileMenu.AddItem(TEXT("E&xit\tAlt+X"), OnExit);
  return fileMenu;
}
```

The standard **Edit** menu holds the **Cut, Copy, Paste,** and **Delete** menu items:

```
Menu StandardDocument::StandardEditMenu() {
  Menu editMenu(this, TEXT("&Edit"));
  editMenu.AddItem(TEXT("C&ut\tCtrl+X"), OnCut, CutEnable);
  editMenu.AddItem(TEXT("&Copy\tCtrl+C"), OnCopy, CopyEnable);
  editMenu.AddItem(TEXT("&Paste\tCtrl+V"), OnPaste,PasteEnable);
  editMenu.AddSeparator();
  editMenu.AddItem(TEXT("&Delete\tDelete"),
                   OnDelete, DeleteEnable);
  return editMenu;
}
```

The standard **Help** menu holds the **About** menu item with the help of the application name:

```
Menu StandardDocument::StandardHelpMenu() {
  Menu helpMenu(this, TEXT("&Help"));
  helpMenu.AddItem(TEXT("About ") +
                   Application::ApplicationName() +
                   TEXT(" ..."), OnAbout);
  return helpMenu;
}
```

File management

The TryClose method checks whether the dirty flag is true when the user tries to close the window. If it is true, the user is asked if they want to save the document before closing it. If they answer yes, the document is saved as if the user has selected the **Save** menu item. If the dirty flag is set to false after that, it means that the save operation went well and true is returned. If the user answers no, true is returned and the window is closed without saving. If the answer is cancel, false is returned and the closing is aborted:

```
bool StandardDocument::TryClose() {
  if (IsDirty()) {
    switch (MessageBox(TEXT("Do you want to save?"),
                       TEXT("Unsaved Document"), YesNoCancel)) {
      case Yes:
        OnSave();
        return !IsDirty();

      case No:
        return true;

      case Cancel:
        return false;
    }
  }

  return true;
}
```

The OnExit method calls TryClose and deletes the application's main window, which eventually sends a quit message to the message loop that terminates the application, if TryClose returns true:

```
void StandardDocument::OnExit() {
  if (TryClose()) {
    delete Application::MainWindowPtr();
  }
}
```

The OnNew method is called when the user selects the **New** menu item. It tries to close the window by calling TryClose. If TryClose returns true, the document, dirty flag, and name are cleared, and the window is invalidated and updated. The ClearDocument method is indented to be overridden by subclasses to clear the application-specific contents of the document:

```
void StandardDocument::OnNew() {
  if (TryClose()) {
    ClearDocument();
    ClearPageSetupInfo();
    SetZoom(1.0);
    SetDirty(false);
    SetName(TEXT(""));
    Invalidate();
    UpdateWindow();
    UpdateCaret();
  }
}
```

The OnOpen method is called when the user selects the **Open** menu item. It tries to close the window by calling TryClose and displays the standard open dialog to establish the path of the file if it succeeds. If OpenDialog returns true and the input stream is valid, the page setup information is read and the methods ClearDocument and ReadDocumentFromStream, which are intended to be overridden by subclasses, are called:

```
void StandardDocument::OnOpen() {
  if (TryClose()) {
    String name = GetName();

    if (StandardDialog::OpenDialog(this, name, fileFilter,
                                   fileSuffixList)) {
      ClearDocument();
      Invalidate();
      UpdateWindow();
      ifstream inStream(name.c_str());

      if (inStream && ReadDocumentFromStream(name, inStream)) {
        SetName(name);
      }
```

```
    else {
      MessageBox(TEXT("Could not open ") +
                 name + TEXT("."));
    }
  }
}

SetDirty(false);
SetZoom(1.0);
Invalidate();
UpdateWindow();
UpdateCaret();
}
```

The **Save** menu item is enabled if the dirty flag is true:

```
bool StandardDocument::SaveEnable() const {
  return IsDirty();
}
```

When saving the file, we call `SaveFileWithName` if the file has a name. If the file has not yet been given a name, `SaveFileWithoutName` is called instead:

```
void StandardDocument::OnSave() {
  String name = GetName();

  if (!name.empty()) {
    SaveFileWithName(name);
  }
  else {
    SaveFileWithoutName();
  }
}
```

When the user selects **Save As**, `SaveFileWithoutName` is called and the **Save** standard dialog is displayed, regardless of whether the document has a name:

```
void StandardDocument::OnSaveAs() {
  SaveFileWithoutName();
}
```

The `SaveFileWithoutName` method displays the save dialog. If the user presses the **Ok** button, the `SaveDialog` call returns true, the new name is set, and `SaveFileWithName` is called to do the actual writing of the document file:

```
void StandardDocument::SaveFileWithoutName() {
  String name = GetName();
```

```
    if (StandardDialog::SaveDialog(this, name, fileFilter,
                                    fileSuffixList)) {
      SaveFileWithName(name);
    }
  }
```

The `SaveFileWithName` method tries to open the document file for writing and calls `WriteDocumentToStream`, which is intended to be overridden by subclasses, to do the actually writing of the document's content. If the writing of both the page setup information and the contents of the document succeeds, the dirty flag is cleared:

```
void StandardDocument::SaveFileWithName(String name) {
  ofstream outStream(name.c_str());

  if (outStream && WriteDocumentToStream(name, outStream)) {
    SetName(name);
    SetDirty(false);
    SetZoom(1.0);
  }
}

void StandardDocument::ClearPageSetupInfo() {
  pageSetupInfo.ClearPageSetupInfo();
}

bool StandardDocument::ReadPageSetupInfoFromStream
                       (istream &inStream) {
  pageSetupInfo.ReadPageSetupInfoFromStream(inStream);
  return ((bool) inStream);
}

bool StandardDocument::WritePageSetupInfoToStream
                       (ostream &outStream) const {
  pageSetupInfo.WritePageSetupInfoToStream(outStream);
  return ((bool) outStream);
}
```

When the user selects the **About** menu item in the **Help** standard menu, a message box with a message including the name of the application is displayed:

```
void StandardDocument::OnAbout() {
  String applicationName = Application::ApplicationName();
  MessageBox(applicationName + TEXT(", version 1.0"),
             applicationName, Ok, Information);
}
```

Cut, copy, and paste

The default behavior for `CutEnable` and `DeleteEnable` is to simply call `CopyEnable`, since it is likely that they are enabled under the same conditions:

```
bool StandardDocument::CutEnable() const {
  return CopyEnable();
}

bool StandardDocument::DeleteEnable() const {
  return CopyEnable();
}
```

The default behavior for `OnCut` is to simply call `OnCopy` and `OnDelete`, which is the common action for cutting:

```
void StandardDocument::OnCut() {
  OnCopy();
  OnDelete();
}
```

The `OnDelete` method is empty and intended to be overridden by subclasses:

```
void StandardDocument::OnDelete() {
  // Empty.
}
```

The `CopyEnable` method iterates through the paste format list and calls `IsCopyAsciiReady`, `IsCopyUnicodeReady`, or `IsCopyGenericReady` depending on the formats. As soon as one of the methods returns `true`, `CopyEnable` returns `true`, implying that it is enough that copying is allowed for one of the formats. When the actual copying occurs in `OnCopy`, the ready methods are called again:

```
bool StandardDocument::CopyEnable() const {
  for (unsigned int format : pasteFormatList) {
    switch (format) {
      case AsciiFormat:
        if (IsCopyAsciiReady()) {
          return true;
        }
        break;

      case UnicodeFormat:
        if (IsCopyUnicodeReady()) {
          return true;
        }
        break;
```

```
      default:
        if (IsCopyGenericReady(format)) {
          return true;
        }
        break;
    }
  }
  return false;
}
```

The `OnCopy` method iterates through the copy format list given in the constructor and calls appropriate methods depending on the formats:

```
void StandardDocument::OnCopy() {
  if (Clipboard::Open(this)) {
    Clipboard::Clear();
    for (unsigned int format : copyFormatList) {
      switch (format) {
```

If the ASCII format applies and if `IsCopyAsciiReady` returns `true`, `CopyAscii` is called, which is intended to be overridden by subclasses to fill `asciiList` with ASCII text. When the list has been copied, it is passed on to `WriteAscii` in `Clipboard`, which stores the text on the global clipboard:

```
        case AsciiFormat:
          if (IsCopyAsciiReady()) {
            vector<String> asciiList;
            CopyAscii(asciiList);
            Clipboard::WriteText<AsciiFormat,char>(asciiList);
          }
          break;
```

If the Unicode format applies and if `IsCopyUnicodeReady` returns `true`, `CopyUnicode` is called, which is intended to be overridden by subclasses to fill `unicodeList` with Unicode text. When the list has been copied, it is passed on to `WriteUnicode` in `Clipboard`, which stores the text on the global clipboard:

```
        case UnicodeFormat:
          if (IsCopyUnicodeReady()) {
            vector<String> unicodeList;
            CopyUnicode(unicodeList);
            Clipboard::WriteText<UnicodeFormat,wchar_t>
                              (unicodeList);
          }
          break;
```

If neither ASCII nor Unicode applies and if `IsCopyGenericReady` returns `true`,

`CopyGeneric` is called, which is intended to be overridden by subclasses to fill the character list with generic information. In C++, a value of type `char` always holds one byte; it is therefore used in the absence of a more generic byte type. When the information has been copied to `infoList`, it is passed on to `WriteGeneric` in `Clipboard` to store the information on the global Clipboard:

```
    default:
      if (IsCopyGenericReady(format)) {
        InfoList infoList;
        CopyGeneric(format, infoList);
        Clipboard::WriteGeneric(format, infoList);
      }
      break;
  }
}
Clipboard::Close();
  }
}
```

The `PasteEnable` method iterates through the paste format list given in the constructor and returns `true` if at least one of the formats is available on the global Clipboard:

```
bool StandardDocument::PasteEnable() const {
  if (Clipboard::Open(this)) {
    for (unsigned int format : pasteFormatList) {
      if (Clipboard::Available(format)) {
        switch (format) {
          case AsciiFormat: {
              vector<String> asciiList;
              if (Clipboard::ReadText<AsciiFormat,char>
                                    (asciiList) &&
                 IsPasteAsciiReady(asciiList)) {
                Clipboard::Close();
                return true;
              }
            }
            break;
          case UnicodeFormat: {
              vector<String> unicodeList;
              if (Clipboard::ReadText<UnicodeFormat,wchar_t>
                                    (unicodeList) &&
                 IsPasteUnicodeReady(unicodeList)) {
                Clipboard::Close();
                return true;
              }
            }
            break;
```

```
                    default: {
                        InfoList infoList;
                        if (Clipboard::ReadGeneric(format, infoList) &&
                            IsPasteGenericReady(format, infoList)) {
                          Clipboard::Close();
                          return true;
                        }
                    }
                }
            }
        }

    Clipboard::Close();
    }

    return false;
}
```

The OnPaste method iterates through the paste format list given in the constructor and, for each format, checks whether it is available on the global Clipboard. If it is, an appropriate method is called. Note that, while OnCopy iterates through the whole copy format list, OnPaste quits after the first format available on the Clipboard, which makes the order of the paste format list significant:

```
void StandardDocument::OnPaste() {
  if (Clipboard::Open(this)) {
    for (unsigned int format : pasteFormatList) {
      bool quit = false;
      if (Clipboard::Available(format)) {
        switch (format) {
```

In the case of the ASCII format, ReadAscii in Clipboard is called, which reads the text list from the global clipboard and, if IsPasteAsciiReady returns true, calls PasteAscii, which is intended to be overridden by subclasses to do the actual application-specific pasting:

```
            case AsciiFormat: {
                vector<String> asciiList;
                if (Clipboard::ReadText<AsciiFormat,char>
                              (asciiList) &&
                    IsPasteAsciiReady(asciiList)) {
                  PasteAscii(asciiList);
                  quit = true;
                }
            }
            break;
```

In the case of the Unicode format, ReadUnicode in Clipboard is called, which reads the text list from the global clipboard and, if IsPasteUnicodeReady returns true, it calls PasteUnicode, which is intended to be overridden by subclasses to do the actual application-specific pasting:

```
case UnicodeFormat: {
    vector<String> unicodeList;
    if (Clipboard::ReadText<UnicodeFormat,wchar_t>
                         (unicodeList) &&
        IsPasteUnicodeReady(unicodeList)) {
      PasteUnicode(unicodeList);
      quit = true;
    }
  }
  break;
```

If neither ASCII nor Unicode applies, ReadGeneric in Clipboard is called to read the generic information from the global clipboard and, if IsPasteGenericReady returns true, it calls PasteGeneric, which is intended be overridden by subclasses to do the actual pasting.

One difference between copying and pasting in the generic case is that OnCopy uses a character list since it does not know the size in advance (if we used a memory block, we would need two methods: one that calculates the size of the block and one that does the actual reading, which would be cumbersome), while OnPaste uses a memory block, which cannot be converted into a character list since we do not know the size. Only the document-specific overridden version of PasteGeneric can decide the size of the memory block:

```
default: {
    InfoList infoList;
    if (Clipboard::ReadGeneric(format, infoList) &&
        IsPasteGenericReady(format, infoList)) {
      PasteGeneric(format, infoList);
      quit = true;
    }
  }
  break;
  }
  if (quit) {
    break;
  }
  }
  }
  Clipboard::Close();
  }
}
```

Drop files

When the user drops one or several files in the client area of the window, we check the file suffix of each filename. If we find exactly one file with one of the file suffixes of the document (the `fileSuffixList` field) we open it in the same way as if the user had opened it with the standard **Open** dialog:

```
void StandardDocument::OnDropFile(vector<String> pathList) {
  set<String> pathSet;
```

We iterate through the path list and add every path with the file suffix to `pathSet`:

```
for (String path : pathList) {
  for (String suffix : fileSuffixList) {
    if (EndsWith(path, TEXT(".") + suffix)) {
      pathSet.insert(path);
      break;
    }
  }
}
```

If `pathSet` is empty, no files with the file suffix have been dropped.

```
if (pathSet.empty()) {
  MessageBox(TEXT("No suitable dropped file."),
             TEXT("Drop File"), Ok, Stop);
}
```

If `pathSet` holds more than one file, too many files with the file suffix have been dropped:

```
else if (pathSet.size() > 1) {
  MessageBox(TEXT("To many suitable dropped files."),
             TEXT("Drop File"), Ok, Stop);
}
```

If `pathSet` holds exactly one file, it is read in the same way as if the user has selected the **Open** menu item:

```
else {
  String path = *pathSet.begin();

  if (TryClose()) {
    ClearDocument();
    ReadDocumentFromStream(path, ifstream(path));
    SetName(path);
    SetDirty(false);
    SetZoom(1.0);
```

```
        Invalidate();
        UpdateWindow();
        UpdateCaret();
    }
  }
}
```

Page size

The PageOuterSize method returns the page size with no regard to the margins. There are two page sizes, depending on the orientation in the **Page Setup** dialog. The page size given in the constructor refers to the Portrait orientation. In the case of the Landscape orientation, the width and height of the page are swapped:

```
Size StandardDocument::PageOuterSize() const {
  if (pageSetupInfo.GetOrientation() == Landscape) {
    return Size(pageSize.Height(), pageSize.Width());
  }

  return pageSize;
}
```

The PageInnerSize method returns the page size with regard to the margins. The width is subtracted by the left and right margins. The height is subtracted by the top and bottom margins. Remember that the margins are given in millimeters and the logical units are in hundredths of millimeters. Therefore, we multiply the margins by 100:

```
Size StandardDocument::PageInnerSize() const {
  Size outerSize = PageOuterSize();

  int innerWidth = outerSize.Width() -
                   (100 * (pageSetupInfo.LeftMargin() +
                   pageSetupInfo.RightMargin())),
      innerHeight = outerSize.Height() -
                   (100 * (pageSetupInfo.TopMargin() +
                   pageSetupInfo.BottomMargin()));

  return Size(innerWidth, innerHeight);
}
```

The PageInnerWidth and PageInnerHeight methods return the width and height of the document after the margins have been subtracted. As the margins are given in millimeters and one millimeter is one hundred logical units, we multiply the margins by 100 in order to obtain logical units:

```
int StandardDocument::PageInnerWidth() const {
  return PageOuterSize().Width() -
         (100 * (pageSetupInfo.LeftMargin() +
                 pageSetupInfo.RightMargin()));
}

int StandardDocument::PageInnerHeight() const {
  return PageOuterSize().Height() -
         (100 * (pageSetupInfo.TopMargin() +
                 pageSetupInfo.BottomMargin()));
}
```

Page setup

The OnPageSetup method is called when the user selects the **Page Setup** menu item. It displays the **Page Setup** dialog (refer to Chapter 12, *The Auxiliary Classes*) and calls OnPageSetup, which is intended to be overridden by subclasses, to notify the application that the page setup information has been changed:

```
void StandardDocument::OnPageSetup() {
  PageSetupDialog pageSetupDialog(this, &pageSetupInfo);

  if (pageSetupDialog.DoModal()) {
    OnPageSetup(pageSetupInfo);
  }
}
```

Printing

The OnPrintPreview method is called when the user selects the **Print Preview** menu item. It displays the print preview document, which is more closely described in Chapter 12, *The Auxiliary Classes*. The GetTotalPages method returns the current number of pages in the document:

```
void StandardDocument::OnPrintPreview() {
  new PrintPreviewDocument(this, GetTotalPages());
}
```

The OnPrintItem method is called when the user selects the **Print** menu item. It displays the standard **Print** dialog and prints the pages of the document in accordance with the page interval and the order and number of copies specified by the user in the dialog.

The method is named OnPrintItem so that it is not confused with OnPrint in Window, which is called when the window receives the WM_PAINT message. However, both methods could have been named OnPrint since they have different parameter lists:

```
void StandardDocument::OnPrintItem() {
    int totalPages = GetTotalPages(), firstPage, lastPage, copies;
    bool sorted;
```

The PrintDialog method creates and returns a pointer to a Graphics object, if the user presses the **Ok** button, or a null pointer if the user presses the **Cancel** button. The totalPages parameters indicate the last possible page that the user can choose (the first possible page is 1). In the case of the **Ok** button, firstPage, lastPage, copies, and sorted are initialized: firstPage and lastPage are the page intervals to be printed, copies is the number of copies to be printed, and sorted indicates whether the copies (if more than one) will be sorted:

```
Graphics* graphicsPtr =
    StandardDialog::PrintDialog(this, totalPages, firstPage,
                                lastPage, copies, sorted);
```

The Win32 API function StartDoc initializes the printing process. It takes the device context connected to the printer by the Graphics object and a DOCINFO structure that only needs to be initialized with the document name. If StartDoc returns a value greater than zero, we are clear to print the pages. We prepare the device context and disable the window while the printing occurs:

```
if (graphicsPtr != nullptr) {
    static DOCINFO docInfo;
    docInfo.cbSize = sizeof docInfo;
    docInfo.lpszDocName = GetName().c_str();

    if (::StartDoc(graphicsPtr->GetDeviceContextHandle(),
                   &docInfo) > 0) {
        PrepareDeviceContext
            (graphicsPtr->GetDeviceContextHandle());
        EnableWindow(false);
```

If sorted is true, the pages are printed in the sorted order. For instance, let's assume that firstPage is set to 1, lastPage is set to 3, and copies is set to 2. If sorted is true, the pages are printed in order 1, 2, 3, 1, 2, 3. If sorted is false, they are printed in the order 1, 1, 2, 2, 3, 3. PrintPage is called for each page and the printing continues as long as it returns true; printOk keeps track of whether the loop continues:

```
              if (sorted) {
                bool printOk = true;
                for (int copy = 1; (copy <= copies) && printOk; ++copy){
                  for (int page = firstPage;
                       (page <= lastPage) && printOk; ++page){
                    printOk = PrintPage(graphicsPtr, page,
                                        copy, totalPages);
                  }
                }
              }
              else {
                bool printOk = true;
                for (int page = firstPage;
                     (page <= lastPage) && printOk; ++page) {
                  for (int copy = 1; (copy <= copies) && printOk;
                       ++copy) {
                    printOk = PrintPage(graphicsPtr, page,
                                        copy, totalPages);
                  }
                }
              }
```

The Win32 API function `EndDoc` is used to finish printing:

```
            ::EndDoc(graphicsPtr->GetDeviceContextHandle());
        }
      }
    }
```

The `PrintPage` method calls the Win32 API functions `StartPage` and `EndPage` before and after the printing of the page. If they both return values greater than zero, it indicates that the printing went well, `true` is returned, and more pages can be printed. `OnPrint` (overridden from `Window`) is called to do the actual printing, `page` and `copy` are the current page and copy, and `totalPages` is the number of pages in the document:

```
    bool StandardDocument::PrintPage(Graphics* graphicsPtr,
                                     int page, int copy, int totalPages){
      if (::StartPage(graphicsPtr->GetDeviceContextHandle()) > 0) {
        OnPrint(*graphicsPtr, page, copy, totalPages);
        return (::EndPage(graphicsPtr->GetDeviceContextHandle())>0);
      }

      return false;
    }
```

The `OnPrint` method prints the information given by the `pageSetupInfo` field. Then, the contents of the documents are clipped and drawn by calling `OnDraw`, and finally the frame enclosing the contents of the document is drawn, if present:

```
void StandardDocument::OnPrint(Graphics& graphics, int page,
                               int copy, int totalPages) const {
```

The document is cleared by being painted white.

```
graphics.FillRectangle(Rect(0, 0, PageOuterSize().Width(),
                       PageOuterSize().Height()), White, White);

int left = 100 * pageSetupInfo.LeftMargin(),
    top = 100 * pageSetupInfo.TopMargin();
int right = left + PageInnerWidth(),
            bottom = top + PageInnerHeight();
```

The header text is written unless it is empty; if the current page is the first page, it is not written:

```
if (!pageSetupInfo.HeaderText().empty() &&
    !((page == 1) && (!pageSetupInfo.HeaderFirst())))) {
  Rect headerRect(left, 0, right, top);
  String headerText =
    Template(this, pageSetupInfo.HeaderText(),
             copy, page, totalPages);
  Color textColor = pageSetupInfo.HeaderFont().FontColor();
  Color backColor = textColor.Inverse();
  graphics.DrawText(headerRect, headerText,
          pageSetupInfo.HeaderFont(), textColor, backColor);
}
```

Similar to the header text, the footer text is written unless it is empty; if the current page is the first page, it is not written:

```
if (!pageSetupInfo.FooterText().empty() &&
    !((page == 1) && (!pageSetupInfo.HeaderFirst())))) {
  Rect footerRect(left, bottom, right,
                  PageOuterSize().Height());
  String footerText =
    Template(this, pageSetupInfo.FooterText(),
             copy, page, totalPages);
  Color textColor = pageSetupInfo.FooterFont().FontColor();
  Color backColor = textColor.Inverse();
  graphics.DrawText(footerRect, footerText,
          pageSetupInfo.FooterFont(), textColor, backColor);
}
```

The current state of the device context is saved, the origin is set to the top-left corner of the current page, the area of the current page is clipped, OnDraw is called to draw the current page, and the paint area is finally restored:

```
int save = graphics.Save();
Point centerPoint(-left,
                  ((page - 1) * PageInnerHeight()) - top);
graphics.SetOrigin(centerPoint);
Rect clipRect(0, (page - 1) * PageInnerHeight(),
              PageInnerWidth(), page * PageInnerHeight());
graphics.IntersectClip(clipRect);
OnDraw(graphics, Print);
graphics.Restore(save);
```

Finally, the page is enclosed by a rectangle if the frame field of the page setup information is true:

```
if (pageSetupInfo.Frame()) {
  graphics.DrawRectangle(Rect(left, top, right, bottom),
                         Black);
}
  }
};
```

Summary

In this chapter, we studied the document classes of Small Windows: Document, Menu, Accelerator, and StandardDocument. In Chapter 12, *The Auxiliary Classes*, we continue by looking into to the auxiliary classes of Small Windows.

12
The Auxiliary Classes

Small Windows includes a set of auxiliary classes, which are as follows:

- `Size`, `Point`, `Rect`, `Color`, and `Font`: These wrap the Win32 API structures which are `SIZE`, `POINT`, `RECT`, `COLORREF`, and `LOGFONT`. They are equipped with methods to communicate with files, the clipboard, and the registry. The Registry is a database in the Windows system that we can use to store values between the executions of our applications.
- `Cursor`: is a type representing the Windows cursor.
- `DynamicList`: holds a list of dynamic size with a set of callback functions.
- `Tree`: holds a recursive tree structure.
- `InfoList`: holds a list of generic information that can be transformed to and from a memory buffer.
- There is also a small set of string manipulation functions.

The Size class

The `Size` class is a small class holding the width and height:

Size.h

```
namespace SmallWindows {
```

The `ZeroSize` object is an object with its width and height set to zero:

```
class Size;
extern const Size ZeroSize;
class Size {
  public:
```

The default constructor initializes the width and height to zero. The size can be initialized by, and assigned to, another size. The `Size` class uses the assignment operator to assign a size to another size:

```
Size();
Size(int width, int height);
Size(const Size& size);
Size& operator=(const Size& size);
```

A `Size` object can be initialized and assigned to a value of the Win32 API `SIZE` structure, and a `Size` object can be converted to a `SIZE`:

```
Size(const SIZE& size);
Size& operator=(const SIZE& size);
operator SIZE() const;
```

When comparing two sizes, the widths are compared first. If they are equal, the heights are then compared:

```
bool operator==(const Size& size) const;
bool operator!=(const Size& size) const;
bool operator<(const Size& size) const;
bool operator<=(const Size& size) const;
bool operator>(const Size& size) const;
bool operator>=(const Size& size) const;
friend Size Min(const Size& left, const Size& right);
friend Size Max(const Size& left, const Size& right);
```

The multiplication operators multiply both the width and height with the factor. Note that even though the factor is a double, the resulting width and height are always rounded to integers:

```
Size operator*=(double factor);
friend Size operator*(const Size& size, double factor);
friend Size operator*(double factor, const Size& size);
```

It is also possible to multiply the size with a pair of values, where the first value is multiplied by the width and the second value is multiplied by the height. Also, in this case, the resulting width and height are integers:

```
Size operator*=(pair<double,double> factorPair);
friend Size operator*(const Size& size,
                      pair<double,double> factorPair);
friend Size operator*(pair<double,double> factorPair,
                      const Size& size);
```

The first set of addition operators adds and subtracts the distance to both the width and height:

```
Size operator+=(int distance);
Size operator-=(int distance);
friend Size operator+(const Size& size, int distance);
friend Size operator-(const Size& size, int distance);
```

The second set of addition operators adds and subtracts the widths and heights separately:

```
Size operator+=(const Size& size);
Size operator-=(const Size& size);
friend Size operator+(const Size& left, const Size& right);
friend Size operator-(const Size& left, const Size& right);
```

The size can be written to, and read from, a file stream, the clipboard, and the registry:

```
bool WriteSizeToStream(ostream& outStream) const;
bool ReadSizeFromStream(istream& inStream);
void WriteSizeToClipboard(InfoList& infoList) const;
void ReadSizeFromClipboard(InfoList& infoList);
void WriteSizeToRegistry(String key) const;
void ReadSizeFromRegistry(String key,
                          Size defaultSize = ZeroSize);
```

The width and height are inspected by the constant methods and modified by the non-constant methods:

```
    int Width() const {return width;}
    int Height() const {return height;}
    int& Width() {return width;}
    int& Height() {return height;}

  private:
    int width, height;
  };
};
```

The implementation of the `Size` class is rather straightforward:

Size.cpp

```
#include "SmallWindows.h"
namespace SmallWindows {
  Size::Size()
   :width(0),
```

```
  height(0) {
  // Empty.
}

Size::Size(int width, int height)
 :width(width),
  height(height) {
  // Empty.
}

Size::Size(const Size& size)
 :width(size.width),
  height(size.height) {
  // Empty.
}

Size& Size::operator=(const Size& size) {
  if (this != &size) {
    width = size.width;
    height = size.height;
  }
  return *this;
}

Size::Size(const SIZE& size)
 :width(size.cx),
  height(size.cy) {
  // Empty.
}

Size& Size::operator=(const SIZE& size) {
  width = size.cx;
  height = size.cy;
  return *this;
}

Size::operator SIZE() const {
  SIZE size = {width, height};
  return size;
}

bool Size::operator==(const Size& size) const {
  return (width == size.width) && (height == size.height);
}

bool Size::operator!=(const Size& size) const {
  return !(*this == size);
}
```

As mentioned earlier, when comparing two sizes, the widths are compared first. If they are equal the heights are then compared:

```
bool Size::operator<(const Size& size) const {
  return (width < size.width) ||
          ((width == size.width) && (height < size.height));
}

bool Size::operator<=(const Size& size) const {
  return ((*this < size) || (*this == size));
}

bool Size::operator>(const Size& size) const {
  return !(*this <= size);
}

bool Size::operator>=(const Size& size) const {
  return !(*this < size);
}
```

Note that Min and Max return the right-hand side value if the values are equal. We could let it return the left-hand side value instead. However, since the Size objects in that case hold the same *x* and *y* values and the methods return objects rather than references to an object, it does not matter. The same value is returned:

```
Size Min(const Size& left, const Size& right) {
  return (left < right) ? left : right;
}

Size Max(const Size& left, const Size& right) {
  return (left > right) ? left : right;
}
```

As mentioned earlier, the resulting width and height are always rounded to integers, even though the factor is a double:

```
Size Size::operator*=(double factor) {
  width = (int) (factor * width);
  height = (int) (factor * height);
  return *this;
}

Size operator*(const Size& size, double factor) {
  return Size((int) (size.width * factor),
              (int) (size.height * factor));
}
```

```
Size operator*(double factor, const Size& size) {
  return Size((int) (factor * size.width),
              (int) (factor * size.height));
}

Size Size::operator*=(pair<double,double> factorPair) {
  width = (int) (factorPair.first * width);
  height = (int) (factorPair.second * height);
  return *this;
}

Size operator*(const Size& size,
               pair<double,double> factorPair) {
  return Size((int) (size.width * factorPair.first),
              (int) (size.height * factorPair.second));
}

Size operator*(pair<double,double> factorPair,
               const Size& size) {
  return Size((int) (factorPair.first * size.width),
              (int) (factorPair.second * size.height));
}

Size Size::operator+=(int distance) {
  width += distance;
  height += distance;
  return *this;
}
Size Size::operator-=(int distance) {
  width -= distance;
  height -= distance;
  return *this;
}

Size operator+(const Size& size, int distance) {
  return Size(size.width + distance, size.height + distance);
}

Size operator-(const Size& size, int distance) {
  return Size(size.width - distance, size.height - distance);
}

Size Size::operator+=(const Size& size) {
  width += size.width;
  height += size.height;
  return *this;
}
```

```
Size Size::operator-=(const Size& size) {
  width -= size.width;
  height -= size.height;
  return *this;
}

Size operator+(const Size& left, const Size& right) {
  return Size(left.width + right.width,
              right.height + right.height);
}

Size operator-(const Size& left, const Size& right) {
  return Size(left.width - right.width,
              right.height - right.height);
}

bool Size::WriteSizeToStream(ostream& outStream) const {
  outStream.write((char*) &width, sizeof width);
  outStream.write((char*) &height, sizeof height);
  return ((bool) outStream);
}

bool Size::ReadSizeFromStream(istream& inStream) {
  inStream.read((char*) &width, sizeof width);
  inStream.read((char*) &height, sizeof height);
  return ((bool) inStream);
}

void Size::WriteSizeToClipboard(InfoList& infoList) const {
  infoList.AddValue<int>(width);
  infoList.AddValue<int>(height);
}

void Size::ReadSizeFromClipboard(InfoList& infoList) {
  infoList.GetValue<int>(width);
  infoList.GetValue<int>(height);
}
```

When writing the size to the registry, we convert the size to a SIZE structure that is sent to WriteBuffer in Registry:

```
void Size::WriteSizeToRegistry(String key) const {
  SIZE sizeStruct = (SIZE) *this;
  Registry::WriteBuffer(key, &sizeStruct, sizeof sizeStruct);
}
```

When reading the size from the registry, we convert the default size to a SIZE structure that is sent to ReadBuffer in Registry. The result is then converted back to a Size object:

```
    void Size::ReadSizeFromRegistry(String key,
                                    Size defaultSize /*=ZeroSize*/){
      SIZE sizeStruct, defaultSizeStruct = (SIZE) defaultSize;
      Registry::ReadBuffer(key, &sizeStruct, sizeof sizeStruct,
                           &defaultSizeStruct);
      *this = Size(sizeStruct);
    }
    const Size ZeroSize(0, 0);
};
```

The Point class

The `Point` class is a small class holding the *x* and *y* position of a two-dimensional point:

Point.h

```
namespace SmallWindows {
  class Point {
    public:
```

The default constructor initializes the *x* and *y* value to zero. The point can be initialized by, and assigned to, another point:

```
      Point();
      Point(int x, int y);
      Point(const Point& point);
```

Similar to the `Size` class mentioned earlier, `Point` uses the assignment operator:

```
      Point& operator=(const Point& point);
```

Similar to `SIZE` in the preceding section, there is a `POINT` Win32 API structure. A `Point` object can be initialized by, and assigned to, a `POINT` structure, and a `Point` object can be converted to `POINT`:

```
      Point(const POINT& point);
      Point& operator=(const POINT& point);
      operator POINT() const;
```

When comparing two points, the *x* values are first compared. If they are equal, the *y* values are then compared:

```
      bool operator==(const Point& point) const;
      bool operator!=(const Point& point) const;
      bool operator<(const Point& point) const;
      bool operator<=(const Point& point) const;
```

```
bool operator>(const Point& point) const;
bool operator>=(const Point& point) const;
friend Point Min(const Point& left, const Point& right);
friend Point Max(const Point& left, const Point& right);
```

Similar to the `Size` class mentioned earlier, the *x* and *y* values of the point can be multiplied by a factor. Note that even though the factor is a double, the resulting *x* and *y* values are always rounded to integers:

```
Point& operator*=(double factor);
friend Point operator*(const Point& point, double factor);
friend Point operator*(double factor, const Point& point);
```

It is also possible to multiply the point with a pair of values, where the first value is multiplied with the *x* value and the second value is multiplied with the *y* value. Also, in this case, the resulting *x* and *y* values are integers:

```
Point& operator*=(pair<double,double> factorPair);
friend Point operator*(const Point& point,
                       pair<double,double> factorPair);
friend Point operator*(pair<double,double> factorPair,
                       const Point& point);
```

The first set of addition operators adds and subtracts the integer distance to both the *x* and *y* value of the point:

```
Point& operator+=(const int distance);
Point& operator-=(const int distance);
friend Point operator+(const Point& left, int distance);
friend Point operator-(const Point& left, int distance);
```

The second set of addition operators adds and subtracts the width and height of the size to the *x* and *y* values of the point:

```
Point& operator+=(const Size& size);
Point& operator-=(const Size& size);
friend Point operator+(const Point& point,const Size& size);
friend Point operator-(const Point& point,const Size& size);
```

The third set of addition operators adds and subtracts the *x* and *y* values of the points:

```
Point& operator+=(const Point& point);
Point& operator-=(const Point& point);
friend Point operator+(const Point&left, const Point&right);
friend Size operator-(const Point& left, const Point&right);
```

The point can be written to, and read from, a file stream, the clipboard, and the registry:

```
      bool WritePointToStream(ostream& outStream) const;
      bool ReadPointFromStream(istream& inStream);
      void WritePointToClipboard(InfoList& infoList) const;
      void ReadPointFromClipboard(InfoList& infoList);
      void WritePointToRegistry(String key) const;
      void ReadPointFromRegistry(String key,
                    Point defaultPoint /* = ZeroPoint */);
```

The *x* and *y* value of the point are inspected by the constant methods and modified by the non-constant methods:

```
      int X() const {return x;}
      int Y() const {return y;}
      int& X() {return x;}
      int& Y() {return y;}

   private:
      int x, y;
 };

 extern const Point ZeroPoint;
};
```

The implementation of the `Point` class is also rather straightforward:

Point.cpp

```
#include "SmallWindows.h"

namespace SmallWindows {
  Point::Point()
   :x(0), y(0) {
     // Empty.
  }

  Point::Point(int x, int y)
   :x(x), y(y) {
     // Empty.
  }

  Point::Point(const Point& point)
   :x(point.x),
    y(point.y) {
     // Empty.
  }
```

In the assignment operator, it is a good custom to verify that we do not assign the same object. However, it is not completely necessary in this case since we just assign the integer values of *x* and *y*:

```cpp
Point& Point::operator=(const Point& point) {
  if (this != &point) {
    x = point.x;
    y = point.y;
  }

  return *this;
}

Point::Point(const POINT& point)
 :x(point.x),
  y(point.y) {
  // Empty.
}

Point& Point::operator=(const POINT& point) {
  x = point.x;
  y = point.y;
  return *this;
}

Point::operator POINT() const {
  POINT point = {x, y};
  return point;
}

bool Point::operator==(const Point& point) const {
  return ((x == point.x) && (y == point.y));
}

bool Point::operator!=(const Point& point) const {
  return !(*this == point);
}

bool Point::operator<(const Point& point) const {
  return (x < point.x) || ((x == point.x) && (y < point.y));
}

bool Point::operator<=(const Point& point) const {
  return ((*this < point) || (*this == point));
}

bool Point::operator>(const Point& point) const {
  return !(*this <= point);
}
```

```
bool Point::operator>=(const Point& point) const {
  return !(*this < point);
}

Point Min(const Point& left, const Point& right) {
  return (left < right) ? left : right;
}

Point Max(const Point& left, const Point& right) {
  return (left > right) ? left : right;
}

Point& Point::operator*=(double factor) {
  x = (int) (factor * x);
  y = (int) (factor * y);
  return *this;
}

Point operator*(const Point& point, double factor) {
  return Point((int) (point.x * factor),
               (int) (point.y * factor));
}

Point operator*(double factor, const Point& point) {
  return Point((int) (factor * point.x),
               (int) (factor * point.y));
}

Point& Point::operator*=(pair<double,double> factorPair) {
  x = (int) (factorPair.first * x);
  y = (int) (factorPair.second * y);
  return *this;
}

Point operator*(const Point& point,
                pair<double,double> factorPair) {
  return Point((int) (point.x * factorPair.first),
               (int) (point.y * factorPair.second));
}

Point operator*(pair<double,double> factorPair,
                const Point& point) {
  return Point((int) (factorPair.first * point.x),
               (int) (factorPair.second * point.y));
}
```

```
Point& Point::operator+=(const int distance) {
  x += distance;
  y += distance;
  return *this;
}

Point& Point::operator-=(const int distance) {
  x -= distance;
  y -= distance;
  return *this;
}

Point& Point::operator+=(const Size& size) {
  x += size.Width();
  y += size.Height();
  return *this;
}

Point& Point::operator-=(const Size& size) {
  x -= size.Width();
  y -= size.Height();
  return *this;
}

Point& Point::operator+=(const Point& point) {
  x += point.x;
  y += point.y;
  return *this;
}

Point& Point::operator-=(const Point& point) {
  x -= point.x;
  y -= point.y;
  return *this;
}

Point operator+(const Point& left, int distance) {
  return Point(left.x + distance, left.y + distance);
}

Point operator-(const Point& left, int distance) {
  return Point(left.x - distance, left.y - distance);
}

Point operator+(const Point& point, const Size& size) {
  return Point(point.x + size.Width(), point.y + size.Height());
}
```

```
Point operator-(const Point& point, const Size& size) {
  return Point(point.x - size.Width(), point.y - size.Height());
}

Point operator+(const Point& left, const Point& right) {
  return Point(left.x + right.x, left.y + right.y);
}

Size operator-(const Point& left, const Point& right) {
  return Size(left.x - right.x, left.y - right.y);
}

bool Point::WritePointToStream(ostream& outStream) const {
  outStream.write((char*) &x, sizeof x);
  outStream.write((char*) &y, sizeof y);
  return ((bool) outStream);
}

bool Point::ReadPointFromStream(istream& inStream) {
  inStream.read((char*) &x, sizeof x);
  inStream.read((char*) &y, sizeof y);
  return ((bool) inStream);
}

void Point::WritePointToClipboard(InfoList& infoList) const {
  infoList.AddValue<int>(x);
  infoList.AddValue<int>(y);
}

void Point::ReadPointFromClipboard(InfoList& infoList) {
  infoList.GetValue<int>(x);
  infoList.GetValue<int>(y);
}

void Point::WritePointToRegistry(String key) const {
  POINT pointStruct = (POINT) *this;
  Registry::WriteBuffer(key, &pointStruct, sizeof pointStruct);
}

void Point::ReadPointFromRegistry(String key,
                      Point defaultPoint /* = ZeroPoint */) {
  POINT pointStruct, defaultPointStruct = (POINT) defaultPoint;
  Registry::ReadBuffer(key, &pointStruct, sizeof pointStruct,
                    &defaultPointStruct);
  *this = Point(pointStruct);
}
```

```
    const Point ZeroPoint(0, 0);
};
```

The Rect class

The Rect class holds the four borders of a rectangle: left, top, right, and bottom.

Rect.h

```
namespace SmallWindows {
  class Rect;
  extern const Rect ZeroRect;

  class Rect {
    public:
```

The default constructor sets all the four borders to zero. The rectangle can be initialized by, or assigned to, another rectangle. It is also possible to initialize the rectangle with the top-left and bottom-right corners, as well as the top-left corner and a size holding the width and height of the rectangle:

```
        Rect();
        Rect(int left, int top, int right, int bottom);
        Rect(const Rect& rect);
        Rect& operator=(const Rect& rect);
        Rect(Point topLeft, Point bottomRight);
        Rect(Point topLeft, Size size);
```

Similar to SIZE and POINT in the previous sections, a rectangle can be initialized and assigned to a value of the Win32 API RECT structure. A Rect object can also be converted to a RECT:

```
        Rect(const RECT& rect);
        Rect& operator=(const RECT& rect);
        operator RECT() const;
```

The compare operators first compare the top-left corners. If they are equal, the bottom-right corners are then compared:

```
        bool operator==(const Rect& rect) const;
        bool operator!=(const Rect& rect) const;
        bool operator<(const Rect& rect) const;
        bool operator<=(const Rect& rect) const;
        bool operator>(const Rect& rect) const;
        bool operator>=(const Rect& rect) const;
```

The multiplication operators multiply all sides with the factor. Even though the factor is a double, the border values are always integers, similar to the `Size` and `Point` cases of the previous sections:

```
Rect& operator*=(double factor);
friend Rect operator*(const Rect& rect, double factor);
friend Rect operator*(double factor, const Rect& rect);
```

It is also possible to multiply the rectangle with a pair of values, where the first value is multiplied with `left` and `right`, and the second value is multiplied with `top` and `bottom`. Also, in this case, the resulting values are integers:

```
Rect& operator*=(pair<double,double> factorPair);
friend Rect operator*(const Rect& rect,
                      pair<double,double> factorPair);
friend Rect operator*(pair<double,double> factorPair,
                      const Rect& rect);
```

The following operators are a little bit special: the addition operator adds the size to the bottom-right corner and leaves the top-left corner unchanged while the subtraction operator subtracts the size from the top-left corner and leaves the bottom-right corner unchanged:

```
Rect& operator+=(const Size& size);
Rect& operator-=(const Size& size);
```

However, the following operators add and subtract the size to and from both the top-left and bottom-right corners:

```
friend Rect operator+(const Rect& rect, const Size& size);
friend Rect operator-(const Rect& rect, const Size& size);
```

The following operators take a point as a parameter and add the point to, and subtract it from, both the top-left and bottom-right corner:

```
Rect& operator+=(const Point& point);
Rect& operator-=(const Point& point);
friend Rect operator+(const Rect& rect, const Point& point);
friend Rect operator+(const Point& point, const Rect& rect);
friend Rect operator-(const Rect& rect, const Point& point);
```

The width of a rectangle is the absolute difference between the left and right border, and its height is the absolute difference between the top and bottom border:

```
int Width() const {return abs(right - left);}
int Height() const {return abs(bottom - top);}
```

The `GetSize` method returns the width and height of the rectangle. It is not possible to name it `Size`, since there is a class with that name. However, it is still possible to define an operator returning a `Size` object. The `Size` and `Point` operators return the size and top-left corner of the rectangle:

```
Size GetSize() const {return Size(Width(), Height());}
operator Size() const {return GetSize();}
operator Point() const {return TopLeft();}
```

The top-left and bottom-right corner can both be inspected and modified. It is not appropriate to define methods returning a reference to a point since there are no corresponding fields for the corners:

```
Point TopLeft() const {return Point(left, top);}
Point BottomRight() const {return Point(right, bottom);}

void SetTopLeft(Point topLeft) {left = topLeft.X();
                                right = topLeft.Y();}
void SetBottomRight(Point bottomRight)
                {right = bottomRight.X();
                 bottom = bottomRight.Y();}
```

The `Clear` method sets all four corners to zero, `Normalize` swaps the left and right borders and the top and bottom borders if they appear in the wrong order, and `PointInside` returns `true` if the point is located inside the rectangle, assuming that it has been normalized:

```
void Clear();
void Normalize();
bool PointInside(Point point) const;
```

The rectangle can be written to and read from a file stream, the clipboard, and the registry:

```
bool WriteRectToStream(ostream& outStream) const;
bool ReadRectFromStream(istream& inStream);
void WriteRectToClipboard(InfoList& infoList) const;
void ReadRectFromClipboard(InfoList& infoList);
void WriteRectToRegistry(String key) const;
void ReadRectFromRegistry(String key,
                          Rect defaultRect = ZeroRect);
```

The four corners are inspected by the constant methods and modified by the non-constant methods:

```
int Left() const {return left;}
int Right() const {return right;}
int Top() const {return top;}
int Bottom() const {return bottom;}
```

```
          int& Left() {return left;}
          int& Right() {return right;}
          int& Top() {return top;}
          int& Bottom() {return bottom;}

      private:
        int left, top, right, bottom;
    };
};
```

Similar to `Size` and `Point`, the implementation of `Rect` is rather straightforward.

Rect.cpp

```
#include "SmallWindows.h"

namespace SmallWindows {
  Rect::Rect()
   :left(0), top(0), right(0), bottom(0) {
    // Empty.
  }

  Rect::Rect(int left, int top, int right, int bottom)
   :left(left),
    top(top),
    right(right),
    bottom(bottom) {
    // Empty.
  }

  Rect::Rect(const Rect& rect)
   :left(rect.left),
    top(rect.top),
    right(rect.right),
    bottom(rect.bottom) {
    // Empty.
  }

  Rect& Rect::operator=(const Rect& rect) {
    if (this != &rect) {
      left = rect.left;
      top = rect.top;
      right = rect.right;
      bottom = rect.bottom;
    }

    return *this;
  }
```

```
Rect::Rect(Point topLeft, Point bottomRight)
 :left(topLeft.X()),
  top(topLeft.Y()),
  right(bottomRight.X()),
  bottom(bottomRight.Y()) {
  // Empty.
}

Rect::Rect(Point topLeft, Size size)
 :left(topLeft.X()),
  top(topLeft.Y()),
  right(topLeft.X() + size.Width()),
  bottom(topLeft.Y() + size.Height()) {
  // Empty.
}

Rect::Rect(const RECT& rect)
 :left(rect.left),
  top(rect.top),
  right(rect.right),
  bottom(rect.bottom) {
  // Empty.
}

Rect& Rect::operator=(const RECT& rect) {
  left = rect.left;
  top = rect.top;
  right = rect.right;
  bottom = rect.bottom;
  return *this;
}

Rect::operator RECT() const {
  RECT rect = {left, top, right, bottom};
  return rect;
}

bool Rect::operator==(const Rect& rect) const {
  return (left == rect.left) && (top == rect.top) &&
         (right == rect.right) && (bottom == rect.bottom);
}

bool Rect::operator!=(const Rect& rect) const {
  return !(*this == rect);
}
```

```
bool Rect::operator<(const Rect& rect) const {
  return (TopLeft() < rect.TopLeft()) ||
         ((TopLeft() == rect.TopLeft()) &&
          (BottomRight() < rect.BottomRight()));
}

bool Rect::operator<=(const Rect& rect) const {
  return ((*this < rect) || (*this == rect));
}

bool Rect::operator>(const Rect& rect) const {
  return !(*this <= rect);
}

bool Rect::operator>=(const Rect& rect) const {
  return !(*this < rect);
}

Rect& Rect::operator*=(double factor) {
  left = (int) (factor * left);
  top = (int) (factor * top);
  right = (int) (factor * right);
  bottom = (int) (factor * bottom);
  return *this;
}

Rect operator*(const Rect& rect, double factor) {
  return Rect(rect.TopLeft() * factor,
              rect.BottomRight() * factor);
}

Rect operator*(double factor, const Rect& rect) {
  return Rect(factor * rect.TopLeft(),
              factor * rect.BottomRight());
}

Rect& Rect::operator*=(pair<double,double> factorPair) {
  left = (int) (factorPair.first * left);
  top = (int) (factorPair.second * top);
  right = (int) (factorPair.first * right);
  bottom = (int) (factorPair.second * bottom);
  return *this;
}
```

```
Rect operator*(const Rect& rect,
               pair<double,double> factorPair) {
  return Rect(rect.TopLeft() * factorPair,
              rect.BottomRight() * factorPair);
}

Rect operator*(pair<double,double> factorPair,
               const Rect& rect) {
  return Rect(factorPair * rect.TopLeft(),
              factorPair * rect.BottomRight());
}

Rect& Rect::operator+=(const Size& size) {
  right += size.Width();
  bottom += size.Height();
  return *this;
}

Rect& Rect::operator-=(const Size& size) {
  left -= size.Width();
  top -= size.Height();
  return *this;
}

Rect operator+(const Rect& rect, const Size& size) {
  return Rect(rect.left + size.Width(),
              rect.top + size.Height(),
              rect.right + size.Width(),
              rect.bottom + size.Height());
}

Rect operator-(const Rect& rect, const Size& size) {
  return Rect(rect.left - size.Width(),
              rect.top - size.Height(),
              rect.right - size.Width(),
              rect.bottom - size.Height());
}

Rect& Rect::operator+=(const Point& point) {
  left += point.X();
  top += point.Y();
  right += point.X();
  bottom += point.Y();
  return *this;
}
```

```
Rect& Rect::operator-=(const Point& point) {
  left -= point.X();
  top -= point.Y();
  right -= point.X();
  bottom -= point.Y();
  return *this;
}

Rect operator+(const Rect& rect, const Point& point) {
  return Rect(rect.left + point.X(), rect.top + point.Y(),
              rect.right + point.X(), rect.bottom + point.Y());
}

Rect operator+(const Point& point, const Rect& rect) {
  return Rect(point.X() + rect.left, point.Y() + rect.top,
              point.X() + rect.right, point.Y() + rect.bottom);
}

Rect operator-(const Rect& rect, const Point& point) {
  return Rect(rect.left - point.X(), rect.top - point.Y(),
              rect.right - point.X(), rect.bottom - point.Y());
}

void Rect::Clear() {
  left = top = right = bottom = 0;
}

void Rect::Normalize() {
  int minX = min(left, right), minY = min(top, bottom),
      maxX = max(left, right), maxY = max(top, bottom);
  left = minX;
  top = minY;
  right = maxX;
  bottom = maxY;
}

bool Rect::PointInside(Point point) const {
  return ((left <= point.X()) && (point.X() <= right) &&
          (top <= point.Y()) && (point.Y() <= bottom));
}

bool Rect::WriteRectToStream(ostream& outStream) const {
  outStream.write((char*) &left, sizeof left);
  outStream.write((char*) &top, sizeof top);
  outStream.write((char*) &right, sizeof right);
  outStream.write((char*) &bottom, sizeof bottom);
  return ((bool) outStream);
}
```

```
bool Rect::ReadRectFromStream(istream& inStream) {
  inStream.read((char*) &left, sizeof left);
  inStream.read((char*) &top, sizeof top);
  inStream.read((char*) &right, sizeof right);
  inStream.read((char*) &bottom, sizeof bottom);
  return ((bool) inStream);
}

void Rect::WriteRectToClipboard(InfoList& infoList) const {
  infoList.AddValue<int>(left);
  infoList.AddValue<int>(top);
  infoList.AddValue<int>(right);
  infoList.AddValue<int>(bottom);
}

void Rect::ReadRectFromClipboard(InfoList& infoList) {
  infoList.GetValue<int>(left);
  infoList.GetValue<int>(top);
  infoList.GetValue<int>(right);
  infoList.GetValue<int>(bottom);
}

void Rect::WriteRectToRegistry(String key) const {
  RECT pointStruct = (RECT) *this;
  Registry::WriteBuffer(key, &pointStruct, sizeof pointStruct);
}

void Rect::ReadRectFromRegistry(String key,
                       Rect defaultRect /* = ZeroRect */) {
  RECT rectStruct, defaultRectStruct = (RECT) defaultRect;
  Registry::ReadBuffer(key, &rectStruct, sizeof rectStruct,
                     &defaultRectStruct);
  *this = Rect(rectStruct);
}

const Rect ZeroRect(0, 0, 0, 0);
};
```

The Color class

The Color class is a wrapper class for the Win32 API COLORREF structure, which holds a color in accordance with the Red-Green-Blue (RGB) standard. Each component of the color is represented by a value between 0 and 255, inclusive, which gives a theoretical total number of 256^3 = 16,777,216 different colors, among which Color defines 142 standard colors.

Color.h

```
namespace SmallWindows {
  class Color;
  extern const Color SystemColor;
```

The default constructor initializes the color with zero for each of the red, green, and blue values, which corresponds to black. A color object can also be initialized by, and assigned to, another color:

```
class Color {
  public:
    Color();
    Color(int red, int green, int blue);
    Color(const Color& color);
    Color& operator=(const Color& color);
```

The equality operators compare the red, green, and blue values:

```
    bool operator==(const Color& color) const;
    bool operator!=(const Color& color) const;
```

The `Inverse` function returns the inverted color and `GrayScale` returns the corresponding grayscale color:

```
    Color Inverse();
    void GrayScale();
```

The color can be written to, and read from, a file stream, the clipboard, and the registry:

```
    bool WriteColorToStream(ostream& outStream) const;
    bool ReadColorFromStream(istream& inStream);
    void WriteColorToClipboard(InfoList& infoList) const;
    void ReadColorFromClipboard(InfoList& infoList);
    void WriteColorToRegistry(String key) const;
    void ReadColorFromRegistry(String key,
                        Color defaultColor =SystemColor);
```

The wrapped `COLORREF` structure value is inspected by the constant method and modified by the non-constant method:

```
    COLORREF ColorRef() const {return colorRef;}
    COLORREF& ColorRef() {return colorRef;}

  private:
    COLORREF colorRef;
};
```

The predefined colors are constant objects:

```
extern const Color
  AliceBlue, AntiqueWhite, Aqua, Aquamarine,
  Azure, Beige, Bisque, Black, BlanchedAlmond,
  Blue, BlueViolet, Brown, Burlywood, CadetBlue,
  Chartreuse, Chocolate, Coral, CornflowerBlue,
  Cornsilk, Crimson, Cyan, DarkBlue, DarkCyan,
  DarkGoldenRod, DarkGray, DarkGreen, DarkKhaki,
  DarkMagenta, DarkOliveGreen, DarkOrange, DarkOrchid,
  DarkRed, DarkSalmon, DarkSeaGreen, DarkSlateBlue,
  DarkSlateGray, DarkTurquoise, DarkViolet, DeepPink,
  DeepSkyBlue, DimGray, DodgerBlue, FireBrick,
  FloralWhite, ForestGreen, Fuchsia, Gainsboro,
  GhostWhite, Gold, GoldenRod, Gray, Green, GreenYellow,
  HoneyDew, HotPink, IndianRed, Indigo, Ivory, Khaki,
  Lavender, LavenderBlush, Lawngreen, LemonChiffon,
  LightBlue, LightCoral, LightCyan, LightGoldenRodYellow,
  LightGreen, LightGray, LightPink, LightSalmon,
  LightSeaGreen, LightSkyBlue, LightSlateGray,
  LightSteelBlue, LightYellow, Lime, LimeGreen, Linen,
  Magenta, Maroon, MediumAquamarine, MediumBlue,
  MediumOrchid, MediumPurple, MediumSeaGreen,
  MediumSlateBlue, MediumSpringGreen, MediumTurquoise,
  MediumVioletRed, MidnightBlue, MintCream, MistyRose,
  Moccasin, NavajoWhite, Navy, Navyblue, OldLace, Olive,
  OliveDrab, Orange, OrangeRed, Orchid, PaleGoldenRod,
  PaleGreen, PaleTurquoise, PaleVioletRed, PapayaWhip,
  PeachPuff, Peru, Pink, Plum, PowderBlue, Purple,
  Red, RosyBrown, RoyalBlue, SaddleBrown, Salmon,
  SandyBrown, SeaGreen, SeaShell, Sienna, Silver, SkyBlue,
  SlateBlue, SlateGray, Snow, SpringGreen, SteelBlue,
  SystemColor, Tan, Teal, Thistle, Tomato, Turquoise,
  Violet, Wheat, White, WhiteSmoke, Yellow, YellowGreen;
};
```

The implementation of `Color` is rather straightforward. The Win32 `RGB` macro creates a `COLORREF` value based on the three color components.

Color.cpp

```
#include "SmallWindows.h"

namespace SmallWindows {
  Color::Color()
   :colorRef(RGB(0, 0, 0)) {
    // Empty.
  }
```

```
Color::Color(COLORREF colorRef)
 :colorRef(colorRef) {
  // Empty.
}

Color::Color(int red, int green, int blue)
 :colorRef(RGB(red, green, blue)) {
  // Empty.
}

Color::Color(const Color& color)
 :colorRef(color.colorRef) {
  // Empty.
}

Color& Color::operator=(const Color& color) {
  if (this != &color) {
    colorRef = color.colorRef;
  }

  return *this;
}
```

Two colors are equal if their wrapped COLORREF structures are equal, and they are compared with the C standard function memcpy.

```
bool Color::operator==(const Color& color) const {
  return (colorRef == color.colorRef);
}

bool Color::operator!=(const Color& color) const {
  return !(*this == color);
}
```

The Inverse function returns the inverted color with each component subtracted from 255, and GrayScale returns the corresponding grayscale color with each component holding the average value of the red, green, and blue components. GetRValue, GetGValue, and GetBValue are Win32 API macros that extract the red, green, and blue components:

```
Color Color::Inverse() {
  int inverseRed = 255 - GetRValue(colorRef);
  int inverseGreen = 255 - GetGValue(colorRef);
  int inverseBlue = 255 - GetBValue(colorRef);
  return Color(inverseRed, inverseGreen, inverseBlue);
}
```

```
void Color::GrayScale() {
  int red = GetRValue(colorRef);
  int green = GetGValue(colorRef);
  int blue = GetBValue(colorRef);

  int average = (red + green + blue) / 3;
  colorRef = RGB(average, average, average);
}

bool Color::WriteColorToStream(ostream& outStream) const {
  outStream.write((char*) &colorRef, sizeof colorRef);
  return ((bool) outStream);
}

bool Color::ReadColorFromStream(istream& inStream) {
  inStream.read((char*) &colorRef, sizeof colorRef);
  return ((bool) inStream);
}

void Color::WriteColorToClipboard(InfoList& infoList) const {
  infoList.AddValue<COLORREF>(colorRef);
}

void Color::ReadColorFromClipboard(InfoList& infoList) {
  infoList.GetValue<COLORREF>(colorRef);
}

void Color::WriteColorToRegistry(String key) const {
  Registry::WriteBuffer(key, &colorRef, sizeof colorRef);
}

void Color::ReadColorFromRegistry(String key,
                     Color defaultColor /*=SystemColor */) {
  Registry::ReadBuffer(key, &colorRef, sizeof colorRef,
                  &defaultColor.colorRef);
}
```

Each of the predefined colors calls the constructor that takes the red, green, and blue components:

```
const Color
  AliceBlue(240, 248, 255), AntiqueWhite(250, 235, 215),
  Aqua(0, 255, 255), Aquamarine(127, 255, 212),
  Azure(240, 255, 255), Beige(245, 245, 220),
  Bisque(255, 228, 196), Black(0, 0, 0),
  BlanchedAlmond(255, 255, 205), Blue(0, 0, 255),
  BlueViolet(138, 43, 226), Brown(165, 42, 42),
  Burlywood(222, 184, 135), CadetBlue(95, 158, 160),
```

Chartreuse(127, 255, 0), Chocolate(210, 105, 30),
Coral(255, 127, 80), CornflowerBlue(100, 149, 237),
Cornsilk(255, 248, 220), Crimson(220, 20, 60),
Cyan(0, 255, 255), DarkBlue(0, 0, 139),
DarkCyan(0, 139, 139), DarkGoldenRod(184, 134, 11),
DarkGray(169, 169, 169), DarkGreen(0, 100, 0),
DarkKhaki(189, 183, 107), DarkMagenta(139, 0, 139),
DarkOliveGreen(85, 107, 47), DarkOrange(255, 140, 0),
DarkOrchid(153, 50, 204), DarkRed(139, 0, 0),
DarkSalmon(233, 150, 122), DarkSeaGreen(143, 188, 143),
DarkSlateBlue(72, 61, 139), DarkSlateGray(47, 79, 79),
DarkTurquoise(0, 206, 209), DarkViolet(148, 0, 211),
DeepPink(255, 20, 147), DeepSkyBlue(0, 191, 255),
DimGray(105, 105, 105), DodgerBlue(30, 144, 255),
FireBrick(178, 34, 34), FloralWhite(255, 250, 240),
ForestGreen(34, 139, 34), Fuchsia(255, 0, 255),
Gainsboro(220, 220, 220), GhostWhite(248, 248, 255),
Gold(255, 215, 0), GoldenRod(218, 165, 32),
Gray(127, 127, 127), Green(0, 128, 0),
GreenYellow(173, 255, 47), HoneyDew(240, 255, 240),
HotPink(255, 105, 180), IndianRed(205, 92, 92),
Indigo(75, 0, 130), Ivory(255, 255, 240),
Khaki(240, 230, 140), Lavender(230, 230, 250),
LavenderBlush(255, 240, 245), Lawngreen(124, 252, 0),
LemonChiffon(255, 250, 205), LightBlue(173, 216, 230),
LightCoral(240, 128, 128), LightCyan(224, 255, 255),
LightGoldenRodYellow(250, 250, 210),
LightGreen(144, 238, 144), LightGray(211, 211, 211),
LightPink(255, 182, 193), LightSalmon(255, 160, 122),
LightSeaGreen(32, 178, 170), LightSkyBlue(135, 206, 250),
LightSlateGray(119, 136, 153), LightSteelBlue(176, 196, 222),
LightYellow(255, 255, 224), Lime(0, 255, 0),
LimeGreen(50, 205, 50), Linen(250, 240, 230),
Magenta(255, 0, 255), Maroon(128, 0, 0),
MediumAquamarine(102, 205, 170), MediumBlue(0, 0, 205),
MediumOrchid(186, 85, 211), MediumPurple(147, 112, 219),
MediumSeaGreen(60, 179, 113), MediumSlateBlue(123, 104, 238),
MediumSpringGreen(0, 250, 154), MediumTurquoise(72, 209, 204),
MediumVioletRed(199, 21, 133), MidnightBlue(25, 25, 112),
MintCream(245, 255, 250), MistyRose(255, 228, 225),
Moccasin(255, 228, 181), NavajoWhite(255, 222, 173),
Navy(0, 0, 128), Navyblue(159, 175, 223),
OldLace(253, 245, 230), Olive(128, 128, 0),
OliveDrab(107, 142, 35), Orange(255, 165, 0),
OrangeRed(255, 69, 0), Orchid(218, 112, 214),
PaleGoldenRod(238, 232, 170), PaleGreen(152, 251, 152),
PaleTurquoise(175, 238, 238), PaleVioletRed(219, 112, 147),
PapayaWhip(255, 239, 213), PeachPuff(255, 218, 185),

```
      Peru(205, 133, 63), Pink(255, 192, 203),
      Plum(221, 160, 221), PowderBlue(176, 224, 230),
      Purple(128, 0, 128), Red(255, 0, 0),
      RosyBrown(188, 143, 143), RoyalBlue(65, 105, 225),
      SaddleBrown(139, 69, 19), Salmon(250, 128, 114),
      SandyBrown(244, 164, 96), SeaGreen(46, 139, 87),
      SeaShell(255, 245, 238), Sienna(160, 82, 45),
      Silver(192, 192, 192), SkyBlue(135, 206, 235),
      SlateBlue(106, 90, 205), SlateGray(112, 128, 144),
      Snow(255, 250, 250), SpringGreen(0, 255, 127),
      SteelBlue(70, 130, 180), SystemColor(0, 0, 0),
      Tan(210, 180, 140), Teal(0, 128, 128),
      Thistle(216, 191, 216), Tomato(255, 99, 71),
      Turquoise(64, 224, 208), Violet(238, 130, 238),
      Wheat(245, 222, 179), White(255, 255, 255),
      WhiteSmoke(245, 245, 245), Yellow(255, 255, 0),
      YellowGreen(139, 205, 50);
  };
```

The Font class

The Font class is a wrapper class for the Win32 API LOGFONT structure. The structure holds a large set of properties; however, we only take into consideration the fields for the font's name and size and whether the font is italic, bold, or underlined; the other fields are set to zero. The system font is the font where all fields in the LOGFONT structure are set to zero, which results in the standard font of the system. Finally, the Font class also includes a Color object.

Font.h

```
namespace SmallWindows {
  class Font;
  extern const Font SystemFont;

  class Font {
    public:
```

The default constructor sets the name to the empty string and all other values to zero, resulting in the system font, usually 10 points Arial. The size of the font is given in typographic points (1 point = 1/72 of an inch = 1/72 * 25.4 mm ≈ 0.35 mm). A font can also be initialized by, or assigned to, another font:

```
      Font();
      Font(String name, int size,
           bool italic = false, bool bold = false);
```

```
Font(const Font& Font);
Font& operator=(const Font& font);
```

Two fonts are equal if they hold the same name and size as well as the same italic, bold, and underline status (all other fields are assumed to be zero):

```
bool operator==(const Font& font) const;
bool operator!=(const Font& font) const;
```

The font can be written to, and read from, a file stream, the clipboard, and the registry:

```
bool WriteFontToStream(ostream& outStream) const;
bool ReadFontFromStream(istream& inStream);
void WriteFontToClipboard(InfoList& infoList) const;
void ReadFontFromClipboard(InfoList& infoList);
void WriteFontToRegistry(String key);
void ReadFontFromRegistry(String key,
                          Font defaultFont = SystemFont);
```

The PointToMeters function converts a typographic point to logical units (hundredths of millimeters):

```
void PointsToLogical(double zoom = 1.0);
```

The wrapped LOGFONT structure is inspected by the constant method and modified by the non-constant method:

```
LOGFONT LogFont() const {return logFont;}
LOGFONT& LogFont() {return logFont;}
```

The color field can also be inspected by the constant method and modified by the non-constant method:

```
Color FontColor() const {return color;}
Color& FontColor() {return color;}
```

```
  private:
    LOGFONT logFont;
    Color color;
  };
};
```

Font.cpp

```
#include "SmallWindows.h"

namespace SmallWindows {
  Font::Font() {
    memset(&logFont, 0, sizeof logFont);
  }

  Font::Font(String name, int size, bool italic, bool bold) {
    memset(&logFont, 0, sizeof logFont);
    wcscpy_s(logFont.lfFaceName, LF_FACESIZE, name.c_str());
    logFont.lfHeight = size;
    logFont.lfItalic = (italic ? TRUE : FALSE);
    logFont.lfWeight = (bold ? FW_BOLD : FW_NORMAL);
  }

  Font::Font(const Font& font) {
    logFont = font.LogFont();
    color = font.color;
  }

  Font& Font::operator=(const Font& font) {
    if (this != &font) {
      logFont = font.LogFont();
      color = font.color;
    }

    return *this;
  }
```

Two fonts are equal if their wrapped LOGFONT structures and their Color fields are equal:

```
  bool Font::operator==(const Font& font) const {
    return (::memcmp(&logFont, &font.logFont,
                     sizeof logFont) == 0) &&
           (color == font.color);
  }

  bool Font::operator!=(const Font& font) const {
    return !(*this == font);
  }
```

The write and read methods write and read the wrapped LOGFONT structure and call the Color write and read methods:

```
bool Font::WriteFontToStream(ostream& outStream) const {
  outStream.write((char*) &logFont, sizeof logFont);
  color.WriteColorToStream(outStream);
  return ((bool) outStream);
}

bool Font::ReadFontFromStream(istream& inStream) {
  inStream.read((char*) &logFont, sizeof logFont);
  color.ReadColorFromStream(inStream);
  return ((bool) inStream);
}

void Font::WriteFontToClipboard(InfoList& infoList) const {
  infoList.AddValue<LOGFONT>(logFont);
  color.WriteColorToClipboard(infoList);
}

void Font::ReadFontFromClipboard(InfoList& infoList) {
  infoList.GetValue<LOGFONT>(logFont);
  color.ReadColorFromClipboard(infoList);
}

void Font::WriteFontToRegistry(String key) {
  Registry::WriteBuffer(key, &logFont, sizeof logFont);
  color.WriteColorToRegistry(key);
}

void Font::ReadFontFromRegistry(String key,
                  Font defaultFont /* = SystemFont */) {
  Registry::ReadBuffer(key, &logFont, sizeof logFont,
                  &defaultFont.logFont);
  color.ReadColorFromRegistry(key);
}
```

A typographic point is $1/72^{th}$ of an inch, and an inch is 25.4 millimeters. To transform a font typographical unit to logical units (hundredths of millimeters), we divide the width and height by 72, multiply by 2,540 (2,540 logical units equals 25.4 millimeters) and the zoom factor:

```
void Font::PointsToLogical(double zoom /* = 1.0 */) {
  logFont.lfWidth =
    (int) (zoom * 2540.0 * logFont.lfWidth / 72.0);
  logFont.lfHeight =
    (int) (zoom * 2540.0 * logFont.lfHeight / 72.0);
}

const Font SystemFont;
};
```

The Cursor class

There is a set of cursors available in the Win32 API, all with names starting with IDC_. In Small Windows, they have been given other names, which are hopefully easier to understand. Unlike other cases, we cannot use an enumeration for the cursors, since they are actually zero-terminated C++ strings (character pointers). Instead, every cursor is a pointer to a zero-terminated string. LPCTSTR stands for **Long Pointer to Constant TChar String**.

The reason the cursor has its own class, while the caret has a method in the Document class is that the caret does need a window handle to be set, while the cursor does not.

Cursor.h

```
namespace SmallWindows {
  typedef LPCTSTR CursorType;

  class Cursor {
    public:
      static const CursorType Normal;
      static const CursorType Arrow;
      static const CursorType ArrowHourGlass;
      static const CursorType Crosshair;
      static const CursorType Hand;
      static const CursorType ArrowQuestionMark;
      static const CursorType IBeam;
      static const CursorType SlashedCircle;
      static const CursorType SizeAll;
      static const CursorType SizeNorthEastSouthWest;
      static const CursorType SizeNorthSouth;
      static const CursorType SizeNorthWestSouthEast;
      static const CursorType SizeWestEast;
      static const CursorType VerticalArrow;
      static const CursorType HourGlass;

      static void Set(CursorType cursor);
  };
};
```

Cursor.cpp

```
#include "SmallWindows.h"

namespace SmallWindows {
  const CursorType Cursor::Normal = IDC_ARROW;
  const CursorType Cursor::Arrow = IDC_ARROW;
  const CursorType Cursor::ArrowHourGlass = IDC_APPSTARTING;
```

```
const CursorType Cursor::Crosshair = IDC_CROSS;
const CursorType Cursor::Hand = IDC_HAND;
const CursorType Cursor::ArrowQuestionMark = IDC_HELP;
const CursorType Cursor::IBeam = IDC_IBEAM;
const CursorType Cursor::SlashedCircle = IDC_NO;
const CursorType Cursor::SizeAll = IDC_SIZEALL;
const CursorType Cursor::SizeNorthEastSouthWest = IDC_SIZENESW;
const CursorType Cursor::SizeNorthSouth = IDC_SIZENS;
const CursorType Cursor::SizeNorthWestSouthEast = IDC_SIZENWSE;
const CursorType Cursor::SizeWestEast = IDC_SIZEWE;
const CursorType Cursor::VerticalArrow = IDC_UPARROW;
const CursorType Cursor::HourGlass = IDC_WAIT;
```

The Set method sets the cursor by calling the Win32 API functions LoadCursor and SetCursor:

```
void Cursor::Set(CursorType cursor) {
  ::SetCursor(::LoadCursor(nullptr, cursor));
}
};
```

The DynamicList class

The DynamicList class can be regarded as a more advanced version of the C++ standard classes list and vector. It varies its size dynamically:

DynamicList.h

```
namespace SmallWindows {
  template <class Type>
  class DynamicList {
    public:
```

The IfFuncPtr pointer is a function prototype that is used when testing (without changing) a value in the list. It takes a constant value and a void pointer and returns a Boolean value. DoFuncPtr is used when changing a value in the list and takes a (non-constant) value and a void pointer. The void pointers are sent by the calling methods; they hold additional information:

```
typedef bool (*IfFuncPtr)(const Type& value, void* voidPtr);
typedef void (*DoFuncPtr)(Type& value, void* voidPtr);
```

The list can be initialized by, and assigned to, another list. The default constructor creates an empty list, and the destructor deallocates the memory from the list:

```
DynamicList();
DynamicList(const DynamicList& list);
DynamicList& operator=(const DynamicList& list);
~DynamicList();
```

The `Empty` function returns `true` if the list is empty, `Size` returns the number of values in the list, `Clear` removes every value in the list, and `IndexOf` gives the zero-based index of the given value, or returns minus one if there is no such value in the list:

```
bool Empty() const;
int Size() const;
void Clear();
int IndexOf(Type& value) const;
```

The `begin` and `end` methods return pointers to the beginning and end of the list. They are included in order for the list to be iterated by the `for` statement:

```
Type* begin();
const Type* begin() const;
Type* end();
const Type* end() const;
```

The index method inspects or modifies the value with the given zero-based index in the list:

```
Type operator[](int index) const;
Type& operator[](int index);
```

The `Front` and `Back` methods inspect and modify the first and the last value of the list by calling the index methods mentioned previously:

```
Type Front() const {return (*this)[0];}
Type& Front() {return (*this)[0];}
Type Back() const {return (*this)[size - 1];}
Type& Back() {return (*this)[size - 1];}
```

The `PushFront` and `PushBack` methods add a value or a list at the beginning or at the end of the list, and `Insert` inserts a value or a list at the given index:

```
void PushBack(const Type& value);
void PushBack(const DynamicList& list);
void PushFront(const Type& value);
void PushFront(const DynamicList& list);
void Insert(int index, const Type& value);
void Insert(int index, const DynamicList& list);
```

The `Erase` function deletes the value at the given index, and `Remove` deletes the list from `firstIndex` to `lastIndex`, inclusive, or the end of the list if `lastIndex` is minus one. If `firstIndex` is zero and `lastIndex` is minus one, the whole list is deleted. The methods have been given different names since `lastIndex` in `Remove` is a default parameter. Giving the methods the same name would be a violation of the overload rules:

```
void Erase(int deleteIndex);
void Remove(int firstIndex = 0, int lastIndex = -1);
```

The `Copy` function copies the list from `firstIndex` to `lastIndex`, inclusive, to `copyList` or the rest of the list if `lastIndex` is minus one, which implies that the whole list is copied if `firstIndex` is zero and `lastIndex` is minus one:

```
void Copy(DynamicList& copyList, int firstIndex = 0,
          int lastIndex = -1) const;
```

The `AnyOf` function returns `true` if at least one value satisfies `ifFuncPtr`. That is, if `ifFuncPtr` returns `true` when called with the value as parameter. The `AllOf` function returns `true` if all values satisfy `ifFuncPtr`:

```
bool AnyOf(IfFuncPtr ifFuncPtr, void* ifVoidPtr = nullptr)
        const;
bool AllOf(IfFuncPtr ifFuncPtr, void* ifVoidPtr = nullptr)
        const;
```

The `FirstOf` and `LastOf` methods set the `value` parameter to the first and last value satisfying `ifFuncPtr`; they return `false` is there are no such values:

```
bool FirstOf(IfFuncPtr ifFuncPtr, Type& value,
             void* ifVoidPtr = nullptr) const;
bool LastOf(IfFuncPtr ifFuncPtr, Type& value,
            void* ifVoidPtr = nullptr) const;
```

The `Apply` method calls `doFuncPtr` for all values in the list, and `ApplyIf` calls `doFuncPtr` for each value in the list that satisfies `ifFuncPtr`:

```
void Apply(DoFuncPtr doFuncPtr, void* ifVoidPtr = nullptr);
void ApplyIf(IfFuncPtr ifFuncPtr, DoFuncPtr doFuncPtr,
             void* ifVoidPtr = nullptr,
             void* doVoidPtr = nullptr);
```

The `CopyIf` method copies each value in the list satisfying `ifFuncPtr` to `copyList`. `RemoveIf` removes the values satisfying `ifFuncPtr`:

```
void CopyIf(IfFuncPtr ifFuncPtr, DynamicList& copyList,
            void* ifVoidPtr = nullptr) const;
void RemoveIf(IfFuncPtr ifFuncPtr,
              void* ifVoidPtr = nullptr);
```

The `ApplyRemoveIf` method calls `doFuncPtr` to each value satisfying `ifFuncPtr` and then removes them. It may seem strange to apply a function to values that are to be removed. However, it is useful when removing dynamically allocated values, where `doFuncPtr` deallocates the memory of each value before it is removed from the list. It would not work to simply call `ApplyIf` and `RemoveIf`. When the values have been deleted by `ApplyIf`, they cannot be parameters to `ifFuncPtr` calls in `RemoveIf`:

```
void ApplyRemoveIf(IfFuncPtr ifFuncPtr, DoFuncPtr doFuncPtr,
                   void* ifVoidPtr=nullptr,
                   void* doVoidPtr=nullptr);
```

The size is the number of values in the list and the buffer holds the values themselves. The size of the buffer is dynamic and changes when values are added to, or removed from, the list. When the list is empty, the buffer points are null:

```
  private:
    int size;
    Type* buffer;
};

template <class Type>
DynamicList<Type>::DynamicList()
 :size(0),
  buffer(nullptr) {
  // Empty.
}
```

The default constructor and assignment operator iterates through the given list and copies each value. For this to work, the type must support the assignment operator, which all types, except arrays, do:

```
template <class Type>
DynamicList<Type>::DynamicList(const DynamicList& list)
 :size(list.size),
  buffer(new Type[list.size]) {
  assert(buffer != nullptr);
  for (int index = 0; index < size; ++index) {
    buffer[index] = list.buffer[index];
  }
}
```

In the assignment operator, we first delete the buffer, as it may hold values. If the list is empty, the buffer points are null and the delete operator does nothing:

```
template <class Type>
DynamicList<Type>& DynamicList<Type>::operator=
                                    (const DynamicList& list) {
```

```
      if (this != &list) {
        delete[] buffer;
        size = list.size;
        assert((buffer = new Type[size]) != nullptr);

        for (int index = 0; index < size; ++index) {
          buffer[index] = list.buffer[index];
        }
      }

      return *this;
    }
```

The destructor simply deletes the buffer. Again, if the list is empty, the buffer points are null and the delete operator does nothing:

```
    template <class Type>
    DynamicList<Type>::~DynamicList() {
      delete[] buffer;
    }

    template <class Type>
    bool DynamicList<Type>::Empty() const {
      return (size == 0);
    }

    template <class Type>
    int DynamicList<Type>::Size() const {
      return size;
    }
```

The Clear method sets the size to zero and the buffer to null:

```
    template <class Type>
    void DynamicList<Type>::Clear() {
      size = 0;
      delete[] buffer;
      buffer = nullptr;
    }
```

The IndexOf method iterates through the list and returns the index of the found value, or it returns minus one if there is no such value:

```
    template <class Type>
    int DynamicList<Type>::IndexOf(Type& value) const {
      for (int index = 0; index < size; ++index) {
```

```
        if (buffer[index] == value) {
          return index;
        }
      }

      return -1;
    }
```

The `begin` method returns the address of the first value in the list:

```
    template <class Type>
    Type* DynamicList<Type>::begin() {
      return &buffer[0];
    }

    template <class Type>
    const Type* DynamicList<Type>::begin() const {
      return &buffer[0];
    }
```

The `end` method returns the address one step beyond the last value in the list, which is the convention of list iterators in C++:

```
    template <class Type>
    Type* DynamicList<Type>::end() {
      return &buffer[size];
    }

    template <class Type>
    const Type* DynamicList<Type>::end() const {
      return &buffer[size];
    }
```

An assertion occurs if the index is beyond the list:

```
    template <class Type>
    Type DynamicList<Type>::operator[](int index) const {
      assert((index >= 0) && (index < size));
      return buffer[index];
    }

    template <class Type>
    Type& DynamicList<Type>::operator[](int index) {
      assert((index >= 0) && (index < size));
      return buffer[index];
    }
```

When adding a value at the end of the original list, we need to allocate a new list with one extra value and add the new value at the end:

```cpp
template <class Type>
void DynamicList<Type>::PushBack(const Type& value) {
  Type* newBuffer = new Type[size + 1];
  assert(newBuffer != nullptr);

  for (int index = 0; index < size; ++index) {
    newBuffer[index] = buffer[index];
  }

  newBuffer[size++] = value;
  delete[] buffer;
  buffer = newBuffer;
}
```

When adding a new list at the end of the original list, we need to allocate a new list with the size of the original and new lists, and copy the values from the original list to the new list:

```cpp
template <class Type>
void DynamicList<Type>::PushBack(const DynamicList& list) {
  Type* newBuffer = new Type[size + list.size];
  assert(newBuffer != nullptr);

  for (int index = 0; index < size; ++index) {
    newBuffer[index] = buffer[index];
  }

  for (int index = 0; index < list.size; ++index) {
    newBuffer[size + index] = list.buffer[index];
  }

  delete[] buffer;
  buffer = newBuffer;
  size += list.size;
}
```

When inserting a new value at the beginning of the list, we need to copy all the values in the original list one step forward to make room for the new value:

```cpp
template <class Type>
void DynamicList<Type>::PushFront(const Type& value) {
  Type* newBuffer = new Type[size + 1];
  assert(newBuffer != nullptr);
  newBuffer[0] = value;
```

```
    for (int index = 0; index < size; ++index) {
      newBuffer[index + 1] = buffer[index];
    }

    delete[] buffer;
    buffer = newBuffer;
    ++size;
  }
```

When inserting a new list, at the beginning of the list, we need to copy all its values and the number of steps corresponding to the size of the new list to make room for its values:

```
  template <class Type>
  void DynamicList<Type>::PushFront(const DynamicList& list) {
    Type* newBuffer = new Type[size + list.size];
    assert(newBuffer != nullptr);
```

We move the values of the original list in order to make room for the new list:

```
    for (int index = 0; index < list.size; ++index) {
      newBuffer[index] = list.buffer[index];
    }
```

When we have made room for the new list, we copy it to the original list at the beginning:

```
    for (int index = 0; index < size; ++index) {
      newBuffer[index + list.size] = buffer[index];
    }

    delete[] buffer;
    buffer = newBuffer;
    size += list.size;
  }
```

The `Insert` method works in ways similar to `PushFront`. We need to allocate a new list and copy values in the original list to make room for the new values, and then copy the new values into the original list:

```
  template <class Type>
  void DynamicList<Type>::Insert(int insertIndex,
                                 const Type& value) {
    assert((insertIndex >= 0) && (insertIndex <= size));
    Type* newBuffer = new Type[size + 1];
    assert(newBuffer != nullptr);

    for (int index = 0; index < insertIndex; ++index) {
      newBuffer[index] = buffer[index];
    }
```

```
    newBuffer[insertIndex] = value;

    for (int index = 0; index < (size - insertIndex); ++index) {
      newBuffer[insertIndex + index + 1] =
        buffer[insertIndex + index];
    }

    delete[] buffer;
    buffer = newBuffer;
    ++size;
}

template <class Type>
void DynamicList<Type>::Insert(int insertIndex,
                               const DynamicList& list){
    assert((insertIndex >= 0) && (insertIndex <= size));
    Type* newBuffer = new Type[size + list.size];
    assert(newBuffer != nullptr);

    for (int index = 0; index < insertIndex; ++index) {
      newBuffer[index] = buffer[index];
    }

    for (int index = 0; index < list.size; ++index) {
      newBuffer[insertIndex + index] = list.buffer[index];
    }

    for (int index = 0; index < (size - insertIndex); ++index) {
      newBuffer[insertIndex + index + list.size] =
        buffer[insertIndex + index];
    }

    delete[] buffer;
    buffer = newBuffer;
    size += list.size;
}
```

When erasing a value in the list, we allocate a new smaller list and copy the remaining values to that list:

```
template <class Type>
void DynamicList<Type>::Erase(int eraseIndex) {
    assert((eraseIndex >= 0) && (eraseIndex < size));
    Type* newBuffer = new Type[size - 1];
    assert(newBuffer != nullptr);
```

First, we copy the values before the delete index:

```
for (int index = 0; index < eraseIndex; ++index) {
  newBuffer[index] = buffer[index];
}
```

Then, we copy the values after the delete index:

```
for (int index = 0; index < (size - (eraseIndex + 1));
     ++index) {
  newBuffer[eraseIndex + index] =
    buffer[eraseIndex + index + 1];
}

delete[] buffer;
buffer = newBuffer;
--size;
}
```

The Remove method works in the same way as Delete; the difference is that more than one value can be removed from the list; removeSize holds the number of values to be removed:

```
template <class Type>
void DynamicList<Type>::Remove(int firstIndex /* = 0 */,
                               int lastIndex /* = -1 */) {
  if (lastIndex == -1) {
    lastIndex = size - 1;
  }

  assert((firstIndex >= 0) && (firstIndex < size));
  assert((lastIndex >= 0) && (lastIndex < size));
  assert(firstIndex <= lastIndex);

  int removeSize = lastIndex - firstIndex + 1;
  Type* newBuffer = new Type[size - removeSize];
  assert(newBuffer != nullptr);
  for (int index = 0; index < firstIndex; ++index) {
    newBuffer[index] = buffer[index];
  }

  for (int index = 0;
       index < (size - (firstIndex + removeSize)); ++index){
    newBuffer[firstIndex + index] =
      buffer[firstIndex + index + removeSize];
  }

  delete[] buffer;
  buffer = newBuffer;
```

```
      size -= removeSize;
   }
```

The `Copy` method simply calls `PushBack` for each value to be copied:

```
template <class Type>
void DynamicList<Type>::Copy(DynamicList& copyList,
                             int firstIndex/* =0 */,
                             int lastIndex /* = -1 */) const {
   if (lastIndex == -1) {
     lastIndex = size - 1;
   }

   assert((firstIndex >= 0) && (firstIndex < size));
   assert((lastIndex >= 0) && (lastIndex < size));
   assert(firstIndex <= lastIndex);

   for (int index = firstIndex; index <= lastIndex; ++index) {
     copyList.PushBack(buffer[index]);
   }
}
```

The `AnyOf` method iterates through the list and returns `true` if at least one value satisfies the function:

```
template <class Type>
bool DynamicList<Type>::AnyOf(IfFuncPtr ifFuncPtr,
                             void* ifVoidPtr /* = nullptr */) const {
   for (int index = 0; index < size; ++index) {
     if (ifFuncPtr(buffer[index], ifVoidPtr)) {
       return true;
     }
   }

   return false;
}
```

The `AllOf` method iterates through the list and returns `false` if at least one value does not satisfy the function:

```
template <class Type>
bool DynamicList<Type>::AllOf(IfFuncPtr ifFuncPtr,
                             void* ifVoidPtr /* = nullptr */) const {
   for (int index = 0; index < size; ++index) {
     if (!ifFuncPtr(buffer[index], ifVoidPtr)) {
       return false;
     }
   }
```

```
    return true;
  }
```

The `FirstOf` method finds the first value in the list that satisfies the function, copies it to the value parameter, and returns `true`. If it does not find any value satisfying the function, `false` is returned:

```
template <class Type>
bool DynamicList<Type>::FirstOf(IfFuncPtr ifFuncPtr,
          Type& value, void* ifVoidPtr /* = nullptr */) const{
  for (int index = 0; index < size; ++index) {
    if (ifFuncPtr(buffer[index], ifVoidPtr)) {
      value = buffer[index];
      return true;
    }
  }

  return false;
}
```

The `LastOf` method finds the last value satisfying the function in the same way as `FirstOf`; the difference is that the search is performed backward:

```
template <class Type>
bool DynamicList<Type>::LastOf(IfFuncPtr ifFuncPtr, Type& value,
                      void* ifVoidPtr /* = nullptr */) const {
  for (int index = (size - 1); index >= 0; --index) {
    if (ifFuncPtr(buffer[index], ifVoidPtr)) {
      value = buffer[index];
      return true;
    }
  }

  return false;
}
```

The `Apply` method iterates through the list and calls `doFuncPtr` for each value, the value may be modified (actually, the point of `Apply` is that the value is modified) since the parameter to `doFuncPtr` is not constant:

```
template <class Type>
void DynamicList<Type>::Apply(DoFuncPtr doFuncPtr,
                        void* doVoidPtr /* = nullptr */) {
  for (int index = 0; index < size; ++index) {
    doFuncPtr(buffer[index], doVoidPtr);
  }
}
```

The `ApplyIf` method iterates through the list and calls `doFuncPtr` for each value that satisfies `ifFuncPtr`:

```
template <class Type>
void DynamicList<Type>::ApplyIf(IfFuncPtr ifFuncPtr,
      DoFuncPtr doFuncPtr, void* ifVoidPtr /* = nullptr */,
      void* doVoidPtr /* = nullptr */){
  for (int index = 0; index < size; ++index) {
    if (ifFuncPtr(buffer[index], ifVoidPtr)) {
      doFuncPtr(buffer[index], doVoidPtr);
    }
  }
}
```

The `CopyIf` method copies every value that satisfies `ifFuncPtr` to `copyList` by calling `PushBack`:

```
template <class Type>
void DynamicList<Type>::CopyIf(IfFuncPtr ifFuncPtr,
                        DynamicList& copyList,
                        void* ifVoidPtr /* = nullptr */) const {
  for (int index = 0; index < size; ++index) {
    if (ifFuncPtr(buffer[index], ifVoidPtr)) {
      copyList.PushBack(buffer[index]);
    }
  }
}
```

The `RemoveIf` method removes every value that satisfies `ifFuncPtr` by calling `Delete` for each value:

```
template <class Type>
void DynamicList<Type>::RemoveIf(IfFuncPtr ifFuncPtr,
                        void* ifVoidPtr /* = nullptr */) {
  for (int index = 0; index < size; ++index) {
    if (ifFuncPtr(buffer[index], ifVoidPtr)) {
      Erase(index--);
    }
  }
}
```

The `ApplyRemoveIf` method applies `doFuncPtr` to each value that satisfies `ifFuncPtr`. We cannot simply call `Apply` and `RemoveIf`, since `doFuncPtr` may deallocate the values in `Apply`, and `ifFuncPtr` in `RemoveIf` would not work when called on deleted values. Instead, we call `doFuncPtr` and call `Erase` immediately after. In this way, the values are not accessed after the call to `doFuncPtr`:

```
template <class Type>
void DynamicList<Type>::ApplyRemoveIf(IfFuncPtr ifFuncPtr,
        DoFuncPtr doFuncPtr, void* ifVoidPtr /* = nullptr */,
        void* doVoidPtr /* = nullptr */) {
  for (int index = 0; index < size; ++index) {
    if (ifFuncPtr(buffer[index], ifVoidPtr)) {
      doFuncPtr(buffer[index], doVoidPtr);
      Erase(index--);
    }
  }
}
};
```

The Tree class

The C++ standard library hold a set of container classes for arrays, lists, vectors, sets, and maps. However, there is no class for a tree structure. Therefore, the `Tree` class has been added to Small Windows. A tree is made up of a set of nodes, among which, one is the root node. Each node holds a (possibly empty) list of child nodes:

Tree.h

```
namespace SmallWindows {
  template <class NodeType>
  class Tree {
    public:
      Tree();
      Tree(NodeType nodeValue,
          initializer_list<Tree<NodeType>*> childList = {});
      Tree(const Tree& tree);
      Tree& operator=(const Tree& tree);
      void Init(const Tree& tree);
      ~Tree();
```

The tree can be written to, and read from, a file stream or the clipboard:

```
bool WriteTreeToStream(ostream& outStream) const;
bool ReadTreeFromStream(istream& inStream);
void WriteTreeToClipboard(InfoList& infoList) const;
void ReadTreeFromClipboard(InfoList& infoList);
```

Each tree node holds a value that is inspected by the constant method and modified by the non-constant method:

```
NodeType NodeValue() const {return nodeValue;}
NodeType& NodeValue() {return nodeValue;}
```

The tree node also holds a list of child nodes, which is inspected by the constant method and modified by the non-constant method:

```cpp
    const DynamicList<Tree*>& ChildList() const
                                        {return childList;}
    DynamicList<Tree*>& ChildList() {return childList;}

  private:
    NodeType nodeValue;
    DynamicList<Tree*> childList;
};

template <class NodeType>
Tree<NodeType>::Tree() {
  // Empty.
}
```

The child list is an initializer list of tree nodes; it is empty by default:

```cpp
template <class NodeType>
Tree<NodeType>::Tree(NodeType nodeValue,
        initializer_list<Tree<NodeType>*> childList /* = {} */)
 :nodeValue(nodeValue) {
  for (Tree<NodeType>* childNodePtr : childList) {
    this->childList.PushBack(childNodePtr);
  }
}
```

The default constructor and the assignment operator call Init to do the actual initialization of the tree:

```cpp
template <class NodeType>
Tree<NodeType>::Tree(const Tree& tree) {
  Init(tree);
}

template <class NodeType>
Tree<NodeType>& Tree<NodeType>::operator=(const Tree& tree) {
  if (this != &tree) {
    Init(tree);
  }

  return *this;
}
```

```
template <class NodeType>
void Tree<NodeType>::Init(const Tree& tree) {
  nodeValue = tree.nodeValue;

  for (Tree* childPtr : tree.childList) {
    Tree* childClonePtr = new Tree(*childPtr);
    assert(childClonePtr != nullptr);
    childList.PushBack(childClonePtr);
  }
}
```

The destructor deletes the children recursively:

```
template <class NodeType>
Tree<NodeType>::~Tree() {
  for (Tree* childPtr : childList) {
    delete childPtr;
  }
}
```

The WriteTreeToStream method writes the node value and the number of children to the stream, and then calls itself recursively for each child:

```
template <class NodeType>
bool Tree<NodeType>::WriteTreeToStream(ostream& outStream)const{
  nodeValue.WriteTreeNodeToStream(outStream);

  int childListSize = childList.Size();
  outStream.write((char*) &childListSize, sizeof childListSize);

  for (Tree* childPtr : childList) {
    childPtr->WriteTreeToStream(outStream);
  }

  return ((bool) outStream);
}
```

The ReadTreeFromStream method reads the node value and the number of children from the stream, creates the children, and calls itself recursively for each child:

```
template <class NodeType>
bool Tree<NodeType>::ReadTreeFromStream(istream& inStream) {
  nodeValue.ReadTreeNodeFromStream(inStream);

  int childListSize;
  inStream.read((char*) &childListSize, sizeof childListSize);
```

```
      for (int count = 0; count < childListSize; ++count) {
        Tree* childPtr = new Tree();
        assert(childPtr != nullptr);
        childPtr->ReadTreeFromStream(inStream);
        childList.PushBack(childPtr);
      }

      return ((bool) inStream);
    }
```

The `WriteTreeToClipboard` and `ReadTreeFromClipboard` methods work in ways similar to `WriteTreeToStream` and `ReadTreeFromStream`:

```
    template <class NodeType>
    void Tree<NodeType>::WriteTreeToClipboard(InfoList& infoList)
                                                      const {
      nodeValue.WriteTreeNodeToClipboard(infoList);

      infoList.AddValue<int>( childList.Size());

      for (Tree* childPtr : childList) {
        childPtr->WriteTreeToClipboard(infoList);
      }
    }

    template <class NodeType>
    void Tree<NodeType>::ReadTreeFromClipboard(InfoList& infoList) {
      nodeValue.ReadTreeNodeFromClipboard(infoList);

      int childListSize;
      infoList.GetValue<int>(childListSize);

      for (int count = 0; count < childListSize; ++count) {
        Tree* childPtr = new Tree();
        assert(childPtr != nullptr);
        childPtr->ReadTreeFromClipboard(infoList);
        childList.PushBack(childPtr);
      }
    }
    };
```

The InfoList class

The `InfoList` class is an auxiliary class with template methods that stores information in a character list; information can be added and extracted; or written to, or read from, a buffer.

InfoList.h

```
namespace SmallWindows {
  class InfoList {
    public:
      template <class AlignType> void Align();
      template <class ListType>
        void AddValue(const ListType value);
      template <class ListType>
        void PeekValue(ListType& value, int index);
      template <class ListType> void GetValue(ListType& value);
      template <class CharType>
        void AddString(basic_string<CharType> text);
      template <class CharType>
        basic_string<CharType> GetString();
      void FromBuffer(const void* voidBuffer, int size);
      void ToBuffer(void* voidBuffer);
      int Size() const {return list.Size();}

    private:
      DynamicList<char> list;
  };
```

The `Align` function increases the list one byte at a time until the size of the align type is a divisor of the list size:

```
template <class AlignType>
void InfoList::Align() {
  int size = sizeof(AlignType);

  while ((list.Size() % size) > 0) {
    list.PushBack(0);
  }
}
```

The `AddValue` function adds a value of the template type by adding its value byte by byte to the list, while `GetValue` gets the value at the beginning of the list by extracting it byte by byte from the list:

```
template <class ListType>
void InfoList::AddValue(const ListType value) {
  int size = sizeof(ListType);
  const char* buffer = (char*) &value;

  for (int count = 0; count < size; ++count) {
    list.PushBack(*(buffer++));
  }
}
```

```
template <class ListType>
void InfoList::PeekValue(ListType& value, int index) {
  int size = sizeof(ListType);
  char* buffer = (char*) &value;

  for (int count = 0; count < size; ++count) {
    *(buffer++) = list[index + count];
  }
}

template <class ListType>
void InfoList::GetValue(ListType& value) {
  int size = sizeof(ListType);
  char* buffer = (char*) &value;

  for (int count = 0; count < size; ++count) {
    *(buffer++) = list.Front();
    list.Erase(0);
  }
}
```

The AddString function adds the characters of the text to the list along with a terminating
zero character, while GetString reads the text from the list until it encounters the
terminating zero character:

```
template <class CharType>
void InfoList::AddString(basic_string<CharType> text) {
  for (CharType c : text) {
    AddValue<CharType>(c);
  }

  AddValue<CharType>(0);
}

template <class CharType>
basic_string<CharType> InfoList::GetString() {
  bacic_string<CharType> text;

  CharType c, zero = (CharType) 0;
  while ((c = GetValue<CharType>()) != zero) {
    text.append(c);
  }

  return text;
}
};
```

InfoList.cpp

```
#include "SmallWindows.h"
```

The `FromBuffer` function adds each byte of the buffer to the list, while `ToBuffer` extracts and copies each byte of the list to the buffer:

```
void InfoList::FromBuffer(const void* voidBuffer, int size) {
  const char* charBuffer = (const char*) voidBuffer;

  for (int count = 0; count < size; ++count) {
    list.PushBack(*(charBuffer++));
  }
}

void InfoList::ToBuffer(void* voidBuffer) {
  char* charBuffer = (char*) voidBuffer;

  for (char c : list) {
    *(charBuffer++) = c;
  }
}
```

Strings

There are a small set of string functions:

- `CharPtrToGenericString`: This takes text as a `char` character pointer and returns the same text as a generic `String` object. Remember that the `String` class holds values of the `TCHAR` type, of which many are `char` or `wchar_t` depending on system settings.
- `Split`: This takes a string and returns a list of strings holding the space-separated words of the text.
- `IsNumeric`: This returns `true` if the text holds a numeric value.
- `Trim`: This removes spaces at the beginning and at the end of the text.
- `ReplaceAll`: This replaces one string with another string.
- `WriteStringToStream` and `ReadStringFromStream`: These write and read a string to and from a stream.
- `StartsWith` and `EndsWith`: These return `true` if the text starts or ends with the subtext.

String.h

```
namespace SmallWindows {
  extern String CharPtrToGenericString(char* text);
  extern vector<String> Split(String text, TCHAR c = TEXT(' '));
  extern bool IsNumeric(String text);
  extern String Trim(String text);
  void ReplaceAll(String& text, String from, String to);
  extern bool WriteStringToStream(const String& text,
                                  ostream& outStream);
  extern bool ReadStringFromStream(String& text,
                                   istream& inStream);
  extern bool StartsWith(String text, String part);
  extern bool EndsWith(String text, String part);
};
```

String.cpp

```
#include "SmallWindows.h"

namespace SmallWindows {
  String CharPtrToGenericString(char* text) {
    String result;

    for (int index = 0; text[index] != '\0'; ++index) {
      result += (TCHAR) text[index];
    }

    return result;
  }

  vector<String> Split(String text, TCHAR c /* = TEXT(' ') */) {
    vector<String> list;
    int spaceIndex = -1, size = text.size();

    for (int index = 0; index < size; ++index) {
      if (text[index] == c) {
        String word =
          text.substr(spaceIndex + 1, index - spaceIndex - 1);
        list.push_back(word);
        spaceIndex = index;
      }
    }

    String lastWord = text.substr(spaceIndex + 1);
    list.push_back(lastWord);
    return list;
  }
```

The `IsNumeric` method uses the `IStringStream` method to read the value of the string and compare the number of characters read with the length of the text. If all the characters of the text are read, the text will hold a numeric value and `true` will be returned:

```
    bool IsNumeric(String text) {
  IStringStream stringStream(Trim(text));
  double value;
  stringStream >> value;
  return stringStream.eof();
}

String Trim(String text) {
  while (!text.empty() && isspace(text[0])) {
    text.erase(0, 1);
  }

  while (!text.empty() && isspace(text[text.length() - 1])) {
    text.erase(text.length() - 1, 1);
  }

  return text;
}

void ReplaceAll(String& text, String from, String to) {
  int index, fromSize = from.size();

  while ((index = text.find(from)) != -1) {
    text.erase(index, fromSize);
    text.insert(index, to);
  }
}

bool WriteStringToStream(const String& text,ostream& outStream){
  int size = text.size();
  outStream.write((char*) &size, sizeof size);

  for (TCHAR tChar : text) {
    outStream.write((char*) &tChar, sizeof tChar);
  }

  return ((bool) outStream);
}

bool ReadStringFromStream(String& text, istream& inStream) {
  int size;
  inStream.read((char*) &size, sizeof size);
```

```
    for (int count = 0; count < size; ++count) {
      TCHAR tChar;
      inStream.read((char*) &tChar, sizeof tChar);
      text.push_back(tChar);
    }

    return ((bool) inStream);
  }

  bool StartsWith(String text, String part) {
    return (text.find(part) == 0);
  }

  bool EndsWith(String text, String part) {
    int index = text.rfind(part),
        difference = text.length() - part.length();
    return ((index != -1) && (index == difference));
  }
};
```

Summary

In this chapter, we studied the auxiliary classes used by Small Windows. In Chapter 13, *The Clipboard, Standard Dialogs, and Print Preview*, we will look into the registry, the clipboard, standard dialogs, and print preview.

13

The Registry, Clipboard, Standard Dialogs, and Print Preview

This chapter describes the implementation of:

- **The Registry:** A Windows database holding information between application executions.
- **The Clipboard:** A Windows database holding information that has been cut, copied, and pasted.
- **The standard dialogs**: This is used for saving and opening documents, for colors and fonts, and for printing.
- **Print preview:** In the `StandardDocument` class, it is possible to view the document on the screen as if it is being printed.

The registry

The static write, read, and erase methods in the `Registry` class operate on values of the `Integer`, `Double`, `Boolean`, and `String` types, as well as memory blocks in the Windows Registry.

Registry.h:

```
namespace SmallWindows {
  class Registry {
    public:
```

```
      static void WriteInteger(String key, const int value);
      static void WriteDouble(String key, const double value);
      static void WriteBoolean(String key, const bool value);
      static void WriteString(String key, const String text);

      static void WriteBuffer(String key, const void* buffer,
                              int size);

      static int ReadInteger(String key, const int defaultValue);
      static double ReadDouble(String key,
                               const double defaultValue);
      static bool ReadBoolean(String key,
                              const bool defaultValue);
      static String ReadString(String key,
                               const String defaultText);
      static void ReadBuffer(String key, void* buffer, int size,
                             const void* defaultBuffer);

      static void Erase(String key);
  };
};
```

Registry.cpp:

```
  #include "SmallWindows.h"

  namespace SmallWindows {
```

The global constant `RegistryFileName` holds the path to the registry domain of Small Windows:

```
  const String RegistryFileName = TEXT(".\\SmallWindows.ini");
```

The `WriteInteger`, `WriteDouble`, and `WriteBoolean` functions simply convert the value to a string and call `WriteString`:

```
  void Registry::WriteInteger(String key, const int intValue) {
    WriteBuffer(key, &intValue, sizeof intValue);
  }

  void Registry::WriteDouble(String key,
                             const double doubleValue) {
    WriteBuffer(key, &doubleValue, sizeof doubleValue);
  }

  void Registry::WriteBoolean(String key, const bool boolValue) {
    WriteBuffer(key, &boolValue, sizeof boolValue);
  }
```

The WriteString function calls the Win32 API function WritePrivateProfileString, which writes the string to the registry. All the C++ String objects need to be converted to zero-terminated C strings (char pointers) by c_str:

```
void Registry::WriteString(String key, const String text) {
  ::WritePrivateProfileString
      (Application::ApplicationName().c_str(),
        key.c_str(), text.c_str(), RegistryFileName.c_str());
}
```

The WriteBuffer function calls the Win32 API function WritePrivateProfileStruct, which writes the memory block to the registry:

```
void Registry::WriteBuffer(String key, const void* buffer,
                           int size) {
  ::WritePrivateProfileStruct
      (Application::ApplicationName().c_str(),
        key.c_str(), (void*) buffer, size,
        RegistryFileName.c_str());
}
```

The ReadInteger, ReadDouble, and ReadBoolean functions convert the default value to a string and call ReadString. The return value of ReadString is then converted and returned; _tstoi and _tstof are the generic versions of the standard C functions atoi and atof:

```
int Registry::ReadInteger(String key, const int defaultValue) {
  int intValue;
  ReadBuffer(key, &intValue, sizeof intValue, &defaultValue);
  return intValue;
}

double Registry::ReadDouble(String key,
                            const double defaultValue) {
  double doubleValue;
  ReadBuffer(key, &doubleValue, sizeof doubleValue,
            &defaultValue);
  return doubleValue;
}

bool Registry::ReadBoolean(String key, const bool defaultValue){
  bool boolValue;
  ReadBuffer(key, &boolValue, sizeof boolValue, &defaultValue);
  return boolValue;
}
```

The `ReadString` function calls the Win32 API function `GetPrivateProfileString`, which reads the string value to `text` and returns the number of characters read. If the number of read characters is greater than zero, the text is converted to a `string` object and returned; otherwise, the default text is returned:

```
String Registry::ReadString(String key,
                            const String defaultText) {
  TCHAR text[MAX_PATH];
  int count =
    ::GetPrivateProfileString
        (Application::ApplicationName().c_str(), key.c_str(),
          nullptr, text, MAX_PATH, RegistryFileName.c_str());
  return (count > 0) ? String(text) : defaultText;
}
```

The `ReadBuffer` function calls the Win32 API function `ReadPrivateProfileStruct`, which reads the memory block from the registry. If it returns zero, it means that the reading failed and the default buffer is copied to the buffer:

```
void Registry::ReadBuffer(String key, void* buffer, int size,
                          const void* defaultBuffer) {
  int result =
    ::GetPrivateProfileStruct
        (Application::ApplicationName().c_str(), key.c_str(),
          buffer, size, RegistryFileName.c_str());

  if (result == 0) {
    ::memcpy(buffer, defaultBuffer, size);
  }
}
```

When erasing a value from the registry, we call `WritePrivateProfileString` with a null pointer instead of a string, which erases the value:

```
void Registry::Erase(String key) {
  ::WritePrivateProfileString
      (Application::ApplicationName().c_str(),
        key.c_str(),nullptr,RegistryFileName.c_str());
  }
};
```

The Clipboard class

The `Clipboard` class is an interface to the global Windows Clipboard, which makes it possible to cut, copy, and paste information between different kinds of applications. There are two forms of clipboard operations: ASCII and Unicode text and generic (application-specific) information.

Clipboard.h:

```
namespace SmallWindows {
```

The formats for ASCII and Unicode lines are predefined.

```
enum {AsciiFormat = CF_TEXT, UnicodeFormat = CF_UNICODETEXT};
```

`Open` and `Close` open and close the clipboard. They return `true` if they succeed. `Clear` clears the clipboard when it has been opened. More specifically, it removes any potential information with the specified format and `Available` returns `true` if there is information with the format stored on the clipboard.

Information in different formats may be stored on the clipboard. For instance, when the user copies text in an application, the text may be stored on the clipboard as ASCII and Unicode text, as well as a more advanced application-specific format. `Available` returns `true` if information is stored on the clipboard with the specified format:

```
class Clipboard {
  public:
    static bool Open(const Window* windowPtr);
    static bool Close();
    static bool Clear();
    static bool Available(unsigned int format);
```

The `WriteText` and `ReadText` functions write and read a list of strings, while the `WriteGeneric` and `ReadGeneric` functions write and read generic information:

```
        template<int Format, class CharType>
        static bool WriteText(vector<String>& lineList);
        template<int Format, class CharType>
        static bool ReadText(vector<String>& lineList);

        static bool WriteGeneric(unsigned int format,
                                 InfoList& infoList);
        static bool ReadGeneric(unsigned int format,
                                InfoList& infoList);
    };
```

Clipboard.cpp:

```
#include "SmallWindows.h"

namespace SmallWindows {
```

The `Open`, `Close`, and `Clear` functions call the Win32 API functions `OpenClipboard`, `CloseClipboard`, and `EmptyClipboard`. They all return integer values; a non-zero value indicates success:

```
bool Clipboard::Open(const Window* windowPtr) {
  return (::OpenClipboard(windowPtr->WindowHandle()) != 0);
}

bool Clipboard::Close() {
  return (::CloseClipboard() != 0);
}

bool Clipboard::Clear() {
  return (::EmptyClipboard() != 0);
}
```

The `Available` function examines whether there is data with the format available on the clipboard by calling the Win32 API function `FormatAvailable`:

```
bool Clipboard::Available(unsigned int format) {
  return (::IsClipboardFormatAvailable(format) != 0);
}
```

ASCII and Unicode lines

As `WriteText` and `ReadText` are template methods, they are included in the header file instead of the implementation file. `WriteText` takes a list of generic strings and writes them in any format to the clipboard; `AsciiFormat` (one byte/character) and `UnicodeFormat` (two bytes/character) are predefined.

Clipboard.h:

```
template<int Format, class CharType>
bool Clipboard::WriteText(vector<String>& lineList) {
```

First, we need to find the buffer size, which we calculate by adding the total number of characters in the lines. We also add one for each line since each line also holds a terminating character. The terminating character is the return character ($\backslash r$) for each line, except the last line, which is terminated by a zero character ($\backslash 0$):

```
int bufferSize = 0;

for (String line : lineList) {
  bufferSize += line.size();
}

int listSize = lineList.size();
bufferSize += listSize;
```

When we have calculated the buffer size, we can call the Win32 API `GlobalAlloc` function to allocate the buffer in the global clipboard. We will later connect it to the format. We use the size of the template character type for the buffer:

```
HGLOBAL globalHandle =
  ::GlobalAlloc(GMEM_MOVEABLE, bufferSize * sizeof(CharType));
```

If the allocation succeeds, we receive a handle to the buffer. Since the clipboard and its buffers can be used by several processes at the same time, we need to lock the buffer by calling the Win32 API function `GlobalLock`. As long as the buffer is locked, no other processes can access it. When we lock the buffer we receive a pointer to it, which we can use when writing information to the buffer:

```
if (globalHandle != nullptr) {
  CharType* buffer = (CharType*) ::GlobalLock(globalHandle);

  if (buffer != nullptr) {
    int bufferIndex = 0;
```

We write the characters of the line to the buffer, and we add a `return` character unless it is the last line in the list:

```
for (int listIndex = 0; listIndex < listSize;++listIndex) {
  for (TCHAR tChar : lineList[listIndex]) {
    buffer[bufferIndex++] = (CharType) tChar;
  }

  if (listIndex < (listSize - 1)) {
    buffer[bufferIndex++] = (CharType) '\r';
  }
}
```

We add a zero character at the end of the buffer to mark its ending:

```
buffer[bufferIndex] = (CharType) '\0';
```

When the buffer has been loaded with information, we only need to unlock the buffer so that other processes can access it and associate the buffer with the format:

```
      ::GlobalUnlock(globalHandle);
      ::SetClipboardData(Format, globalHandle);
```

Finally, we return true to indicate that the operation succeeded:

```
      return true;
   }
}
```

If we were not able to allocate a buffer to write the line list to, we indicate that the operation did not succeeded by returning false:

```
   return false;
}
```

When reading the line list with ReadText, we use Format (which usually is AsciiFormat or UnicodeFormat) to receive a handle from the clipboard, which we then use to lock the buffer and receive its pointer, which in turn allows to us read from the buffer:

```
template<int Format,class CharType>
bool Clipboard::ReadText(vector<String>& lineList) {
   HGLOBAL globalHandle = ::GetClipboardData(Format);

   if (globalHandle != nullptr) {
     CharType* buffer = (CharType*) ::GlobalLock(globalHandle);

     if (buffer != nullptr) {
       String currentLine;
```

Note that we have to divide the buffer size with the template character type size (which may be greater than 1) in order to find the number of characters:

```
       int charCount =
         ::GlobalSize(globalHandle) / (sizeof(CharType));

       for (int count = 0; count < charCount; ++count) {
         CharType cChar = (*buffer++);
```

When we encounter a return character ($\backslash$r), the current line is finished; we add it to the line list and then clear it in order for it to be ready for the next line:

```
         switch (cChar) {
           case ((CharType) '\r') :
             lineList.push_back(currentLine);
             currentLine.clear();
             break;
```

When we encounter a return character ('$\backslash$0'), we also add the current line to the line list.

However, there is no need to clear the current line, since the zero character is the last character in the buffer:

```
case ((CharType) '\0') :
  lineList.push_back(currentLine);
  break;
```

If the character is neither a return nor a zero character, we add it to the current line. Note that we read a character of the template `CharType` type and convert it to a generic character of the `TCHAR` type:

```
default:
  currentLine += (TCHAR) cChar;
  break;
      }
    }
```

Finally, we unlock the buffer and return `true` to indicate that the operation succeeded:

```
    ::GlobalUnlock(globalHandle);
    return true;
  }
}
```

If we do not receive a buffer for the format, we return `false` to indicate that the operation did not succeed:

```
  return false;
  }
};
```

Generic information

The `WriteGeneric` function is actually simpler than the preceding `WriteText` function, since it does need to take line lists into consideration. We simply lock the clipboard buffer, write each byte in `infoList` to the buffer, unlock the buffer, and associate it with the format.

Clipboard.cpp:

```
bool Clipboard::WriteGeneric(unsigned int format,
                             InfoList& infoList) {
  int bufferSize = infoList.Size();
  HGLOBAL globalHandle = GlobalAlloc(GMEM_MOVEABLE, bufferSize);
```

```
      if (globalHandle != nullptr) {
        void* buffer = ::GlobalLock(globalHandle);
```

The `ToBuffer` object in the `InfoList` function writes its bytes to the buffer:

```
      if (buffer != nullptr) {
        infoList.ToBuffer(buffer);
        ::GlobalUnlock(globalHandle);
        ::SetClipboardData(format, globalHandle);
        return true;
      }
    }
```

If we do not manage to allocate the global buffer, we return `false` to indicate that the operation did not succeed:

```
    return false;
  }
```

The `ReadGeneric` function locks the clipboard buffer, writes each byte in the buffer to `infoList`, unlocks the buffer, and returns `true` to indicate that the operation succeeded:

```
  bool Clipboard::ReadGeneric(unsigned int format,
                             InfoList& infoList) {
    HGLOBAL globalHandle = ::GetClipboardData(format);

    if (globalHandle != nullptr) {
      void *buffer = ::GlobalLock(globalHandle);
      int bufferSize = ::GlobalSize(globalHandle);
      infoList.FromBuffer(buffer, bufferSize);
      ::GlobalUnlock(globalHandle);
      return true;
    }
```

If we do not receive the global handle, we return `false` to indicate that the operation did not succeed:

```
    return false;
  }
};
```

Standard dialogs

In Windows, it's possible to define **dialogs**. Unlike windows, dialogs are intended to be populated with controls such as buttons, boxes, and text fields. A dialog may be **modal**, which means that the other windows of the application become disabled until the dialog is closed. In the next chapter, we will look into how we build our own dialogs.

However, in this section, we will look into the Windows **standard dialogs** for saving and opening files, choosing fonts and colors, and printing. Small Windows supports standard dialogs by wrapping the Win32 API function, which provides us with the dialogs.

The Save dialog

The `SaveDialog` function displays the standard **Save** dialogs.

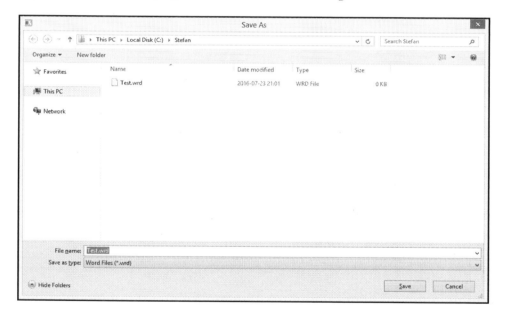

The `filter` parameters filter the file types to be displayed. Each file format is defined in two parts: the text displayed in the dialog and the default file suffix. The parts are separated by a zero character and the filter is terminated with two zero characters. For instance, consider the following:

```
Word Files (*.wrd)\0*.drw\0Text Files(*.txt)\0*.txt\0\0
```

The `fileSuffixList` parameter gives the allowed file suffixes and `saveFlags` holds the flags of the operation. The following two flags are available:

- `PromptBeforeOverwrite`: This flag is a warning message that is displayed if the file does already exist
- `PathMustExist`: This flag is an error message that is displayed if the path does not exist

StandardDialog.h:

```
namespace SmallWindows {
  class Window;
  class Graphics;

  class StandardDialog {
    public:
      enum SaveFlags {NoSaveFlag = 0,
                      PromptBeforeOverwrite = OFN_OVERWRITEPROMPT,
                      PathMustExist = OFN_PATHMUSTEXIST,
                      NormalSaveFlags = OFN_OVERWRITEPROMPT |
                                        OFN_PATHMUSTEXIST};

      static bool SaveDialog(Window* windowPtr, String& path,
                             const TCHAR* filter,
                             const vector<String> fileSuffixList,
                             StandardDialog::SaveFlags saveFlags =
                               NormalSaveFlags);
```

StandardDialog.cpp:

```
#include "SmallWindows.h"

namespace SmallWindows {
  bool StandardDialog::SaveDialog(Window* windowPtr, String& path,
                                  const TCHAR* filter,
                                  const vector<String> fileSuffixList,
                                  SaveFlags saveFlags
                                    /* = NormalSaveFlags */) {
```

The Win32 API `OPENFILENAME` structure `saveFileName` is loaded with appropriate values: `hwndOwner` is set to the window's handle, `hInstance` is set to the application instance handle, `lpstrFilter` is set to the `filter` parameter, `lpstrFile` is set to `pathBuffer`, which in turn holds the `path` parameter, and `Flags` is set to the `saveFlags` parameter:

```
OPENFILENAME saveFileName;
memset(&saveFileName, 0, sizeof saveFileName);

TCHAR pathBuffer[MAX_PATH];
wcscpy_s(pathBuffer, MAX_PATH, path.c_str());

saveFileName.lStructSize = sizeof saveFileName;
saveFileName.hwndOwner = windowPtr->WindowHandle();
saveFileName.hInstance = Application::InstanceHandle();
saveFileName.lpstrFilter = filter;
saveFileName.lpstrFile = pathBuffer;
saveFileName.nMaxFile = MAX_PATH;
saveFileName.Flags = saveFlags;

if (!fileSuffixList.empty()) {
  saveFileName.lpstrDefExt = fileSuffixList.front().c_str();
}
else {
  saveFileName.lpstrDefExt = nullptr;
}
```

When `saveFileName` is loaded, we call the Win32 API function `GetSaveFileName`, which displays the standard **Save** dialog and returns a non-zero value if the user terminates the dialog by clicking on the **Save** button or pressing the **Return** key. In that case, we set the `path` parameter to the chosen path, check whether the path ends with one of the suffixes in `fileSuffixList`, and return `true` if it does. If the path suffix is not present in the list, we display an error message and the saving process starts over again. If the user cancels the process, `false` is returned. In fact, the only way for the user to finish the process is to choose a file with a suffix in the list or to cancel the dialog:

```
while (true) {
  if (::GetSaveFileName(&saveFileName) != 0) {
    path = pathBuffer;

    for (String fileWithSuffix : fileSuffixList) {
      if (EndsWith(path, TEXT(".") + fileWithSuffix)) {
        return true;
      }
    }

    windowPtr->MessageBox(TEXT("Undefined file suffix."));
  }
  else {
    return false;
  }
}
```

The Open dialog

The `OpenDialog` function displays the standard **Open** dialog.

The `filter` and `fileSuffixList` parameters work in the same way as in the preceding `SaveDialog` function. There are three flags available:

- `PromptBeforeCreate`: This flag displays a warning message if the file already exists
- `FileMustExist`: The opened file must exist
- `HideReadOnly`: This flag indicates that read-only files are hidden in the dialog

OpenDialog.h:

```
enum OpenFlags {NoOpenFlag = 0,
                PromptBeforeCreate = OFN_CREATEPROMPT,
                FileMustExist = OFN_FILEMUSTEXIST,
                HideReadOnly = OFN_HIDEREADONLY,
                NormalOpenFlags = OFN_CREATEPROMPT |
                                  OFN_FILEMUSTEXIST |
                                  OFN_HIDEREADONLY};
```

```
static bool OpenDialog(Window* windowPtr, String& path,
                       const TCHAR* filter,
                       const vector<String> fileSuffixList,
                       StandardDialog::OpenFlags openFlags =
                           NormalOpenFlags);
```

The implementation of `OpenDialog` is similar to the preceding `SaveDialog` function. We use the same `OPENFILENAME` structure; the only difference is that we call `GetOpenFileName` instead of `GetSaveFileName`.

OpenDialog.cpp:

```
bool StandardDialog::OpenDialog(Window* windowPtr, String& path,
                                const TCHAR* filter,
                                const vector<String> fileSuffixList,
                                StandardDialog::OpenFlags openFlags
                                    /*=NormalOpenFlags */) {
  OPENFILENAME openFileName;
  memset(&openFileName, 0, sizeof openFileName);

  TCHAR pathBuffer[MAX_PATH];
  wcscpy_s(pathBuffer, MAX_PATH, path.c_str());

  openFileName.lStructSize = sizeof openFileName;
  openFileName.hwndOwner = windowPtr->WindowHandle();
  openFileName.hInstance = Application::InstanceHandle();
  openFileName.lpstrFilter = filter;
  openFileName.lpstrFile = pathBuffer;
  openFileName.nMaxFile = MAX_PATH;
  openFileName.Flags = openFlags;

  if (!fileSuffixList.empty()) {
    openFileName.lpstrDefExt = fileSuffixList.front().c_str();
  }
  else {
    openFileName.lpstrDefExt = nullptr;
  }

  while (true) {
    if (::GetOpenFileName(&openFileName) != 0) {
      path = pathBuffer;

      for (String fileWithSuffix : fileSuffixList) {
        if (EndsWith(path, TEXT(".") + fileWithSuffix)) {
          return true;
        }
      }
```

```
            windowPtr->MessageBox(TEXT("Undefined file suffix."));
        }
        else {
            return false;
        }
    }
}
```

The Color dialog

The `ColorDialog` function displays a standard **Color** dialog.

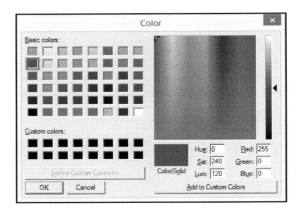

StandardDialog.h:

```
static COLORREF customColorArray[];
static bool ColorDialog(Window* windowPtr, Color& color);
```

The static `COLORREF` array `customColorArray` is used by the user in the color dialog to store the chosen colors. Since it is static, the `customColorArray` array is reused between dialog display sessions.

The `ColorDialog` function uses the Win32 API `CHOOSECOLOR` structure to initialize the dialog. The `hwndOwner` function is set to the window's handle, `rgbResult` is set to the color's `COLORREF` field, and `lpCustColors` is set to the custom color array. The `CC_RGBINIT` and `CC_FULLOPEN` flags initialize the dialog with the given color so that it is fully extended.

StandardDialog.cpp:

```
COLORREF StandardDialog::customColorArray[16];

bool StandardDialog::ColorDialog(Window* windowPtr,
                                 Color& color) {
  CHOOSECOLOR chooseColor;
  chooseColor.lStructSize = sizeof chooseColor;
  chooseColor.hwndOwner = windowPtr->WindowHandle();
  chooseColor.hInstance = nullptr;
  chooseColor.rgbResult = color.ColorRef();
  chooseColor.lpCustColors = customColorArray;
  chooseColor.Flags = CC_RGBINIT | CC_FULLOPEN;
  chooseColor.lCustData = 0;
  chooseColor.lpfnHook = nullptr;
  chooseColor.lpTemplateName = nullptr;
```

The Win32 `ChooseColor` function displays the **Color** dialog and returns a non-zero value if the user terminates the dialog by clicking on the **OK** button. In that case, we set the chosen color and return `true`:

```
if (::ChooseColor(&chooseColor) != 0) {
  color.ColorRef() = chooseColor.rgbResult;
  return true;
}
```

If the user cancels the dialog, we return `false`:

```
  return false;
}
```

The Font dialog

The `FontDialog` function displays a standard **Font** dialog.

StandardDialog.h:

```
static bool FontDialog(Window* windowPtr, Font& font);
```

FontDialog.cpp:

```
bool StandardDialog::FontDialog(Window* windowPtr, Font& font) {
  LOGFONT logFont = font.LogFont();
```

The Win32 API CHOOSEFONT structure `chooseFont` is loaded with appropriate values. The `lpLogFont` object is set to the font's LOGFONT field and `rgbColors` is set to the color's COLORREF field:

```
CHOOSEFONT chooseFont;
memset(&chooseFont, 0, sizeof chooseFont);

chooseFont.lStructSize = sizeof(CHOOSEFONT);
chooseFont.hInstance = Application::InstanceHandle();
chooseFont.hwndOwner = windowPtr->WindowHandle();
chooseFont.Flags = CF_INITTOLOGFONTSTRUCT |
                   CF_SCREENFONTS | CF_EFFECTS;
chooseFont.lpLogFont = &logFont;
chooseFont.rgbColors = font.FontColor().ColorRef();
```

The Win32 `ChooseFont` function displays the **Font** dialog and returns a non-zero value if the user clicks on the **OK** button. In that case, we set the chosen font and color and return `true`:

```
if (::ChooseFont(&chooseFont) != 0) {
  font.LogFont() = logFont;
  font.FontColor() = Color(chooseFont.rgbColors);
  return true;
}
```

If the user cancels the dialog, we return `false`:

```
  return false;
}
```

The Print dialog

The `PrintDialog` function displays a standard**Print** dialog.

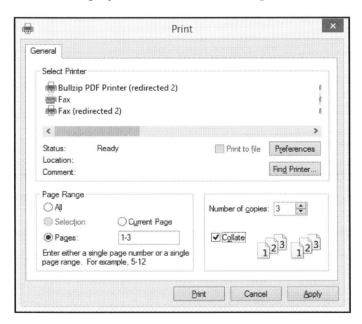

If the user clicks on the **Print** button, the chosen print settings are saved in the `PrintDialog` parameters:

PrintDialog.h:

```
        static Graphics* PrintDialog(Window* parentPtr,
                                     int totalPages,
                                     int& firstPage, int& lastPage,
                                     int& copies, bool& sorted);
    };
};
```

The `PrintDialog` function loads the Win32 API `PRINTDLG` structure `printDialog` with appropriate values, `nFromPage` and `nToPage` are set to the first and last page to be printed (whose default values are 1 and the number of pages respectively), `nMaxPage` is set to the number of pages, and `nCopies` is set to 1 (the default value).

PrintDialog.cpp:

```
Graphics* StandardDialog::PrintDialog(Window* parentPtr,
                                      int totalPages,
                                      int& firstPage, int& lastPage,
                                      int& copies, bool& sorted) {
    PRINTDLG printDialog;
    memset(&printDialog, 0, sizeof printDialog);
    printDialog.lStructSize = sizeof printDialog;
    printDialog.hwndOwner = parentPtr->WindowHandle();
    printDialog.hDevMode = nullptr;
    printDialog.hDevNames = nullptr;
    printDialog.hDC = nullptr;
    printDialog.Flags = PD_ALLPAGES | PD_COLLATE |
                        PD_RETURNDC | PD_NOSELECTION;
    printDialog.nFromPage = 1;
    printDialog.nToPage = totalPages;
    printDialog.nMinPage = 1;
    printDialog.nMaxPage = totalPages;
    printDialog.nCopies = 1;
    printDialog.hInstance = nullptr;
    printDialog.lCustData = 0L;
    printDialog.lpfnPrintHook = nullptr;
    printDialog.lpfnSetupHook = nullptr;
    printDialog.lpPrintTemplateName = nullptr;
    printDialog.lpSetupTemplateName = nullptr;
    printDialog.hPrintTemplate = nullptr;
    printDialog.hSetupTemplate = nullptr;
```

The Win32 API function `PrintDlg` displays the standard print dialog and returns a non-zero value if the user finishes the dialog by pressing the **Print** button. In that case, the first and last page to be printed, the number of copies, and whether the copies will be sorted are stored in the parameters, and the pointer to the `Graphics` object to be used when printing is created and returned.

If the user has chosen a page interval, we use the `nFromPage` and `nToPage` fields; otherwise, all pages are selected and we use the `nMinPage` and `nMaxPage` fields to set the first and last page to be printed:

```
if (::PrintDlg(&printDialog) != 0) {
  bool pageIntervalSelected =
    ((printDialog.Flags & PD_SELECTION) != 0);

  if (pageIntervalSelected) {
    firstPage = printDialog.nFromPage;
    lastPage = printDialog.nToPage;
  }
  else {
    firstPage = printDialog.nMinPage;
    lastPage = printDialog.nMaxPage;
  }
```

If the `PD_COLLATE` flags is present, the user has chosen to sort the pages:

```
  copies = printDialog.nCopies;
  sorted = (printDialog.Flags & PD_COLLATE) != 0;
```

Finally, we create and return a pointer to the `Graphics` object to be used when painting to the printer.

```
  return (new Graphics(parentPtr, printDialog.hDC));
}
```

If the user terminates the dialog by pressing the **Cancel** button, we return null:

```
  return nullptr;
  }
};
```

Print preview

The `PrintPreviewDocument` class displays the pages of the document parent window. The `OnKeyDown` method closes the document when the user presses the *Esc* key. The `OnSize` method adjusts the physical size of the page so that the page always fits inside the window. The `OnVerticalScroll` method shifts the pages when the user scrolls up or down, and `OnPaint` calls `OnPrint` of the parent document for each page.

PrintPreviewDocument.h:

```
namespace SmallWindows {
  class PrintPreviewDocument : Document {
    public:
      PrintPreviewDocument(StandardDocument* parentDocument,
                  int page = 1, Size pageSize = USLetterPortrait);
      bool OnKeyDown(WORD key, bool shiftPressed,
                  bool controlPressed);
```

The OnSize function is overridden only to neutralize its functionality in Document. In Document, OnSize modifies the scroll bars, but we do not want that to happen in this class:

```
.         void OnSize(Size clientSize) {/* Empty. */}
          void OnVerticalScroll(WORD flags, WORD thumbPos = 0);
          void OnPaint(Graphics& graphics) const;
```

The page field holds the current page number and totalPages holds the total number of pages:

```
    private:
      void SetHeader();
      int page, totalPages;
  };
};
```

PrintPreviewDocument.cpp

```
#include "SmallWindows.h"
```

The constructor sets the page and totalPages fields to appropriate values.

```
namespace SmallWindows {
  PrintPreviewDocument::PrintPreviewDocument
    (StandardDocument* parentDocument, int totalPages /* = 1 */,
     Size pageSize/* = USLetterPortrait */)
   :Document(PreviewCoordinate, pageSize, parentDocument),
    page(1),
    totalPages(totalPages) {
```

The horizontal scroll bar is always set to the width of the window, which means that the user cannot change its setting:

```
    SetHorizontalScrollPosition(0);
    SetHorizontalScrollPageWidth(pageSize.Width());
    SetHorizontalScrollTotalWidth(pageSize.Width());
```

The vertical scroll bar is set to match the number of pages of the document, and the scroll thumb corresponds to one page:

```
  SetVerticalScrollPosition(0);
  SetVerticalScrollPageHeight(pageSize.Height());
  SetVerticalScrollTotalHeight(totalPages * pageSize.Height());

  SetHeader();
  ShowWindow(true);
}
```

The header displays the current and total number of pages:

```
void PrintPreviewDocument::SetHeader() {
  SetName(TEXT("Print Preview: Page ") + to_String(page) +
          TEXT(" out of ") + to_String(totalPages));
}
```

Keyboard input

The OnKeyDown function is called when the user presses a key. If they press the *Esc* key, the preview window is closed and destroyed, and the input focus is returned to the main window of the application. If they press the *Home, End, Page Up,* or *Page Down* keys or the up and down arrow keys, OnVerticalScroll is called to take the appropriate action:

```
bool PrintPreviewDocument::OnKeyDown
      (WORD key, bool shiftPressed, bool controlPressed) {
  switch (key) {
    case KeyEscape: {
        Window* parentWindow = ParentWindowPtr();
        ::CloseWindow(WindowHandle());
        parentWindow->SetFocus();
      }
      break;

    case KeyHome:
      OnVerticalScroll(SB_TOP);
      break;

    case KeyEnd:
      OnVerticalScroll(SB_BOTTOM);
      break;

    case KeyUp:
    case KeyPageUp:
      OnVerticalScroll(SB_LINEUP);
      break;
```

```
      case KeyDown:
      case KeyPageDown:
        OnVerticalScroll(SB_LINEDOWN);
        break;
    }
```

We return `true` to indicate that the keyboard input has been used:

```
    return true;
  }
```

Scroll bar

The `OnVerticalScroll` function is called when the user scrolls the vertical bar. If they click on the scroll bar itself, above or below the scroll thumb, the previous or next page is displayed. And if they drag the thumb to a new position, the corresponding page is calculated. The `SB_TOP` and `SB_BOTTOM` cases are included to accommodate the *Home* and *End* keys from the preceding `OnKeyDown` function rather than to accommodate any scroll movements; they set the page to the first or last page:

```
    void PrintPreviewDocument::OnVerticalScroll(WORD flags,
                                    WORD thumbPos /* = 0 */) {
      int oldPage = page;

      switch (flags) {
        case SB_LINEUP:
        case SB_PAGEUP:
          page = max(1, page - 1);
          break;

        case SB_LINEDOWN:
        case SB_PAGEDOWN:
          page = min(page + 1, totalPages);
          break;

        case SB_THUMBTRACK:
        case SB_THUMBPOSITION:
          page = (thumbPos / pageSize.Height()) + 1;
          break;

        case SB_TOP:
          page = 1;
          break;
```

```
case SB_BOTTOM:
  page = totalPages;
  break;
}
```

If the scroll movement has resulted in a new page, we set the header and the scroll bar position and invalidate and update the window:

```
if (oldPage != page) {
  SetHeader();
  SetVerticalScrollPosition((page - 1) * pageSize.Height());
  Invalidate();
  UpdateWindow();
  }
}
```

The `OnPaint` function in `PrintPreviewDocument` calls `OnPaint` in the parent standard document window in order to paint the contents of the preview window:

```
void PrintPreviewDocument::OnPaint(Graphics& graphics) const {
  StandardDocument* parentDocument =
    (StandardDocument*) ParentWindowPtr();
  parentDocument->OnPrint(graphics, page, 1, totalPages);
  }
};
```

Summary

In this chapter, we looked into the registry, the clipboard, standard dialogs, and print preview. In `Chapter 14`, *Dialogs, Controls, and Page Setup*, we will look into custom dialogs, controls, converters, and page setup.

14

Dialogs, Controls, and Page Setup

In this chapter, we look into the implementation of the following:

- **Custom dialogs**: The `Dialog` class is intended to be inherited by subclasses and equipped with controls.
- **Controls**: The `Control` class and its subclasses. There are controls for edit fields, check boxes, radio buttons, list boxes, and combo boxes.
- **Converters**: Between strings and other values. For instance, when the user inputs text that represents a numerical value, it is possible to add a converter that converts the text to a value, or gives an error message if the text does not hold a valid value.
- **Page Setup**: Where we extend the `Dialog` class. The dialog is used when setting page settings for a document of the `StandardDocument` class. It handles information for headers, footers, and margins.

Custom dialogs

The `Dialog` class handles a set of **controls**, which are added to the dialog by the `AddControl` method. For a subclass of the `Dialog` class, refer to `PageSetupDialog` in the last section of this chapter. The Dialog class provides a modal dialog, which means that all other windows in the application become disabled until the dialog is closed.

The user may navigate between controls with the *Tab* key and between radio buttons in the same group with the arrow keys. They can also use mnemonics to access controls.

Dialog.h

```
namespace SmallWindows {
```

The `dialogMap` field is used by `DialogProc` to look up the dialog receiving the messages:

```
extern map<HWND,Dialog*> dialogMap;
extern Font DialogFont;
```

The `Dialog` class is a subclass of `Window` even though it calls the default `Window` constructor, which does not call the Win32 API function `CreateWindowEx`. Instead, `DoModal` collects information about the dialog and its controls and calls the Win32 API function `DialogBoxIndirectParam`:

```
class Dialog : public Window {
  public:
    Dialog(String name, Point topLeft,
           Window* parentPtr = nullptr,
           WindowStyle style = OverlappedWindow,
           WindowStyle extendedStyle = NoStyle,
           Font font = DialogFont);
```

As the name implies, `DoModal` disables its parent window for as long as the dialog is visible. That is, until the user closes the dialog:

```
bool DoModal();
```

The destructor deletes all controls, which implies that a subclass to `Dialog` should add dynamically allocated controls to the dialog without deleting them:

```
~Dialog();
```

The `AddControl` method assigns an identity number to the control and adds it to `idMap`.

```
int AddControl(Control* controlPtr);
```

The `OnSize` function is called each time the user changes the size of the dialog, it iterates through the controls and adjusts their size so that they keep their size relative to the size of the dialog client area.

```
void OnSize(Size windowSize);
```

When the user presses the *Return* key `OnReturn` is called, and when they press the *Esc* key `OnEscape` is called. Their default behavior is to close the dialog and return control to `DoModal` with 1 and 0 as the return code; 1 is interpreted as `true` and 0 as `false`.

```
void OnReturn();
void OnEscape();
```

The `OnControlInit` method is intended to be overridden by subclasses and is called when the dialog is being initialized (when it receives the `WM_INITDIALOG` message).

```
virtual void OnDialogInit() {/* Empty. */}
```

The `TryClose` method is intended to be overridden by subclasses and its default behavior is to return `true`. The `OnClose` method is called when the user tries to close the dialog, and its default behavior is to call `TryClose` and close the dialog if it returns `true`, in which case `OnDestroy` is also called:

```
virtual bool TryClose() const {return true;}
virtual void OnClose();
virtual void OnDestroy() {/* Empty. */}
```

Each control is assigned an identity number when added to the dialog, which is mapped to a pointer to the control in `idMap`:

```
map<WORD,Control*> IdMap() const {return idMap;}
map<WORD,Control*>& IdMap() {return idMap;}

private:
    map<WORD,Control*> idMap;
```

The dialog has a header text, top-left position, font, regular style, and extended style, which are stored by the constructor and used by `DoModal` in the `DialogBoxIndirectParam` call. However, the size of the dialog is not a constructor parameter; instead, the size is based on the control dimensions:

```
String header;
Point topLeft;
Font font;
WindowStyle style;
WindowStyle extendedStyle;
```

The `leftMargin`, `maxWidth`, `topMargin`, and `maxHeight` fields are used when calculating the size of the dialog. The idea is that its size will be adjusted so that the left and right margins as well as the top and bottom margins for the closest control are equal:

```
int leftMargin, maxWidth, topMargin, maxHeight;
```

The first control is not assigned the identity number of 0, since it will cause confusion when handling messages if the control with identity 0 is a push button. Instead, we initialize `currentId` with 1000, and decrease its value with each new control. It is necessary to decrease the value in order for the *Tab* key to work correctly in the dialog:

```
int currentId = 1000;
```

When the dialog is initialized (by receiving the WM_INITDIALOG message), its size is stored in originalClientSize to be used by OnSize when calculating the size of the controls:

```
Size originalClientSize;
```

The DialogProc method is called every time the dialog receives a message. Unlike WindowProc, it will return TRUE if the message has been handled and does not need further processing. Moreover, it will not call DefWindowProc at the end; instead it will return FALSE if the message has not been handled:

```
    friend INT_PTR CALLBACK
      DialogProc(HWND windowHandle, UINT message,
                 WPARAM wordParam, LPARAM longParam);
  };
};
```

Dialog.cpp

```
#include "SmallWindows.h"

namespace SmallWindows {
  map<HWND,Dialog*> dialogMap;
```

The default dialog font is set to 12-point Times New Roman.

```
Font DialogFont(TEXT("Times New Roman"), 12);
```

The constructor calls the Window constructor, which sets the parent window pointer and does nothing else. That is, it does not call the Win32 API function CreateWindowEx. The header, topLeft, style, extendedStyle, and font fields are stored to be used by DoModal:

```
Dialog::Dialog(String header, Point topLeft,
               Window* parentPtr /*=nullptr*/,
               WindowStyle style /* = OverlappedWindow */,
               WindowStyle extendedStyle /* = NoStyle */,
               Font font /* = DialogFont */)
  :Window(parentPtr),
   header(header),
   topLeft(topLeft),
   style(style),
   extendedStyle(extendedStyle),
```

```
font(font) {
// Empty.
}
```

The `DoModal` function makes the dialog enter the modal state. That is, its parent window becomes disabled until the dialog is destroyed. But, it first loads information to `infoList`. The `AddValue` method is a template method of the `InfoList` class and adds values of different types to the list:

```
bool Dialog::DoModal() {
  InfoList infoList;
```

First, we need to add the value 1 in order to set the version of the dialog template we want to work with:

```
infoList.AddValue<WORD>(1);
```

The `0xFFFF` value indicates that we want to work with the extended dialog template:

```
infoList.AddValue<WORD>(0xFFFF);
```

The next word is intended for a help identity; however, we do not use it so we just set it to 0:

```
infoList.AddValue<DWORD>(0);
```

Then comes the extended and regular style. Besides the style sent to the constructor, we set the dialog to have a caption, a system menu, a modal frame, and a font. Due to the `DS_SETFONT` flag, we will later add information about the dialog font:

```
infoList.AddValue<DWORD>(extendedStyle);
infoList.AddValue<DWORD>(style | WS_CAPTION | WS_SYSMENU |
                        DS_MODALFRAME | DS_SETFONT);
```

The next value is the number of controls in the dialog, which is given by the size of `idMap`:

```
infoList.AddValue<WORD>(idMap.size());
```

The top-left position is given by the `topLeft` field:

```
infoList.AddValue<WORD>(topLeft.X());
infoList.AddValue<WORD>(topLeft.Y());
```

The size of the client area of the dialog is set by `maxWidth`, `leftMargin`, `maxHeight`, and `topMargin`, which has been calculated in `AddControl`. The width of the client area is the maximum width of the control set plus its left margin. In this way, we adjust the dialog to hold the controls with equal left and right margins as well as top and bottom margins to the closest control:

```
infoList.AddValue<WORD>(maxWidth + leftMargin);
infoList.AddValue<WORD>(maxHeight + topMargin);
```

The next two zeros indicate that we do not want to use a menu and that we use the default dialog `Windows` class:

```
infoList.AddValue<WORD>(0);
infoList.AddValue<WORD>(0);
```

Then, we set the header of the dialog. The `AddString` method is an `InfoList` template method that adds the string with a terminating 0 to the information list:

```
infoList.AddString<TCHAR>(header);
```

Finally, we set the font of the dialog. We extract the `LOGFONT` structure of the `Font` class and extract its size (`lfHeight`), whether it is bold (`lfWeight`) or italics, its character set (which is 0 since we do not use it), and the font name:

```
LOGFONT logFont = font.LogFont();
infoList.AddValue<WORD>((WORD) logFont.lfHeight);
infoList.AddValue<WORD>((WORD) logFont.lfWeight);
infoList.AddValue<BYTE>(logFont.lfItalic);
infoList.AddValue<BYTE>(logFont.lfCharSet);
infoList.AddString<TCHAR>(logFont.lfFaceName);
```

When the dialog information has been added to the information list, we call `AddControlInfo` for each control in order for the control information to be added to the list:

```
for (pair<WORD,Control*> entry : idMap) {
  Control* controlPtr = entry.second;
  controlPtr->AddControlInfo(infoList);
}
```

When the list has been fully loaded, we allocate a global buffer and load it with the list. The `ToBuffer` method copies the list into the buffer:

```
HGLOBAL globalHandle = ::GlobalAlloc(0, infoList.Size());
if (globalHandle != nullptr) {
  char* buffer = (char*) ::GlobalLock(globalHandle);

  if (buffer != nullptr) {
    infoList.ToBuffer(buffer);
```

We need the handle to the parent window, if present, and then we create the dialog by calling the Win32 API function `DialogBoxIndirectParam`, which will not return until the user closes the dialog. The last parameter is a pointer to the `Dialog` object that will be sent with the `WM_INITDIALOG` message. The return value stored in `result` is the second parameter to an `EndDialog` call:

```
HWND parentHandle = (parentPtr != nullptr) ?
                    parentPtr->WindowHandle() : nullptr;
INT_PTR result =
  ::DialogBoxIndirectParam(Application::InstanceHandle(),
            (DLGTEMPLATE*) buffer, parentHandle,
            DialogProc, (LPARAM) this);
::GlobalUnlock(globalHandle);
```

We return `true` if the result value does not equal 0:

```
      return (result != 0);
  }
}
```

If the global buffer allocation does not succeed, we return `false`:

```
    return false;
}
```

The destructor iterates through `idMap` and deletes each control of the dialog:

```
Dialog::~Dialog() {
  for (pair<WORD,Control*> entry : idMap) {
    Control* controlPtr = entry.second;
    delete controlPtr;
  }
}
```

The `AddControl` method adds a control to the dialog. If it is the first control to be added (`idMap` is empty), `leftMargin` and `topMargin` are set to the top-left corner of the control, and `maxWidth` and `maxHeight` are set to the top-left corner plus the control width or height. However, if it is not, the first control we need to compare is its top-left corner and size, with the current values, in order to find the margins and maximum size of the control set:

```
int Dialog::AddControl(Control* controlPtr) {
  Point topLeft = controlPtr->TopLeft();
  Size controlSize = controlPtr->GetSize();
```

```
    if (idMap.empty()) {
      leftMargin = topLeft.X();
      topMargin = topLeft.X();
      maxWidth = topLeft.X() + controlSize.Width();
      maxHeight = topLeft.Y() + controlSize.Height();
    }
    else {
      leftMargin = min(leftMargin, topLeft.X());
      topMargin = min(topMargin, topLeft.Y());
      maxWidth = max(maxWidth, topLeft.X() + controlSize.Width());
      maxHeight = max(maxHeight,topLeft.Y()+controlSize.Height());
    }
```

The identity number of the control is set to currentId, which is returned and decreased:

```
    idMap[currentId] = controlPtr;
    return currentId--;
}
```

The OnSize method compares the new size of the client area with its original size. The ratio between them is stored in factorPair:

```
void Dialog::OnSize(Size newClientSize) {
  pair<double, double> factorPair
    (((double) newClientSize.Width() /
    originalClientSize.Width()),
    ((double) newClientSize.Height() /
    originalClientSize.Height()));
```

The controls of idMap are iterated and the original size of each control is multiplied with factorPair, the ratio between the new and original client area size. In this way, the control will keep their sizes relative to the size of the dialog client area when the user changes the dialog size.

```
    for (pair<WORD,Control*> entry : idMap) {
      Control* controlPtr = entry.second;
      Rect originalRect = controlPtr->OriginalRect();
      controlPtr->SetWindowDeviceRect(factorPair * originalRect);
    }
}
```

The OnReturn method is called when the user presses the *Return* key, OnEscape is called when they press the *Esc* key, and OnClose is called when they close the dialog. The default behavior is to call TryClose and, if it returns true, call the Win32 API function EndDialog, which causes the DialogBoxIndirectParam call in DoModal to return the integer value given as the second parameter to EndDialog:

```
void Dialog::OnReturn() {
  if (TryClose()) {
    ::EndDialog(windowHandle, 1);
  }
}

void Dialog::OnEscape() {
  if (TryClose()) {
    ::EndDialog(windowHandle, 0);
  }
}

void Dialog::OnClose() {
  if (TryClose()) {
    ::EndDialog(windowHandle, 0);
  }
}
```

The `DialogProc` method is called each time the dialog receives a message. The first parameter is a handle to the dialog, which is mapped to a `Dialog` pointer by `dialogMap`:

```
INT_PTR CALLBACK DialogProc(HWND dialogHandle, UINT message,
                            WPARAM wordParam, LPARAM longParam){
  switch (message) {
```

The `WM_INITDIALOG` case is called when the dialog is created, but before it becomes visible. When the dialog was created by the `DialogBoxIndirectParam` method, the last parameter was a pointer to the encapsulating `Dialog` object. That pointer is given in the `longParam` parameter, it is translated into a pointer to `Dialog`, and added to `dialogMap`:

```
case WM_INITDIALOG: {
    Dialog* dialogPtr = (Dialog*) longParam;
    dialogMap[dialogHandle] = dialogPtr;
```

The Win32 API window handle of the dialog is assigned to `dialogHandle`, the original size of the client area is calculated and stored in `originalClientSize`, and `OnDialogInit` is called:

```
dialogPtr->WindowHandle() = dialogHandle;
dialogPtr->originalClientSize =
  dialogPtr->GetClientDeviceSize();
dialogPtr->OnDialogInit();
```

For each control in the dialog, its window handle is set by calling the Win32 API function `GetDlgItem`, which takes the dialog window handle and the control identity number, set by `AddControl`. Similar to the original client size of the dialog, the original size and position of the controls are also stored. Finally, `OnControlInit` is called for each control:

```
for (pair<WORD,Control*> entry : dialogPtr->IdMap()) {
  WORD controlId = entry.first;
  Control* controlPtr = entry.second;
  controlPtr->WindowHandle() =
    ::GetDlgItem(dialogHandle,controlId);
  controlPtr->OriginalRect() =
    controlPtr->GetWindowDeviceRect();
  controlPtr->OnControlInit(dialogPtr);
}
}
```

Since the message is handled, TRUE is returned:

```
return TRUE;
```

The WM_SIZE case is sent to the dialog each time its size has been changed. The width and height are stored in the lower and upper word of the `longParam` parameter. The `OnSize` method is called in order to handle the message:

```
case WM_SIZE: {
  Dialog* dialogPtr = dialogMap[dialogHandle];
  assert(dialogPtr != nullptr);
  Size clientSize =
    {LOWORD(longParam), HIWORD(longParam)};
  dialogPtr->OnSize(clientSize);
}
return TRUE;
```

The WM_CLOSE case is called when the user tries to close the dialog. The `OnClose` method is called to handle the message, which may or may not close the dialog:

```
case WM_CLOSE: {
  Dialog* dialogPtr = dialogMap[dialogHandle];
  assert(dialogPtr != nullptr);
  dialogPtr->OnClose();
}
return TRUE;
```

The WM_DESTROY case is called when the dialog is being destroyed. Unlike WM_CLOSE, there is no way to prevent the dialog from being destroyed. Since WM_DESTROY is the last message sent to the dialog, the dialog is removed from `dialogMap`:

```
case WM_DESTROY: {
   Dialog* dialogPtr = dialogMap[dialogHandle];
   dialogPtr->OnDestroy();
   dialogMap.erase(dialogHandle);
}
return TRUE;
```

The WM_COMMAND case is sent to the dialog when the user has performed some action with one of the controls. In cases where the action involves a control, its identity number is stored in the lower word of wordParam:

```
case WM_COMMAND: {
   Dialog* dialogPtr = dialogMap[dialogHandle];
   WORD controlId = LOWORD(wordParam);
```

If the identity number is IDOK or IDCANCEL, the user has pressed the *Return* or *Esc* key:

```
switch (controlId) {
  case IDOK:
    dialogPtr->OnReturn();
    break;

  case IDCANCEL:
    dialogPtr->OnEscape();
    break;
```

If the identity number is not IDOK or IDCANCEL, we look up the control with idMap and the notification code in the higher word of wordParam. The notification code may have the same value as IDOK or IDCANCEL, which is why we use this somewhat cumbersome construction to handle the code:

```
default: {
   Control* controlPtr =
     dialogPtr->IdMap()[controlId];
   WORD notificationCode = HIWORD(wordParam);
```

When a control gains or loses input focus, OnGainFocus or OnLoseFocus is called; when they change the input text of a text field, OnChange is called; when they change the selection of a combo box, list box, or multiple list box, OnSelect is called; and when they click on a push button, checkbox, or radio button, OnClick is called:

```
switch (notificationCode) {
  case EN_SETFOCUS:
    controlPtr->OnGainFocus(dialogPtr);
    break;
```

```
                     case EN_KILLFOCUS:
                       controlPtr->OnLoseFocus(dialogPtr);
                       break;

                     case EN_CHANGE:
                       controlPtr->OnChange(dialogPtr);
                       break;

                     case CBN_SELCHANGE:
                       controlPtr->OnSelect(dialogPtr);
                       break;

                     case BN_CLICKED:
                       controlPtr->OnClick(dialogPtr);
                       break;
                   }
                 }
               }
             }
```

When the command message has been handled, there is no need to further process it. Therefore, we return `true`:

```
             return TRUE;
           }
```

If the message has not been handled, we returns `false` in order for the message to be further processed by the Windows system:

```
           return FALSE;
         }
       };
```

Controls

Here is the Small Windows control hierarchy:

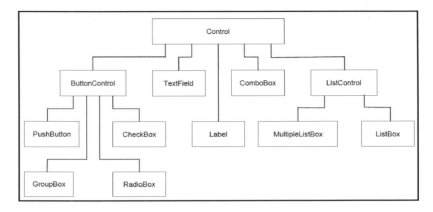

Control.h

```
namespace SmallWindows {
  class Dialog;
```

The constructor sends the parent window pointer to the `Window` constructer and stores the other values until it is added to the dialog information list by `AddControlInfo`:

```
class Control : public Window {
  public:
    Control(Dialog* parentPtr, Point topLeft, Size controlSize,
            String className, String text, int style);
    void AddControlInfo(InfoList& infoList) const;

    Point TopLeft() const {return topLeft;}
    Size GetSize() const {return controlSize;}
```

The following methods are intended to be overridden by subclasses and are by default empty:

```
        virtual void OnControlInit(Dialog* dialogPtr) {/* Empty. */}
        virtual void OnGainFocus(Dialog* dialogPtr) {/* Empty. */}
        virtual void OnLoseFocus(Dialog* dialogPtr) {/* Empty. */}
        virtual void OnChange(Dialog* dialogPtr) {/* Empty. */}
        virtual void OnSelect(Dialog* dialogPtr)  {/* Empty. */}
        virtual void OnClick(Dialog* dialogPtr) {/* Empty. */}
```

The rectangle holding the original size and position is set by `Dialog` when it receives the
`MW_INITDIALOG` message:

```
Rect OriginalRect() const {return originalRect;}
Rect& OriginalRect() {return originalRect;}

private:
  Rect originalRect;
```

Each control has an identity number, given by `AddControl` in `Dialog`. It has a regular
style; the extended style is always 0. The style, top-left corner and control size, class name,
and control text are added to the information list when `DoModal` in `Dialog` calls
`AddControlInfo`:

```
    int controlId, style;
    Point topLeft;
    Size controlSize;
    String className;
    String text;
  };
};
```

Control.cpp

```
#include "..\\SmallWindows.h"
```

The constructor calls `AddControl` for its parent dialog to add the control to the dialog and
to receive the control's identity number:

```
namespace SmallWindows {
  Control::Control(Dialog* parentPtr, Point topLeft,
                   Size controlSize, String className,
                   String text, int style)
   :Window(parentPtr),
    topLeft(topLeft),
    controlSize(controlSize),
    className(className),
    text(text),
    style(style) {
    controlId = parentPtr->AddControl(this);
  }
```

The `AddControlInfo` method, which is called by `DoModal` in `Dialog`, adds the
information of the control. First, we need to align the information list with the size of a
double word (4 bytes):

```
void Control::AddControlInfo(InfoList& infoList) const {
  infoList.Align<DWORD>();
```

The help identity and extended style are always 0:

```
infoList.AddValue<DWORD>(0);
infoList.AddValue<DWORD>(0);
```

The style is extended with the child and visible flags, indicating that the control is a child window of the dialog and that it becomes visible when the dialog becomes visible:

```
infoList.AddValue<DWORD>(WS_CHILD | WS_VISIBLE | style);
```

The top-left corner and size of the control are given in **dialog units,** which are based on the dialog font and are translated into device units:

```
infoList.AddValue<WORD>(topLeft.X());
infoList.AddValue<WORD>(topLeft.Y());
infoList.AddValue<WORD>(controlSize.Width());
infoList.AddValue<WORD>(controlSize.Height());
```

The control identity number is given in order to identify the control when the user performs some action, such as clicking on a button or selecting a list item:

```
infoList.AddValue<DWORD>(controlId);
```

Each control has a class name, which is button, list, combo, static (label), or edit (text field), and text, which is the text of a text field or the label of a box or button, but is ignored for list and combo boxes:

```
infoList.AddString<TCHAR>(className);
infoList.AddString<TCHAR>(text);
```

Finally, it is possible to send extra data with the control. However, we pass on that opportunity and just send 0:

```
    infoList.AddValue<WORD>(0);
  }
};
```

The button controls

There are four kinds of button controls: group box, push button, checkbox, and radio button. The checkbox and radio button can be checked; the `Check` and `IsChecked` methods are defined in `ButtonControl`.

ButtonControl.h

```
namespace SmallWindows {

  class ButtonControl : public Control {
    public:
      ButtonControl(Dialog* parentPtr, Point topLeft,
                    Size controlSize, String text, int style);

    protected:
      void Check(bool check) const;
      bool IsChecked() const;
  };
};
```

ButtonControl.cpp

```
#include "..\\SmallWindows.h"

namespace SmallWindows {
  ButtonControl::ButtonControl(Dialog* parentPtr, Point topLeft,
                    Size controlSize, String text, int style)
   :Control(parentPtr, topLeft, controlSize,
            TEXT("button"), text, style) {
    // Empty.
  }
```

We send the `BM_SETCHECK` message to a check, a checkbox, or a radio button and the `BM_GETCHECK` message to find out whether it is checked:

```
  void ButtonControl::Check(bool check) const {
    ::SendMessage(windowHandle, BM_SETCHECK, check ? 1 : 0, 0);
  }

  bool ButtonControl::IsChecked() const {
    return (::SendMessage(windowHandle, BM_GETCHECK, 0, 0) != 0);
  }
};
```

A group box is quite simple; it encapsulates a set of other controls and has no functionality besides its graphical appearance.

GroupBox.h

```
namespace SmallWindows {
  class GroupBox : public ButtonControl {
    public:
      GroupBox(Dialog* parentPtr, Point topLeft,
              Size controlSize, String text);
  };
};
```

GroupBox.cpp

```
#include "..\\SmallWindows.h"

namespace SmallWindows {
  GroupBox::GroupBox(Dialog* parentPtr, Point topLeft,
                     Size controlSize, String text)
   :ButtonControl(parentPtr, topLeft, controlSize,
                  text, BS_GROUPBOX) {
    // Empty.
  }
};
```

The clickListener constructor parameter is a listener called when the user clicks on the button. The OnClick method is overridden from Control.

PushButton.h

```
namespace SmallWindows {
  class PushButton : public ButtonControl {
    public:
      PushButton(Dialog* parentPtr, Point topLeft,
                Size controlSize, String text,
                VoidListener clickListener,
                bool default = false);
      void OnClick(Dialog* dialogPtr);

    private:
      VoidListener clickListener;
  };
};
```

PushButton.cpp

```cpp
#include "..\\SmallWindows.h"

namespace SmallWindows {
  PushButton::PushButton(Dialog* parentPtr, Point topLeft,
                         Size controlSize, String text,
                         VoidListener clickListener,
                         bool default /* = false */)
   :ButtonControl(parentPtr, topLeft, controlSize, text,
                  WS_BORDER | WS_GROUP| WS_TABSTOP |
                  (default ? BS_DEFPUSHBUTTON : BS_PUSHBUTTON)),
    clickListener(clickListener) {
    // Empty.
  }

  void PushButton::OnClick(Dialog* dialogPtr) {
    clickListener(dialogPtr);
  }
};
```

A checkbox works independently of other checkboxes. The `checkPtr` parameter is a pointer to a `Boolean` value set to `true` or `false`, depending on whether the checkbox is checked.

CheckBox.h

```cpp
namespace SmallWindows {
  class CheckBox : public ButtonControl {
    public:
      CheckBox(Dialog* parentPtr, Point topLeft,
               Size controlSize, String text, bool* checkPtr);

    private:
      void OnControlInit(Dialog* dialogPtr);
      void OnClick(Dialog* dialogPtr);
      bool* checkPtr;
  };
};
```

CheckBox.cpp

```cpp
#include "..\\SmallWindows.h"

namespace SmallWindows {
  CheckBox::CheckBox(Dialog* parentPtr, Point topLeft,
                     Size controlSize, String text, bool* checkPtr)
```

```
    :ButtonControl(parentPtr, topLeft, controlSize, text,
                   BS_AUTOCHECKBOX | WS_GROUP | WS_TABSTOP),
      checkPtr(checkPtr) {
    }
```

The `OnControlInit` method is overridden from `Control` and checks the box in accordance with the value that `checkPtr` points at. `OnClick` is also overridden from `Control` and sets the value to `true` if the box is checked:

```
    void CheckBox::OnControlInit(Dialog* dialogPtr) {
      Check(*checkPtr);
    }

    void CheckBox::OnClick(Dialog* dialogPtr) {
      *checkPtr = IsChecked();
    }
};
```

A radio button is intended to work in a group with other radio buttons, with exactly one button checked at the time. When the user checks one button in the group, it gets checked and the previously checked box get unchecked. Each radio button in the group has a zero-based index; `indexPtr` points to an integer value, common to all radio buttons in the group, which is set to the index of the button currently checked.

RadioButton.h

```
namespace SmallWindows {
  class RadioButton : public ButtonControl {
    public:
      RadioButton(Dialog* parentPtr, Point topLeft, Size size,
                  String text, int* indexPtr, int index);
      void OnControlInit(Dialog* dialogPtr);
      void OnClick(Dialog* dialogPtr);

    private:
      int *indexPtr, index;
  };
};
```

RadioButton.cpp

```
#include "..\\SmallWindows.h"
```

The constructor sends the group and tab stop styles to the `Control` constructor if the index is 0, since the first button is the first button in the group. All buttons in the group will not be accessed by the *Tab* key, but only the first button. The `group` style indicates that the button starts a group and all additional radio buttons are considered members of the group, until another button with the `group` style is added:

```
namespace SmallWindows {
  RadioButton::RadioButton(Dialog* parentPtr, Point topLeft,
                           Size size, String text, int* indexPtr,
                           int index)
   :ButtonControl(parentPtr, topLeft, size, text,
                  BS_AUTORADIOBUTTON |
                  ((index == 0) ? (WS_GROUP | WS_TABSTOP) : 0)),
    indexPtr(indexPtr),
    index(index) {
    // Empty.
  }
```

The radio button is checked if it has the same index as the value that `indexPtr` points at, and the value is set to the index of the button that is checked:

```
  void RadioButton::OnControlInit(Dialog* dialogPtr) {
    Check((*indexPtr) == index);
  }

  void RadioButton::OnClick(Dialog* dialogPtr) {
    *indexPtr = index;
  }
};
```

List controls

There are two kinds of list box: single list box and multiple list box. The single list box selects exactly one item at a time, and the multiple list box selects one or several (or none at all) items at the same time. The constructor takes a string list that is loaded to the list box by `LoadList`.

ListControl.h

```
namespace SmallWindows {
  class ListControl : public Control {
    public:
      ListControl(Dialog* parentPtr, Point topLeft,
                  Size controlSize, int style,
                  list<String> textList);

    protected:
      void LoadList() const;
```

```
    private:
      list<String> textList;
  };
};
```

ListControl.cpp

```
#include "..\\SmallWindows.h"

namespace SmallWindows {
  ListControl::ListControl(Dialog* parentPtr, Point topLeft,
                           Size controlSize, int style,
                           list<String> textList)
   :Control(parentPtr, topLeft, controlSize,
            TEXT("listbox"), TEXT(""), style),
    textList(textList) {
    // Empty.
  }
```

The `LoadList` method adds the item text in `textList` to the (single or multiple) list box by calling the `LB_ADDSTRING` message:

```
  void ListControl::LoadList() const {
    for (String text : textList) {
      ::SendMessage(windowHandle, LB_ADDSTRING,
                    0, (LPARAM) text.c_str());
    }
  }
};
```

A (single) list box is a box holding a list of visible items, as opposed to a combo box where the items are dropped down. If necessary, the list can be scrolled. Only one item can be selected at a time, as opposed to the multiple list. Similar to the radio box group, the constructor takes the `indexPtr` pointer pointing at an integer value holding the zero-based index of the currently selected item. Moreover, the constructor also takes a string list that is loaded into the list box by `LoadList` in `ListControl`.

ListBox.h

```
namespace SmallWindows {
  class ListBox : public ListControl {
    public:
      ListBox(Dialog* parentPtr, Point topLeft, Size controlSize,
              initializer_list<String> textList, int* indexPtr);
      void OnControlInit(Dialog* dialogPtr);
      void OnSelect(Dialog* dialogPtr);
```

```
      private:
        void SelectList(int index) const;
        int GetListSelection() const;
        int* indexPtr;
    };
};
```

ListBox.cpp

```cpp
#include "..\\SmallWindows.h"

namespace SmallWindows {
  ListBox::ListBox(Dialog* parentPtr, Point topLeft,
              Size controlSize, initializer_list<String>  textList,
              int* indexPtr)
    :ListControl(parentPtr, topLeft, controlSize, WS_VSCROLL |
                WS_BORDER | LBS_NOTIFY | WS_GROUP | WS_TABSTOP,
                textList),
    indexPtr(indexPtr) {
    // Empty.
  }

  void ListBox::OnControlInit(Dialog* dialogPtr) {
    LoadList();
    SelectList(*indexPtr);
  }

  void ListBox::OnSelect(Dialog* dialogPtr) {
    *indexPtr = GetListSelection();
  }
```

We send the LB_SETCURSEL message to select an item and LB_GETCURSEL to get the index of the currently selected item:

```cpp
  void ListBox::SelectList(int index) const {
    ::SendMessage(windowHandle, LB_SETCURSEL, index, 0);
  }

  int ListBox::GetListSelection() const {
    return ::SendMessage(windowHandle, LB_GETCURSEL, 0, 0);
  }
};
```

A multiple list box is a list box where the user can select more than one value, or no value at all; therefore, the indexSetPtr parameter is a pointer to a set of indexes rather than a pointer to one index.

MultipleListBox.h

```
namespace SmallWindows {
  class MultipleListBox : public ListControl {
    public:
      MultipleListBox(Dialog* parentPtr, Point topLeft,
              Size controlSize, initializer_list<String> textList,
              set<int>* indexSetPtr);
      void OnControlInit(Dialog* dialogPtr);
      void OnSelect(Dialog* dialogPtr);

    private:
      void SelectMultiple(set<int>& indexSet) const;
      set<int> GetSelectionMultiple() const;
      set<int>* indexSetPtr;
  };
};
```

MultipleListBox.cpp

```
#include "..\\SmallWindows.h"

namespace SmallWindows {
  MultipleListBox::MultipleListBox(Dialog* parentPtr,
              Point topLeft, Size controlSize,
              initializer_list<String> textList,
              set<int>* indexSetPtr)
    :ListControl(parentPtr, topLeft, controlSize, LBS_MULTIPLESEL |
                WS_VSCROLL | WS_BORDER | LBS_NOTIFY | WS_GROUP |
                WS_TABSTOP, textList),
     indexSetPtr(indexSetPtr) {
    // Empty.
  }

  void MultipleListBox::OnControlInit(Dialog* dialogPtr) {
    LoadList();
    SelectMultiple(*indexSetPtr);
  }

  void MultipleListBox::OnSelect(Dialog* dialogPtr) {
    *indexSetPtr = GetSelectionMultiple();
  }
```

When the user selects 0 or several values in the multiple list, we iterate through the indexes and send the LB_SETSEL message for each index with a Boolean value indicating whether its item will be set:

```
void MultipleListBox::SelectMultiple(set<int>& indexSet) const {
  int size = ::SendMessage(windowHandle, LB_GETCOUNT, 0, 0);
  for (int index = 0; index < size; ++index) {
    BOOL selected = (indexSet.count(index) > 0) ? TRUE : FALSE;
    ::SendMessage(windowHandle, LB_SETSEL, selected, index);
  }
}
```

When checking which values are currently selected, we send the LB_GETSEL message for each index and add the indexes of the selected items to the set, which is then returned:

```
set<int> MultipleListBox::GetSelectionMultiple() const {
  int size = ::SendMessage(windowHandle, LB_GETCOUNT, 0, 0);

  set<int> indexSet;
  for (int index = 0; index < size; ++index) {
    if (::SendMessage(windowHandle, LB_GETSEL, index, 0) != 0) {
      indexSet.insert(index);
    }
  }

  return indexSet;
}
};
```

Combo box

A combo box is a drop-down list of items, from which the user can select one. The functionality of a combo box is equal to a list box, only their graphical appearance differs. Moreover, the functionality is also equivalent to a radio button group. Similar to ListBox and Radiobutton, the constructor takes the indexPtr parameter, which is a pointer to an integer value, holding the zero-based index of the item currently selected.

ComboBox.h

```
namespace SmallWindows {
  class ComboBox : public Control {
    public:
      ComboBox(Dialog* parentPtr, Point topLeft, Size controlSize,
               initializer_list<String> textList, int* indexPtr);
      void OnControlInit(Dialog* dialogPtr);
      void OnSelect(Dialog* dialogPtr);
```

```
   private:
     void LoadCombo() const;
     void SelectCombo(int index) const;
     int GetComboSelection() const;
     list<String> textList;
     int* indexPtr;
  };
};
```

ComboBox.cpp

```
#include "..\\SmallWindows.h"

namespace SmallWindows {
  ComboBox::ComboBox(Dialog* parentPtr, Point topLeft,
            Size controlSize, initializer_list<String> textList,
            int* indexPtr)
   :Control(parentPtr, topLeft, controlSize, TEXT("combobox"),
            TEXT(""), CBS_DROPDOWN | CBS_HASSTRINGS | LBS_NOTIFY |
            LBS_COMBOBOX | WS_GROUP | WS_TABSTOP),
    textList(textList),
    indexPtr(indexPtr) {
    // Empty.
  }

  void ComboBox::OnControlInit(Dialog* dialogPtr) {
    LoadCombo();
    SelectCombo(*indexPtr);
  }

  void ComboBox::OnSelect(Dialog* dialogPtr) {
    *indexPtr = GetComboSelection();
  }
```

The CB_ADDSTRING message loads the combo box with items, CB_SETCURSEL sets the selected item, and CB_GETCURSEL returns the index of the selected item:

```
  void ComboBox::LoadCombo() const {
    for (String text : textList) {
      ::SendMessage(windowHandle, CB_ADDSTRING,
                    0, (LPARAM) text.c_str());
    }
  }

  void ComboBox::SelectCombo(int index) const {
    ::SendMessage(windowHandle, CB_SETCURSEL, index, 0);
  }
```

```
    int ComboBox::GetComboSelection() const {
      return ::SendMessage(windowHandle, CB_GETCURSEL, 0, 0);
    }
};
```

Label

A label is a displayed text that often serves as a prompt to a text field; it has no functionality besides its graphical appearance.

Label.h

```
namespace SmallWindows {
  class Label : public Control {
    public:
      Label(Dialog* parentPtr, Point topLeft,
            Size controlSize, String text);
  };
};
```

Label.cpp

```
#include "..\\SmallWindows.h"

namespace SmallWindows {
  Label::Label(Dialog* parentPtr, Point topLeft,
               Size controlSize, String text)
   :Control(parentPtr, topLeft, controlSize,
            TEXT("static"), text, 0) {
  }
};
```

The TextField class

The TextField class is a template for a text field; it takes the type of the value stored in the text field; an integer base for octal, decimal, or hexadecimal integers (ignored for non-integer types); and a converter of the Converter class in the next section, which converts between values and text. The constructor's valuePtr parameter is a pointer to the value to be edited in the text field.

TextField.h

```
namespace SmallWindows {
  enum EditStyle {LeftEdit = ES_LEFT, CenterEdit = ES_CENTER,
                  RightEdit = ES_RIGHT, DigitsOnly = ES_NUMBER,
                  ReadOnly = ES_READONLY, Password = ES_PASSWORD,
                  Uppercase = ES_UPPERCASE, Lowercase=ES_LOWERCASE,
                  AutoScroll = ES_AUTOHSCROLL};

  enum {oct = 8, dec = 10, hex = 16};

  template <class Type = String, int Base = dec,
            class TheConverter = Converter<Type>>
  class TextField : public Control {
    public:
      TextField(Dialog* parentPtr, Point topLeft,
                Size controlSize, Type* valuePtr,
                int size = 100, EditStyle style = AutoScroll);
```

The `OnControlInit` method is called when the text field has been created. It converts the value to the text displayed in the text field. The `OnLoseFocus` method is called when the user leaves the text field and converts its text to a value of the template type if the text is valid. If it is not valid, the text field is set to the text converted from the latest valid value:

```
      void OnControlInit(Dialog* dialogPtr);
      void OnLoseFocus(Dialog* dialogPtr);

    protected:
      String GetText() const;
      void SetText(String text);

    private:
      Type* valuePtr;
  };

  template <class Type = String, int Base = dec,
            class TheConverter = Converter<Type>>
  TextField<Type,Base,TheConverter>::TextField
    (Dialog* parentPtr, Point topLeft, Size controlSize,
     Type* valuePtr, int size /* = 100 */,
     EditStyle style /* = AutoScroll */)
   :Control(parentPtr, topLeft, controlSize, TEXT("edit"),
            TEXT(""), style | WS_BORDER | WS_GROUP | WS_TABSTOP),
     valuePtr(valuePtr) {
     // Empty.
   }
```

The Win32 API function `GetWindowText` gets the text of the text field and `SetWindowText` sets its text. We need to convert from a zero-terminated character pointer string to a `String` object by calling the `String` constructor, and from a `String` object to a zero-terminated character pointer by calling the `c_str` method of the `String` class:

```
template <class Type = String, int Base = dec,
          class TheConverter = Converter<Type>>
String TextField<Type,Base,TheConverter>::GetText() const {
  TCHAR buffer[MAX_PATH];
  ::GetWindowText(windowHandle, buffer, MAX_PATH);
  return String(buffer);
}

template <class Type = String, int Base = dec,
          class TheConverter = Converter<Type>>
void TextField<Type,Base,TheConverter>::SetText(String text) {
  ::SetWindowText(windowHandle, text.c_str());
}
```

When the text field has been initialized, the `ValueToText` method of the `Converter` class is called to convert the value pointed to by `valuePtr` to the text displayed in the text field:

```
template <class Type = String, int Base = dec,
          class TheConverter = Converter<Type>>
void TextField<Type,Base,TheConverter>::OnControlInit
                                      (Dialog* dialogPtr) {
  SetText(TheConverter::ValueToText(*valuePtr, Base));
}
```

When the text field loses input focus, the text is evaluated by the `Check` method in order to decide whether it is suitable to be converted to a value. If it is suitable, the `ValueToText` method is called to do the actual converting, and then the text is loaded to the text field:

```
template <class Type = String, int Base = dec,
          class TheConverter = Converter<Type>>
void TextField<Type,Base,TheConverter>::OnLoseFocus
                                      (Dialog* dialogPtr) {
  String text = GetText();

  if (TheConverter::Check(text, Base)) {
    *valuePtr = TheConverter::TextToValue(text, Base);
  }

  SetText(TheConverter::ValueToText(*valuePtr, Base));
}
};
```

Converters

The `Converter` class is a template class intended to be specialized by type. Its task is to convert values between the template type and the `String` objects. The `Check` variable takes a string and returns `true` if it holds a valid value, `TextToValue` converts a text to a value, and `ValueToText` converts a value to a text.

Converter.h

```
namespace SmallWindows {
  template <class Type>
  class Converter {
    public:
      static bool Check(String& text, int base);
      static Type TextToValue(String& text, int base);
      static String ValueToText(Type& value, int base);
  };
```

Signed integers

Small Windows comes equipped with a set of predefined converters, which are specializations of `Converter`. One of these handles signed integer values of the type `int`.

Converter.h

```
  template <>
  class Converter<int> {
    public:
      static bool Check(String& text, int base);
      static int TextToValue(String& text, int base);
      static String ValueToText(int& value, int base);
  };
```

Converter.cpp

```
  #include "SmallWindows.h"
```

When checking whether the given string holds a valid integer value, we create an `IStringStream` object (the generic version of the Standard C++ class `istringstream`, with `TCHAR` instead of `char`) initialized with the trimmed text (initial and terminating white spaces are removed). Then, we read the text into an integer variable with the base parameter and test whether the stream has reached end-of-file (`eof`). If it has, all characters of the text have been read, which implies that the text holds a valid integer value and `true` is returned:

```
namespace SmallWindows {
  bool Converter<int>::Check(String& text, int base) {
    IStringStream stringStream(Trim(text));
    int value;
    stringStream >> setbase(base) >> value;
    return stringStream.eof();
  }
```

The conversion from a string to an integer is similar to Check, which we covered earlier, with the difference that we return the integer value assuming that Check has confirmed that the text holds a valid integer value:

```
  int Converter<int>::TextToValue(String& text, int base) {
    IStringStream stringStream(Trim(text));
    int value;
    stringStream >> setbase(base) >> value;
    return value;
  }
```

When converting an integer to a string, we use the OStringStream method (the generic version of ostringstream), write the value to the stream, and return the stream converted to a string by str:

```
  String Converter<int>::ValueToText(int& value, int base) {
    OStringStream outputStream;
    outputStream << setbase(base) << value;
    return outputStream.str();
  }
```

Unsigned integers

Unsigned integers work in the same way as signed integers, the only difference is that int has been replaced by unsignedint:

Converter.h

```
  template <>
  class Converter<unsigned int> {
    public:
      static bool Check(String& text, int base);
      static unsigned int TextToValue(String& text, int base);
      static String ValueToText(unsigned int& value, int base);
  };
```

Converter.cpp

```
bool Converter<unsigned int>::Check(String& text, int base) {
  IStringStream stringStream(Trim(text));
  unsigned int value;
  stringStream >> setbase(base) >> value;
  return stringStream.eof() && (text.find(TEXT("-")) == -1);
}
unsigned int Converter<unsigned int>::TextToValue(String& text,
                                                  int base) {
  IStringStream stringStream(Trim(text));
  unsigned int value;
  stringStream >> setbase(base) >> value;
  return value;
}
String Converter<unsigned int>::ValueToText(unsigned int&value,
                                            int base) {
  OStringStream outputStream;
  outputStream << setbase(base) << value;
  return outputStream.str();
}
```

Double values

Double values ignore the base parameter and do not use the setbase manipulator; otherwise, the test and conversions work in the same way as in integer cases.

Converter.h

```
template <>
class Converter<double> {
  public:
    static bool Check(String& text, int /* base */);
    static double TextToValue(String& text, int /* base */);
    static String ValueToText(double& value, int /* base */);
};
```

Converter.cpp

```
bool Converter<double>::Check(String& text, int /* base */) {
  IStringStream stringStream(Trim(text));
  double value;
  stringStream >> value;
  return stringStream.eof();
}
```

```
double Converter<double>::TextToValue(String& text,
                                     int /* base */) {
  IStringStream stringStream(Trim(text));
  double value;
  stringStream >> value;
  return value;
}
String Converter<double>::ValueToText(double& value,
                                     int /* base */) {
  OStringStream outputStream;
  outputStream << value;
  return outputStream.str();
}
```

Strings

The string case is trivial, since a string can always be converted to another string.

Converter.h

```
template <>
class Converter<String> {
  public:
    static bool Check(String& text, int /* base */)
                    {return true;}
    static String TextToValue(String& text, int /* base */)
                            {return String(text);}
    static String ValueToText(String& value, int /* base */)
                            {return String(value);}
};
```

Rational numbers

A **rational number** is a number that can be expressed as a fraction of two integers, where the second integer is non-zero. We do not really use rational numbers in this section or complex numbers in the next section, in our applications. They are included only to demonstrate the converter, and they are implemented in the Appendix at the end of the book.

Converter.h

```
template <>
class Converter<Rational> {
```

```
public:
  static bool Check(String& text, int /* base */);
  static Rational TextToValue(String& text, int /* base */);
  static String ValueToText(Rational& value, int /* base */);
};
```

When checking whether the text holds a valid rational number, we simply create an object of the Rational class. If the constructor accepts the text without throwing a NotaRationalNumber exception, we return true. If it throws the exception, the text is not acceptable and we return false.

Converter.cpp

```
bool Converter<Rational>::Check(String& text, int /* base */) {
  try {
    Rational value(text);
    return true;
  }
  catch (NotaRationalNumber) {
    return false;
  }
}
```

When converting a string to a rational number, we create and return a Rational object, assuming that Check has confirmed that the text holds a valid rational number:

```
Rational Converter<Rational>::TextToValue(String& text,
                                          int /* base */) {
  return Rational(text);
}
```

When converting a rational number to a string we call the String conversion operator of the Rational class.

```
String Converter<Rational>::ValueToText(Rational& value,
                                        int /* base */) {
  return ((String) value);
}
```

Complex numbers

A complex number is the sum $z = x + yi$ of a real number x and a real number y multiplied by the **imaginary unit** i, which is the solution of the equation $x^2 + 1 = 0$. The specialization of Converter with regard to the Complex class is similar to the Rational specialization.

Converter.h

```
template <>
class Converter<Complex> {
  public:
    static bool Check(String& text, int /* base */);
    static Complex TextToValue(String& text, int /* base */);
    static String ValueToText(Complex& value, int /* base */);
  };
};
```

Converter.cpp

```
bool Converter<Complex>::Check(String& text, int /* base */) {
  try {
    Complex value(text);
    return true;
  }
  catch (NotAComplexNumber) {
    return false;
  }
}

Complex Converter<Complex>::TextToValue(String& text,
                                        int /* base */) {
  return Complex(text);
}

String Converter<Complex>::ValueToText(Complex& value,
                                       int /* base */) {
  return ((String) value);
}
};
```

Page setup

The final section describes page setup functionality, divided into the `PageSetupInfo` class, which handles page setup information, the `PageSetupDialog`, which is a subclass of `Dialog` displayed for the user to input page setup information, and the `Template` function, which translates code input by the user in the **Page Setup** dialog to actual values.

Page setup information

The `PageSetupInfo` class holds information about the page: portrait or landscape orientation, the margins, the text and font of the header and footer, whether the header and footer will be present on the first page, and whether the pages will be enclosed by a frame.

PageSetupInfo.h

```
namespace SmallWindows {
  enum Orientation {Portrait, Landscape};

  class PageSetupInfo {
    public:
      PageSetupInfo();
      PageSetupInfo(const PageSetupInfo& pageSetupInfo);
      bool operator==(const PageSetupInfo& pageSetupInfo);
      bool operator!=(const PageSetupInfo& pageSetupInfo);

      void ClearPageSetupInfo();
      bool WritePageSetupInfoToStream(ostream& outStream) const;
      bool ReadPageSetupInfoFromStream(istream& inStream);

      Orientation& GetOrientation() {return orientation;}
      int& LeftMargin() {return leftMargin;}
      int& TopMargin() {return topMargin;}
      int& RightMargin() {return rightMargin;}
      int& BottomMargin() {return bottomMargin;}
      String& HeaderText() {return headerText;}
      String& FooterText() {return footerText;}
      bool& HeaderFirst() {return headerFirst;}
      bool& FooterFirst() {return footerFirst;}
      bool& Frame() {return frame;}
      Font& HeaderFont() {return headerFont;}
      Font& FooterFont() {return footerFont;}

      Orientation GetOrientation() const {return orientation;}
      int LeftMargin() const {return leftMargin;}
      int TopMargin() const {return topMargin;}
      int RightMargin() const {return rightMargin;}
      int BottomMargin() const {return bottomMargin;}
      String HeaderText() const {return headerText;}
      String FooterText() const {return footerText;}
      bool HeaderFirst() const {return headerFirst;}
      bool FooterFirst() const {return footerFirst;}
      bool Frame() const {return frame;}
      Font HeaderFont() const {return headerFont;}
      Font FooterFont() const {return footerFont;}
```

```
    private:
      Orientation orientation;
      int leftMargin, topMargin, rightMargin, bottomMargin;
      String headerText, footerText;
      bool headerFirst, footerFirst, frame;
      Font headerFont, footerFont;
  };
};
```

PageSetupInfo.cpp

```
#include "..\\SmallWindows\\SmallWindows.h"
```

The default constructor initializes the default member values by calling `PageSetupInfo`.

```
namespace SmallWindows {
  PageSetupInfo::PageSetupInfo() {
    ClearPageSetupInfo();
  }
```

The default constructor and assignment operator copy the member values.

```
PageSetupInfo::PageSetupInfo(const PageSetupInfo& pageSetupInfo)
 :orientation(pageSetupInfo.orientation),
  leftMargin(pageSetupInfo.leftMargin),
  topMargin(pageSetupInfo.topMargin),
  rightMargin(pageSetupInfo.rightMargin),
  bottomMargin(pageSetupInfo.bottomMargin),
  headerText(pageSetupInfo.headerText),
  footerText(pageSetupInfo.footerText),
  headerFirst(pageSetupInfo.headerFirst),
  footerFirst(pageSetupInfo.footerFirst),
  frame(pageSetupInfo.frame),
  headerFont(pageSetupInfo.headerFont),
  footerFont(pageSetupInfo.footerFont) {
    // Empty.
}
```

The equality operators compare all the fields:

```
bool PageSetupInfo::operator==
      (const PageSetupInfo& pageSetupInfo) {
  return (orientation == pageSetupInfo.orientation) &&
         (leftMargin == pageSetupInfo.leftMargin) &&
         (topMargin == pageSetupInfo.topMargin) &&
         (rightMargin == pageSetupInfo.rightMargin) &&
         (bottomMargin == pageSetupInfo.bottomMargin) &&
         (headerText == pageSetupInfo.headerText) &&
         (footerText == pageSetupInfo.footerText) &&
```

```
               (headerFirst == pageSetupInfo.headerFirst) &&
               (footerFirst == pageSetupInfo.footerFirst) &&
               (frame == pageSetupInfo.frame) &&
               (headerFont == pageSetupInfo.headerFont) &&
               (footerFont == pageSetupInfo.footerFont);
  }

  bool PageSetupInfo::operator!=
          (const PageSetupInfo& pageSetupInfo) {
    return !(*this == pageSetupInfo);
  }
  void PageSetupInfo::ClearPageSetupInfo() {
    orientation = Portrait;
    leftMargin = 25;
    topMargin = 25;
    rightMargin = 25;
    bottomMargin = 25;
    headerText = TEXT("");
    footerText = TEXT("");
    headerFirst = true;
    footerFirst = true;
    frame = true;
    headerFont = Font(TEXT("Times New Roman"), 12, false, true);
    footerFont = Font(TEXT("Times New Roman"), 12, false);
  }
```

Page setup information can be written to, or read from, a stream:

```
  bool PageSetupInfo::WritePageSetupInfoToStream
                     (ostream& outStream) const {
    outStream.write((char*) &orientation, sizeof orientation);
    outStream.write((char*) &leftMargin, sizeof leftMargin);
    outStream.write((char*) &topMargin, sizeof topMargin);
    outStream.write((char*) &rightMargin, sizeof rightMargin);
    outStream.write((char*) &bottomMargin, sizeof bottomMargin);
    WriteStringToStream(headerText, outStream);
    WriteStringToStream(footerText, outStream);
    outStream.write((char*) &headerFirst, sizeof headerFirst);
    outStream.write((char*) &footerFirst, sizeof footerFirst);
    outStream.write((char*) &frame, sizeof frame);
    headerFont.WriteFontToStream(outStream);
    footerFont.WriteFontToStream(outStream);
    return ((bool) outStream);
  }

  bool PageSetupInfo::ReadPageSetupInfoFromStream
                     (istream& inStream) {
    inStream.read((char*) &orientation, sizeof orientation);
```

```
    inStream.read((char*) &leftMargin, sizeof leftMargin);
    inStream.read((char*) &topMargin, sizeof topMargin);
    inStream.read((char*) &rightMargin, sizeof rightMargin);
    inStream.read((char*) &bottomMargin, sizeof bottomMargin);
    ReadStringFromStream(headerText, inStream);
    ReadStringFromStream(footerText, inStream);
    inStream.read((char*) &headerFirst, sizeof headerFirst);
    inStream.read((char*) &footerFirst, sizeof footerFirst);
    inStream.read((char*) &frame, sizeof frame);
    headerFont.ReadFontFromStream(inStream);
    footerFont.ReadFontFromStream(inStream);
    return ((bool) inStream);
  }
};
```

The Page Setup dialog

The PageSetupDialog class is a part of Small Windows and is displayed by the StandardDocument framework when the user selects the **Page Setup** menu item. The word processor earlier in this book gives an example. The PageSetupDialog class is a subclass of Dialog and provides the user with the possibility to input the information in PageSetupInfo. Note that the header and footer text can be annotated with blocks of code, explained in the next section.

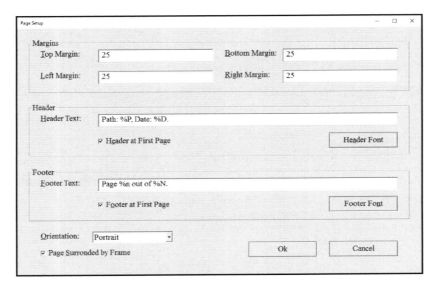

PageSetupDialog.h

```
namespace SmallWindows {
  class PageSetupDialog : public Dialog {
    public:
      PageSetupDialog(Window* parentPtr, PageSetupInfo* infoPtr);
```

Each push button has its own listener:

```
      DEFINE_VOID_LISTENER(PageSetupDialog, OnHeaderFont);
      DEFINE_VOID_LISTENER(PageSetupDialog, OnFooterFont);
      DEFINE_VOID_LISTENER(PageSetupDialog, OnOk);
      DEFINE_VOID_LISTENER(PageSetupDialog, OnCancel);
```

The page setup information is pointed at by `infoPtr`, which is modified when the user changes the state of the controls. There is also `backupInfo`, in case the user cancels the dialog:

```
    private:
      PageSetupInfo *infoPtr, backupInfo;
  };
};
```

PageSetupDialog.cpp

```
#include "SmallWindows.h"
```

The constructor sets the pointer `infoPtr` to point at the page setup information. The information is also stored in `backupInfo`, which will be used if the user cancels the dialog; refer to `OnCancel`:

```
namespace SmallWindows {
  PageSetupDialog::PageSetupDialog(Window* parentPtr,
                                   PageSetupInfo* infoPtr)
   :Dialog(TEXT("Page Setup"), Point(0, 0), parentPtr),
    infoPtr(infoPtr),
    backupInfo(*infoPtr) {
```

Each control gives the **Page Setup** dialog (`this`) as its parent dialog, which means that the controls will be deleted by the dialog's destructor. This implies that we do need to keep track of the controls in order to delete them manually. Actually, we will not delete them manually as it would result in dangling pointers:

```
      new GroupBox(this, Point(10, 10),
                   Size(330, 50), TEXT("Margins"));
      new Label(this, Point(20, 20), Size(50, 10),
                TEXT("&Top Margin:"));
```

Note that we give a pointer as a reference for the value of the top margin. This value will be modified when the user changes the value:

```
new TextField<int>(this, Point(70, 20), Size(100, 12),
                   &infoPtr->TopMargin());
new Label(this, Point(180, 20), Size(50, 10),
          TEXT("&Bottom Margin:"));
new TextField<int>(this, Point(230, 20), Size(100, 12),
                   &infoPtr->BottomMargin());
new Label(this, Point(20, 40), Size(50, 10),
          TEXT("&Left Margin:"));
new TextField<int>(this, Point(70, 40), Size(100, 12),
                   &infoPtr->LeftMargin());
new Label(this, Point(180, 40), Size(50, 10),
          TEXT("&Right Margin:"));
new TextField<int>(this, Point(230, 40), Size(100, 12),
                   &infoPtr->RightMargin());

new GroupBox(this, Point(10, 70),
             Size(330, 50), TEXT("Header"));
new Label(this, Point(20, 80), Size(50, 10),
          TEXT("&Header Text:"));
new TextField<>(this, Point(70, 80), Size(260, 12),
                &infoPtr->HeaderText());
```

Similar to the `TextField` case, we give a pointer to a reference of the `HeaderFirst` value, which is a `Boolean` value. It will be modified when the user checks the box:

```
new CheckBox(this, Point(70, 100), Size(100, 10),
             TEXT("H&eader at First Page"),
             &infoPtr->HeaderFirst());
```

The `OnHeaderFont` listener is called when the user presses the button:

```
new PushButton(this, Point(270, 98), Size(60, 15),
               TEXT("He&ader Font"), OnHeaderFont);

new GroupBox(this, Point(10, 130),
             Size(330, 50), TEXT("Footer"));
new Label(this, Point(20, 140), Size(50, 10),
          TEXT("&Footer Text:"));
new TextField<>(this, Point(70, 140), Size(260, 12),
                &infoPtr->FooterText());
new CheckBox(this, Point(70, 160), Size(100, 10),
             TEXT("F&ooter at First Page"),
             &infoPtr->FooterFirst());
new PushButton(this, Point(270, 158), Size(60, 15),
               TEXT("Footer Fo&nt"), OnFooterFont);
```

```
      new Label(this, Point(20, 190), Size(40, 10),
             TEXT("&Orientation:"));
      new ComboBox(this, Point(65, 190), Size(70, 30),
               {TEXT("Portrait"), TEXT("Landscape")},
               (int*) &infoPtr->GetOrientation());
      new CheckBox(this, Point(20, 205), Size(100, 10),
              TEXT("Page &Surrounded by Frame"),
              &infoPtr->Frame());
      new PushButton(this, Point(200, 200),
                Size(60, 15), TEXT("Ok"), OnOk);
      new PushButton(this, Point(270, 200), Size(60, 15),
                TEXT("Cancel"), OnCancel);
   }
```

The `OnHeaderFont` and `OnFooterFont` methods display font dialogs:

```
   void PageSetupDialog::OnHeaderFont() {
      StandardDialog::FontDialog(this, infoPtr->HeaderFont());
   }

   void PageSetupDialog::OnFooterFont() {
      StandardDialog::FontDialog(this, infoPtr->FooterFont());
   }
```

The `OnOk` and `OnCancel` methods terminate the dialog. The `OnCancel` method also copies the backup information that was stored by the constructor at the beginning, since no new information will be returned when the user cancels the dialog:

```
   void PageSetupDialog::OnOk() {
      Dialog::OnReturn();
   }

   void PageSetupDialog::OnCancel() {
      *infoPtr = backupInfo;
      Dialog::OnEscape();
   }
};
```

The Template function

When the user inputs text in the header and footer fields in the **Page Setup** dialog, they can insert code in the text, which needs to be translated into valid values. The code is shown in the following table:

Code	Description	Example
%P	Path with suffix	`C:\Test\Test.wrd`
%p	Path without suffix	`C:\Test\Test`
%F	File with suffix	`Test.wrd`
%f	File without suffix	Test
%N	Total number of pages	7
%n	Current page	5
%c	Current Copy	3
%D	Date with full month	January 1, 2016
%d	Date with abbreviated month	Jan 1, 2016
%T	Time with seconds	07:08:09
%t	Time without seconds	07:08
%%	Percent character	%

The task of the `Template` function is to replace the code with valid values. It takes the `templateText` string with template code and returns the text with the code replaced by valid values. It needs the current copy and page number as well as the total number of pages.

For instance, the `Page %n out of %N` text can be translated to **Page 3 out of 5** and `File: %F, date: %d` can be translated to **File: Text.txt, date: Dec 31, 2016**.

Template.h

```
namespace SmallWindows {
   String Template(const Document* documentPtr, String templateText,
                   int copy = 0, int page = 0, int totalPages = 0);
};
```

Template.cpp

```
#include "SmallWindows.h"

namespace SmallWindows {
   String Template(const Document* documentPtr, String templateText,
                   int copy /* = 0 */, int page /* = 0 */,
                   int totalPages /* = 0 */) {
```

We start by replacing the c, n, and N code with the number of copies and the current and total pages. The numerical values are translated into strings by `to_String`:

```
ReplaceAll(templateText, TEXT("%c"), to_String(copy));
ReplaceAll(templateText, TEXT("%n"), to_String(page));
ReplaceAll(templateText, TEXT("%N"), to_String(totalPages));
```

The file of the path is its text after the last backslash (\) and the suffix is its text after the last dot (.). If there is no backslash, the file is the same as the path; if there is no dot, the path and file without the suffix is the same as the file and path with the suffix:

```
String pathWithSuffix = documentPtr->GetName();
ReplaceAll(templateText, TEXT("%P"), pathWithSuffix);

int lastPathDot = pathWithSuffix.find_last_of(TEXT('.'));
String pathWithoutSuffix =
  pathWithSuffix.substr(0, lastPathDot);
ReplaceAll(templateText, TEXT("%p"), pathWithoutSuffix);

int lastBackslash = pathWithSuffix.find_last_of(TEXT(''));
String fileWithSuffix =
  pathWithSuffix.substr(lastBackslash + 1);
ReplaceAll(templateText, TEXT("%F"), fileWithSuffix);

int lastFileDot = fileWithSuffix.find_last_of(TEXT('.'));
String fileWithoutSuffix =
  fileWithSuffix.substr(0, lastFileDot);
ReplaceAll(templateText, TEXT("%f"), fileWithoutSuffix);
```

The current date and time are obtained by calling the Standard C functions `time` and `localtime_s`:

```
time_t t = ::time(nullptr);
struct tm time;
::localtime_s(&time, &t);
```

The current time with and without seconds and the current date with whole and abbreviated month names are written to string output streams. The `setw` manipulator makes sure that two characters are always written, `setfill` fills with zeros if necessary, and `ios::right` writes the value in a right-aligned manner:

```
{ OStringStream timeWithoutSeconds;
  timeWithoutSeconds << std::setw(2) << setw(2)
                     << setiosflags(ios::right)
                     << setfill(TEXT('0')) << time.tm_hour
                     << TEXT(":") << setiosflags(ios::right)
                     << setw(2) << setfill(TEXT('0'))
                     << time.tm_min;
```

```
      ReplaceAll(templateText, TEXT("%t"),
               timeWithoutSeconds.str());

      OStringStream timeWithSeconds;
      timeWithSeconds << timeWithoutSeconds.str() << TEXT(":")
                      << setiosflags(ios::right) << setw(2)
                      << setfill(TEXT('0')) << time.tm_sec;
      ReplaceAll(templateText, TEXT("%T"), timeWithSeconds.str());
   }

   { static const String longMonths[] =
        {TEXT("January"), TEXT("February"), TEXT("March"),
         TEXT("April"), TEXT("May"), TEXT("June"), TEXT("July"),
         TEXT("August"), TEXT("September"), TEXT("October"),
         TEXT("November"), TEXT("December")};
      OStringStream dateFullMonth;
      dateFullMonth << longMonths[time.tm_mon] << TEXT(" ")
                    << time.tm_mday << TEXT(", ")
                    << (1900 + time.tm_year);
      ReplaceAll(templateText, TEXT("%D"), dateFullMonth.str());
   }

   { static const String shortMonths[] =
        {TEXT("Jan"), TEXT("Feb"), TEXT("Mar"), TEXT("Apr"),
         TEXT("May"), TEXT("Jun"), TEXT("Jul"), TEXT("Aug"),
         TEXT("Sep"), TEXT("Oct"), TEXT("Nov"), TEXT("Dec")};
      OStringStream dateShortMonth;
      dateShortMonth << shortMonths[time.tm_mon] << TEXT(" ")
                     << time.tm_mday << TEXT(", ")
                     << (1900 + time.tm_year);
      ReplaceAll(templateText, TEXT("%d"), dateShortMonth.str());
   }
```

Finally, we need to replace each instance of %% with %:

```
      ReplaceAll(templateText, TEXT("%%"), TEXT("%"));
      return templateText;
   }
};
```

Summary

In this chapter, we looked into custom dialogs, controls, converters, and the Page Setup dialog. The only remaining part of the book is the implementation of the rational and complex classes.

Rational and Complex Numbers

This Appendix defines the `Rational` and `Complex` classes from the *Converters* section in the previous chapter.

Rational numbers

A **rational number** can be expressed as a fraction of two integers, called the **numerator** and **denominator**.

Rational.h

```
namespace SmallWindows {
  class NotaRationalNumber : public exception {
    public:
      NotaRationalNumber() {/* Empty. */}
  };
```

The default constructor initializes the numerator and denominator to 0 and 1, respectively. The second constructor takes a string and throws a `NotaRationalNumber` exception if the string does not hold a valid rational number. The copy constructor and the assignment operator take another rational number. The `String` conversion operator returns the rational number as a string:

```
class Rational {
  public:
    Rational(int numerator = 0, int denominator = 1);
    Rational(const String& text);
    Rational(const Rational &rational);
    Rational operator=(const Rational &complex);
    operator String() const;
    bool operator==(const Rational &rational) const;
```

```
bool operator!=(const Rational &rational) const;
bool operator< (const Rational &rational) const;
bool operator<=(const Rational &rational) const;
bool operator> (const Rational &rational) const;
bool operator>=(const Rational &rational) const;
Rational operator+(const Rational &rational) const;
Rational operator-(const Rational &rational) const;
Rational operator*(const Rational &rational) const;
Rational operator/(const Rational &rational) const;
```

A rational number is always normalized when it has been created by the constructor or any of the arithmetic operators: the numerator and the denominator are divided by their **Greatest Common Divisor (GCD)**:

```
   private:
     void Normalize();
     int GCD(int iNum1, int iNum2);
     int numerator, denominator;
  };
};
```

Rational.cpp

```
#include "SmallWindows.h"
```

The default constructor initializes the numerator and the denominator, and throws an exception if the denominator is zero. This constructor and the next constructor that takes a string are actually the only places where the denominator can be zero. The following constructors and arithmetic operators always produce a rational number with non-zero denominators:

```
namespace SmallWindows {
  Rational::Rational(int numerator /* = 0 */,
                     int denominator /* = 1 */)
   :numerator(numerator),
    denominator(denominator) {
    if (denominator == 0) {
      throw NotaRationalNumber();
    }
    Normalize();
  }
```

Text can hold a rational number in two formats: as an integer followed by a slash (/) and another integer, or as a single integer. We start by initializing the numerator and the denominator to 0 and 1:

```
Rational::Rational(const String& text)
 :numerator(0),
  denominator(1) {
  String trimText(Trim(text));
```

First, we try two integers and a slash; we read the numerator, slash, and denominator. Before the slash we set the `skipws` flag, which causes the stream to skip any potential white spaces before the slash. If we have reached the end of the line, the denominator is not 0, the character read into the `slash` variable really is a slash, the text holds a rational number, and we have read the numerator and denominator, then we are done and we return:

```
{ IStringStream totalStream(trimText);
  TCHAR slash;
  totalStream >> numerator >> setiosflags(ios::skipws)
              >> slash >> denominator;
  if (totalStream.eof() && (denominator != 0) &&
      (slash == TEXT('/'))) {
    Normalize();
    return;
  }
}
```

If using two integers and a slash does not work, we try the case of a single integer. We create a new stream and read the numerator. If we have reached the end of the stream after that, the string holds a valid integer. We let the numerator hold its initialized value, which was 1, and return.

```
{ IStringStream numeratorStream(trimText);
  numeratorStream >> numerator;
  if (numeratorStream.eof()) {
    return;
  }
}
```

If two integers and a slash as well as a single integer both failed, we have to draw the conclusion that the string does not hold a valid rational number, and we throw a `NotaRationalNumber` exception:

```
  throw NotaRationalNumber();
}
```

The copy constructor simply copies the numerator and denominator of the rational number:

```
Rational::Rational(const Rational &rational)
  :numerator(rational.numerator),
   denominator(rational.denominator) {
   // Empty.
}
```

The assignment operator also copies the numerator and denominator of the rational number and returns its own Rational object (*this):

```
Rational Rational::operator=(const Rational &rational) {
   numerator = rational.numerator;
   denominator = rational.denominator;
   return *this;
}
```

The String conversion operator creates an OStringStream object and looks into the denominator. If it is 1, the rational number can be expressed as a single integer; otherwise, it needs to be expressed as a fraction of the numerator and denominator. Finally, the stream is converted into a string that is returned:

```
Rational::operator String() const {
   OStringStream outStream;

   if (denominator == 1) {
     outStream << numerator;
   }
   else {
     outStream << numerator << TEXT("/") << denominator;
   }

   return outStream.str();
}
```

As rational numbers are always normalized, we can conclude that two rational numbers are equal if they have the same numerator and denominator:

```
bool Rational::operator==(const Rational &rational) const {
   return (numerator == rational.numerator) &&
          (denominator == rational.denominator);
}

bool Rational::operator!=(const Rational &rational) const {
   return !(*this == rational);
}
```

When deciding whether a rational number is smaller than another rational number, in order not to involve floating values, we multiply both sides by the denominator and compare the products:

$$\frac{n_1}{d_1} < \frac{n_2}{d_2} \Leftrightarrow n_1 d_2 < n_2 d_1$$

```
bool Rational::operator<(const Rational &rational) const {
    return ((numerator * rational.denominator) <
            (rational.numerator * denominator));
}

bool Rational::operator<=(const Rational &rational) const {
    return ((*this < rational) || (*this == rational));
}

bool Rational::operator>(const Rational &rational) const {
    return !(*this <= rational);
}

bool Rational::operator>=(const Rational &rational) const {
    return !(*this < rational);
}
```

When adding two rational numbers, we multiply the numerator by the opposite denominator in each term:

$$\frac{n_1}{d_1} + \frac{n_2}{d_2} = \frac{n_1 d_2}{d_1 d_2} + \frac{n_2 d_1}{d_2 d_1} = \frac{n_1 d_2 + n_2 d_1}{d_1 d_2}$$

```
Rational Rational::operator+(const Rational &rational) const {
    Rational result((numerator * rational.denominator) +
                    (rational.numerator * denominator),
                    denominator * rational.denominator);
    result.Normalize();
    return result;
}
```

When subtracting two rational numbers, we also multiply the numerator by the opposite denominator in each term:

$$\frac{n_1}{d_1} - \frac{n_2}{d_2} = \frac{n_1 d_2}{d_1 d_2} - \frac{n_2 d_1}{d_2 d_1} = \frac{n_1 d_2 - n_2 d_1}{d_1 d_2}$$

```
Rational Rational::operator-(const Rational &rational) const {
  Rational result((numerator * rational.denominator) -
                  (rational.numerator * denominator),
                  denominator * rational.denominator);


  result.Normalize();
  return result;
}
```

When multiplying two rational numbers, we simply multiply the numerators and denominators:

$$\frac{n_1}{d_1}\frac{n_2}{d_2} = \frac{n_1 n_2}{d_1 d_2}$$

```
Rational Rational::operator*(const Rational &rational) const {
  Rational result(numerator * rational.numerator,
                  denominator * rational.denominator);
  result.Normalize();
  return result;
}
```

When dividing two rational numbers, we invert the second operand and then multiply the numerators and denominators:

$$\frac{n_1}{d_1} / \frac{n_2}{d_2} = \frac{n_1}{d_1}\frac{d_2}{n_2} = \frac{n_1 d_2}{d_1 n_2}$$

```
Rational Rational::operator/(const Rational &rational) const {
  assert(rational.numerator != 0);
  Rational result(numerator * rational.denominator,
                  denominator * rational.numerator);
  result.Normalize();
  return result;
}
```

When normalizing the rational number, we first look into the numerator. If it is 0, we set the denominator to 1 regardless of its previous value and return:

```
void Rational::Normalize() {
  if (numerator == 0) {
    denominator = 1;
    return;
  }
```

However, if the numerator is not 0, we look into the denominator. If it is less than 0, we switch the sign of both the numerator and denominator so that the denominator is always greater than 0:

```
if (denominator < 0) {
  numerator = -numerator;
  denominator = -denominator;
}
```

Then we calculate the Greatest Common Divisor by calling GCD, and then we divide both the numerator and denominator by the Greatest Common Divisor:

```
  int gcd = GCD(abs(numerator), denominator);
  numerator /= gcd;
  denominator /= gcd;
}
```

The GCD method calls itself recursively by comparing the numbers and subtracting the smaller number from the larger number. When they are equal, we return the number. The GCD algorithm is regarded as the world's oldest non-trivial algorithm.

```
int Rational::GCD(int number1, int number2) {
  if (number1 > number2) {
    return GCD(number1 - number2, number2);
  }
  else if (number1 < number2) {
    return GCD(number1, number2 - number1);
  }
  else {
    return number1;
  }
}
};
```

Complex numbers

A **complex number** $z = x + yi$ is the sum of a real number x and a real number y multiplied by the **imaginary unit** i, $i^2 = -1 \Rightarrow i = \pm\sqrt{(-1)}$, which is the solution of the equation $x^2 + 1 = 0$.

Complex.h

```
namespace SmallWindows {
  class NotaComplexNumber : public exception {
    public:
      NotaComplexNumber() {/* Empty. */}
```

```
  };

  extern double Square(double value);
```

The constructors, assignment operators, and the `String` conversion operator are similar to their counterparts in `Rational`:

```
class Complex {
  public:
    Complex(double x = 0, double y = 0);
    Complex(const Complex &complex);
    Complex operator=(const Complex &complex);
    bool ReadStream(const String& text);
    Complex(const String& text);
    operator String() const;
```

When comparing two complex number, their absolute values (refer to `Abs`) are compared.

```
    bool operator==(const Complex &complex) const;
    bool operator!=(const Complex &complex) const;
    bool operator<(const Complex &complex) const;
    bool operator<=(const Complex &complex) const;
    bool operator>(const Complex &complex) const;
    bool operator>=(const Complex &complex) const;
```

The arithmetic operators apply to complex numbers and double values:

```
    Complex operator+=(double x);
    Complex operator+=(Complex &complex);
    friend Complex operator+(double x, const Complex &complex);
    friend Complex operator+(const Complex &complex, double x);
    friend Complex operator+(const Complex &complex1,
                             const Complex &complex2);

    Complex operator-=(double x);
    Complex operator-=(Complex &complex);
    friend Complex operator-(double x, const Complex &complex);
    friend Complex operator-(const Complex &complex, double x);
    friend Complex operator-(const Complex &complex1,
                             const Complex &complex2);

    Complex operator*=(double x);
    Complex operator*=(Complex &complex);
    friend Complex operator*(double x, const Complex &complex);
    friend Complex operator*(const Complex &complex, double x);
    friend Complex operator*(const Complex &complex1,
                             const Complex &complex2);
```

```
Complex operator/=(double x);
Complex operator/=(Complex &complex);
friend Complex operator/(double x, const Complex &complex);
friend Complex operator/(const Complex &complex, double x);
friend Complex operator/(const Complex &complex1,
                         const Complex &complex2);
```

The absolute value of a complex number (and its value converted to a `double`) is the Pythagoras theorem of the real and imaginary part, that is, the square root of the sum of the squares of the parts:

```
double Abs() const {return sqrt(Square(x) + Square(y));}
operator double() const {return Abs();}

  private:
    double x, y;
};
};
```

Complex.cpp

```
#include "SmallWindows.h"

namespace SmallWindows {
  double Square(double value) {
    return value * value;
  }

  Complex::Complex(double x, double y)
   :x(x), y(y) {
    // Empty.
  }

  Complex::Complex(const Complex &complex)
   :x(complex.x),
    y(complex.y) {
    // Empty.
  }

  Complex Complex::operator=(const Complex &complex) {
    x = complex.x;
    y = complex.y;
    return *this;
  }
```

When interpreting a text holding a rational number, we read the text from a stream, and we need some auxiliary functions to start with. The `ReadWhiteSpaces` method reads (and disposes of) all white spaces at the beginning of the stream:

```
void ReadWhiteSpaces(IStringStream& inStream) {
  while (true) {
    TCHAR tChar = inStream.peek();


    if ((tChar >= 0) && (tChar <= 255) && isspace(tChar)) {
      inStream.get();
    }
    else {
      break;
    }
  }
}
```

The `Peek` method reads the white spaces and returns the zero character (\0) if it has reached the end of the stream. If not, we look into what comes next in the stream by calling `peek`, and return its resulting value. Note that `peek` does not consume the character from the stream; it just checks out the next character:

```
TCHAR Peek(IStringStream& inStream) {
  ReadWhiteSpaces(inStream);

  if (inStream.eof()) {
    return TEXT('\0');
  }
  else {
    return (TCHAR) inStream.peek();
  }
}
```

The `ReadI` method verifies whether the next character in the stream is **i** or **I**. If it is, it reads the character from the stream and returns `true`:

```
bool ReadI(IStringStream& inStream) {
    if (tolower(Peek(inStream)) == TEXT('i')) {
      inStream.get();
      return true;
    }
    return false;
}
```

The ReadSign method verifies that the next character in the stream is a plus or minus sign. If it is, it reads the character from the stream, sets the sign parameter to + or −, and returns true:

```
bool ReadSign(IStringStream& inStream, TCHAR& sign) {
  TCHAR tChar = Peek(inStream);
  switch (tChar) {
    case TEXT('+'):
      inStream.get();
      sign = TEXT('+');
      return true;

    case TEXT('-'):
      inStream.get();
      sign = TEXT('-');
      return true;

    default:
      return false;
  }
}
```

The ReadValue method verifies that the next two characters in the stream are a plus or a minus sign followed by a digit or a dot, or whether the first character is a digit or a dot. If the latter is the case, it reads the value parameter from the beginning of the stream and returns true:

```
bool ReadValue(IStringStream& inStream, double& value) {
  TCHAR tChar = Peek(inStream);

  if ((tChar == TEXT('+')) || (tChar == TEXT('-'))) {
    inStream.get();
    tChar = Peek(inStream);
    inStream.unget();

    if (isdigit(tChar) || (tChar == TEXT('.'))) {
      inStream >> value;
      return true;
    }
  }
  else if (isdigit(tChar) || (tChar == TEXT('.'))) {
    inStream >> value;
    return true;
  }

  return false;
}
```

The `EndOfLine` method simply returns `true` if the next character in the stream is the zero character (\0), in which case we have reached the end of the string:

```
bool EndOfLine(IStringStream& inStream) {
  return Peek(inStream) == TEXT('\0');
}
```

Now we are ready to interpret a string as a rational number. We have the following ten cases, where *x* and *y* are real values, *i* is the imaginary unit, and ± is plus or minus. All ten cases represent valid complex numbers:

1. $x \pm yi$
2. $x \pm \pm i$
3. $x \pm i$
4. $yi \pm x$
5. $\pm i \pm x$
6. $i \pm x$
7. yi
8. $\pm i$
9. i
10. x

The `ReadStream` method creates an input stream from the text and tries to interpret it as one of the preceding ten cases. The idea is that we read the stream and try one part of the potential complex number at a time:

```
bool Complex::ReadStream(const String& text) {
  IStringStream inStream(Trim(text));
  double value1, value2;
  TCHAR sign1, sign2;
```

If the stream is made up of a value, a sign, another value, and i or I, we set *x* and *y* in accordance with case 1 ($x \pm yi$) and return `true`. The *y* field is negative if the sign is minus. However, the second value may also be negative, in which case *y* is positive:

```
if (ReadValue(inStream, value1)) {
  if (ReadSign(inStream, sign1)) {
    if (ReadValue(inStream, value2) && ReadI(inStream) &&
        EndOfLine(inStream)) {
      x = value1;
      y = (sign1 == TEXT('-')) ? -value2 : value2;
      return true;
    }
```

If the sign is not followed by a value, but by another sign and i or I, case 2 ($x \pm \pm i$) applies and we return true. In this case, we actually have to adjust the value of y twice in accordance with both signs:

```
else if (ReadSign(inStream, sign2)) {
  if (ReadI(inStream) && EndOfLine(inStream)) {
    x = value1;
    y = (sign1 == TEXT('-')) ? -1 : 1;
    y = (sign2 == TEXT('-')) ? -y : y;
    return true;
  }
}
```

If the sign is not followed by a value or another sign, but by i or I, case 3 ($x \pm i$) applies and we return true:

```
else if (ReadI(inStream) && EndOfLine(inStream)) {
  x = value1;
  y = (sign1 == TEXT('-')) ? -1 : 1;
  return true;
  }
}
```

If the value is not followed by a sign but by i or I, another sign, and another value, case 4 ($yi \pm x$) applies and we return true:

```
else if (ReadI(inStream)) {
  if (ReadSign(inStream, sign1)) {
    if (ReadValue(inStream, value2) && EndOfLine(inStream)){
      y = value1;
      x = (sign1 == TEXT('-')) ? -value2 : value2;
      return true;
    }
  }
}
```

If the value is followed by i or I and nothing else, case 7 (yi) applies and we return true:

```
else if(EndOfLine(inStream)) {
  y = value1;
  x = 0;
  return true;
  }
}
```

If the value is followed by nothing else, case 10 (*x*) applies and we return `true`:

```
else if (EndOfLine(inStream)) {
  x = value1;
  y = 0;
  return true;
 }
}
```

If the stream does not start with a value, but with a sign followed by i or I, another sign and another value, case 5 (±*i* ± *x*) applies and we return `true`:

```
else if (ReadSign(inStream, sign1)) {
  if (ReadI(inStream)) {
    if (ReadSign(inStream, sign2)) {
      if (ReadValue(inStream, value2) && EndOfLine(inStream)){
        y = (sign1 == TEXT('-')) ? -1 : 1;
        x = (sign2 == TEXT('-')) ? -value2 : value2;
        return true;
      }
    }
```

If the stream starts with a sign followed by i or I and nothing else, case 8 (±*i*) applies and we return `true`:

```
else if (EndOfLine(inStream)) {
  y = (sign1 == TEXT('-')) ? -1 : 1;
  x = 0;
  return true;
 }
}
}
```

If the stream does not start with a value or a sign, but with i or I followed by a sign and a value, case 6 (*i* ± *x*) applies and we return `true`:

```
else if (ReadI(inStream)) {
  if (ReadSign(inStream, sign2)) {
    if (ReadValue(inStream, value2) && EndOfLine(inStream)) {
      y = 1;
      x = (sign2 == TEXT('-')) ? -value2 : value2;
      return true;
    }
  }
```

If the stream is made up by i or I and nothing else, case 9 (*i*) applies and we return `true`:

```
      else if (EndOfLine(inStream)) {
         y = 1;
         x = 0;
         return true;
      }
   }
```

Finally, if none of the above cases apply, the text does not hold a complex number and we return `false`:

```
      return false;
   }
```

The constructor that takes a text simply calls `ReadStream` and throws a `NotaComplexNumber` exception if `ReadStream` returns `false`. However, if `ReadStream` returns `true`, x and y are set to the appropriate values:

```
Complex::Complex(const String& text) {
   if (!ReadStream(text)) {
      throw NotaComplexNumber();
   }
}
```

In the `String` conversion operator, we look into several different cases:

1. $x + i$
2. $x - i$
3. $x \pm i$
4. x
5. $+i$
6. $-i$
7. yi
8. 0

If the real part x is not 0, we write its value on the stream and look into the first four cases with regard to the imaginary part, y. If y is plus or minus 1, we simply write $+i$ or $-i$. If it is not plus or minus 1, and not 0, we write its value with the `showpos` flag, which forces the plus sign to be present in the case of a positive value. Finally, if y is 0, we do not write it at all:

```
Complex::operator String() const {
   OStringStream outStream;

   if (x != 0) {
```

```
      if (y == 1) {
        outStream << x << TEXT("+i");
      }
      else if (y == -1) {
        outStream << x << TEXT("-i");
      }
      else if (y != 0) {
        outStream << x << setiosflags(ios::showpos)
                  << y << TEXT("i");
      }
      else {
        outStream << x;
      }
    }
```

If *x* is zero, we omit it and write the value of *y* in the same manner as we did earlier. However, if *y* is zero, we write 0; otherwise, nothing will be written if both *x* and *y* are 0. Moreover, we omit the showpos flag, since it is not necessary to write the plus sign in the case of a positive value:

```
    else {
      if (y == 1) {
        outStream << TEXT("i");
      }
      else if (y == -1) {
        outStream << TEXT("-i");
      }
      else if (y != 0) {
        outStream << y << TEXT("i");
      }
      else {
        outStream << TEXT("0");
      }
    }
    return outStream.str();
  }
```

Two complex numbers are equal if their real and imaginary parts are equal:

```
bool Complex::operator==(const Complex &complex) const {
  return ((x == complex.x) && (y == complex.y));
}

bool Complex::operator!=(const Complex &complex) const {
  return !(*this == complex);
}
```

When deciding whether a complex number is smaller than another complex number, we chose to compare their absolute values, which is given by the `Abs` method:

```
bool Complex::operator<(const Complex &complex) const {
  return (Abs() < complex.Abs());
}

bool Complex::operator<=(const Complex &complex) const {
  return ((*this < complex) || (*this == complex));
}

bool Complex::operator>(const Complex &complex) const {
  return !(*this <= complex);
}

bool Complex::operator>=(const Complex &complex) const {
  return !(*this < complex);
}
```

The addition operators all call the following final operator, which works for all four arithmetic operators:

```
Complex Complex::operator+=(double x) {
  *this = (*this + Complex(x));
  return *this;
}

Complex Complex::operator+=(Complex &complex) {
  *this = (*this + complex);
  return *this;
}

Complex operator+(double x, const Complex &complex) {
  return (Complex(x) + complex);
}

Complex operator+(const Complex &complex, double x) {
  return (complex + Complex(x));
}
```

When adding two complex numbers, we add the real and imaginary parts separately:

```
Complex operator+(const Complex &complex1,
                  const Complex &complex2) {
  return Complex(complex1.x + complex2.x,
                 complex1.y + complex2.y);
}
```

```
Complex Complex::operator-=(double x) {
  return (*this - Complex(x));
}

Complex Complex::operator-=(Complex &complex) {
  return (*this - complex);
}

Complex operator-(double x, const Complex &complex) {
  return (Complex(x) - complex);
}

Complex operator-(const Complex &complex, double x) {
  return (complex - Complex(x));
}
```

When subtracting two complex numbers, we subtract the real and imaginary parts separately:

```
Complex operator-(const Complex &complex1,
                  const Complex &complex2) {
  return Complex(complex1.x - complex2.x,
                 complex1.y - complex2.y);
}

Complex Complex::operator*=(double x) {
  *this = (*this * Complex(x));
  return *this;
}

Complex Complex::operator*=(Complex &complex) {
  *this = (*this * complex);
  return *this;
}

Complex operator*(double x, const Complex &complex) {
  return (Complex(x) * complex);
}

Complex operator*(const Complex &complex, double x) {
  return (complex * Complex(x));
}
```

The product of two complex numbers can be established by some algebra:

$$(x_1 + y_1 i)(x_2 + y_2 i) = x_1 x_2 + x_1 y_2 i + y_1 i x_2 + y_1 y_2 i^2 = x_1 x_2 + x_1 y_2 i + y_1 i x_2 + y_1 y_2 (-1) = x_1 x_2 + x_1 y_2 i + x_2 y_1 i - y_1 y_2 = (x_1 x_2 - y_1 y_2) + (x_1 y_2 + x_2 y_1)i$$

```
Complex operator*(const Complex &complex1,
                  const Complex &complex2) {
  return Complex((complex1.x * complex2.x) -
                 (complex1.y * complex2.y),
                 (complex1.x * complex2.y) +
                 (complex2.x * complex1.y));
}



Complex Complex::operator/=(double x) {
  *this = (*this / Complex(x));
  return *this;
}

Complex Complex::operator/=(Complex &complex) {
  *this = (*this / complex);
  return *this;
}

Complex operator/(double x, const Complex &complex) {
  return (Complex(x) / complex);
}

Complex operator/(const Complex &complex, double x) {
  return (complex / Complex(x));
}
```

The quotient between two complex numbers can also be established by some algebra. The **conjugate** of a complex number $x_2 + y_2i$ is $x_2 - y_2i$, which we can use in the conjugate rule:

$$(x_2 + y_2i)(x_2 - y_2i) = x_2^2 - x_2y_2i + x_2y_2i - y_2^2(-1) = x_2^2 - x_2y_2i + x_2y_2i + y_2^2 = x_2^2 + y_2^2$$

We can use the conjugate rule when dividing two complex numbers by multiplying the conjugate by both the numerator and the denominator:

$$\frac{x_1 + y_1i}{x_2 + y_2i} = \frac{x_1 + y_1i}{x_2 + y_2i}\frac{x_2 - y_2i}{x_2 - y_2i} = \frac{(x_1 + y_1i)(x_2 - y_2i)}{(x_2 + y_2i)(x_2 - y_2i)} = \frac{x_1x_2 - x_1y_2i + x_2y_1i - y_1y_2i^2}{x_2^2 + y_2^2} =$$

$$\frac{x_1x_2 - x_1y_2i + x_2y_1i - y_1y_2(-1)}{x_2^2 + y_2^2} = \frac{x_1x_2 - x_1y_2i + x_2y_1i + y_1y_2}{x_2^2 + y_2^2} = \frac{(x_1x_2 + y_1y_2) + (x_2y_1 - x_1y_2)i}{x_2^2 + y_2^2} =$$

$$\frac{x_1x_2 + y_1y_2}{x_2^2 + y_2^2} + \frac{x_2y_1 - x_1y_2}{x_2^2 + y_2^2}i$$

```
    Complex operator/(const Complex &complex1,
                     const Complex &complex2) {
      double sum = Square(complex2.x) + Square(complex2.y);
      double x = ((complex1.x * complex2.x) +
                  (complex1.y * complex2.y)) / sum,
             y = ((complex2.x * complex1.y) +
                  (complex1.x * complex2.y)) / sum;
      return Complex(x, y);
    }
};
```

Summary

By reading this book you have learned how to develop applications in Windows with Small Windows, a C++ object-oriented class library for graphical applications in Windows. I hope you have enjoyed the book!

Index

visible characters, finding 197

L

LineFigure class 101, 104, 106, 108
logical units 16
Long Pointer to Constant TChar String (LPCTSTR) 453
look-ahead parser 282

M

MainWindow function 38, 329
Matrix class 292, 297, 298
Menu class 389
modes, applicationMode
  Idle 73
  ModifyRectangle 73
  ModifySingle 73
  MoveMultiple 73

N

non-terminals 278

P

Page Break 158
page setup
  about 503, 536
  information, fetching 537
  PageSetupdialog class 540
  Template function 543
painting functions
  Add menu 93
  cursor 94
  Modify menu 90, 91, 92
  OnDraw 85
  OnPaint 85
  OnPrint 85
parse tree 279
Parser 268
parser generators 282
parser table 282
parser
  bottom-up parser 282
  top-down parser 282
  writing 282

print preview
  about 497
  keyboard input 499
  scroll bars, using 500

R

RectangleFigure class 116, 119, 120, 122
Reference class 292, 293, 295
registry 477

S

Scanner 268
Small Windows
  about 8
  overview 323
source sets
  about 257
  breadth-first approach 261
  depth first approach 261
spreadsheet application, building
  about 209
  alignments, adjusting 252, 253
  CalcDocument class, using 210, 211, 212, 213, 214, 218
  caret, updating 227, 229
  client area, repainting 223
  color, changing 250
  copy methods, using 243, 244, 246, 247, 249, 250
  cut methods, using 243, 245, 248, 250
  Down method, using 219
  files, managing 239, 242
  font, changing 250
  IsCellVisible method, using 225, 227
  keyboard input, using 229, 232, 234, 236, 238
  MainWindow class, using 209
  mouse inputs, using 219
  OnCharDown method, using 229, 232, 234, 237
  OnDraw method, using 223, 224
  OnHorizontalScroll method, using 220
  OnMouseMove methods, using 219, 221
  OnVerticalScroll method 221
  OnVerticalScroll method, using 220
  paste method, using 243, 244, 246, 248, 250
  UpdateCaret method, using 227, 229

Printed in Great Britain
by Amazon

85954476R00334